THE
CHOSEN

Just Show us a Sign
...And We Will Believe
In You...

LEN TITOW

SWEETSPIRE **LITERATURE**
—— MANAGEMENT ——

THE CHOSEN

...None Believed
Even Though They Witnessed
the Miracles...

CHAPTER 1

THE NOISE OF EXPLODING GLASS with a man being thrown through a shop window, closely followed by a chair, disrupted a peaceful evening.

Silence.

Then a gun being fired, the noise bellowed down the street, and then all went quiet again.

All that could be heard was a woman weeping over the body of her dead husband.

Men stood around the body, but none would help or defend the shop owner, who was shot for not paying protection money. An outright killing.

Peter Marlow stood over the body momentarily with his gun in his hand and then placed the gun back into its holster under his jacket. He walked out of the shop and got into his expensive car and drove off. He did not worry about whether anyone was going to call the police or accuse him of killing the owner of the store. He knew that his reputation was enough to ensure there were no witnesses to the killing and that other store owners would get the message loud and clear as to what will happen to them if they didn't pay their share of extortion money.

Peter drove to his office and noted that the car park was full. He had arranged a meeting with his men, and they were all early. He parked his car in his reserved spot and walked to his office. About twenty men were waiting for him in the boardroom. He moved to the head of the table and filled a glass with water and drank it. The meeting came to order, and Peter remained standing. Peter said, 'Our take on prostitution and gambling has fallen considerably. Why?' No one spoke. 'Well, I will tell you why. It is because mugs like you are allowing your territory to be sliced up by newcomers who are getting the bulk of the business, and you blokes seem to do nothing about it. This is to stop, and you are to regain all the territory we have lost, or I will have you replaced with someone who has the guts to do the job. I do not intend to sit back and allow the business to slip through my fingers—the business that I built up over the years, which is now being controlled by outsiders.'

A gang member asked, 'What do you want us to do—kill them?'

Peter replied, 'Yes, if you have to.'

The gang member said, 'That will only lead to an outright gang war amongst ourselves, with each one of us killing the other until there is no one left.'

Peter said, 'There are three influential families controlling the city. If we kill them, the others will run, leaving the city for us to control. I want a plan as to who is going after the heads of the families, as each will have to be eliminated at the same time.'

The gang member said, 'Difficult, as we don't know where they are at anyone time, so we will need to make enquiries as to their movements and come back in a week's time to coordinate the plan.'

Peter replied, 'All right. Find out where they are going to be in a few weeks' time, and we will meet again next week to set a plan.'

The meeting broke up with everyone going to their cars and driving out of the car park.

One of the territory bosses, Judas Reveal, headed straight for the headquarters of the gang that over the years, had gained the bulk of the business. He drove into their car park and was met by several men who took his gun from him and escorted him upstairs to the family's head, Vincent Marconi.

Judas said, 'They are planning on killing all the heads of the three families that control the bulk of the trade, including you, Vince.'

Vince asked, 'when are they going to do this?'

Judas replied, 'they have not completed the plan. We agreed we would adjourn for a week to find out where the family heads were going to be so we can arrange for all to be dealt with at one time.'

Vince asked, 'if we get rid of Peter, will his lieutenants come over to us and join our family?'

Judas replied, 'I believe they will, as they hate Peter and consider him to be a killer who will stop at nothing to stay on top. Are you going to kill him, Vince?'

Vince said, 'If we have to, we will, but if we can plan for the State to do it for us, then this would be all the better. We cannot just kill Peter, as there will be too many questions asked. We have to arrange for him to be put out of the way so we can take over.'

Judas asked, 'How can we do that?'

Vince replied, 'Knowing Peter, he will do it for us, as he thinks he can do anything and not pay the price. I will arrange for a team of police to shadow him wherever he goes, and if he does something stupid, like kill someone, we can lock him up for a long time and get our people in the jail to take care of him.'

Vince made several phone calls and then came out of his office to advise that the police will follow Peter and, if he does something stupid, arrest him. In the meantime, he would provide Judas with false details as to where he will be over the next week and beyond, so it would look like Judas was doing his job.

Judas stayed for a while and collected his gun at the front desk and walked out of the building and got into his car. He drove off but failed to see that there was a car parked along the side of the road taking pictures of him leaving Vince's home.

Peter, in the meantime, drove to his sister's house to see how she was. His sister, Helen, lived on her own. Her husband left her when their daughter was born. He wanted Helen to have an abortion, as they were told that their daughter would be very disabled and would not live beyond her teens. Helen refused, as she was a religious person and believed it was wrong to end a life. Her daughter, Alice Waters, suffered from several muscular and medical conditions, including MS. To look at her would bring tears to your eyes. She could not go to the toilet by herself or even stand up or walk. She could not speak and could only utter grunts or shrieks to communicate.

Alice relied on her mother for everything, including feeding her and changing her nappies after she had soiled herself. Helen stayed home on a carer's allowance looking after Alice. Her allowance was not enough to pay for all their bills, and she relied on Peter to help her out when things got tough, and money was scarce. She knew of Peter's reputation but ignored what people were saying, as he gave her the money, which she needed to keep the roof over her head, help feed both her and Alice, and pay the doctor's bills.

Peter had frequently been forced to confront doctors and other creditors who were keen to get paid when Helen ran out of money. Sometimes he had to persuade them it would be in their best interest to forgo the debt rather than their lives.

Peter walked into Alice's room and stared at her sitting in her wheelchair and felt helpless. All the money and influence he had could not help her one bit. He had already paid for the best medical opinion as to what could be done. All concluded nothing could be done to help her, as she had too many complications and would die before she turned twenty.

The only way out was to shoot her and allow her to escape her mangled body. To Peter, there was no way Alice would overcome her disability, and death would be the only way out for her. The only question to be answered would be, when does he do it, or will nature take care of it before he does?

As he was standing at the doorway, Helen came into the room. She would not let Peter stay with Alice, as she knew he would most likely take her life to set her soul free from her mangled body. Peter was not a religious man, anything but one, and considered religion a waste of time. He considered a god that allowed his people to suffer was not a god to respect or worship but a fake god and should be opposed whenever confronted with life-and-death issues. To him, the church was just a business established to take money from the poor, as the rich would not contribute to any religious cause. The rich did not need religion, as they have everything they would ever want, according to Peter.

Helen and Peter had spoken about Alice frequently and each time disagreed as to the best course of action for both mother and daughter. Peter had set up a trust for Alice to ensure she was looked after should something happen to him and left money with Helen to ensure she was also taken care of.

Peter stayed for dinner, and at about eight, left to go home. The next morning, Peter phoned Judas and arranged to meet him at one of his upmarket restaurants for lunch. Judas agreed and prepared himself, thinking this was just another catch-up meeting, which they often had.

Peter arrived at the restaurant and positioned himself at his usual spot in the corner and took out his gun and slid it under the table in a bracket he had permanently fixed to the under section of the table to hold his gun. He ordered a beer and waited. After about ten minutes, Judas arrived, and Peter greeted him, and both settled down to business.

Peter said, 'I understand you visited Vince Marconi yesterday. why?'

Judas, caught off guard, said, 'what makes you think it was me?'

Peter took out a brown envelope and turned it upside down. The photos fell out, showing Judas and Vince having drinks together and smiling at each other.

Peter asked, 'were you planning on eliminating me instead of Vince?'

Judas replied, 'No. We were just talking about his increase in the prostitution business and that he intends to bring in more girls to take the bulk of the business from us.'

Peter said, 'You're lying. You went to sell us out and didn't expect to be caught with your hands around my throat.'

Judas said, 'No, you have it wrong. All I wanted to do is to get some information.'

Peter said, 'You could have gotten that from one of his men, not from the boss himself. You're a liar. You were there to tip him off regarding our plan and have been caught selling us down the drain to the Marconi family. Do you think they will look after you the same way we have?'

Judas was not sure what to say. He recognised he had been caught out and did not know how to reply to the questions being asked; however, he knew that there was a good possibility he would end up in the morgue.

Peter pulled the gun from under the table and pointed it at Judas. Judas stood up to grab it from him, as he had not expected this, and wanted to reach for his gun and put a bullet into Peter so he could get the credit for killing a notorious gang member. In the struggle, Peter's gun went off and hit Judas in the heart, and he went down, grabbing his chest. Immediately, the restaurant was packed with police, who swarmed in with their guns drawn.

'Put your gun down or we will shoot, and you will go the way Judas went.'

Peter, realising that this was a set-up, put his gun down on the table, which was quickly taken up in a handkerchief by the officer in charge, and he was handcuffed and led out of the restaurant. He was taken to the police station and, after hours of being questioned, was charged for the murder of Judas Reveal. The next morning, Peter met with his lawyers, who advised him that the entire scene was taped and there might be a possibility of him getting the death sentence, as this was just an outright cold-blooded killing of an unarmed man.

The lawyers established their case based on "Entrapment" which it was, as the police were there within minutes, and no one called them. They convinced Peter to plead guilty based on "Entrapment " and "Self-defence" as he thought Judas was armed as all of his men were and that he would use his weapon on him once Judas found out that he had been spotted collaborating with the enemy.

Peter followed these instructions and, after a lengthy trial, ended up with a sentence of twenty years with a non-parole period of ten years. They sent Peter to the maximum-security prison, MSP for short, where all hardened criminals were sent. The prison had an outer perimeter wall and barbwire fencing on top to prevent prisoners from escaping. No one had ever made a successful escape from this prison.

He was processed and placed in a cell with another prisoner and told what they expected of him and the daily routine he was to follow while in prison.

CHAPTER 2

Peter found it hard to settle down in prison. He was a custom to giving orders and not taking them from monkeys, who in his opinion, were dressed up as prison guards. His cellmate turned out to be a hired killer and, one night while Peter was in bed, tried to kill him with a knife he stole from the kitchen.

Peter was stabbed in the stomach and, in the struggle, pulled the knife out of his gut and cut his cellmate's throat, killing him instantly. There was little doubt that the prison guards were in on the plot, as none of them were in that wing when it happened. After that instance, a clear message was sent to the Marconi family that Peter would not be eliminated easily. Peter told the guard to tell Vince Marconi that he will come after him personally if ever he was released from prison or would arrange for a contract to be put out on him if another attempt was made on his life while he was in jail.

Marconi was determined to kill Peter to make sure he did not come back to being the supremo or godfather of the families. He knew Peter had friends that held high places in Congress and the judiciary, and they would support him when necessary. He also knew that Peter could have his treats carried out even while he was in jail.

Life in jail was not a picnic, and you always had to watch out for the attempt on your life or someone set to do you an injury, which happened often and at the most unexpected times.

One morning, Peter was in the library looking for a book to read in his cell when he was confronted by two inmates, one from each end of the aisle. Both moved in on Peter at once, and he could see they were after him. He hit the first one right in the face with his book, while the other one threw a punch, which landed on Peter's chest, which only took the wind out of him. Peter grabbed a thick book from the shelf just in time to stop the second man from trying to thrust a knife into him.

The knife penetrated the cover of the book. Peter hit the man on his arm with the book he grabbed from the shelf, forcing him to drop the knife. He quickly picked the knife up and stabbed the first man in the chest, who fell to the floor. The second man made another attempt to hit Peter, and as he deflected his punch, he thrust the knife into his chest, causing him to also fall to the floor. Peter dropped his book over the second man and left the library, and stayed outside to see what was going to happen.

After about twenty minutes, the guards moved into the library in numbers after someone discovered the two men. They brought in body bags, and they eventually took both to the prison morgue. Guards looked for Peter and found him outside the library. They questioned him to see if he had been in the library. Peter said he was on his way to exchange a book. Why? They would not answer him.

A week later, Peter was assigned to the road gang where daily he would go out to the state highways and, with a crew of ten prisoners and five guards, repair the highways and crash barriers that were erected to prevent cars from coming off the highway and rolling down embankments. He had served five years' imprisonment and had settled down to the routine, always watching over his shoulder to make sure he did not end up dead.

One day, the men were told to move to a new section of the highway, while Peter stayed back with two guards. He knew that something was up, possibly another attempt to kill him. He was working on a barrier replacing a damaged section. He was told to unbolt the damaged section at a bend. He realised he was being set up for something and noticed the guards were well away from him, which meant that whatever was going to happen was going to be a split-second job. He yelled out to the guard to come over to hold a rail, but the guard would not come near. Peter figured out that possibly he was set up for a car or truck to come around the corner and to take him out while he was unbolting the rail.

He went down into the gully and found a tree that had fallen from strong winds and dragged it up to the road and placed it over the rail as if the rail was removed.

A guard who could not see what Peter was doing came up to him to see where he had disappeared to. As the guard approached him, Peter hit him in the head with his shovel and knocked the guard out. He quickly leaned the guard over the tree and put his hat on the guard's head and shovel in his hand, allowing the shovel to hold the guard up as if it were him looking over the rail. Sure enough, a truck came around the corner and headed straight towards the guard, running him down and stopping before he went over the gully. The guard was sent flying down the gully along with the tree and barrier, damaging the truck to the extent that it could not be reversed or be driven away. The driver tried to get out of the truck and make a run for it, but Peter got to him just as he stepped out of the cabin. He gave the driver a punch to the face, knocking him out. He then scrambled down the embankment as if he had been thrown down there with the guard.

A few minutes later, police came from everywhere, assuming Peter was dead. It surprised them to find him at the bottom of the embankment with a dead guard. Peter advised he was knocked out and did not know what had happened. He was working on the rail when the truck hit him and his guard, sending both flying. They took him to hospital, and he stayed there for a week under observation and was then sent back to his cell. Everyone put it down to good luck as to why Peter was not killed by the guard that day.

About two months after this event, Peter and his gang were working on a straight stretch of the highway when two men in an expensive car pulled up near to where his team was repairing the shoulder of the road. One got out of the car and put up the bonnet of the car as if they were attending to a repair. The man that got out walked up to the guard and asked if any of the men knew anything about cars. The guard yelled out to Peter to help the man start his car. Peter kept working as if he did not hear the guard. The guard walked up to Peter and told him to go over to help the man. Peter said he knew nothing about cars and was not a mechanic.

One of the other men said he was a mechanic, and before the guard said anything, he immediately dropped his shovel and walked up to the car. The guard yelled out to him to join the gang, but the prisoner kept walking towards the car. As he approached the car, the man under the bonnet pulled out a gun and shot the prisoner in the head and immediately put down the bonnet and got into his car, and both men drove off at high speed, leaving the dead prisoner lying face down on the highway.

Peter knew it would only be time before they got him, as no doubt the set-ups were not working, and they would have to kill him and then come up with a reason for his death in prison.

Summer ended, and the temperature got cold, especially in the mornings. One morning, the gang was in a small town repairing a section of the highway that had given way, leaving a big hole in the left lane that was dangerous, as it caused a lot of blowouts. The sun had just risen, but the temperature was minus three degrees. Peter was told to drive a small excavator and to get a bucket of gravel to fill the hole. As he approached the pile of gravel, he noticed a man sitting nearby, warming himself near a fire comprising a burning bush. Peter yelled out, 'Good morning!' and kept working, keeping an eye on the old man to ensure this was not another trap. As he approached the old man, he noticed he was waving to Peter to join him. Peter ignored him and continued to scoop up gravel and take it back to the damaged section in the road. Peter dumped the gravel into the hole and moved away to allow the roller to compact the gravel.

After around five minutes had passed, the lead guard instructed Peter to bring back yet another load. Peter returned to the stockpile and filled his bucket up with another batch before heading back to the part of the road that needed repair. Just then, the man near the fire got up and blocked Peter's machine from advancing. Peter yelled out for the man to move out of the way, but the man stood his ground and would not move. Peter got off his machine and moved towards the man, intending to push him aside, but he immediately found himself unable to move or say a word.

The man came up to Peter and said, 'You are Satan's disciple, and you live a wasteful life, as he has instructed you to do. You worship him and glorify the material things he gives you, and you have frequently knelt before him, paying homage to him as you spill the blood of men without concern. You have been with your master for the last thirty years, and he does not want you to leave him as you have served him well, and the ground he walks on testifies the amount of blood you have spilt in his name.'

'In the past, you had power, influence, and wealth beyond comparison and possessions that others would envy, but now you have nothing, which is the way of your master and his world, and yet you have learnt nothing from the years you have spent with him and in prison. Your thoughts and expectations are to regain the material things you have lost, and you refuse to understand that again you will lose them upon death, as you will soon depart this life with nothing. You have refused to follow Me, for you believe the material things in this life are the only things that count, yet repeatedly you have lost them and have been left with nothing but still do not understand they are only temporary, not yours to keep, and you will never possess them permanently.'

'Your previous wealth has not allowed you to do good but only waste money on yourself with little to show for it. You have despised Me, your Creator, and have followed Satan instead of My teachings. I will, in the next three days, set you free from this prison, and you will witness the glory of my work and see the things that money cannot buy. For one year, you will follow My ways and see what it means to be a Christian, the power of the Holy Spirit, and the gifts you have rejected that I can bestow upon you.

Peter said, 'I am not one of your believers, and my life has not been based on your teachings. I have killed many and have lived a life of sin, contrary to your teachings. To me, the wealth of this world is all that there is, not some future promise or eternal life. It is useless to tell me about heaven, as my sins can never be forgiven for what I have done.'

God said, 'I will show you My way and a life that is far more rewarding, things that money cannot buy and things that can only be done in My name, irrespective of the wealth you possess.' Peter said, 'I can't follow you. I am a prisoner and must stay in prison for another four years before I am due to be paroled. Anyhow, if the Marconi family will have their way, I will be dead before I am paroled.'

God said, 'In three days', I will release you from prison and you will be free for one year. Thereafter, you will be brought back to prison to finish your sentence. Once you are set free, you will be collected outside the prison and taken to a place where I will wait for you.'

Peter said, 'No, I am not going anywhere, your mad to think otherwise. The Marconi family are too powerful and won't let me leave prison alive.'

The guard staring at Peter asked, 'what are you doing? Get the gravel and get on with your work. Are you going mad talking to yourself? There is no one there. Your imagination is getting the better of you. Get back to work.'

Peter looked around and saw the guard yelling at him and then turned around and looked for the old man and the burning bush, but neither was to be seen. He put it down to being out in the cold for too long and got back to his work.

The second day, the gang is back to finish the repair on the highway. Peter looked around and could not see the old man that was there yesterday and put it down to his mind playing tricks on him—mirages, as they often refer to.

The third day, Peter got ready to move out with his gang. He had had breakfast and waited for the guards to release him from his cell. Two guards came to his door and told him to stand at the back of his cell. He thought this was unusual, as normally they unlock the door and allow him to make his own way out to the assembly point in the car park. The guards entered his cell and informed Peter he was being released from prison and for him to get out of his prison clothes and to put on the clothes they brought down for him to wear, which were the clothes he wore when he entered prison, some five years ago. He undressed and changed into his street clothes and went to collect his personal items from the front desk.

Peter thought this was another attempt to kill him. He was worried about what was around the corner, as he knew he still had four or five more years to complete his sentence.

He asked for the release papers, however the guards refused to give them to him and said they would process his release in the main office. Peter walked several corridors and went up multiple flights of stairs before reaching the main office. He was told to sit and wait until his name was called.

After about twenty minutes, his name was called out, and he was asked to go into a room. His prison records showed him to be the right person. They advised him he was being released and was handed the watch and cash he had on him when he was arrested. He was given a copy of his release papers and told that a bus was waiting to take all those being released into town, where they can make their way to the train station or airport.

Peter walked out of the main building and momentarily waited to see if anyone was going to take a shot at him. He looked to see if there were any other cars around but could not see any and stepped onto the bus and walked to the back and sat down. A few other people got on the bus, and it moved off.

About half an hour later, the bus pulled up at a bus station in the centre of town, and everyone got up and moved out of the bus. Peter got out and walked away from the bus, not sure what he was doing. He recognised this was a blunder, but understood he had to leave before they knew of the mistake and came after him. He did not want to call on his old mates, as no doubt they would call the police, and he would be arrested again. He walked down to the train station and bought a ticket to where his sister lived and eventually got on the train to take him to her suburb.

About an hour later, he got off the train and walked to his sister's house. As he was approaching her place, he could see his sister being confronted by two men who did not seem to be neighbours but more like two punks who were giving her a rough time. He approached them slowly as if he was just walking down the street, and he could hear his sister was being picked on by the two, and one of them pushed her to the ground. Peter walked up to them and gave the first a hit in the head, which sent him flying across the front lawn. The second he grabbed and hit his midsection, making him bend over, and then laid a punch to the side of his face. Both were out cold. Peter went up to his sister, who was in tears, who grabbed hold of Peter and would not let him go. She was shaking with fear and sobbing.

After about five minutes, Peter calmed Helen down and sat her on the steps. He went through the pockets of the men and took out their wallets and their guns. He loaded the men into their car, which was parked nearby, and drove it to the local police station and left it there. He walked back to his sister's place after he had made several stops at different ATMs, as the men had credit cards with credit balances. He cashed their credit cards out fully and left their cards in the receipt bin at the ATM. He ended up with about five thousand dollars, which he took from the men's wallets and their bank accounts. He walked to his sister's place and knocked on the door. His sister opened, and he stepped in.

His sister never told Peter that she was finding it very hard to get by while he was in prison and was always behind in the rent and with bills. She did her best, but there was never enough money to go around, and she would end up owing someone money at the end of each month. The two thugs were not debt collectors but selling protection—you pay up or get beaten up. Peter had come at the right time. He did not tell his sister that he had got out of prison by mistake.

He went into his niece's room, and she was asleep. Her mangled body was twisted, and she was a terrible sight to look upon. He uttered the word 'mangled, what a terrible state to be in,' as a stared at her.

He walked out of her room back into the kitchen where his sister was sitting. He said to her, 'I want you to catch a bus and go to the supermarket and buy some groceries. I noticed you don't have any milk or bread.'

The sister said, 'No. We had to pay the rent with the last of our money and haven't any money for food. We have been living off charities, but today they do not seem to want to help us. They are there for the recognition and donations and not the christian support they say they will give.'

Peter stood up and said to his sister, 'Here is two thousand dollars. I want you to put most of it way, buy what you and Alice need in the way of food and medicine. I will stay here while you do the shopping. Take a bus to the shopping centre and catch a cab back with the groceries. I will stay and look after Alice, as she is asleep and most probably will be like that for a while.'

Helen was very excited when she saw Peter's two thousand dollars and burst into tears. She took the money with her trembling hand and went into her bedroom and, after about fifteen minutes, came out all dressed up, ready to go shopping. She had a smile on her face and was quite excited about being able to buy some groceries for Alice and herself, especially not having to put it on credit or explain why her card registered 'dishonoured'. She knew there was nothing in the house to eat and was quite eager to buy what they needed before Alice woke up. She took her bag and went off to the bus stop. She waited about ten minutes for a bus and when one arrived, went on board to the shopping centre.

After about ten minutes, she had some bad thoughts. She wondered whether Peter would kill Alice as he often thought of doing before he went to prison. She kept thinking about it and decided that she could trust him not to touch her while she was away. However, she had this nagging feeling that she should not have left him there but did not have a choice, as they had to get some food.

The bus stopped outside of the shopping centre, and Helen went inside to the supermarket and took a trolley and began walking up and down the aisles. After about half an hour, she had the trolley full and made her way to the checkout and waited for her turn. The checkout attendant recognised her, as she had been in before, when her card was rejected as she was 'maxed out.' She thought to herself, *here we go again, another argument as to why her card will register 'dishonoured'.* Eventually, she got to the checkout, and the girl stared at her, thinking, *this will be a waste of time.*

Helen kept her cool, as she knew this girl was going to make it as difficult for her as she had in the past. The checkout girl was too young to know how it feels when you have no money, and your credit card was 'dishonoured'. No doubt life will teach her, and hopefully she reflects what she did to those people in the past who had their card dishonoured. The girl scanned all the groceries and then stared at Helen and said, 'Your card, madam?'

Helen instinctively reached for her purse to take out her card, but then realised that it was cashed out and, on this occasion, Peter had given her cash to buy the groceries. With the girl staring at her, Helen moved forward and said, 'No. I will pay by cash. Thank you.'

At that time, the store manager was walking by and stood at the checkout where Helen was counting out her money. She saw him there and said to him, 'It would be nice if your girls were civil and didn't prejudge customers. This girl has not been courteous towards me and look how she has packed my bags.' The store manager glanced at the bags, which were all over the place, with items falling out of them and nothing fitting squarely in the bags. The manager said, 'Madam, we apologise. It seems that this girl needs some further training in packing. I will have someone repack your bags and have them delivered to your home for free.'

'If someone can repack them, that will be good enough. I intend to catch a taxi so I can take them with me.' Helen finished paying for her groceries while the manager looked on and waited while they repacked the bags. The checkout girl was replaced and accompanied the manager to his office. With the aid of a store assistant, Helen took the trolley and groceries to a taxi stand and waited her turn. The taxi driver was kind enough to load the bags into his boot, and the attendant took the trolley back into the supermarket.

Helen was concerned as to what she would find back home but kept convincing herself that it was the devil's work to put those bad thoughts into her mind. Twenty minutes later, they were outside her home. She leapt from the cab and rushed inside to find Peter sitting in the lounge watching television. She went into Alice's room, which was dark, as the blinds were closed, but she could see Alice breathing and knew nothing had happened. She came back out and said to Peter, 'Come on, lend a hand to bring in the groceries.' Peter got up and brought in the bags from the boot of the cab. After five or six trips, the groceries were in the kitchen, and Helen unpacked the bags and put everything away. She yelled out to Peter, 'Pay the taxi driver!' Peter went out and paid the driver, who was happy to get cash instead of a credit card.

About an hour later, when everything had been put away, Helen went to Alice's room and noticed a light from under the door. She called out to Peter, and both entered Helen's room and were blinded by a bright white light, which flooded the room. Alice was in bed trying to reach out and say something but could only make noises. At the end of her bed stood what seemed to be an elderly man dressed in pure white robes. Peter recognised the man as being the same one who told him they would release him from prison in three days' time, and he was right.

Peter asked, 'what are you doing here? Who are you?'

The old man replied, 'I have appeared so you may understand who I am and, in Helen's case, answer her prayers and strengthen her faith. In Peter's case, to show him that there are things beyond this world that cannot be done on this earth, even if you had all the money and power this world could give you. Peter, you have spent a small fortune on having specialists give you opinions regarding Alice, and they have told you that her condition is extensive and incurable. You have consulted not only local doctors and specialists but also overseas specialists that lecture and teach their expertise here at universities. They have all told you she is a hopeless case.'

Peter asked, 'How do you know this? Who are you? How did you get into this room when we didn't see anyone come past us?'

The old man replied, 'Peter, move to the head of the bed and put your hands on Alice's head. Helen, go to the end of the bed where you can see Alice and she can see you.'

Peter was not willing to be ordered around and stood his ground but was being propelled to the head of the bed. His hands were being forced to rest on Alice's head, and he could not break away. Some spirit was controlling his body.

The old man raised his right hand and made the sign of the cross over Alice and held up his right arm, bent at the elbow.

Peter, not able to set himself free or say anything, uttered the words, 'In the, the name of Jesus Christ, I command you, you to be free of evil, evil spirits and healed.'

A white cross appeared on Alice as she lay in bed, motionless. There was a rushing noise as if several people just rushed out of the room, and then Alice started to wriggle and move her twisted body, arms, and legs. She unwound the locked arm with her leg, and her arms and legs straightened out slowly at first and then turned and bent until they took the shape of normal body parts. Her back, which was humped and bent over, straightened up, and her twisted body turned to reveal Alice's hips. Her face, which was screwed up and twisted, took shape, and her facial features began appearing. Her skin took on its natural colour. As the miracle was happening, Helen stood motionless, witnessing all that was happening and praying. Peter could not move and kept his eyes on the old man, who had his eyes fixed on Alice and right hand pointed to heaven.

When everything seemed to be completed, all eyes were fixed on Alice, who lay motionless in bed. Peter realised he could move and immediately took his hands off Alice's head. Helen said, 'where did the old man go?'

Peter replied, 'I don't know, but the white light has gone off with him.'

Peter went to the window and opened the blinds to let some light in. He turned to look at Alice and could see she had the body features of a young woman of her age. Alice was staring at her mother, who was at the end of her bed, not believing the beauty she was seeing in her daughter and the miracle she had just witnessed.

Alice, in a slow and slurred manner, said, 'Mum, Mum, it is me.'

Helen went to Alice, hugged and kissed her, and helped her to sit up, crying while she hugged her daughter and refusing to let her go.

Helen, after a considerable time, said, 'You look beautiful.

Can you speak?' while still sobbing.

Alice replied, 'Yes.'

Helen asked, 'Can you get up?' Alice said, 'Help me, Peter.'

Peter lifted her up and sat her on the end of the bed. He then lifted her up and stood her upright on her own legs. She made small steps in a shuffle fashion and then took some small strides. Helen took her hand, and she walked out of the bedroom into the lounge room still in a shuffle fashion.

Peter stood in the bedroom to figure out what had just happened and to comprehend the miracle that he had just witnessed but did not understand. He kept saying to himself, *this is not real. No, this did not happen. But it did happen, as Alice is walking and speaking.* Peter went into the lounge room to join the others.

Helen sat at on the lounge with Alice, and both were giving a prayer of thanks to the Lord for His miracle. Peter waited for them to finish and then said, 'Can anyone make sense of what has happened?'

Helen said, 'Peter, look at Alice. She has been miraculously healed. That is all that counts. The Lord Himself was in that room and healed Alice. You were there and witnessed everything that happened, and yet you question what you have seen, and that Alice is here with us, healed. What other explanation can you give it? You know the condition Alice was in. Look at her now.'

Peter looked dumfounded and bewildered, not knowing what to say, nor could he understand it.

Alice made a move to get up, and Helen assisted her. She said, 'Toilet,' and Helen helped her to the bathroom and went inside to help her.

After about five minutes, both came out, and Helen said, 'well, in the future, you will make it on your own now that you are getting stronger.'

Helen said, 'I will have to buy you some clothes and underwear for you so you can change into something that fits you better than your old clothes and nappies. You cannot walk around in nappies all day now that you can stand and move around. I have some money left from what Peter gave me, so I should be all right. We can go shopping later during the week, and you can choose some clothes for yourself.'

Peter said, 'Yes, but you will have to buy some clothes for her now so she can wear around the house.'

Helen took her bag and again made her way to the bus stop and caught a bus into the shopping centre. She looked around and bought two pairs of slacks, socks, two shirts, underwear, a pair of slippers, slip-on flat shoes, and a cardigan. As she was loaded up with bags, she caught a cab back home and hailed one that had just driven past her.

Half an hour later, she was home showing Alice what she had bought her. All the clothes were unpacked and put in the washing machine and then in the drier to ensure Alice had something to wear. As soon as the clothes were dry, Alice went into the bathroom with Helen and had her first shower. After twenty minutes, she came out wearing her new clothes, which looked stunning on her. They threw her old clothes in the garbage bin. Alice went to sit in the lounge, as it was a long day and she was getting tired.

Helen went to the kitchen and prepared dinner, while Peter sat opposite Alice, staring at her, still trying to understand what could have transformed her. All the money he spent on her achieved nothing other than allowing some doctors to profit from her condition. Helen came back into the room and handed Peter a beer and sat down with Alice.

Peter asked, 'Where did you get this from? Not another miracle. This type I like and would like more and more often.'

Helen and Alice burst out laughing, while Peter gulped down what seemed half the bottle.

Peter said, 'Thanks, Helen. That was good. Now, Alice, tell us what you remember. Did you hear and understand when we were talking to you while you lay there in your wheelchair and in bed, or were you brain-dead and don't remember what has happened over the last twenty years?'

Alice replied, 'everything that was said to me and everything I saw I remember, and even the television programs on literacy and numbers I remember. I will have to go to a library and get some books so I can improve on my reading, but I know the alphabet and numbers, so I have not missed out on the basics. I will just have to get myself up to speed as I get stronger. As for the conversations, I remember them all and recognise all of Mum's friends. Boy, are they going to get a surprise! What do we tell them?'

Peter said, 'Yes, what are you going to say to those who know, Alice?'

Helen said, 'The truth. It is a miracle. They can either believe it or not. Why should I lie about it?' God did it, so why shouldn't He get the credit for it? I know normally he doesn't. What He usually gets is the criticism.'

Helen got up and went into the kitchen and began preparing dinner. About half an hour later, she called everyone to the dining room table, and they sat down to dinner. Alice was asked to say grace, which she did, and they all ate. Helen helped Alice cut up her meal, as she still had not regained all her movements and strength. After dinner, Peter helped wash the dishes and put them away and then went into the lounge room to watch a move. Once it was over, everyone went off to bed. Helen helped Alice get into her pyjamas and into bed and then went to bed herself.

The next day, Peter got up early as usual, made coffee, and took a stroll around the block. He passed several people who thought they recognised him but could not be sure, as everyone thought he still was in jail. He found a newspaper lying around and picked it up to read at home. He came home just when Helen got up and put the toast on so they could have breakfast.

Helen asked, 'what are you going to do today?'

Peter replied, 'I don't know. I'm not sure of what is expected of me—whether I should get a job or what I should do. I still do not know how I got out of jail and ended up here. I still cannot explain what happened to Alice or who was that old man. A lot of questions with very few answers. I might just see if any of my old associates are around and find out what happened to my assets after I ended up in jail.'

Helen said, 'I will stay around here for the day helping Alice get her strength. We might go shopping sometime next week if she feels up to it.'

Peter went off and had his shower, dressed, and walked to the bus stop. He caught the bus and got off in the entertainment section of town where the nightclubs were. He decided to just walk along the block to see what had changed and see if he could recognise anyone.

Alice had woken up and got out of bed and ambled to the kitchen. Helen greeted her with a kiss and said, 'I will make you some breakfast,' which she did.

After breakfast, Alice went and had her shower and got dressed in her new clothes and sat herself on the lounge, while Helen put the dirty clothes in the washing machine to wash.

While Alice was sitting watching television, the doorbell rang. Since Helen was busy, Alice went and see who was at the front door. She moved cautiously towards the door and opened it. She recognised the man and woman standing there. She said, 'Reverend Charmers, Mrs Charmers, won't you come in?'

Both stared at Alice and said, 'Thank you,' and walked into the house.

The reverend said, 'We haven't met before. I am Reverend Charmers, and this is my wife, Jean. Is Helen around?'

Alice replied, 'Yes, she is just putting things in the washing machine and should be out shortly.'

The reverend said, 'That is good. Since she is tied up, I'll just pop on in and see how Alice is doing.'

Before Alice could say a word, both disappeared and went into Alice's bedroom. Shortly they came out looking bewildered. In the meantime, Helen came into the lounge room just as the reverend and his wife came in.

The reverend said, 'I see you put Alice into respite. She is not in her room.'

Helen said, 'But you have already spoken to Alice.'

The reverend asked, 'When? I haven't seen her. I went into her room, but she wasn't there.'

Helen said, 'But this is Alice. Don't you recognise her?' The reverend replied, 'No. You must be another Alice, not Helen's Alice, the one that was deformed.'

Helen said, 'Reverend, Jean, you better sit down. We have something to tell you.'

Both the reverend and his wife sat down, and Helen explained everything to them. They were disbelievers at first and then walked up to where Alice was sitting and stared at her. They asked her a few questions as to what the sermon was about last week, as Helen and Alice attended church that day, and Alice replied, but the reverend could not remember himself and therefore did not know whether it was Alice. Eventually, he conceded it was her and fell on his knees and prayed to the Lord, giving thanks for His miracle.

Helen asked, 'What are we to say to other members of the church? They will not believe us, just like you.' The reverend replied, 'whether they believe will be up to them. If you like, I will make an announcement on your behalf on Sunday after I have given my sermon, which will have to be on the subject "Give us a sign, Lord, and we will believe". 'Alice, the Lord has done a wonderful job on you. You were a mangled mess before, and look at you now, a very beautiful woman. I just regret that I was not present to experience it. It would have helped to tell others.'

The reverend and his wife stayed a few more minutes and then moved on to see other parishioners, talking out loud while glancing back at Alice to make sure it was her. Alice saw them to the door and then came back to the lounge room.

Alice said, 'well, they didn't have much faith, did they? They didn't believe what you had said to them.'

Helen said, 'no. I guess miracles are rare these days. Or is it that the reverend does not believe in God? Or believes in God but believes miracles are something that took place during the biblical period and does not happen these days?'

Helen and Alice went into the kitchen to make a cup of tea. Both pondered on the lack of belief by the reverend as to the miracle that they saw in Alice's transformation and the constant cry by those believers who question God's existence and who constantly say, 'Give us a sign and we will believe Lord.'

Alice said, 'Fat chance. These are the people who only believe in themselves while still cannot make a cup of tea out of boiled water. That's the miracle they are looking for in themselves.'

CHAPTER 3

PETER CAUGHT THE BUS INTO town and walked down the side streets that he knew well, hoping to meet some of his old friends so he could find out what had happened rather than having to call on members of his previous family. He walked past several restaurants but did not recognise them, as they had been recently renovated and looked as if they did not seem to be owned by any of the underworld families. He walked on until he came across a building he recognised as one of his old nightclubs and went in to see who owned it. He opened the door and walked in. There were a couple of people inside cleaning up and two women behind the bar stacking glasses. One woman spotted Peter and yelled out to him, 'we are closed! Come back tonight about eight.'

Peter ignored her and kept looking around until she yelled out, 'Security!' and there appeared a man from a rear office who spotted Peter and walked up to him.

He yelled out, 'Mate, we are closed! Didn't you hear the girl yell out to you?'

Peter immediately recognised the man as being one of his lieutenants. His name was Brutus, and he was one of those men that would hit first and then ask questions rather than the other way around. Brutus stopped about a meter away from Peter and said, 'Get out. We're not open,' and reached for Peter to grab him and throw him out.

Peter immediately grabbed Brutus's arm and twisted it behind his back while grabbing him in a headlock and said, 'now, Brutus, that's not the right way of welcoming an old friend, or have you become an enemy?'

Brutus asked, 'who are you?'

Peter said, 'You don't remember me?' Brutus asked, 'Peter?'

Peter let Brutus go and said, 'What? You have already forgotten me, haven't you?'

Brutus said, 'Peter, you're the last person I would expect to walk in at this hour. How did you get out of jail?'

Peter said, 'Iit is a long and complicated story, which I doubt you will believe me if I told you. Let us just say I am out until someone wakes up to themselves. What has happened to the team we had?'

Brutus replied, 'We have lost a lot of turf and are currently being run by Joe Maratelli. Remember him? He was your second in charge. He now runs the business. Let me take you to him.'

'Sorry, Peter, I must frisk you first.' with that, Peter raised his hands and was body-searched by Brutus. Once he finished, he led the way into a hallway behind the stages and down to an office where a man was seated. Brutus knocked on the door and opened it and said, 'Boss, a man wants to speak to you.' He opened the door wider to let Peter into the office.

Joe didn't believe his eyes and momentarily hesitated and then said, 'Peter? How did you get out?'

Peter stepped forward and said, 'Joe, the years have been good to you. You're looking good.'

Joe asked, 'How did you get out? We understood you were to be locked up for another five years, minimum.'

Peter said, 'it's a long story, which I will tell you some other time. What has happened while I have been locked up?'

Joe asked, 'Are you coming back to take over?'

Peter said, 'Not at all. What has happened to the families and the territory?'

Joe replied, 'After you were locked up, there was a turf war with Vince Marconi's family coming out on top, and we were forced to merge our interest on the east side with a few nightclubs in the centre of town, like this one. Are you back to take over?'

Peter said, 'Not now. I just wanted to catch up to see what had happened. Why didn't you kill Vince and take control?'

Joe said, 'Vince controlled all the police, courts, and public servants, so we had no support and could trust no one, not even our own team, as there were a lot of Judases in our own camp. Once you left, all our contacts dropped us, as they were not getting paid. Vince controls most of the territories and gaming places, while we have most of the clubs and brothels. All we could do is take what we had and try to keep hold of this until we could change things. We are in a good position and are left alone by the other families if we do not muscle in their territory. Are you coming in?'

Peter replied, 'No, Joe, just catching up to see what has happened while I have been in the clink.'

Joe asked, 'what are you going to do with yourself while you're out?'

Peter replied, 'Keep a low profile to make sure the parties that are after me and have tried to kill me in jail, don't try while I am out.'

Joe asked, 'Do you need money or a handout?'

Peter, not wanting to be obligated to Joe, said, 'no thanks. I get an allowance for the first three months from the government, which allows me to buy pizzas. Thanks anyhow. It looks like you have everything under control and don't need me to interfere.' Joe said, 'Call us if you need any help. You know where we are. Brutus knows what you look like now, so you shouldn't have any problems next time you come.'

Peter got up and shook Joe's hand and walked out of the club, noticing two men standing nearby with guns in their hands. He knew the next time Joe might put a bullet into him, as he knew Joe did not want to relinquish control and wanted to stay as the head of the gang that he ran for the last five years. Peter went out of the club and decided to see what they have done to his home. He knew the government confiscated all his assets, but he wondered if it had been sold and renovated. He walked down several streets, turning left and then right, and as he approached his old house, he could smell smoke, which seemed to thicken as he got closer. When he got in sight of his house, he noticed the left side was on fire. In his days, this was where the bedrooms were located. As he approached the house, he noticed neighbours were out looking on, but no one was hosing the fire down or checking to see if anyone was inside. He yelled out to one neighbour, 'Anyone inside?'

The neighbour said, 'Yes, the mother with their three children.'

Peter grabbed the front hose and turned it on and pushed the front door open and went in, squirting water at the fire as he went into the house. The fire took hold, and he searched for anyone. He went into the main bedroom, but no one was there. He proceeded on to the next room, checking each room as best as he could, but he was running out of hose and water pressure was dropping. He finally had to leave the house and search the last rooms without water. He ran into one room and could see no one there and moved to another room. The fire took hold, and he knew he had to get out as the heat was intensifying. He decided this would be his last room, and as he approached the entrance, he could see what seemed to be four individuals in the far corner.

As he got closer, he could see that one of those huddled in the group was the old man that had told him about leaving prison and who was present when Alice was cured. The old man was sheltering the mother and the three children, and while the fire was blazing all around him. It was not coming near him. He yelled out to Peter to take the mother and children and escort them out of the building. Peter yelled out, 'what about you?' when he took another look, he could not see the old man. He grabbed the mother and placed one child in her arms while grabbing the other two under his arms and racing off down the hallway. There was a wall of fire in front of him, and the old man stood between him and the fire, urging him to go through the fire, which he did, and he eventually found the entrance and got out of the burning house.

As Peter burst through the fire and out of the house carrying the two children, the television crew who were setting themselves up, to broadcast. Peter was overwhelmed with the smoke and lost his footing as he exited the house with the two children. He got to the lawn and collapsed on the lawn, dropping the children and falling face down. Paramedics rushed to his aid just when the mother came out of the house carrying the youngest child. All cameras were on her and not on Peter. The paramedics quickly put Peter onto a stretcher and took him and the two children into the ambulance and sped off to the hospital. One paramedic in the back of the ambulance quickly gave the children oxygen and worked on Peter, who had breathed in a lot of smoke.

None of the reporters could get pictures of Peter, who was described as a hero. This was fortunate for him, for if they showed his face in the press, the prison guards would know where Peter was and would come and arrest him. The mother and the third child were also taken to the hospital to be checked out for smoke inhalation and were eventually reunited with the other two children.

Helen and Alice, who were in their lounge room watching the news on television, recognised the person who saved the children as Peter even though his face was not shown. They decided to go to the hospital to see if he was all right or if they could help him. They gathered their things together and telephoned for a cab. Half an hour later, they arrived at the hospital and eventually were told to wait in one of the waiting rooms, as doctors were working on Peter, who had taken in a lot of smoke. Eventually, Peter was placed in a room, and Helen and Alice could go in and speak to him. Peter could not talk much, as he had damaged his oesophagus through breathing in the smoke.

He managed, with some difficulty, to tell Helen and Alice what had happened and that it was a miracle they got out of the house as it collapsed around them. He told them he saw the old man standing in the centre of the fire protecting the children, who were not afraid when they were with him. The old man was sheltering the children and their mother, and none of the flames or fire would go near him. 'He called out for me, and I ran towards the children, thinking he needed a hand. He told me to lead everyone out of the burning building, so I grabbed two of the children and led the way out. I do not know what happened to the old man after that.'

While Peter was explaining what had happened, a man came into his compartment where his bed was and introduced himself to him as the father of the children. His name was Roger O'Brien, the owner of the largest bank in town. Roger said, 'I would like to thank you for what you did for my wife and children. No one else would lend a hand and just stood around. You went in at personal risk to save them. The person in charge on the scene told me that my whole family would have died in the house if you had not saved them then, as the roof caved in shortly after you carried the children out.' Helen said, 'it is nice of you to come over, but as you can see, Peter cannot talk now, as the smoke damages his oesophagus. Unfortunately, he will be asked to leave the hospital, as he does not have health insurance and they cannot find him a public bed. He cannot work for a few weeks until he can breathe properly. But it is good to see your family was saved. What does your wife say about the fire?'

Roger replied, 'I think she is still hallucinating. When she is asked what had happened, she continually tells reporters and others that it is a miracle she and the children were saved and says that an old man saved them by ensuring the flames never got close to them by ordering them away until Peter came and took them out of the burning house. She believes the old man to be an angel or God Himself. She said the old man called you Peter, and it was strange that he knew your name. He also knew my wife's name and my children's names. No doubt after a good night's sleep, she will come to her senses.'

Helen asked, 'Where will you live now that your house has been destroyed?'

Roger replied, 'We own a property near to our house that we recently renovated. We will move into there until our home is rebuilt. It has beds and the basic needs of a family. It will do until we have time to look around for new furniture.'

Helen said, 'I hope your wife gets better.'

Roger said, 'Yes, so do I. All that I can do is keep telling her it is her imagination and for her to stop telling people about God saving her and the children. Our local minister, unfortunately, is of no help in that he believes her and keeps telling her she saw God. Unbelievable, isn't it?'

Helen asked, 'Are you a Christian? Do you believe in God?'

Roger replied, 'Yes, I do, but to think God would come down on earth to save my wife and children, well, that is ridiculous. He would not do that. When you ask for God's help, you never get it, do you? And all that the ministers tell you is all rubbish. God has not done a thing for me. All that I have earned is through my own hard work, not by the grace of God.'

Helen said, 'Thank you for coming and seeing Peter, and we hope your wife has a speedy recovery. We will pray for her and the children.'

Roger walked out of Peter's compartment in emergency, and Helen turned to Peter and said, 'Thank God I am not his wife. I would tell him quickly that the only god he believes in is himself or his money. Notice he did not offer to assist you with some reward or money to carry you over while you are in hospital or to compensate you for lost earnings while you are getting on your feet. No, he couldn't think of departing with his money.'

Peter said, 'I agree he believes only in himself, yet you can never tell that type of person the truth. They will never want to hear it. His wife told the truth that the old man was there, and he saved them. The white cross was between them and the flames. This is the second time I have seen him. There must be some plan or reason these things are happening. He was there to show me something and said to me, "It was done in the name of the Father."

'The miracles started off with Alice and look at her—she is walking perfectly now without a stumble and can charm anyone with her smile and conversation—and now this fire and the saving of four lives. I can't see where it is leading, but there must be a message there somewhere.'

Helen said, 'Yes, and I am sure we will get to know of His plan when He is ready.'

Alice asked, 'what have the doctors told you, as to what will happen to you?'

Peter replied, 'They haven't said what they intend to do, only that they are holding me for observation.'

At that time, a doctor came in and said to Peter, 'How do you feel?'

Peter replied, 'My throat is still sore to swallow, but other than that, I am all right.'

The doctor said, 'Well, that's good. We will give you some tablets that will ease the pain in your throat, and after a few days, you should be all right. You can get dressed and go home when you are ready. I will have your discharge papers ready in about five minutes. I understand that the newspaper reporters are on their way here to interview you and should arrive in about ten minutes.'

Peter said, 'I am not in the mood to speak to them. They will really irritate my throat. Is there any way we can go now and avoid them?'

The doctor replied, 'Yes, I guess I can discharge you now, and you can go out of the hospital through the back way. I will give your papers to a nurse and have her show you the way out, so you don't have to confront them.'

Peter said, 'That would be helpful.'

Peter waited while the doctor prepared his discharge papers, and within a few minutes, a nurse escorted him out of the hospital. Just as they came out of the rear section of the hospital, they spotted the news contingent arriving and walking into the front entrance. Helen flagged a cab, and all piled into it, and they drove home.

Nothing was said on the way home, and everyone was thinking about the event that evening and about why these things were happening. They arrived home, and all went inside. It being late, all went to bed, except Peter, who showered first before going to bed.

CHAPTER 4

EVERYONE GOT UP REASONABLY EARLY and, over breakfast, decided to go into town to see the parade that was celebrating the town's anniversary. Peter did not want to go but was convinced to come to make sure no one injured Alice as she still could not walk fast. They caught the bus into town and positioned themselves in the centre of town at an intersection of two main roads. They had water and food with them in a bag and therefore did not need to go away from their position.

While they stood there waiting for the parade to begin and as the crowd was building up, Helen noticed an elderly woman at the opposite side of the intersection trying to cross the road. She had a cane, which showed she was vision impaired. She was walking up to the lights but did not stop when she got to them and continued to cross the road. Motorists blew their horns as she crossed the three-lane highway, but that did not seem to make any difference to her; she just kept walking across. Peter immediately ran out and grabbed her and brought her back to the kerb. He spoke to her, but she was not responding. She handed him a card that stated, 'Please help me. I cannot see or hear; I am blind and deaf.'

Peter was alarmed that she was on her own without help, as she could have been run over or injured by one of the cars. He sat her down on a bench in a bus shelter and stopped for a moment, realising that sitting at the end of the bench was the old man who was at the fire and who saved the children. Helen and Alice joined Peter in the bus shelter, and they also noticed the old man sitting there.

He had a white light around Him and carried a crucifix in his right hand, which radiated the white light.

The old man told Peter to place his hands on the lady's eyes and repeat the words 'In the name of the Father, I command you to see.' Peter, with some hesitancy and trepidation, did what he was instructed to do. Once completed, he was instructed to put his hands over the lady's ears and to say, 'in the name of the Father, I command you to hear.' Again, with some hesitancy, he did this under the watchful eyes of Helen and Alice. The old man raised the crucifix in his right hand as Peter spoke the words.

The old lady saw through blurred vision at the start and slowly, while blinking to clear her sight, saw the world around her clearer to where she could make things out, and she was amazed how, in reality, things appeared. Her hearing was also slowly restored, and the sounds of the world were recognised and heard by her. She could hear noises that she never heard before, which seemed very loud to her at first and made her anxious, especially the screeching from car wheels and the blaring horns.

People around her were astounded to see she could see and hear, and those that knew her came to her and introduced themselves, as they were only recognised in the past by name and the tone of their voice.

Peter wondered why they did not come to her aid sooner, presumably hoping she would kill herself and not be a burden to them. When they saw she could see, they wanted to know how this came about.

Peter turned to say something to the old man, but he was not there. The white light had gone out. He had gone, as on previous occasions. Peter, Alice, and Helen left and decided to go and get a cup of coffee as a crowd was gathering around the old lady, who was very excited, as the first time in her life she could see and hear. They were also concerned that reporters would appear, and Peter's photo may be taken and shown on the front page of newspapers and on television.

They walked for about half an hour away from the crowd and the parade and ended up in a small café outside of town and ordered some refreshments. While sitting there, an old man walked up to their table and sat down with them. They were all momentarily shocked to see it was the same old man that was there when Alice was cured, and Peter recognised him as the old man that was in the fire. They were taken aback and speechless. He was not surrounded in pure white as he had been in the past and was only in normal street clothes. He looked like an average Joe.

The old man said, 'No doubt you are wondering who I am and what is the purpose of the miracles I have instructed you to perform in the name of the Father.

'I am your Lord, Jesus Christ, the creator of heaven, earth, and mankind. These miracles enable you to see that I can do things that no other in heaven or on earth can do, miracles that cannot be earned or be bought. You, Peter, have followed Satan's ways up to now, which leads you to gain as much power, materialism, and wealth as you can, because in his world, you can never have enough of these. Now, look at you, penniless and without the fortune you once had, and strived so much to get and keep. Before you went to prison, you had a large fortune and power, as you blackmailed many of the judiciary and politicians, yet they could not arrange for you to get out of prison. Nor could any of them cure Alice. All your money that went to doctors did nothing for her, for they promised much but did very little for her, as they, too, were Satan's disciples. You saw what I have done in the name of the Father.'

'At the fire, I controlled the flames, and not one cinder fell on the heads of those children, and I saved all of them and their mother. The old lady that you rescued that was deaf and blind. I protected her from being run over, and finally I cured her. Why have I done all these things? To show you that there are things outside of this world that you cannot gain or do other than in the name of the Father.

'You were becoming a disciple of Satan, believing all that counts on this world is you and your personal wealth and power, which took you years to get and secure, but you lost them in a minute. I have shown you I could let you out of jail, which Satan could not do, nor wanted to do. All he could do is put you in jail and didn't care what happened to you, as he thought he had you forever and you would continue along your ways to regain the position and wealth you lost when you were sentenced to prison. I made sure that no harm came to you in jail, yet Satan will allow men to kill you to ensure you remained his disciple to death. He still wishes you dead, and more so when he finds out you have rejected him. I will show you another world, one that does not rely on personal wealth but on faith in God the Father.'

Peter said, 'I could never be a follower of yours, as I have killed men and done things you would never support or forgive. My life has not been a holy one or one that recognises or supports you or for what you and the Bible stand for.'

Jesus said, 'I died on the cross so your sins may be forgiven. I died for all mankind who believe in me. The only condition is you have faith in Me and My word and abandon your previous sinful life and follow My word.'

Peter asked, 'What is expected of me?'

Jesus replied, 'I will use you to do work in My name on earth. It will not be easy for you, as Satan will do all in his power to get you back, and if he can't achieve this, then he will try to discredit you so you do not become a thorn in his side or kill you to ensure you do not disrupt his plans on earth. After one year, I will return you to jail to finish your sentence, by which time you must decide whom you will follow, my ways or Satan's.'

Peter asked, 'How am I to live while out of jail? The only trade I know is how I lived in the past, mainly extortion and killing, and you now say that I must stop this and follow a different life, one that doesn't require wealth or power.'

Jesus said, 'You are to stop immediately your old sinful ways. I will ensure you receive a monthly allowance to enable you to live and attend to my work. Should you follow Satan's ways, then I will put you back in jail immediately, and your allowance will cease. You cannot have a foot in both camps. You either follow My word and, in return, I will give you eternal life and treasures in heaven far beyond what Satan could give you on this earth, or you revert to your old ways and follow Satan and live whatever time My Father has allocated to you on this earth in sin and then, at the end, be thrown into the internal fire and live in hell for a thousand years with your master, Satan.

'Helen and Alice know my ways and pray constantly. Both have been blessed by Me. You, Peter, do not know Me or My ways, so I will shortly take you to heaven when you will be instructed in the ways of the Bible. You will see for yourself the glory of heaven and meet those who transformed mankind. I will do this so you may understand who I am and know my word. Understood?'

Peter replied, 'Yes, understood except the heavenly bit. I will follow Your ways.'

The café owner asked, 'Mate, who are you talking to? You seem to mumble to yourself while looking at me. You seem to have a conversation with someone, but no one is here.'

Peter replied, 'Sorry, I was just talking out loud to myself.'

They gave their order and, once delivered to their table, sat there drinking their coffee.

Helen said, 'So you have been the chosen one.'

Peter said, 'And you are the chosen two, whatever that means. I am not sure what is in the Bible and what I am about to do with it.'

Helen said, 'It will not be of benefit for us to discuss the Bible or try to explain it to you. I am not sure I understand it myself totally, but always found the Bible to help when in time of trouble and when I need to pray. I have always believed in God, and even when we had extreme trouble with Alice or money, I understood it was always part of God's plan and I was being used as part of that plan even when things went bad with Alice. Unlike most, I never blamed God for Alice's condition or complained, but asked for His mercy and divine help to overcome the problems confronting us. He never left us, even if it took some time for the problem to be resolved. It was always done in His time.'

Alice said, 'Yes, I agree. You used to read the Bible to me every night so I can just about repeat it to you line by line, but there were many sections I did not quite understand.'

Peter said, 'Good. Then both of you can accompany me to heaven and get instructions when I ask your questions to those in the know.'

Helen said, 'I doubt they will invite us. No, I am sure you are the only one designated, as you seem the only one asked to take part in the miracles in the name of the Father.'

They finished their coffee and caught a bus back home, which took about half an hour.

Peter opened the front door, and as they stepped inside, all immediately were confronted by an immense bright light, and their bodies seemed to be free from the earth's gravity, and they were taken on a journey till they were told to open their eyes and step forward, which they did. Before them was the old man sitting on a pure white granite throne, and around him were other priests, who also were dressed in white robes.

They were told to sit down before those present, which they did, and were taken back to the beginning of Creation and were witnesses to all the events that were written in the Bible. They witnessed the parting of the seas, the birth of Jesus, the feeding of the crowd, the Sermon on the Mount, Christ's Crucifixion, and His Resurrection.

They spoke to Izhar, Elijah, Abraham, David, Solomon, Moses, Ruth, Mark, Luke, Paul, and Peter the disciple. They saw the horrors of the Crucifixion and the agony endured by Jesus when abandoned by His Father at the time he took all our sins upon his shoulders at the Cross and the subsequent Resurrection. History was portrayed before them, and at the end, they opened their eyes and were sitting on the sofa in their lounge room wondering what had happened and where did they go.

They said nothing momentarily and then realised that they had all been on the journey described to them at the café by Jesus. They looked at the time and noted that they had arrived home exactly the moment they entered their house from the bus stop. They checked their calendar and noticed that they had lost three whole days in their heavenly journey. No one said anything, but all knew what had happened and that they could interpret the events of the Bible and recall the exact dates and times when things happened. They could also recall all the sections of the Bible missing none. All were grateful that they witnessed what had happened from Creation to the Resurrection and could speak to those that made Bible history and got answers from them as to what had happened and to see for themselves the glory of God. To speak to those who wrote the Bible was an extreme privilege, and each was speechless regarding the miracle that had happened to them personally.

They were privileged and were humble to know that God considered them justified to stand before His throne and speak to those who had proven themselves faithful followers of God.

Peter mostly could not get his head around why he was chosen, but was extremely thankful, as he would never have believed in God or the kingdom of heaven otherwise. what he saw made him accept that what we have on earth is not worth keeping and is only short term. What heaven offers is far more gratifying and worthy to strive for, rather than materialism and sin offered here on earth and into which we are born.

Peter, a sinner, never thought he would get to speak to the saints and be taught the Bible as he was. Being a sinner, he thought his sins would never be forgiven. But the night before, he prayed to God and asked Him to forgive him for his sins. Being thrust into heaven and presented before Jesus confirmed to him that his prayer had been answered. His sins had been forgiven at the cross.

CHAPTER 5

SUNDAY AND ALL GOT UP, had breakfast, and Helen and Alice prepared themselves for church. Peter sat on the lounge looking at television until Helen said, 'You better get dressed if you are going to church.'

Peter asked, 'Church, why?'

Helen replied, 'You mean to tell me, after what we witnessed, you would not want to go to church?'

Peter said, 'I don't see the association.'

Helen said, 'Then Satan is truly knocking at your door, brother. Please yourself, but we are going and will head off in about five minutes.'

Peter said, 'well, if you think I must, then I will go with you, but it has been a long time since I have been to church. I do not know what to do.'

Helen said, 'Follow all the others. That is all you can do. Sit in the pew and listen to the sermon. You don't have to do anything you don't want to do. There are no rituals, and believe it or not, they do speak English.'

Peter got dressed, and they all walked off to their local church, which was some four blocks away. When they arrived, Reverend Charmers greeted them and they entered the church to wait for other members of the congregation to assemble. After about fifteen minutes, the service began with singing of a hymn, followed by reading from the Bible, and, finally, Reverend Charmers entered the pulpit to deliver his sermon.

Reverend Charmers said, 'Many of you here today in this packed church still do not believe in Jesus Christ. You partly believe in God on Sundays, for an hour when in church, but for the rest of the week, you are back to the ways of this world, and Christ gets put back into the last row of your thoughts until next Sunday, when He is again brought out.

'When I ask you why this is the case, most of you say you cannot feel or see Christ. Yet you get up in the morning and witness a sunrise and at night the sun falls, the stars and moon. During the day, you see and feel the rain, wind, and see the oceans and mountains and witness the birth of your own children and a new generation. And yet you still say to me, we cannot believe unless we see a sign.

'Today we are witnesses in this church. Not one sign, but three.'

'You all have seen each Sunday Helen and Alice coming to church and have seen the condition Alice was in. She was confined to a wheelchair, barely recognisable as a young woman, crippled, and with a twisted body, leaving her little hope of any life of her own. No medical intervention or cure was possible, and yet by the miracle of Jesus Christ, she has been cured and miraculously made a new young woman. Alice, please stand up.' Alice stood up and turned and confronted all those behind her. They did not recognise her, nor did they believe she was the same person. Reverend Charmers placed a picture of how Alice was in the past on the church overhead screen.

'This is how Alice looked before, the one you knew in her wheelchair. The person who is now before you is Alice, after the Lord's miracle. You may not believe it, but they are the same person. If that is running through your mind, then go up to her after the service and have a discussion with her. You will find she is the same person, and she remembers what you said to her in the past and behind her back. Now she can answer you back.'

'But, wait, one miracle may not be enough for the sceptics amongst you. There was a fire last week in a house close to here. Three children and a mother were saved, but no one can explain how Peter took everyone out when the house was totally ablaze. The children and their mother come to this church regularly, and most of you know them. When asked, they will tell you they had no hope of escaping the house as the fire took hold quickly. Yet an elderly man entered the building with none of the flames touching him and sheltered the four, commanding the flames to stay away. When Peter came on the scene, the same person directed him to take all of them out of the burning building, which he did. He was assured that no flame would touch any of them, and that was the case. Now, you may say we are all dreaming this up and have made an event out of an occurrence. Not so. Speak to those who took part in the rescue and find out for yourself.'

'But some will not accept this truth. So, I will mention miracle number three. You all know John Matthews, one of our elderly members of the church. She comes every Sunday and reads the service in Braille and tries to follow the service as best as she can with assistance from her helpers. She has been blind and deaf since birth. Regulars know her and know of her condition. Well, by the grace of God, she, too, has been cured and can now see and hear what is being said. Those that will approach her after the service may ask her questions, and she can respond. However, she speaks in a low voice, her speech will come good in time. So be patient if you want a reply from her. She is eager to meet all those that have known her over the years.'

'We have three concrete examples of nothing less than miracles. Yet I dare say that there will be some of you that will still not believe in Jesus Christ and will still stay the way you were until death, when it will be too late for you, and you will be condemned to hell and forfeit the right of eternal life, which is given to you by Jesus Christ. Others will say, "Yes, but show me a sign that I can witness. Otherwise, no matter how many miracles you show me, I still will not believe them.'

'At the crucifixion, many in the crowd said, "If you are the Christ, then order God to set you free from the cross," while others said, "If you are Christ, then give us a sign. Come on down from the cross, and we will believe you.'

These people had witnessed Jesus revive Lazarist and heal the disabled, yet still demanded a sign. You still believe in yourself and will only trust in yourself and never have faith in God. in doing so, you believe in Satan and are prepared to do his sinful work rather than what God wants of you. You will be the ones that believe in what you have on this earth and will not accept or do not want what God has offered you.

'You have been born into a sinful world and will never look up to heaven and ask for forgiveness, and no matter how much proof is presented to you, it is not enough. However, at the first opportunity, you turn against God and brush Him aside and declare there is no God, as if the miracles presented to you never happened or are mere tricks.'

'We are all condemned to death and, before this, a miserable life, yet most try to shrug this off, as they have found a substitute for God in materiality and wealth and are not prepared to accept God's judgement on mankind. They avoid this by selling their soul to Satan and, in doing so, enjoy life on this earth for whatever time is given to them. But life ends abruptly, and then it is too late to jump ship, and for a thousand years, they will regret their decision. The good life will be no more.

'I urge you to seek those involved in the three miracles. Talk to them and seek God and ask Him to come into your life and forgive you of your sins.'

'Let us pray . . .'

After the service, Peter, Helen, and Alice went outside to have coffee and to confront the expected crowd of parishioners who they believed would want to speak to Alice and confirm the miracle. As they were at the front of the church, it took them the longest time to walk out of the church, but when they exited the church, there were only several people gathered for morning tea to speak to those Reverend Charmers spoke of and to confirm for themselves that these miracles happened. Peter went up to the reverend and said, 'Where are those who wanted a sign?'

The reverend replied, 'They are like the Pharisees—they asked for a sign when the blind was made to see. They even witnessed the resurrection of Lazarus and continually requested a sign 'so we know you are the true God". nothing will ever satisfy these people, and they will never believe or have faith in Jesus Christ. These people are the majority in this world, for what they possess is what they want, and they do not want to be told the purpose of why they have been placed on this earth and what is going to happen to them when they die. They are the disbelievers, and no matter what you say, they will never believe, as what they want, they already have and only want more of it. Wealth and materiality. These have become a substitute for Jesus Christ.'

Alice met several people she remembered, and they agreed it was her. After asking her several questions and looking into her eyes, they could recognise that it was her.

The same with the other people that had experienced the Lord's blessing. They, too, stayed on and met those that knew them and chatted with them, but these were around twenty people out of a congregation of over two hundred.

Peter, Alice, and Helen stayed till the end and then walked back to their home, still talking about the small number of people that stayed to greet them and discuss their miraculous cure. As they approached their home, they noticed an expensive Mercedes car parked on the curb opposite their front door. They all thought it was for the neighbour and walked to the front door and insert their key in the lock when the driver, a chauffeur, got out and opened the door of the car and said, 'Sir, madam, you are expected to accompany me. Please get into the car?'

Peter said, 'Sorry, we do not know anyone who owns such a car and will not accompany you anywhere.'

The chauffeur said, 'Sir, an old man appeared before me, telling me to come to this address and drive you to the home of Sir Richards.'

Helen said, 'We better go, as it seems important.'

All three got into the car and were driven into the countryside along a main highway. After an hour, they turned off on a side street and proceeded along it for approximately ten minutes and then drove into an estate with a large spacious house before them that had a long driveway. The car drove up to the house, and the chauffeur got out and opened the door of the car to let them out. They got out of the car, and the door of the house opened, and a servant stood there waiting for them to get out of the car, which they eventually did, and they walked up to the front door. The servant, under instructions, escorted them to a room where there was a young woman in bed in a similar condition to what Alice was in.

They went into the room and looked around. Alice immediately recognised the physically disabled woman as being with her in respite frequently. Her face and body were deformed and bent in a form that would prevent anyone from recognising the person. As they were looking around, a man entered the room. He was dressed in an expensive suit and looked about fifty years old. He walked up to Peter and said, 'My name is David Richards. I own this property, and this is my daughter, Alexis. I had several dreams that I ignored until I saw an image in my office telling me to send for you, which now I have done.'

Peter said, 'My name is Peter, and this is my sister, Helen, and her daughter, Alice. why have you called for us? What do you want us to do?'

David said, 'I am not sure. I don't expect you can do anything, and I am not sure why I had to summon you here to my house.'

Peter asked, 'Is your wife around? She may know what this is about.'

David replied, 'My wife died some eighteen months ago in a car accident. It was quite odd in that she was a very religious woman and believed in God. In fact, both of us had faith. A lot of good that did us. She got killed by a drunken driver slamming into her and leaving me with a crippled daughter that no one can cure. I have had the best specialists examine her, and they can do nothing for her.'

Peter said, 'I sense you have shown that, you never had much faith in Jesus, and that as soon as you were given a trial, you gave up on him and decided it was of no use to have faith in Christ, as He doesn't exist. I even bet that you stopped going to church, and when the first opportunity presented itself, you declared to one and all that there was no God.'

David said, 'Yes. what is the use when all your life you believe in Jesus Christ and then He allows a drunken driver to slam head-on into my wife and kill her? She meant everything to me.'

Peter said, 'what you have told us leads me to think you idolised your wife to idolatry. She was your god, and you had little faith in Jesus. You have showed to yourself that you, in fact, did not believe in Him at all. You merely went through the motions of being a good Christian to either satisfy your wife or to uphold a good appearance in the community, one that you believe was necessary in line with your position and wealth.'

David said, 'well, I have been proven right, haven't I? My wife is dead, and I am left with a crippled daughter that will never be healed or achieve anything in life.'

Peter asked, 'please close the door and move to the end of your daughter's bed?'

Helen said, 'Peter, are you sure you know what you are doing?'

Peter said, 'You and Alice will have to move aside.'

Peter then placed his hands on Alexis's head as she lay motionless in her bed with her father looking on, not knowing what to expect. Under his breath, Peter said, 'Jesus, I ask for your strength and help to cure Alexis of her deformity and illness. In the name of Jesus Christ, I command any evil spirits to come out of Alexis now and for her to be cured of her deformity and illness.'

Peter looked up, and so did Helen and Alice, as each of them could see the old man standing next to Alexis on the other side of Peter. The old man placed his hands on Alexis and said a silent prayer, mouthing the words, 'Father, I ask in your name that Alexis be cured and healed from her deformity. In the name of the Father.'

A white cross appeared over Alexis and suddenly, there was a gust of wind as if something had just run out of the room, which everyone felt. Then nothing.

David said, 'I told you nothing can be done to help Alexis. nothing or no one on this earth or in heaven can cure her. Your prayers amount to nothing, and we are all wasting our time in standing here hoping for a miracle.'

Peter, with his hands still resting on Alexis's head, continued to pray and could feel that something was happening with Alexis's body. It turned, and her arms straightened out. By this time, David had reached the door of the bedroom and was on his way out when he heard Alexis give a shriek, which made him turn to see her body move left and then right to straighten itself out under her blanket. She was struggling to keep her blanket, her arms outstretched, while her father watched anxiously. After about a further few minutes, everything stopped.

David moved quickly up to Alexis's bed and pulled her blankets to one side to reveal a completely straightened body. Her face also had been straightened out, and all the twisted jaws were straightened out, revealing a beautiful young lady. He paused for a few seconds and then leaned over her to grab her in his arms and gave her a big hug and kiss. Alexis held on to him as she tried to get up, but the best she could do was keep her grip on him as he swung her around and sat her on the edge of her bed.

Everyone stopped and stared at her as she tried to get up, and with David's help, she stood on her own two feet and walked, first in shuffle motions assisted by her father.

Peter, Helen, and Alice stepped aside and allowed David to experience the miracle that had just been performed. After about ten minutes, David sat his daughter on the side of her bed and went over to Peter and said, 'You have performed a miracle. No one on this earth could have cured my daughter. Only you have done it.'

Peter said, 'No, David, I did nothing other than prayed over your daughter. While you did not see Him, Jesus was present here and prayed to His Father to cure your daughter. It was God who cured her, not me, Helen, or Alice.'

'It is the God whom you despised, the one in whom you showed little faith in that did this miracle. When we first came here, you said you did not know the reason we were brought here. We also did not know why we were called here, but now you can see it was to witness the miraculous cure of your daughter, whom you haven't had much to do with since her mother's death, if I read the body language right.'

David said, 'You're right. I have rejected Alexis since her mother's death and have blamed God for the death of my wife. I always said that He could have prevented it, as He could do all things, not recognising that we are all created with a free will and God refuses to intervene in what we decide to do. It was not His doing or lack of intervention that caused the death of my wife, but that drunken driver. He could have laid off the booze, but, no, he got himself full so he could run into someone. It was my wife, and he killed her. Yes, I have had little faith in God, blaming Him for her death, showing what little faith I had in Him. But now He has given me back a beautiful daughter that no one else could cure.'

Alice took Alexis by the hand, and both walked with small steps. After a while, Alice let go of her hands, and Alexis walked unaided with stiff motions first and then becoming more confident as time went by.

Peter said, 'David, I think we better leave you and Alexis alone and let you get yourselves settled down. Could your driver give us a lift to the train station or somewhere where we can get home?'

David replied, 'no, he will take you home, but I wonder whether Helen and Alice could stay a couple of days to help me with Alexis. I understand you went through a similar situation with Alice. Alexis said she recognised Alice from respite, and you can see both get on very well. I will need someone to buy Alexis clothes so she can move around, and I really am not the best person for that kind of thing.'

Helen said, 'We will have to go home and collect some clothes for a few days, if that is all right with Peter.'

David said, 'Peter, can stay here as well. There are enough rooms for everyone.'

Peter replied, 'Thanks, but, no, I don't want to go shopping for dresses and underwear.'

David said, 'My driver will take you home and wait until you pack your things and then will bring Helen and Alice back. 'Alice said, 'Alexis is roughly the same size as me, so we'll bring back some of my things so you can wear today and when we go shopping.'

David said, 'Good. while you are away, we have some praying to do and asking for forgiveness as to my lost faith in the Lord. I will have to get reconnected and most probably will need some help to do this. I will call our local minister, who still drops in from time to time, and give him the good news about Alexis and get some advice from him. What more would a man want to convince him of the existence of a God?'

Peter, Helen, and Alice went out, and the driver was waiting for them to take them home. About an hour later, they were home, and the girls packed their bags and soon had everything ready for their return journey. They said goodbye to Peter and drove off in the chauffeur-driven car to Sir Richards's house. There, the girls unpacked their things and then took Alexis to have a shower and helped her change into proper clothes rather than the gown that she was in. When she came out of the bedroom to walk to the kitchen, her father could hardly believe his eyes as to how straight her body was and how beautiful she looked now that she was wearing proper clothes.

David assembled all the staff in the lounge room and, once everyone was there, declared to them that a miracle had happened and the person before them was Alexis.

The staff doubted the story, as they did not believe in Jesus or miracles, thinking David had done something to Alexis and replaced her with the other girl. They were all surprised, but most still did not believe she had a miraculous cure but said nothing, as it was not their business.

Alexis's speech improved by the hour, and she could speak without slurring her words if she spoke slowly and did not rush her speech. Her walking was still limited, as she was stiff and unaccustomed to bending her knees, but Alice said this would improve over the next few days, as she was the same when she was first cured.

After all the formalities were attended to and Helen and Alice were introduced to the staff, they sat down and had dinner and watched a movie on Sir Richards's large screen and then retired for the night.

The next morning, Sir Richards left to attend to business matters and left the girls to arrange their day. Since Alexis was still getting used to walking, it was agreed to allow her to walk around the house and gardens for the next few days so she could build up her strength.

David had already telephoned all the relatives and advised them about what had happened, but most thought he had been drinking and did not believe him. So, over the following few days, there was a stream of relatives calling in to see for themselves what had happened. At first, they did not believe what David had stated to them, but after having a conversation with Alexis, they had to admit she had been cured and the person they were talking to was the same person who was crippled and laid in bed for most of the day.

One relative, a brother, did not believe what was said to him and called the police, advising them that their brother had most probably killed Alexis and did away with her body and hired a young model to take her place. The police did interview Helen and Alice but did not believe in miracles either, so left the matter to be further investigated and for doctors who were treating Alexis to examine her and file reports.

It finally came down to a DNA examination of Alexis's clothing before and after her cure, which concluded she was the same person.

Over the next week, the entire household was embroiled with doctors and investigators examining Alexis with the news of Alexis's cure, finally reaching the television stations. Alexis and her father gave interviews, and this was broadcasted around the world. The Pope received the message and declared this to be a miracle and prayed for Alexis.

The doctors examined Alexis and again re-examined her DNA samples, which proved she was the same person who was crippled and now healed. As to how this was done, most could not give an opinion, as they did not believe in God and therefore could not agree that it was a miraculous cure. Most said, 'Be reasonable, these things just do not happen.'

Medical scientists were asked to examine the evidence and again could not give an opinion, as most did not believe in miracles or God but knew that it must have been a miracle, as there was no other possibility for the cure to happen. Publicly, all they could say was that their examination was ongoing and currently inconclusive, which did little for their credibility. As the DNA proved Alexis was who she claimed to be, the police could not pursue the matter further and dropped the case, marking the file as not being a homicide matter and therefore could be closed.

Alexis was featured in magazines, and her miraculous cure was raised by many ministers as part of their sermons. Prayers were said for her, and believers gave thanks to God in prayers for curing such a crippled person.

Eventually, things settled down after a few weeks, and Helen, Alice, and Alexis could go shopping with David to get clothes for

Alexis. on the first shopping spree, David became frustrated in waiting for his daughter to decide and wasted a whole day moving from one shop to another and waiting on her to try on various outfits, which she ended up not buying. On the second day, he declared he had an emergency at the office and gave his credit card to Helen with instructions to buy whatever she thought was necessary.

The three spent over a week going into most of the expensive shops and buying outfits that suited Alexis. When they brought them home and showed David, he was very pleased with their selection of garments, shoes, and accessories, even if it ended up costing him substantially more than he planned on.

CHAPTER 6

Peter took the time to relax while the girls were away and, after a couple of days, became bored doing nothing. He went into town to look around, so got himself dressed up and headed for the bus stop. While waiting there for a bus, a car pulled up with two men in it, telling him to get in.

Peter was reluctant at first to get in, as he thought they mistook him for someone else. He thought the faces were familiar but could not remember where he had seen the men. He got in the back seat, and the car drove off. The driver said to Peter, 'Peter, it has been a long time. When did you get out? Why haven't you come to see us?'

Peter replied, 'Well, I have only been out for a few weeks and have to be careful what I do, as the police are monitoring me.'

The driver said, 'Don't worry, we know most of the police and can square things with them. Do you remember us, or have you forgotten us since they set you up?'

Peter replied, 'The faces are familiar, but I can't recall the names.'

The driver said, 'Louise Abbott, Lou, and this fella is Mic Omalos. we used to do work for you when you wanted someone roughened up or taught a lesson. Don't you remember us?'

Peter replied, 'I recognised the faces but couldn't remember your names. What are you doing now besides driving past bus stops and picking up strangers?'

Lou said, 'We work for ourselves doing the same things we did for you, picking up a contract on someone or attending to a heist when we get the word. Are you interested in joining us? We have a big shipment of drugs coming in, and we could use another man that knows how to use a gun. Are you interested in joining us?'

Peter quickly thought about their offer and remembered what the old man has said to him about sin and breaking his pledge to God. He did not want to go back to prison and now had second thoughts about whether his old life was the right one to follow, since he could see what God could do with miracles, things that money can't buy, such as the cure of Alice and Alexis.

Peter replied, 'I think the risk is too great for me. If the police spot me, I will end up in prison for another ten years, and the families will arrange for me to be killed in there. I don't want to, or I can't take the risk.'

Lou said, 'We understand, but this one, we all get to wear hoods so we won't be recognised, and it would be a simple in- and-out job. We already have a buyer lined up for the drugs, so we will get our money the same day, all three million. A million each. Are you in?'

Peter remembered God telling him that Satan would not let him go easily and would not care if he was caught, sent back to prison, or went back to his old trade, as long as he did not follow God's way. He was not too keen to go back to his old life after seeing the miracles God had done and that he, of all people, was chosen to do God's work. While contemplating his answer to Lou, Peter received a premonition with the angel of the Lord telling Peter that Satan was again knocking at his door and for him to go to the local community hospital and to lay his hands on a sister, Mary Partridge, who was dying of late-stage cancer. He was told which floor she was on and her room number and was advised what to do.

Lou said, 'Hey, Peter, are you still with me, or have you dropped off to sleep?'

Peter replied, 'Sorry, Lou, thanks for considering me. I will have to think about it, as the risk is very high. Many people would like to have me locked up for good. I will have to get back to you later today. I have to perform a miracle at the local hospital, so I will have to get you to let me out anywhere here so I can get a bus.'

Lou said, 'A miracle. Yeah, anything done at a hospital is a miracle except for the ones who are carried out in a bag. We will drive you there. It won't be a problem for us.'

Lou drove Peter to the hospital and parked the car. As Peter got out, the other two men get out of the car with him.

Peter said, 'I will be all right from here. You don't have to come.'

Lou said, 'We want to see your miracle, Peter, just to make sure you don't spill the beans on us.'

Peter asked, 'why would I do that? I will still end up in jail if I told the cops.'

Lou said, 'We thought you would jump at our offer. Since you want to think about it, we do not want to take the chance, so we will follow you to see you perform your miracle. Shall we go?'

All three men went to the entrance and caught the lift to the floor where Sister Mary was lying. They came up to the room, and Peter said to Lou, 'You better wait out here.'

Lou said, 'No. We will come in to see your miracle, as I smell a rat.'

Peter said, 'There is a nun in there dying of cancer, and I have been asked to help cure her.'

Lou said, 'You must think we are idiots to believe that rubbish. There is no cure for cancer other than death. So, who do you intend to rub out?'

Peter said, 'I will rub no one out. Just help cure this nun.'

Lou said, 'well, let's see you do it.'

With that, Lou pushed the door open and shoved Peter in. To his surprise, he could see the room was dimly lit, and it had about five or six nuns sitting there praying with Bibles in their hands. They were all startled by Lou as he shoved Peter in and said, 'Well, do your miracle.'

Peter, under the watchful eyes of those present, went to the head of the bed where Sister Mary lay and momentarily hesitated to get his composure. He then placed his hands on the head of Sister Mary and said, 'Lord, I pray for Sister Mary, who has been a loyal servant of yours and has done worthy things in your name. I ask that you cure her of her cancer and allow her to rise. I do this in Jesus's most holy name.'

The sisters present looked up at Peter in surprise and in total disbelief at what he was saying. While they were there praying for Sister Mary, they had no doubt that their prayer was falling on deaf ears and that nothing would change the condition of the terminal illness sister Mary had.

Peter again placed his hands on Sister Mary's forehead and immediately saw the old man dressed in a white robe, who came up to Sister Mary and placed his hands over her hands, which were crossed in front of her. A white cross appeared on sister Mary. No one else could see the old man, but those close to Sister Mary felt as if something brushed against them and they could see the white cross on Sister Mary.

Peter said, 'In the name of Jesus Christ, may God heal you of your cancer, and may you rise and be free from this ailment. In the name of our Lord Jesus Christ, God the Father, I so mercifully ask of the Lord.'

When Peter looked up, the old man had gone. Sister Mary moved at the surprise of the other sisters that were present there. She moved and then tried to get out of bed. The other sisters told her to remain lying down, but she immediately sat up and tried to get out of bed and onto her feet. Lou and his mate, not believing what they were seeing, made a bolt for the door and could be heard running down the hallway to get out of the place. Sister Mary got to her feet and stood there, while the other sisters were calling for the nurse or a doctor. A doctor ran into the room and, seeing Sister Mary standing up, said, 'My god, what are you doing? How did you get up? An hour ago, you were dying, and we thought you would die within a short period. Go back to bed before you fall over.'

Sister Mary said, 'I will not fall over, nor will I go back to bed.'

'There is nothing wrong with me.'

The doctor said, 'Mary, you are dying of cancer, so please go back to bed before you collapse on the floor.'

Sister Mary said, 'There is nothing wrong with me. If you examine me, you will find the cancer has gone.'

The doctor said, 'Just sit in this chair until I examine you.'

It surprised all the other sisters that were there to see Sister Mary standing up and able to speak. They heard what Peter had said but disbelieved that anything miraculous would happen. Seeing Sister Mary stand up still didn't register with them that a miracle had happened. Peter could see that Mary could control the situation and therefore left her after saying a brief prayer of thanks to the Lord for the miracle performed in His name. He then departed, leaving the doctors and nurses to sort out what they had to do.

Peter then made his way to the elevator and went up to the Cardiology Department, where there was a priest dying from a severe heart attack. He entered the room and was spotted by a nurse, who followed him in. She said to Peter, 'You can only stay for a minute.'

Peter said, 'Thank you. That will be all the time I need.' Peter placed his hands on the priest and in a low voice said, 'Jesus, as instructed, I am with Father Brain Rheumy and ask you to heal him from his heart attack.'

On hearing these words, the nurse turned around and stared at Peter as to what he was doing and continued looking at his every movement in total surprise.

After saying these words, Peter noticed the old man in the room, who had moved to where the priest had been lying and placed his hands on the priest. A white light appeared, and a white cross appeared over Father Rheumy.

Peter moved to the head of the bed and placed his hands on the head of Brian Rheumy and said, 'In Jesus's name and in the name of God the Father, I ask the Lord to heal Brother Brian Rheumy and command him to rise and be totally cured of his illness.'

Peter looked up, and the old man had gone, but the nurse was there witnessing what had happened. Within seconds, Brian moved the blankets off himself and was preparing to get up. The nurse leapt forward to stop him, insisting he stay in bed. Peter took the opportunity to remove himself from the room while the nurse was involved with her patient. The nurse, not having much luck in convincing the priest to stay in bed, pressed the button for help and was immediately surrounded by support staff and doctors telling Brian he should stay in bed, or he will have another heart attack. Brian was telling them that there was nothing wrong with him and he was getting up out of bed and just did that to the surprise of the doctors.

The doctors immediately put him back in bed and performed an ECG on him, which showed there was nothing wrong with his heart. They could not believe this and got another machine, which showed the same result. They performed other pathology tests on him, which also showed that there was nothing wrong with him. Finally, they sent him to have an MRI on his heart, which revealed he had a heart of a twenty-year-old and there was nothing wrong with his heart. When they matched this up with the tests done on previous days, they could not come up with an answer as to how he could have been cured in such a short period.

The nurse tried to tell the doctors that there was a man who came to visit Brian who said a prayer over him, and that was when Brian decided he wanted to get out of bed. Brian remembered the man and described God's presence, but no one would believe him, as none of them believed in God or in the power of prayer, and all put it down to Brian hallucinating from medication. They kept saying there must be some scientific reason as to how this cure happened. They immediately discounted God and miracles, as these things do not happen, which really left them with nothing.

Peter walked out of the hospital and made his way to the bus stop and finally home. He made himself some lunch and sat down to watch the news on the television. Sure enough, the news about Sister Mary and Brian Rheumy was all over the news, with the hospital refusing to comment about patients on privacy grounds.

The nuns in the room with Sister Mary were all too willing to describe it as a miracle that she was cured, and the nurse in Father Rheumy's room also said that in his case, there could be no other explanation other than an act of God. Peter listened to the news and thought to himself, *I wonder what had happened with Lou and his mate, whether they would come around again after witnessing what had been done.* As he pondered on the topic, there was a knock at the door, and Lou was there with Mic. Peter gestured them in, and they went inside and sat down.

Lou said, 'Man, that was some performance you did this morning. You had everyone in the room convinced that it was an actual miracle. You nearly fooled me. How much did they pay you to do that trick?'

Peter replied, 'It was not a trick, Lou. God Himself was in the room, whom you could not see, nor could you see standing alongside you was Satan, who was also witnessing the miracle and who was trying to prevent it from happening. But he could not, and it happened. If only you stayed to see it. That's why you bolted because your sinful master, Satan, didn't want you to see the power of God as you may decide that His power is greater than of Satan's or what this world can offer you and you would change your ways.'

Lou said, 'So I take it you will not join us in what we discussed.'

Peter said, 'Like you, I drift towards what this world offers—namely, money, power, and influence — but you can't take these with you once you go to the grave, which could be an hour from now. Yes, you can enjoy life with those things, but you saw the power offered by God, which lasts beyond this world. I prefer to not go back to the past and resume life as it was, but to change and try to live a better life without the prostitution, killing, bashings, and stealing, which were my everyday activities before I ended up in jail. I had it all but went to jail with nothing. God took me out of jail to show me His way. Satan wants me back in there to make sure I do not leave him and change my ways. I can guarantee that if you stay with him, he will not care about you but will make sure you act as he would want you to do, doing what you have always done until someone puts a bullet in you, and then it is too late to change.'

Lou said, 'well, it is too late for me, as I would prefer to live a good life here on earth and enjoy myself while I am here. I do not believe there is anything better after this life, and what I saw this morning does not make me change my mind. To me, it was a magician's act and there is no God. If there was, why is the world so messed up?'

Peter replied, 'I thought the same way until He told me He has given each one of us free choice and He will not override the choice you make. So, if you decide to rape someone or shoot someone, then He will not step in and save that person, as it is your free choice to do so. Yes, the other person, an innocent party, is injured, and you will be made to answer for your actions. But you may decide what you want to do knowing eventually you will pay for these. Remember, Satan has been placed on this earth after being sentenced to hell. You will join him there if you don't change your ways.'

Lou said, ' I don't believe any of what you say and will continue with the life I have carved out for myself. Mic and I have worked together for years and trust each other. We are one of a kind. I take it you will not be coming with us. There is good money for all of us, enough to take care of us for some time in the good life. If you continue your life as it is, receiving handouts and living a beggars' life, you will achieve nothing.'

Peter said, 'I think there is a better life than what Satan is offering. Thanks, but I wish you all the best.'

With that, they shook hands, and Lou and Mic left Peter and drove off.

About a week later, Helen and Alice came home and quickly settled back into their routine. Peter cut the grass and did some work around the yard and then sat down to have a beer in front of the television. Helen and Alice sat down with him to hear the news headlines and were surprised to hear that two men were gunned down trying to steal drugs from the mob on the north side. Both men were known to the police and tried to intercept a shipment of heroin as it left the container terminal. Both were killed at the scene; however, the shipment of drugs eluded police, who had it staked out.

Peter thought to himself, thank God he did not take up Satan's offer to join the two, as he also would be headed for hell. Peter recalled Lou's words, 'nothing can go wrong. It will be a straightforward job.'

Helen looked at Peter and said, 'Did you know anything thing about the robbery?'

Peter replied, 'Yes. while you were away, they came to me to see if I wanted to join them. I told them the risk was to too high and declined. Thank God I did. Otherwise, you would cremate me along with them.'

Helen said, 'Don't risk it, Peter. it is not worth it. We have enough to live on and under the Lord's protection. It is not worth it. Satan has put you in jail, and he will try to keep you there.'

Peter said, 'I know. Do not worry about it. I didn't join them.'

--- ✳ ---

CHAPTER 7

STEVEN BLIGH WAS LOOKING OVER his profit-and-loss statement and was concerned that he was not getting the profits he should and would miss out on his million-dollar bonus unless he did something drastic to address the situation.

The only way he could remedy the slide being experienced is to increase the volume of milk being sold. He could lower his margin to increase volume, but that benefit was unlikely because of the retailers' aggressive strategies, and they would take up the increased profit.

He knew dairy farmers were having trouble breaking even, but they could still make a profit if they monitored their costs. The processors whom the farmer had a contract with to sell his milk to, we're central to making a profit in that the processor could agree or not agree to buy the farmer's milk and could negotiate a price that allowed them to on-sell the milk to the retailers and still make a profit.

Steven contemplated that for him to increase his profit, he would have to export milk to another country. For this to happen, there would have to be a shortage of supply in that country. The only way this could occur is if the local farmers were driven out of business by not being able to get a reasonable farm gate price for their milk, making their business not viable and forcing the farmers off the land.

He researched into the processing conglomerates in other countries and found that there were three large ones controlling 80 percent of the market. He noted one conglomerate which purchased his produce in his own country, which he knew well, as he had extensive dealings with them over many years. He knew the family that ran and owned the company and knew that they were currently in financial strife, as they had lost a lot of money on unit development and their bank had threatened to call in administrators if they didn't improve. He went to speak to them with a plan to kill the local dairy market and export their produce to that market at a higher margin.

The meeting was arranged, and the plan conceived—have one of the major retailers that has market power try to get a greater share of the retail market by dropping the price of one of its basic food components—namely, milk—to a very low price, which will force other smaller retailers to go broke trying to compete against them. Once the smaller players are eliminated, they could get a greater market share of the grocery market. At the same time, it will reduce the farm gate price the processor will pay to the farmer, making it uneconomical for the farmer to remain in business and over time, force him to sell their farm or cows and move off the land.

Steven could see that this plan had a secondary benefit in that the Chinese were very keen to buy up assets in his country and in particular their dairy farms for export of dairy produce to China, as quality milk could be sold at a premium in China.

Steven thought he could buy some of the larger farms himself and then sell them to the Chinese should the farmer be forced off his farm by not being able to meet their mortgage repayments. The bank would get its money and not lose on their loan. In the long run, the processor could get a greater margin or greater profit in that it would get an increase in volume. The retailer would get more profit because it has forced smaller players to go broke and have reduced the farm gate price to the farmer. The only one who misses out is the farmer, and no one cared about him, as he has no political clout or market power to prevent himself from going broke.

The problems in the country are not only in the dairy industry but also in the manipulation of the farming and agricultural industry. For years, politicians have been praising themselves for reviews of waterways and rivers owing to the constant onset of drought, which inflicts enormous pain on the agricultural community. The politicians have for years been reviewing infrastructure projects to build dams and pipelines to bring water from the monsoon areas in the north to the drought areas, and many plans have been proposed and should have begun, but none to date have been committed to. Why? Because it does not meet the desire or plans of the rich and powerful and our member of parliament that have been voted in to represent the farmer but, in reality, represent the influential who donate to their election campaign.

These people have a different agenda, which is not to ensure the farmers benefit from watering our centre, but quite the contrary. The intention is to provide lip service only so the farmers will think that the politician are doing something such as to drought-proofing the country and overcome the crippling effects of the drought.

MPs have declared large grants for farmers and fodder relief for cattle, but the farmer has difficulty in claiming them. The hypocrisy of declaring significant benefits to the farmer when they know the farmer cannot meet the established criteria and thus will not get the grant promised. Why? Quite simple. Like the dairy industry, there are significant movements occurring to ensure farmers go broke.

Those that rely on water allocation cannot get water for their crops and therefore cannot earn a living and go broke. Politicians and companies buy up the farms for a lower price than the farmers owe, making it impossible to pay off debt and resulting in bankruptcy. It is only after these farms are acquired by influential individuals that the infrastructure projects will be commenced, and the value of farms will then increase, as they will be drought-proof in the future. The farmer again is the loser, as is the dairy industry.

CHAPTER 8

I T BEING SUNDAY, PETER, HELEN, and Alice attended church. It was a full congregation, and Rev. Andrew Chalmers was in the pulpit preaching on the theme 'Is the drought a message for us?' Reverend Charmers said, 'Throughout time, there has been reported droughts, and God no doubt has let it be known when a major drought is to happen, as with Joseph when he declared to the pharaoh of Egypt that there was going to be drought for seven years, giving time for preparation for such events. His brothers had to come to Egypt to find fodder and eventually brought their father, Jacob, to establish the Jewish community there.'

'Famine many times is used to show to man faith mankind has in God, as with Abram, who, after a long period of waiting for an answer to his prayers from God, went to Egypt in search of fodder, as he could not find God, nor was God willing to answer his prayers.'

'We currently have a devastating drought that is crippling extensive areas of the central and northern regions of the country. Many have prayed for rain, but very little has been delivered, with many deciding that there is no God and have turned their backs on him. Others have taken their own lives, as they have lost hope and have decided that they cannot take much more of what seems to be a situation that they can never get themselves out of. Many have lost their farms, their homes, which sometimes had been held in families for generations. They also have lost face and belief in themselves.' Peter, hearing all this, wondered what this has to do with him and how God is going to handle this complex matter. He wonders why God allows the powerful to gain while the poor, often the faithful, suffer.

He has heard what had been said on the talkback radio stations and the criticism raised against the politicians in their refusal to take any action other than mouthed words of assurances. Their refusal to begin construction of dams to prevent this from happening repeatedly coupled with the suicides amongst the farming communities has left many bewildered, as they do not know the truth as to what lies behind the politician's inaction. Peter drifted in and out of daydreaming until Helen hit him in the ribs, telling him to stand up as the last song of the service had begun. He stood up and, after the hymn, walked out of the church and stood with the others for morning tea. After a while, all three made their way back home.

Once inside their house, Peter slipped into something more casual and watched the football game on television. He got up from the couch just as Helen and Alice entered the lounge room and just as the old man appeared before them in all his splendour.

The old man said, 'Peter, you wondered why I allowed the drought to take hold and what I intend to do about it as many of my people cry out in My name and many are left with nothing owing to the inactions of some in authority.

'I will send you to these areas so you may speak for Me and bring faith back to My people and oppose those who stand to prosper from their deception. I have chosen you, as you will find yourselves amongst a den of thieves, and you will need to draw upon your experience to overcome them. I have made sure you had the upbringing and skills to handle all that you will confront. At the time, you thought your lifestyle was for your benefit, when in reality I was making sure you had the character, courage and skill to handle what I am now sending you to do.'

Peter said, 'I am not a preacher. I cannot stand up before these people and act as a minister.'

The old man said, 'I have embedded in you the Bible and its interpretation, and each of you knows the Bible better than any minister could ever know. I have instructed you as to the requirement of a minister and how to conduct services should you need to do these things in my name. I will be with you to support you and to protect you from all danger, including the acts of men against you, for they will try to harm you to prevent you from supporting my people.'

'Helen will drive you, as she has a licence, and Alice will help spread my word amongst the young. I will direct you as to where to go and what I require you to do. You will act as my disciples, spreading my word, the Bible, to my people, and you will give them hope. You have the skill and have witnessed miracles to know what can be done in my name. It will not be easy, and you, Peter, will have to draw on your skills learnt from your younger days, but you should not take a life as you have in the past.'

Peter said, 'I will need a car and money if I am to move to the drought areas.'

The old man said, 'A station wagon awaits you outside the local car yards along the main road about four kilometres from here. The car's details are noted on the registration papers found in Helen's bag, along with the registration of the trailer. The car will have a trailer coupled to it, allowing you to stock up on provisions to assist the hungry whom you will encounter. You will give freely but take no money for what you have given in the way of food and water and will take some hay for the starving animals you may encounter. The scene will be bleak and will at times bring you to tears, as my people have suffered at the hands of those that have chosen Satan above me. You will not return to the place you currently live at, so take all your possessions with you. Peter, remember, you will be returned to prison shortly to finish your sentence, so do not think you will remain as a free man.'

There was a knock at the front door, which brought everyone back to reality. The old man was no longer in the living room, only the three occupants. Helen went to the front door to see who was there.

Helen said, 'Mr Thomas, what brings you to our house? We have paid the rent for this month, so it can't be a money issue.' Mr Thomas said, 'Helen, I am sorry to tell you. I must give you notice to vacate these premises. My sister is having a hard time and needs a place to live. Her husband has left her and the children, but she can't manage, and I have brought her back here so I can help her get back on her feet.'

Helen asked, 'when did you want us to move out?'

Mr Thomas replied, 'My sister and her children have already moved in and are living with me now, which is making things very awkward. So, whenever you can find another place, I would appreciate it.'

Helen said, 'We can be out of here in two days' time, if that suits you? You will have to refund our rent for the month, which we paid in advance.'

Mr Thomas replied, 'No problem. I will get the money now and deposit it into the account. When can you be out?'

Helen said, 'Tomorrow at ten o'clock.'

Mr Thomas said, 'That will be great, but where will you go?' 'We can call upon our spiritual leader to find somewhere where we can stay.'

'I appreciate you doing this for me. It will take the pressure off my household and stop the arguments and fights that are occurring between us, as we are all in each other's way. I will call in tomorrow and collect the keys from you. You don't have to vacuum the place, as I will arrange for cleaners to come in and attend to that.'

Mr Thomas then went to his car and drove off a lot happier than when he knocked on Helen's door.

Peter said, 'we better pick up the car and trailer and see what we can do about getting provisions. Alice can stay here, and we will catch the bus to where the car is parked. I think I know where it is located.'

Peter and Helen went off, leaving Alice to pack her belongings and the possessions they owned. The bus stopped straight opposite the car yard, and they could locate the car with no difficulty. The only problem was that the trailer was large, and Helen had never driven with a trailer before. They got into the car and made their way back home. As they drove along the highway, they noticed a large Costco food outlet and pulled into it. They took two trollies and went down the aisles buying basic foods in bulk. When they finished, they had the trailer just about full and could buy some bales of lucerne for any animal that they would encounter. The manager came out after being alerted to their bulk purchases and wanted to know why they were buying in bulk large quantities of basic food items. When told it was for drought relief, the farmers, he ordered four of his team to help load the trailer and gave Peter and Helen 30 percent discount on what they purchased.

Helen was not happy about driving the station wagon with a trailer back home, so Peter had to move into the driver's seat and take over.

Once home, they pulled a tarpaulin over the trailer to ensure if it rained, that water would not get in and to make sure the items were safe from vandals. They packed their belongings and loaded up the station wagon with their items, ready for an early departure the next day. The furniture was the landlords, so they didn't have to worry about this or the household dishes and cutlery.

Everyone went to bed early that evening, as all wanted to get as much rest as possible.

The next day, they loaded up their last items, and Mr Thomas arrived right at ten to collect his keys. He was surprised to see the trailer and believed it contained all their personal furniture.

Mr Thomas said, 'I didn't realise you had so much furniture. You should have asked me to give you a hand loading the furniture up. It must have been very hard for you girls to trolley all of your furniture onto the trailer.'

Helen said, 'We had divine help. It is amazing what a couple of good angels can do.'

Mr Thomas said, 'Yes, of course.'

Mr Thomas inspected the property and was happy as to the condition it was in. Helen gave the keys to Mr Thomas, and everyone got into the station wagon and drove off.

That night, Helen received a premonition that she was about to drive west along the highway, so she knew the direction that was set for them. Along the way, they stopped off to see Reverend Charmers to advise him of their departure.

Reverend Charmers said, 'I appreciate you stopping off and advising me of your departure, as I would have been concerned as to your well-being and what had happened to Alice, who is a walking miracle in herself. I will pray for you and ask the Lord to watch over you. May God be with you.'

With that, they departed, driving along the highway heading west. After four hours, the scenery changed in that the lush green open spaces became dry grey pastures, and, eventually, they were driving through land of bare clay and dust with no grass cover. They stopped that evening in a hotel and the next morning continued their journey.

CHAPTER 9

S ARAH SAT ON HER BED weeping uncontrollably. She is the mother of three young children, one of whom is four months old. She had just come from the barn where she had made a bed of hay for Joshua, her four-month-old baby. The baby would not stop crying, as it was hungry, but there was no food in the house and no formula left for him to eat. Sarah had stopped breastfeeding the baby, as she had no milk and had run out of formula. She had said her goodbyes to Joshua. She would leave him to starve rather than shoot him with the other children.

Sarah went into the children's room where she had previously told them to go, carrying a rifle. The children were scared and were lying on their beds. They, too, were hungry, as they had no breakfast that morning. She felt sick, as she had not eaten for two days. Nothing was left in the house to eat, and the cattle remaining were only bones with very little meat on them.

Sarah and her husband had no money and were up to their eyeballs in debt, with no ability to repay their loan to the bank or credit cards, which were maxed up to their limits.

Sarah's parents were concerned for her and had often rung to see how she was, as they knew how tough things were getting for her. They feared she would snap and do the wrong thing, but they did not have the means to visit them or give them more money or support, as they had also reached their limits.

The politicians did agree to allow payments to be made to her as farm grants, but these had been rejected by the Department because the forms she had complete were poorly filled out and did not contain a full description of their household income and liabilities, as if there were any income during the drought. Common sense did not apply, nor would the department assist the farmer to overcome these hurdles. Sarah had basic schooling and struggled with the 100-page questionnaire for household relief. They sent her a further set of forms and advised that the department would not consider her situation unless the forms were completed to their satisfaction. This had been done to all the farmers in the district, and the tactics were used to ensure no one claimed any of the funds that were allocated to the farmers for relief. In fact, most of the funds were used by the administrators running the department and holding meetings over lunch with politicians and other bureaucrats.

Sarah's husband, John, had gone off to shoot their remaining cattle, as they had no fodder left to feed them. John drove across the parched land and noticed the herd had assembled around the last tree that stood on the property. They cut all the others down to provide some fodder and firewood for Sarah and the children.

He got out of his utility and aimed the gun at the closest cow and pulled the trigger. None of the other cows would run off, as they did not have the energy to do so. One by one, he shot them, saying their names to himself and saying goodbye to his mates, cows that he had known from calf days that were raised for breeding and now skin and bones. When he had shot them all, he stood amongst them, finally deciding he was no better than they were and that he should shoot himself rather than go back to the house and die with Sarah and the kids. He looked at the tree and decided he could not put a bullet in his brains but would hang himself.

He went to his Ute and got a rope and threw it over the branch of the tree and tied a knot at one end. He backed the Ute up to the branch and slipped the rope over his neck, hesitating for a minute as the thoughts of his wife and young children came into his mind. He was in tears and shaking as he knew what he was doing was wrong in the eyes of God, but he had no choice, and no one would help them.

He stood on the back tray and let his feet slip over the side, feeling the rope tightening around his neck as he grasped for oxygen dangling from the rope.

Peter was on the highway driving through the sun haze when he spotted what seemed like a body dangling from a tree in the distance. He quickly sped up and steered the station wagon towards where the man was dangling from the tree. The girls saw what Peter had seen and were saying, 'Go faster. He may still be alive.' Then, suddenly, they lost sight of the dangling body. As they drove closer, they could see that the branch from which the man hung himself broke, forcing him to fall to the ground. They stopped their station wagon close to where the man had fallen and got out and ran up to where the body lay. Peter quickly grabbed the rope and removed it from the man's neck, trying to sense a pulse. There was none. Peter began CPR and hitting the man's heart with the palm of his hand until he finally he gasped for air and breathed. Helen went to the station wagon and got a bottle of water, and brought it over to the man. He took a mouthful and stood up and leaned against the station wagon.

Peter asked, 'Are you all right? Why did you try to hang yourself?'

John replied, 'Don't worry about me. My wife is going to kill our children. We have to get home to stop her.'

John then jumped into his Ute and sped off towards the homestead. Peter got into his station wagon and followed John, not quite understanding what was going on.

Sarah walked into the children's room and stared at them for a moment. She knew she had no alternative. No one cared, and no one would help them. She raised the rifle and aimed it at the younger of her two children lying on the bed. He looked at her and said, 'no, Mummy, no.'

She squeezed the trigger while weeping, knowing it was the only thing to do, as they could not let the kids suffer any more than they have had to. In the back of her mind, she could hear a voice saying, *Yes, do it, do it. They will not suffer anymore. Do it. It's the right thing to do. You know it is the only way out.* She squeezed the trigger harder. Still, no shot fired. She heard a horn blaring in the distance but ignored it.

She increased the pressure on the trigger, convinced it had to reach its end soon. She squeezed more, and finally she pulled it back to its full position. *One more squeeze will do it.* She closed her eyes and squeezed the trigger to its full length. Suddenly, a loud explosive noise rang throughout the room. She opened her eyes and saw John with the barrel of the rifle in his hand, with the rifle pointed to the ceiling of the bedroom. She looked at her son and the other two children on the bed crying and collapsed.

Peter, Helen, and Alice were at the door when John rushed in and grabbed the rifle. They saw what had happened and realised that Sarah was about to shoot her young son and possibly the other two children as well as herself.

Peter and Helen went into the room. They helped John pick up Sarah from the floor and led her out into their lounge room. Peter went out to his car and got a bottle of water, and brought it back for Sarah to drink. She gulped it down as she had had nothing all day.

Alice stepped out of the house and looked around. Everywhere you look was bare, with no grass anywhere. Alice walked around the outside of the house and then went to the barn. As she approached the barn, she thought she could hear a baby crying, but knew this could not be the case. The crying seemed to get louder as she got closer to the barn. She entered the barn and walked to where she believed the noise was coming from. She climbed up a ladder to the top of a mezzanine area and amongst the hay found the baby crying. She took the baby with her and, holding it with one arm close to her chest, manoeuvred down the ladder to ground level. She walked to the house with the baby crying and entered as everyone stared at her.

Alice said, 'it seems you were intending to allow the baby to starve to death in the barn.'

Sarah burst into tears and tried to say, 'I don't have any milk and no formula. We had to shoot our milking cow, as we did not have any fodder to feed her. There was no food for the baby, and I couldn't stand hearing her cry.'

Helen went out to the station wagon and brought in a can of baby formula. She found a baby bottle in the kitchen and made up some formulae with the water she had, which was warm by now, and gave it to Alice to feed the baby. The baby took three gigantic sucks on the bottle and took in the formula quickly. Helen took the bottle from Alice to stop the baby from becoming sick. She took the baby and put it over her shoulder and began patting the baby on the back to bring up the wind, which it did. She then sat down with the baby, allowing it to drink the formula with brakes after several mouthfuls. The baby finished the bottle quickly and settled down and fell asleep.

Peter said, 'It looks like you all decided to commit suicide — first, John killing himself, and Sarah killing the children and then herself. The baby was left in the barn to starve to death. Why? What drove you to this point?'

John replied, 'We didn't plan on doing it. I was in the open area shooting the last of our herd when a voice said, "There is nothing left for you. You might as well shoot yourself and finish the suffering." I did not have any bullets left, so I got a rope from the Ute and hang myself. Fortunately, the branch was rotten and broke just as you drove up to it. When I was swinging from the tree branch, I had a premonition. An old man said to me that Sarah intends to shoot her babies and herself. "Go quickly, save her." I tried to loosen the rope around my neck but could not move, as the blood had drained from by upper body, and I did not have enough oxygen. I saw the old man put his hand on the branch, and it snapped off. You then came along. I quickly jumped into my Ute and drove here just in time to prevent Sarah from shooting our children.'

Sarah said, 'My god, what have I done? Why must they have to suffer? Shoot them so they will not suffer anymore. It is the right thing to do, as there is no other way."

I thought about it and was driven mad the more I was thinking. All that was in my mind was to kill my babies. My god they are the most precious things we have. I kept hearing a voice saying, 'Your children are suffering. What kind of mother are you to allow this? There is no other way for us. We have no food. We have no money. No one wants to help us, and no one cares what happens to us. We were rejected for a grant by the department, as they wanted more forms filled out, which no one can understand. Who do we turn to for help? I looked at the situation and decided to finish it so there would be no more suffering.'

Peter said, 'The person who you each saw, the old man, was God. He cares about you, but you did not care about Him, it seems. He was the one who brought us here.'

'The voices of doom you heard was Satan telling you to end it all. He is a master of deception. God gave you His children to take care of and bring up. Instead of asking for His help, you listened to Satan and did what he told you to do. If God had not intervened, you would all be dead by now. What are you going to do now when we go? Finish what you started?'

Sarah replied, 'We will die anyway. We have no food or water and cannot look after the children. Can you take the children and look after them? They deserve God's mercy. We will starve, as we cannot get help, nor do we have any money to buy food.' Peter said, 'Well, let us go around back, and I will shoot you both myself. I think both of you deserve a bullet each. You have no faith in God at all, have you?'

Sarah said, 'At home, our parents never taught us about God, and we have never searched for Him. We do not understand the Bible and have never been instructed in His ways, only the way of this world, which has a dog-eat-dog attitude towards life.'

'We thought God was only for the rich, as they seem to always prosper and have the power, whereas the poor get nowhere and are taken advantage of. The politicians and bureaucrats only care about themselves and are not there to help us or the farmers. All they try to do is to look as if they are helping while they are ensuring we don't get a cent and go broke so they can buy up our farms, dirt cheap.' Helen said, 'we have a small Primus burner with us. I will make up a quick meal for everyone, and we can then talk about what is going to happen to you and the children. How far are we from the nearest town from here?'

Sarah replied, 'our farm is on the edge of town. It will take you only an hour's drive to get there. Why?'

Helen said, 'no reason other than to see what is there. Do they have a church?'

Sarah replied, 'Yes, but no minister. He died many years ago and was never replaced.'

Helen asked, 'what, about five years ago?' Sarah replied, 'Yes. How did you know?' Helen said, 'Just a thought.'

Helen went to the station wagon and took out what she needed and prepared some rice and canned vegetable meal, which everyone really appreciated. Over the meal, Peter spoke of God and faith and the responsibility a Christian owed to God as compared to the easy way out. Peter made it clear he did not think that John and Sarah were intending to take the easy way out, but they could see no end to the misery they found themselves in. The question then arose, what is going to happen to John and Sarah and their family?

Peter said, 'we will have to move on and see what else we can do to help others in a similar situation to yourself. Are you able to go to your parents for a short time?'

Sarah replied, 'not really. John's parents have passed on, and mine are in housing and on a pension. They are barely making ends meet as it is.'

Peter said, 'what we will have to do is give you enough food and water to carry you over for two weeks. After that time, we will come and see you to make sure you are all right. If you are in trouble, come into town and see us so we can help. If what you say is correct, we will try to get accommodation at the church. You can see us there.'

Peter went out and came in with a lot of groceries comprising canned items and various breakfast foods. Helen got another can of formula for the baby and several large bottles of water. After they sorted everything out, they all bedded down in Sarah's lounge room for the night.

The next morning, everyone had breakfast and said their goodbyes. Peter, Helen, and Alice drove off to see what the town centre looked like and to call into some homesteads if time permitted.

CHAPTER 10

PETER DROVE ALONG THE BROKEN road, which had been damaged by heat and overloaded semitrailers, carrying relief fodder for animals that were kept for breeding. However, most farmers could not keep paying the exorbitant freight costs and had to sell their breeding herds. So now the freight road trains stopped coming, except now and then, bringing in water and groceries for the locals so they could put food on their tables.

Peter drove through what seemed the surface of the moon, as the land was all cracked from the heat and dust swept across its surface. Not a blade of grass in sight, and occasionally you would see the carcase of a dead sheep or cow with its bones sticking out but no visible flesh or hide.

They drove along what seemed an endless scene for an hour, and finally, they came to the edge of town and drove through it first to locate the church that John had mentioned, that was boarded up and unoccupied. They drove past several shops with their doors closed, and you could see that they were unoccupied. Some shops were opened, but no one was in them. They drove past the pub and could see that there were one or two people inside.

They drove on to the end of the town and finally came across the church with its doors nailed together with planks of wood. They stopped around the side and noticed that there was a house on the same parcel of land and a sign reading that enquiries were to be made at the pub.

Peter drove back into town, and everyone got out of the car and entered the pub. All eyes were on them as they went up to the bar. A man on the other side of the counter came up to Peter and said, 'You look as if you're lost. No one comes here intentionally. Are you looking for someone or just passing through?'

Peter replied, 'No, just passing through, but we thought we would stay a few days and see if there are any families in need of our help. Is there any place we can stay around here?'

The barman said, 'There are a lot of places you can stay around here. People have sold their herds and have moved on to find work.'

Peter said, 'We noticed there is a house attached to the church. Are we able to rest up in there?'

The barman replied, 'I guess so, if you take care of it and leave it in its present condition. But I wouldn't recommend staying there, as people around here may decide to burn the church down, and you may be inside it.'

Peter asked, 'Why would they do that?'

The barman replied, 'Because most people hold God responsible for their misery and the drought.'

Peter said, 'That's stupid, isn't it? Climate change has always occurred right from biblical times. They are using God as an excuse, possibly for their own sins.'

The barman said, 'Well, that is the situation here. You're welcome to set up there. I will get you the keys, but don't say I didn't warn you.'

Peter said, 'Thanks for the advice. Can we get a drink from here, or is this the original "pub with no beer"?'

The barman replied, 'we have only one beer and soda.'

Peter said, 'we will have a schooner of beer and two of sodas.'

The barman asked, 'Do you want to pay for them now?'

Peter handed some money over to the barman and went to where the girls were sitting. Shortly after, they brought the drinks over, and the barman dropped the keys in front of Peter. Peter gulped down half his glass in one go, while the girls sipped their drinks.

Helen said, 'They don't seem a friendly lot, do they? Maybe they do not trust strangers. You would think they would be happy to get some trade.'

Peter said, 'Time will tell.'

They finished their drinks and thanked the barman and walked outside. A dust storm was blowing around, so they went to the residence near the church and get themselves settled in and rest for the remainder of the day.

They drove to the church and noticed that there was a large barn attached to the residence that could garage their station wagon. Peter took out his hammer and tools and in no time had all the boards knocked off the doors and windows and fixed the barn door, so it was secure. He drove the station wagon into it and unpacked some provisions they would need to prepare their evening meal. He took out everyone's bags and brought them into the house, so everyone had a change of clothes. He also set up a makeshift alarm system that would let out a shriek if anyone tried to break into the barn and steal their belongings.

Helen prepared the evening meal and, after they washed the plates up, took a walk through the town to get a better idea of what was open. Alice went with her to make sure she was safe. Peter stayed back and opened the church. He knocked out all the woods, boarding up the doors and windows and went inside. He noticed the church was in good condition and was large for such a town. There was dust everywhere, but that could be cleaned up without too much effort. He took a broom and swept the insides clean and then locked the door and went inside the residence to rest. He sat on the bench outside the residence, where it was cooler.

Helen and Alice took their time walking through the town and noticed a car was being driven into town at high speeds. It was a Ute that had two men in the front cabin. As Helen was passing the general store, the Ute stopped, and both men got out and went inside. They came out with the shopkeeper and went to the back of the Ute. All three men went to the back of the Ute, and Helen could hear them saying, 'well, mate, you either take them or I have to shoot them.'

The shopkeeper said, 'I can't afford to take them now. I know I said I would take them, but that was a few months ago and when I had some business in the town. You can see for yourself that there is no business happening now, and like everyone, I am flat broke, and things will not change soon. I cannot take them. Shoot them.'

Helen turned around to see what the men were talking about but couldn't see inside the Ute. She moved on when the man yelled out to Helen, 'And what about you? You seem like a person who would need a dog.'

Helen said, 'A dog? What on earth would I do with a dog?' The driver said, 'Hey, lady, come and have a look at them.

otherwise, I will drive out of town and shoot them and lead the starving dingoes to eat them.'

Helen turned and investigated the Ute and could see that there were two sheepdogs in the back of the Ute and two pups that were about six weeks old. All dogs seemed undernourished and had not eaten for a few days.

Helen asked, 'why are you trying to get rid of them?'

The driver said, 'We don't have any work for them, and we can't afford to feed them. She just had a litter of pups a month ago, and she has no milk to feed them. Two remained out of eight pups. The other pups starved to death. You take them or I will shoot them now.'

Helen said, 'I can't just take them. I don't know what kind of dogs they are and whether they will stay with me or run off back to you after I have fed them.'

The driver said, 'They have only been with us for four months. We took them from another couple who had cleared out of here and left them to starve. We thought things would change so we could look after them, but nothing has changed, and we are now forced to move off the land ourselves and go find work. We cannot get any money from the government to feed ourselves, and I have a young family that is starving. We have no food or milk for the babies. Lady, I am not joking. Take them if you want them or I am forced to shoot them.'

Helen said, 'Drive them up to the church, will you? My brother is there, and we can speak to him.'

The driver said, 'Jump in.'

Helen and Alice got into the second cabin of the Ute, and the men drove them to the church. As they turned, they could see Peter on the veranda of the residence and drove up to him.

The driver said, 'Howdy, mate? Where do you want me to dump the dogs?'

Peter replied, 'At your place, where else? What dogs?' Helen got out of the Ute with Alice.

Helen said, 'Can you give us a minute so I can talk to my brother?'

Helen and Alice explained to Peter what was happening and that the men could not feed their family, let alone the dogs.

Peter said, 'it's quite simple. It is their problem, not yours, so let them do what they want with the animals.'

Helen said, 'They will shoot them. We can't allow that to happen.'

Peter said, 'Yes, we can.'

The driver said, 'You wouldn't have a glass of water we could have, would you?'

Peter asked, 'when was the last time you ate, mate?'

The driver replied, 'Two days ago. We have wives and children. It was agreed the kids would get fed so the adults have to miss out.'

Peter asked, 'How many of you are there?'

The driver replied, 'including my parents and grandparents, there are twelve of us. There are my brother and his family, my family, and our parents, two grandparents in their nineties—all starving because of bureaucrats and lying politicians. Money is available, they say. Just try to get some of it and see what the response is.'

Peter handed the men a small bottle of water each, and they downed it within seconds.

The driver said, 'That was good. I shouldn't have drunk it.' Peter asked, 'why not?'

The driver replied, 'I should have taken it back to the folks.

They haven't had a drink of clean water for a while.'

Peter said, 'we have a small stockpile of canned foods that we can pass on to you to see you through to where you are heading. Give me a hand to load up your Ute.'

The driver asked, 'what about the dogs?'

Peter replied, 'Bring them over here on the veranda and give us a hand with some of these provisions.'

The dogs were taken off the Ute. The pups were in a box but too weak to get out of it. Peter went to where he had a small pile of canned food stored in the kitchen and handed some to the men, including two large bottles of water. The men took the lot and loaded it up in the Ute. They thanked Peter and Helen and drove off.

Peter did not want the men to see the trailer full of provisions, as they might come in the night and steal the lot. Best to give them what they had in the kitchen rather than take them to the barn. Peter went into the barn and brought out some cans of dog food and dry biscuits. He put a small amount into a couple of bowls and fed the two larger dogs. With the three pups, he took the leftovers from their dinner and mashed it and fed the pups. He did the same thing before he went to sleep, leaving a bowl of water out for the dogs to drink. He collected the bowl before he went to bed; otherwise, all the animals around the area would line up for a drink.

The next morning, the two older dogs were on their feet and the pups were sitting up in their box. He fed the animals again, and by about midday, all were on their feet with their tails wagging and following anyone who came near, thinking someone would feed again them.

Over breakfast, they decided to spend the day cleaning up the house and church and to head off the next day to see if they could assist any of the families who might need help. They wiped down the pews and swept the church floor and cleaned its stained-glass window, which was in the presbytery. Their efforts were interrupted throughout the day by people wanting to know what they were doing with the old church. It seems there was an interest in God, and people wanted to get closer to God to get to understand why the drought was inflicted on them. Was it a punishment, and if so, for what reason?

There were several people who came into town seeking help, and since there were no agencies, they always went to the church even though they knew it was closed and the windows and doors had been boarded up. They told much the same story in that they had run out of money and failed to get a grant from the government agency, as the bureaucrats wanted more forms to be filled out and proof of inability to meet their obligations—all designed to ensure no one claimed or can get through the drought. They had run out of food and water and needed help, but no one in town could assist them and their family. They came to the church but were surprised that it was open, and many went inside and sat in the pew and said a prayer. Peter would ask them regarding their circumstances and would give them enough provisions to carry them over for a week or two. All were grateful for the help, and many came back with thanks.

On the second day, they locked everything up and took the trailer out and attached it to the station wagon and headed off to see what the land looked like to the north. They stopped at some homesteads and handed over some provisions. All were grateful for the helping hand.

About a couple of hours' drive north, they came across a large farm that still had some sheep and cattle on bare land. They drove to the homestead and knocked on the front door. A young woman holding a baby came to the door and asked whether they were lost. They told her they were just checking on the farms to ensure they were coping and to provide a handout to those in need. The woman was Jane Omalos. Her husband left that morning to check on the dams and the fences to the north but hadn't returned.

Jane said, 'I am sorry I can't offer you anything, as we don't have any food, only some formula for the baby.' Jane told them they had three children, the youngest eighteen months old and the eldest twelve.

The twelve-year-old spoke up, saying, 'we don't have anything, not even food for the dogs. Dad has taken them with him today to shoot them, as he reckons, he cannot let them starve.'

Jane said, 'we had no choice. We got them when they were puppies, and now it has got to the stage where we must shoot them. What is the world coming to? Lord only knows.'

Peter asked, 'How long has your husband been gone?' Jane replied, 'Too long, and I am worrying.'

Peter said, 'I will uncouple the trailer and see if I can locate him.'

Robert, the twelve-year-old boy, said, 'I will come with you, as I know the area.'

Peter said, 'if that is all right with your mother.'

Jane said, 'Yes, he knows the area well and could guide you. He has had nothing to eat or drink today, so be careful, as he might throw up.'

Peter said, 'Let's fix that right now.'

Peter went to the trailer with Alice and came back with food and formula for the baby. Jane could not have been more excited upon seeing the provisions, which would last them for two to three weeks.

Peter gave Robert some breakfast bars comprising high-energy wheat and, for the other children, made up some milk out of powdered milk, and all the children had breakfast. Helen connected the Primus up and cooked breakfast for Jane, comprising eggs, pancakes, and honey. Peter and Alice then headed off with Robert to see where his father had ended up. They drove for an hour and then came to a dam. They got out to inspect the water level and saw a man face down in the dam. Peter ran into the dam and dragged the man out, who was coughing and splatting as he was dragged from the banks of the dam. Robert looked on as his father regained consciousness. Robert asked, 'Dad, are you all right? What had happened?'

Dad replied, 'It seems I was knocked over by one cow and ended up face down in the dam.'

Robert accepted his father's explanation, but Peter knew better. Peter gave the man some water and could see he was very upset over what he had just done. Peter introduced himself to Robert's father and said very little, as Robert would not leave his father's side.

Peter said, 'I see your Ute is over there. Maybe we should get back to the homestead and see what help you need when we get back there.'

Robert's father introduced himself as Ryan Marconi. He and Robert got into his Ute and headed back to the homestead. Peter followed him. They got back to the homestead, and all got out. The kids were happy to see their father, but Jane knew something was wrong. No one said anything until everyone had their dinner and they washed all up and the kids put to bed.

Peter said, 'Ryan, what had made you decide to take your life? What had happened wasn't an accident.'

Ryan replied, 'no, it wasn't. I drove up to the dam and noticed one cow bogged in there. She was too weak to pull herself out, so I attached a rope to her and pulled her out. When I finished, I stood staring at the last of our water, wondering what I should do when this is gone. Something kept telling me it was over, and it will not get better and I should do myself a favour and drown myself in whatever water was left. I ignored the thought as I remembered Jane and the kids and knew the problems that would face them if I had gone. But the thoughts kept coming into my head, and, finally, they overcame me, and I took the easy way out and drown myself, thinking everyone would be better off without me. I went into the dam and submerged myself face down and then blanked out until Peter came and pulled me out.'

Jane said, 'You took the easy way out, not caring what was to happen to the kids and me. You bloody coward. Me and the kids are going back to my parents. You can do yourself in if that is what you want to do.'

Ryan said, 'no, I don't want to kill myself. It was something that I was encouraged to do to avoid the problem. I also received a phone call from the bank, and they said we had to pay up our mortgage of half a million dollars by the end of the month or they would take possession of the farm and sell it at an auction. We have never fallen behind in our payments and have, in fact, paid three months in advance. I told them they couldn't do this to us, but they said they had a buyer, and he would pay top dollar for our farm. They were not prepared to take any risk and were foreclosing on their mortgage. I thought that if I' am not around, they would have to seek probate before they could sell the farm, which would give you and the kids a roof over your heads for at least six months before they could force you out. By then, you could decide to either go somewhere and rent or go back to your parents. At least they couldn't throw you out straightaway.'

Jane said, 'You didn't tell me any of this?'

Ryan replied, 'No. I didn't want to upset you any more than you were. Things were getting bad for us, and it seems they were to get even worse.'

Peter said, 'So what you are saying is the bank is trying to take your farm from you and sell it to another person even when you are not in default and have paid in advance?'

Ryan replied, 'Yes, and it is an overseas buyer, not a local one. It seems someone who has influence with the bank is using the bank as a front to either launder money or get the bank to do their dirty work for them.'

Peter said, 'I can make a few calls and see what I can do to help you, but it is useless if all you want to do is kill yourself.'

Ryan said, 'No, I won't be doing that again. It was that voice telling me to do it, saying to do it, as no one will care about me dead or alive.'

Peter said, 'That was the devil telling you to do those things, and you should have been smart enough to recognise that he was tempting you and it was not the best thing to do.'

Ryan said, 'Yes, I should have understood it was the wrong thing to do, but when you are depressed and the might of a national bank tells you they are going to smash you, what do you do? They do not care about the farmers, only about their profits and bonuses. They will lie and cheat for a quid and not care about morality or ethics. It is only money and their bonuses.'

Peter said, 'You have to remember they are not on God's side, but give homage to the devil, their king. They want to accumulate as much wealth while they are on this earth, only to lose it at death and be told by God, "Be gone with you, for I do not know you." They will end up in hell, as they believe their money is worth more than God's pledge of eternal life. I will make some phone calls when we get back to town and get back to you in a week or two. Do I have your permission to use your names in a national broadcast?'

Jane replied, 'Yes. But you must remember we are not the only ones they have done this to. We know of three other families in the same predicament.'

Peter said, 'Call them and tell them not to sell. Give us their address, and we will get to them and help them with supplies and water for their families. Give Helen their names, and we will contact them and go out and deliver some supplies to them.' That evening, they had a barbecue. The last of their sheep and lambs that were shot by Ryan and left to hang had to be eaten, so they were barbecued, and everyone enjoyed some meat and canned vegetables.

The next morning, Peter, Helen, and Alice headed off back to town, but they had called on two farms west of where they were. They turned up to the first at about ten in the morning after driving for four hours. They were welcomed, but the folks had nothing they could share with them, as, again, no money had been paid to them and they had no provisions that they could share. Peter, Helen, and

Alice gave them enough to carry them over for close to three weeks and some bottled water and headed for the second place.

After driving three hours, they came to the homestead, and, again; the farmer had recently shot his livestock, as they had no money to keep feeding them, not even their breeding stock. Here, they were asked to help with provisions and water. They were listed by the government department as not being eligible for relief, as the woman's husband was forced off the land and had to get a job in one town to support his family, and because he was working, they were ineligible for relief. They earned enough money only to feed the family. The farmer had to sleep in his Ute, as he could not afford to rent a room for himself. Peter handed over as much provisions as he could and, after a brief stay, started the three-hour drive back to town. They got home at seven in the evening exhausted and had a canned soup each, and went to bed.

CHAPTER 11

THE NEXT MORNING, PETER GOT up early and went to the barn to check on their supplies and see how much was left of the necessities. He took out the list that was prepared when they first purchased their supplies and counted some of the canned foods that were purchased, as he knew they would run low on some of these, as these were the items mostly given out. He was thinking to himself, *I could not give out fresh tomatoes, as they have little shelf life, whereas canned items can be kept for over a year.*

Peter counted the items and compared it against the original list and noted they had the same amount on hand as what they started with. To Peter, this could not be possible. So, he recounted them and found that all the items originally purchased were still there. He questioned his own judgement and looked up and saw the old man standing near the trailer and realised he had restocked all the items.

The old man said, 'You have done well in helping my people. Go north to a township called Castle Hill. There, you will give your trailer load to the charity operating out of the only church in that township. The next day, you are to go west to a township called Rayleigh and, likewise, give a trailer load of provisions to that church. They will expect you.'

Peter looked away momentarily and asked a question but noticed the old man had gone. He walked out of the barn to go into the office of the church when his mobile rang, and the voice on the other end said, 'Peter, this is Vince Marconi. My boys tell me they just killed you in jail last night, but I knew differently. I got your number from a private source who believes you are interstate. Are you located interstate or still in the area, hopefully trying to get back some of your old turf?'

Peter said, 'Well, I didn't expect to hear from you, Vince. My whereabouts I will keep private, if you don't mind, and I better keep this conversation short to make sure you don't locate me, as it seems you are determined to give me my last rites.'

Vince said, 'Not me. The other families believe you will try to regain your turf and, therefore, are determined to rub you out before you become uncontrollable and pay them back for trying to kill you.'

Peter said, 'No, I will not be coming back to that life again, Vince. In fact, I am in the heart of the drought country trying to help the farmers to survive. A lot of them are suiciding and had been forced off their land because of the greed of our politicians and other interested parties. Strange, I saved a young boy who tried to drown himself yesterday in his dam who has the same last name as you have.'

Vince asked, 'is his name Ryan?'

Peter replied, 'Yes. How do you know?' Vince said, 'It is a long story. Is he all right?'

Peter said, 'Health-wise, he is all right, but the big boys are screwing him and trying to take his farm away from him.'

Vince said, 'They can't do that, as I have checked to see, and he is ahead of his repayments.'

Peter said, 'We know, but the bank has given him notice to settle up by the end of the month or they will repossess the farm and throw him off it. I gave him some supplies to carry him over for the next three weeks, but he doesn't have the money to buy things for his family, and he had to shoot all his breeding stock.'

Vince asked, 'How quickly can you meet with me?'

Peter replied, 'I can't, Vince. You or one of your boys will shoot me on sight just as you arranged for whoever is masquerading as me in jail to be killed.'

Vince said, 'It wasn't one of my boys. I give you my word, you will be safe. I understand Helen and Alice are with you. You do not want them involved in anything, do you? All I want to do is to talk to you. I want you to go to the nearest airport and order a ticket on my account. Ring this number when you get there, and we will arrange for your ticket to be paid for. We will have a car ready to pick you up at the airport. I guarantee your safety. If you don't come, I can guarantee your demise.'

Peter said, 'You guarantee to leave Alice and Helen alone.'

Alice and Helen just walked int the office and overheard the last part of the conversation.

Vince said, 'You have my word.'

Peter said, 'I will try to get to an airport today. I will ring you when I get there.'

Helen asked, 'what is going on? Why are we being threatened? Why do we have to be protected?'

Peter said, 'Sit down and let me explain a few things to you. The man whom I was speaking to is the head of a family of gangsters. In fact, he is the man who set me up and has now taken control of all the underworld business where we were staying before we came out here. The other family gangs will not touch him, as he has most of the gambling, racing, prostitution businesses tied up, and he mostly controlled them. Other families control other areas, such as drugs. Last night, the person who was put in my place in jail to cover for me was killed by someone who thinks they have killed me. Vince Marconi didn't believe it was me that got killed, as he has been trying to kill me for the last three years. He is that powerful that he got my mobile number and contact me directly and knows where we are and that you are both with me.'

Helen asked, 'What has that got to do with protecting me and Alice?'

Peter replied, 'Vince wants me to see him now in his office. I said no, as no doubt he will arrange for me to have an accident like fall out of a plane while going to the toilet. He made it clear if I do not come, something nasty will happen to you two. He has left me no choice. He has given me his word if I turn up, nothing will happen to either of you.'

Helen asked, 'What happens if we slip away? He will never find us.'

Peter replied, 'In what you have said and your plan, you are saying you have no faith in God even though you have taken part in His miracles. I was let out of prison by an act of God and kept alive by Him, not the good intentions of Vince. Alice is my daily walking miracle. No, I think God will use Vince in His plan. I am not sure how, but it will be without Vince's knowledge. I think it has something to do with Ryan—remember him? He was the one who tried to drown himself. Vince seemed to become upset when I mentioned we came across a young man who tried to commit suicide who had the same name as his. What a coincidence. No, I trust God, so don't worry about Vince.'

Helen asked, 'If you trust God, why are you going to see Vince?'

Peter replied, 'Trust God, yes. Put His trust to the test, no. Look, head north to a township called Castle Hill with the trailer and take it to the church there. They will distribute it to the needy in that area. They will unload the trailer, and you are to come back here. The next day, you must head west to a township called Rayleigh and hand over the trailer load to the church there and come back here and wait for me. I should be back by then.'

Helen asked, 'How can we take a full load on the trailer to Castle Hill and then to Rayleigh? we have already given over half of the trailer away, so we can't do what you ask.'

Peter replied, 'I went to check this morning as to what we had left, and the old man was waiting for me and told me to ensure these two areas receive their delivery. I was thinking the same as you are, but when I checked as to what we had left, it was the same as when we started off with. It is better than feeding five thousand with twelve baskets of fish and bread or filling barrels with wine that has been drunk.'

Helen and Alice both went to the barn to see for themselves and were astounded to see the trailer was packed to the brim with food items, as Peter had said. In the meantime, Peter went into his room and packed a bag and was waiting for them to come back.

Peter said, 'The airport is on the way to Castle Hill, so you can drop me off. Hopefully, I can get a midday flight. Take the two dogs with you but leave the pups. The dogs will make sure no one does any harm to you. They know you. Hopefully, they will be a deterrent to anyone who wants to take advantage of you. Helen, you know my bank account details, so if anything goes wrong, you can access any money in that account.'

Helen said, 'Thanks. That really makes me feel good.'

The girls packed their things and got some bottles of water for themselves and the dogs and some lunch to eat on the way and piled everything in the station wagon. Peter drove first, and after gathering the dogs and his bag, they ventured off. About two hours later, they came across the airport and noticed there was a flight with suitcases being loaded on board. Peter said his goodbye to Alice and Helen and went into the building to see if he could get on the next flight. The girls waited for a few minutes to see if Peter could get on a flight and went to the toilet.

Peter asked, 'Could you tell me if you have any vacant seats to Sydney?'

The attendant replied, 'I am sorry, sir, we are fully booked.' Peter took out his mobile and phoned Vince and advised him he was at the airport and the flight was fully booked and no seats were expected to become available.

Vince said, 'Just hold on for a minute, Peter.'

Peter could see the girls come out of the toilet, and they saw him standing there with his phone to his ear. They came up to him, saying, 'no luck?' Just at that time, a man came to Peter.

The man said, 'Peter, my name is Jeff Stool, and I am the manager at this airport. I believe you are an associate with Mr Marconi. We have a seat for you on this flight, so if you care to follow me, I will see that you get on board with no problems.'

Peter said, 'But I was told by your assistant over there that you were fully booked.'

Jeff replied, 'we could find you a seat considering you are a friend of the owner of the airline.'

Peter said goodbye again to the girls and asked them to be careful and then followed the manager to the plan where he was seated in the first-class section. The flight was an hour and a half long, and finally, they touched down at the airport. Peter followed all the other passengers out to the terminal and was walking along the causeway when two men came upon him, with one of them saying, 'Come with us.' Peter looked at them and thought they were monkeys in suits. *No, monkeys have more personality.*

He walked along the causeway, waiting until the crowd of people had passed him, and when the opportunity arose, dropped his bag and grabbed one man and threw him down some stairs. The other man he hit him in the face and then another punch to the midsection and a boot to the head as he went down. He felt for his car keys and the person's wallet to see if there was any parking ticket. There was none, which meant he was parked close to the terminal entrance. Peter saw the man had a substantial amount of money in his wallet and took it, just as he would have done in the good days.

Peter walked out of the terminal and saw one charity had set up a table and was asking for donations for the farmers in need. He was not prepared to give, as he saw that many gave donations, but very little ended up on the farmers' table. Administration costs seem to take much of the money being donated, along with greed and lies.

Peter stood at the terminal entrance and pressed the button attached to the keys he borrowed from the man that was currently taking a nap. Sure enough, he heard a pip and looked to see a Mercedes showing it was unlocked. He walked up to the car and opened the door, got inside—*Nice, very nice*—and then drove off and out of the airport. He knew where Vince's office was, as it used to be his old office. He drove around the back and parked the car. He took his bag and locked the car and went inside the building. Vince had mentioned that he was on the fourteenth floor, so he went to the elevators and took the lift to the fourteenth floor.

As he exited the lift, two men, who tried to push him back in the lift grabbed him. He pushed one in as the lift door closed. The other he swung around and hit him right in the face, sending him to the ground. Peter gathered his composure and walked along the corridor until he came to where he thought would be Vince's office. He opened the door and walked in. Vince was waiting for him with two men. One searched Peter and said he was clean, and then both walked out, leaving the two in the room.

Vince asked, 'What happened at the airport? I sent two men to escort you to my office.'

Peter said, 'I think they had other ideas. Besides, I did not believe they were your men. One was short and solid. The other in a brown suit is tall and thin. They were driving an upmarket Mercedes, which I now have.'

Vince said, 'They weren't my men. What was the noise just a moment ago?'

Peter replied, 'Your men tried to push me back into the lift, no doubt to treat me to some hospitality. Whom did you talk to about me coming here? Someone knew and was going to make sure we didn't meet.'

Vince said, 'I thought I could trust my people, but it seems I can't. One of them has told the other families you were coming here, and it seems they were determined to finish you off and no doubt substitute your body for the one lying in the morgue. You know, they killed you early this morning in jail.'

Peter said, 'So I have been told. Well, you brought me here for a reason, so you better get on with it before another one of your loyal employees tries to befriend me.'

Vince said, 'My men are here. I will have a word with them, and then we will go where we can be safe and alone. Have you still got the keys to the Mercedes? Give them here and I will arrange for it to be dumped away from here.'

Peter said, 'I was intending to use it to get back home.' Vince said, 'We will take care of that.'

Peter handed over the keys just when Vince's men walked in. Vince said to the man in front, 'Find out who is the traitor and take care of it. Are these men ours, or have they been bought by the other families?'

Vince did not get a response to his question. Peter knew Vince was on borrowed time and that the other families were going to make a play against him soon. They paid his men to look the other way, which is clear he has no loyalty in his ranks. Vince took Peter to a high-class restaurant he owned and, after allowing him a few minutes to freshen up, asked him questions as to how he got out of prison and what he was doing.

Peter said, 'Vince, if I told you or answered your questions, you would not believe me.' But Vince persisted until finally Peter told him the full story, including the miracles that he had performed.

Peter was right. Vince would not accept what Peter was saying and thought it was a total lie. His only comment was, 'Life is not like that. It could not happen on this earth.'

Vince was very interested in what had happened to Ryan and what the problem was with him, which Peter found to be out of context for a gangster. He told Vince what had happened and that the banks had tried to take Ryan's farm from him even though he was not in default.

Vince asked, 'what are you going to do about it?'

Peter replied, 'See if I can get a couple of people in current affairs programs to take up the cause and shame the banks into backing off in these instances.'

Vince said, 'It won't work because the banks don't care what you think of them. All that their executives care about is their bonuses. They are not named in any moral issues brought up on television. The bank is the only one named, and everyone knows they are already on the nose.'

Peter said, 'So what you are saying is it is a waste of time to shame the banks.'

Vince replied, 'Yes. The banks represent the interest of the rich and powerful who do not care about the farmers. All they care about is how they are going to make more money. They do not care if the farmer goes broke. All they want to do is buy up his farm at the lowest price and sit on it until the government declares it is going to build a dam. Once that happens, the farms will increase in value, and they can sell them off at a higher price. With the dairy, it is the overseas conglomerates that the banks are representing. As soon as our dairy farmers close, we will have to import all our dairy products from overseas, reducing their cost of production and increasing our price for dairy produce, giving them a bigger margin. The government knows this and is intentionally turning a blind eye to what is happening. This is another reason the government is proceeding with these free trade agreements.'

Peter said, 'if that is the case, heaven help us down the track. We will not be a self-sufficient producer of foods. We will have to import all or most of our food products, as our farmland will be held by foreigners or people who only want to hold it for profit and not for agriculture or food production. So, what is going to happen to Ryan?'

Vince replied, 'I will arrange for his loan to be repaid to the bank, and you can tell him you have arranged for it to be refinanced with another company.'

Peter said, 'He won't fall for that. He is not that stupid. Why would you want to do that for him?'

Vince replied, 'What I tell you is to be kept strictly secret and you are to tell no one. Understood? Ryan is my son, and if the other families find out, they will try to get to him to get at me.'

Peter asked, 'How can he be your son?'

Vince replied, 'When Ryan was born, I was just getting on my feet. One day, one family decided to see if they could increase their area by eliminating me. They came to my house and entered through the rear but were confronted by my wife, who screamed out. I came running towards her when one of them fired a shot at me, which I dodged, but the bullet ricocheted and hit my wife, killing her instantly. I drew my pistol and fired at them, hitting one of them in the chest. They carried him out into a waiting car and sped off. None of them knew we had just had a baby.

'I had a brother who was a farmer, and he had a young family who lived on the farm that is currently owned by Ryan. We decided it would be foolish for me to look after Ryan, as they will eventually come after him to get to me. So, my brother took Ryan as one of his children and brought him up as his own. My brother's son died from cancer at an early age, leaving Ryan as the only son. He has a daughter, whom Ryan thinks is his sister. She is married and has gone interstate. 'So, Ryan is my only son, so that is why I am protecting him. Tell him you have transferred the loan to another lender, and he is to keep making the same payments he was making before, except he has three months' grace before he must make his first payment. Tell him the new lender is trying to help the rural community.'

Peter said, 'You will have to give me the bank details so I can tell him, and the name of the lender. He will want to know that.' Vince said, 'I will get that for you before you go back tomorrow. On another matter, today is the day they are burying you. The person they substituted for you got killed, as one family wanted to make sure you were out of the picture for good. I have arranged for you to get a new identity. You are now Peter Andrews, and your driver's licence and papers will arrive tomorrow. You're a new man, and no one will know about you.'

Peter said, 'That is great. I don't have to go back to jail and finish my sentence.'

Vince said, 'You are a free man. You can do what you want. I have arranged for you to stay in a hotel close by. Here are the details. I will pick up the tab, so do not worry about dinner or room service. Relax, and I will see you tomorrow morning before you go back home.'

After some time, Vince and Peter finished their meeting. Vince went back to his office, while Peter made his way to the hotel.

Peter booked himself in, and after a couple of hours, ordered something to eat. He got a beer from the bar in his room and turned the television on to see what was happening. His food arrived after twenty minutes, which he ate, and watched some more television and went to bed early.

The next morning, Peter awoke, showered, had breakfast, and made his way to Vince's office. After waiting a while, he was ordered in and asked to sit down at the desk. Vince took out an envelope from his drawer and handed to Peter and said, 'These are your papers and driver's licence. You do not have to worry. They will stack up to any inspection or check. Your driving record is clean, so try to keep it that way. Remember, your name is Andrews now.'

Peter said, 'Andrews, yes, I have got that.'

Vince said, 'These are the papers regarding Ryan's loan. I discussed the loan with the bank executive yesterday. He would not allow me to pay off the loan, as he had already arranged for the farm to be sold to one of our politicians from the National Party, who was prepared to look after the bank's interest in Parliament. A tit-for-tat arrangement. The farm was going to be registered in a company name that was incorporated in the Canary Islands. The reluctant bank executive is at present recovering in hospital, as one of my men had to drop him off his third-floor balcony to convince him to accept our offer. The bank has replaced him, thinking he has a mental problem and tried to commit suicide. His replacement was more than happy to have the debt paid off. These are the papers you can give Ryan, and this is the bank account he is to pay into each month after the honeymoon period of three months is over.'

Peter said, 'Right, it seems we have everything except my return flight ticket.'

Vince said, 'You're not flying back. Here is the key to a large Ute. it is the latest model RAM and has all the mod cons on it. It has a trailer attached to it full of foodstuffs, which you are to give Ryan. The trailer and Ute are yours. The food provisions are to go totally to Ryan to see him over the next few months.' Peter said, 'He will want to know where the food came from.'

Vince replied, 'Tell him it came from the finance company to switch his loan to them. They are helping farmers that switch.'

Peter said, 'I hope he doesn't get too many others to switch over to you.'

Vince said, 'We will tackle that later if it becomes a problem. You better be off. You have a long drive ahead of you. All your service books are in the car. Look after my boy. I might see him someday.'

Peter replied, 'will do my best. Thanks for the wheels.'

Peter collected the keys and was escorted down to the basement by one of Vince's men and taken to the Ute. it was burgundy coloured and big. Attached to it was a trailer the same size he took to the country, and they packed it with provisions that would last a normal family for six months. He drove out of the building and headed down the highway towards home.

CHAPTER 12

Peter drove west along the highway for about four hours and stopped for a coffee and a break. He pulled into a roadside café and filled his Ute up and parked it and the trailer where he could keep an eye on it. He went to the toilet and then ordered a sandwich and coffee and sat down while his sandwich was being made.

While he was sitting there, he noticed two blokes come up to his Ute, and they examined it and tried the doors to see if it was locked. He moved out of the café and headed towards the Ute. One of them saw him coming and as he moved closer, threw a punch at him without asking who he was. Peter dodged the punch and laid a fist straight into the bloke's face, knocking him off his feet. The other bloke, seeing what had happened, ran in the opposite direction, leaving his mate.

Peter leaned over the bloke he knocked out and saw he was carrying a gun. He reached in and took out his wallet. He noticed the bloke had about a thousand dollars and some credit cards. He dragged the bloke over behind the café and took his wallet from his pocket to teach him a lesson. Hopefully, the bloke would think his mate took it when he ran off.

Peter went back to the café and asked about his order. They were running behind time, but it would be ready in five minutes. He asked for the order to be changed to takeaway, and within a minute, they had it ready. He grabbed a couple of bags of chips and told them he filled up and named the bowser. Once they totalled everything up, he swiped the bloke's credit card, which accepted the charge, and walked out with his purchase. He noticed the bloke was still lying on the ground out cold, so he got into his Ute and drove off.

Peter drove for about fifteen minutes and noticed there was a relief station ahead, which he pulled into, and had his sandwich and coffee. He emptied the bloke's wallet and took the money and put it in his pocket. He placed the wallet in with the wrapper that was around the sandwich and dumped the lot with other garbage in one of the garbage tins. He opened a bag of chips and placed them within picking distance and drove off down the highway until eventually he arrived home at the church.

Helen and Alice had not returned yet from where they headed off to, so he put the Ute and trailer in the barn and locked the door.

The previous day, Helen and Alice headed off to Castle Hill to deliver the trailer load of goods to the church so they could support those farmers in need. They headed off early in the morning and arrived at midday. The minister welcomed them with great joy, and there were a lot of helpers ready to assist in the trailer's unloading. While this was proceeding, Helen and Alice went with the minister into his office and had a soft drink and some conversation.

The minister was taken by Helen's appearance and very interested in whether she was still married (as he knew Alice was her daughter) and where they came from. He advised Helen that his wife died some five years ago from cancer, and he remained in the town to help the farmers who were struggling to understand why the Lord is punishing them in this way.

They emptied the trailer within an hour, and they handed some provisions out to families who were waiting for help. Alice could see that her mother was getting on with the minister, so she did not interfere and took a walk through the town to pass the time. When she came back, they were still talking and laughing, so she sat outside for a further hour and then went in and interrupted them.

Alice said, 'Sorry to interrupt you, but we should head back. It is a long drive, and we don't want to be driving in the dark.'

Helen replied, 'Yes, you're right, we should move on.' The minister said, 'Thank you for delivering the provisions.

How did you know we were urgently in need of them?'

Helen replied, 'An old man advised my brother and directed we should make this trip.'

The minister said, 'Well, please thank the old man on our behalf. We needed them. Many of our farmers have no money or income and could not buy the food.'

The minister thanked them and said he hoped to see Helen again, and they made their way to the car and drove off down the highway, arriving home some three hours later. They parked their car and trailer as Peter told them in the barn and went into the house to get some refreshments. They sat for a while and prepared dinner and, after watching a bit of the news, ended up going to bed.

The next morning, they got up and prepared themselves for their trip west to the church to Rayleigh. They packed their bag of water and sandwiches for the trip and went to the barn, and as Peter had told them, the trailer was packed full of the provisions they started off with. They covered the trailer and drove off west towards Rayleigh.

They drove for three hours and eventually arrived at Rayleigh and, after asking for directions, finally arrived at the church. The Minister Timothy Curtis met them, who they later found out was the son of the minister at Castle Hills. Timothy was glad to see them, as the community desperately needed help, as no one was receiving government grants, even though the government pledged to help the farmers. Timothy arranged for helpers to unload the trailer while he looked after Helen and Alice.

Alice got on well with Timothy, and for the short period they were in Rayleigh, he never left her side. Both were of the same age and got on well together.

Helen left Alice with Timothy and walked down the street of Rayleigh, noting it was much the same as Castle Hill in that there were a lot of shops closed and a lot of places up for rent. After a couple of hours, Helen decided it was time to head back home and found Alice with Timothy in the church talking. She interrupted them to tell Alice that they must start making their way back home. Timothy suggested Alice stay with him for a short period and help with the distribution of the provisions, but Helen would have nothing to do with this and insisted they both drive back, even though Alice wanted to stay and help.

Finally, they got on the highway and after three hours of driving, arrived at home and parked their Ute and trailer in the barn. They noticed a red Ute and trailer parked there and assumed it was Peter's. They went up to the house and greeted Peter and wanted to find out what had happened.

Peter told them everything, including his new identity and driver's licence and the provisions for Ryan, which he intended to take to Ryan tomorrow.

Helen and Alice told Peter about their journeys north and west and about the ministers they met. Helen was very talkative about the minister at Castle Hill, while Alice kept her conversation to the minister at Rayleigh, named Timothy. They had dinner, and after watching television, they all went to bed.

The next morning, Peter got up early and, after breakfast, drove off to Ryan's farm to deliver his provisions. Ryan was glad to hear that they transferred his mortgage to another bank and to receive the provisions. He did not think twice as to why someone would give him a trailer load of provisions just to switch his account to another bank or the fact that he had not signed any mortgage papers. Peter stayed for a while and then left and drove back home.

Peter arrived back home late evening, and after an early dinner, he watched some television and went to bed. The next morning was Sunday. Everyone got up early and were surprised to see the farmers and their family were coming into town to go to church, yet there had been no service for the last four months.

Everyone assumed that since Peter took up residence in the old church that he was an ordained minister, and he would hold a service midmorning. In fact, by ten o'clock, the church was full, and people were standing outside to hear the service.

Helen gathered several women who used to sing in the choir before the previous minister died, and they scoped out a service with singing and Bible readings. Peter was to act as the minister, even though he was not one. He sat in the pew with other members until they urged him to conduct the service. He made it clear he was not a minister, but no one cared.

The service started with several hymns and a Bible reading and then the sermon. Peter stood up and entered the pulpit. He really did not know what to say and, of course, had not prepared a sermon.

Peter said, 'While I appreciate all of you coming and showing your faith in God, I am not sure what you want to hear from me by way of a sermon.'

One from the congregation yelled out, 'Why does God hate us so much that He is crippling us with this drought?'

All the other members of the congregation joined in, saying, 'That's right. What have we done wrong that the Lord has turned against us?'

Peter said, 'I think you all have it wrong. I see it differently. Each of you will have to answer that question yourself. Have you maintained your faith in God? The test is not for God, but for you to get to know the faith you have in Him, not the other way around. I also believe that God is using you for a larger purpose. While it will show you how much faith you have in Christ, you are also being used to show how much faith our politicians have in Christ. God is using you to test them. He is asking you to have faith in Him. Believe in Him, and He will see you through this test. You are a spoke in the wheel, and while we are not privileged to His grand plan, we know we are part of it. What makes this more concerning is when people lose their faith and suicide and do not call upon His mercy and help instead.'

'Think about it. The banks and the rich are after your farms and are trying to buy them up cheap during the drought. They think the government will later declare they will build some dams and water this area, which will make the farms dearer when sold. The Lord will not allow them to get away with their deceit and will use their treachery against them.'

A church patron asked, 'You mean we are part of a grand scheme?'

Peter replied, 'You are. Asked Him to strengthen your faith in Jesus and allow Him to use you in His grand plan. Do not bellyache, but to have faith and believe in Him. It may seem that you are taking all the burden on yourselves, but rest assured it is controlled by God, and His plan will in time, be revealed to you.'

A patron asked, 'what makes you so sure you're right? You could be making this up.'

Peter replied, 'I guess you have no faith in God. They declared it in the book of Revelations that these droughts and disasters would come and intensify over years. It seems as the prediction was correct and possibly we are now entering this phase.'

The patron said, 'What God would put us through hell to let us find out how much faith we have in Him? Some of our neighbours have committed suicide because they couldn't take the pressure of the banks hounding them over their loans, and you tell us this God is using us in the scheme of a bigger development and wants us to trust Him even if we go broke or die from starvation. You're joking, aren't you?'

Peter said, 'I am not saying that God is using you, but there is a possibility of what I have said is true, and you should have faith in Him to show you why the drought has been brought on the land and the purpose as it fits into His plan. Remember Job? He lost his entire fortune and family and was made a beggar to prove he had faith in God. Abram, or Abraham, is another example. Jacob also trusted the Lord, and so should you.'

The patron said, 'I have a son that has been crippled from birth. He has a body that cannot carry his weight, and he cannot think for himself or do anything for himself. He is wheelchair bound for the rest of his life. He is totally reliant on us, his parents, and when we pass on, no one will be there to look after him. We have prayed, but no one answers our prayers, and you tell us that God is in control and will use us in His grand plan. I tell you there is no grand plan and what you are saying is rubbish.'

Peter said, 'Your son is not crippled and has been made well, and you should trust the Lord.'

The patron said, 'Rubbish. He and my wife are both in our van at the back of this church, and he is crippled.'

Peter said, 'Go and see if you do not believe me. I, therefore, take it that if he is as I have stated, then you are a believer in Jesus Christ.'

The patron went out to his van and, within a few minutes, came back with his wife and son.

The patron said, 'It is a miracle. Look at my son, he is normal. He has been healed.'

The son tried to talk but could only make sounds at this point in time.

The patron's son and wife followed the patron and sat down. The son then got up and stepped slowly and uneasily onto the front stage.

The son, at a slow pace, talked. 'I was crippled and could not speak or do anything for myself. An old man in white came up to me and placed his hands on me and said, "I heal you in the name of Jesus Christ." Look at me. It is a miracle.'

Everyone saw it to be a miracle and knew the boy from birth. They could see it was the same person but cured. While he could not speak properly, he could make himself understood.

The patron said, 'what can I say? My wife told me that while I was arguing with Peter, an old man dressed in white appeared and opened the back of the van. He then placed his hands on my son and said, "In the name of the Father, I command you to stand and walk. You are cured." When they turned to look back, he had gone. I cannot but declare this to be an act of God, and you have my support in believing in Him regarding the drought. No matter how much suffering we may go through, my son stands as an example of the Lord's miracle.'

Peter said, 'we will now end the service, but before doing so, I would ask each one of you to think as to what I have said here today and the miracle you have witnessed. I ask you when you get home, pray to the Lord and ask Him to end the drought and to strengthen you and your family so you may have faith in the Lord. If anyone wants to discuss anything that is concerning them, then please ring me or call in, and let us see what can be done. But do not think that the only way out of the drought or to beat the bank is to commit suicide and throw the burden onto your family.'

The service ended with a song, and everyone moved out of the church. Most left to go home, but there were several families who stayed back to see if they could get some provisions and were not disappointed. After everyone left, Peter locked up, and the three settled back at home to a leisurely evening.

At about two in the afternoon, there was a knock at the door, and Peter went to answer it. There stood a young man staring at Peter.

Peter asked, 'Can I help you?'

Tim replied, 'oh, I don't think so. I was looking for Helen and Alice. But I guess I am in the wrong place.'

Peter said, 'They live here. What is your name?'

Tim replied, 'Timothy Curtis. I am the minister at Rayleigh.'

Peter asked, 'Are you the son of Robert Curtis, the minister from Castle Hill?'

Tim replied, 'Yes, he is my father.'

While Peter was giving Tim the third degree, Alice heard Tim say his name and immediately ran to the front door and just about pushed Peter out of the way, knocking him down the front steps.

Alice said, 'Tim, this is a pleasant surprise. Come on in.' Tim said, 'Thank you.'

Tim was taken into the lounge room and immediately recognised Helen and greeted her with a friendly handshake. They introduced Peter to Tim and finally he sat down and accepted a cold drink.

Peter asked, 'well, Tim, what brings you here?'

Tim replied, 'I heard about the miracle and wanted to see the boy for myself, as I know the family.'

Peter said, 'You have missed them. They are headed home and hopefully will pray for rain and show some faith.'

Tim said, 'You sound as if you are a minister, Peter.'

Peter replied, 'No, I am not a minister but have seen quite several miracles recently to tell the disbelievers that they are wrong and are misled on this earth.'

Tim asked, 'Such as?'

Peter replied, 'well, you are sitting next to the first one.' Tim said, 'I would call her an angel, but not a miracle.'

Helen and Peter sensed that there was more than a flirting acquaintance here.

Helen went out and brought in Alice's pictures and began showing Tim what Alice looked like before she was cured. He was gobsmacked and could hardly believe what he was seeing.

Tim said, 'I am impressed with the Lord's work. But how are you involved, Peter?'

Peter replied, 'I am the one that gets to say the prayer after resting my hands on the person.'

Tim asked, 'You mean there have been other miracles?' Peter replied, 'Yes, and you know of the one this morning.'

Tim said, 'we need people to know about these miracles, so they don't lose faith.'

Peter said, 'The miracles will never bring them back to the Lord. They must have faith in Jesus. The drought will show them how much faith they really have or don't have.'

Tim said, 'One reason I came here is to see if you would come to Rayleigh and speak to the farmers there.'

Peter said, 'we can during the week, but it seems the community needs us here on Sunday.'

Tim said, 'They won't leave their farms during the week, only on Sunday.'

Peter said, 'Swell, then we can't leave our locals to attend to yours. You will have to do that.'

Tim said, 'I was going to arrange a festival for the families and wondered whether you would be interested in helping. All the farmers could attend, and we could have it for over two days. I am sure we could get some entertainers to give their time to lift the spirits of our farmers.'

Alice said, 'That is a great idea. I am sure we could help, don't you think, Peter?'

Peter replied, 'I don't want to seem to be a wet blanket, but with all the things going on here, I really don't think I could lend a hand. What with visiting the farms and dropping off food and provisions, well, I just wouldn't have the time.'

Helen said, 'I suppose I could give some time to the preparation but, like Peter, have to help in checking on the farms and the farmers and their family. I might assist.' Alice said, 'I could help. All we really need to do is make some telephone calls to some of the radio stations and see if they could broadcast the event so people from all over the nation will come. We could ask for a donation to help the farmers, and they could help the small shopkeepers by buying locally.'

Tim said, 'It will take some planning, and I am sure we will get support from all over the country.'

Alice said, 'It is going to be hard for me to help being here and you in Rayleigh. It just would not work. You will have to get some support from your area.'

Tim said, 'They are mostly farmers there who would not know what to do. But you folks are from the city and know what it takes to convince businesspeople to open up their hearts and their wallets and lend support to our cause.'

Peter said, 'we can help but not dedicate ourselves to the cause. By the way, what is the cause? What is it you want to put on?'

Tim said a music festival with everyone praying for the rain. Peter replied, 'It would take six months to arrange it. Is this to be a music festival or a religious one?'

Tim said, 'A good question. I don't know.'

Peter asked, 'what is the purpose of the festival? If it is to get together and have a singalong, then it is a music festival. If it is purely to have a big sermon, pray a lot and bring farmers or attendees back to Christ, then it is a religious festival.'

Tim replied, 'I want both. I think the purpose is to bring the farming community together and show them that people care about them and for everyone to pray for rain and show God that we have faith in Him.'

Peter said, 'Then you will only get the relatives of the farmers attending, as most people won't attend if all that you are trying to do is get them to believe in Christ. Most of the population knows of Jesus Christ but does not want Him in their lives. They prefer the material things this world gives them, not the promise of eternal life. Why do you think this drought has been brought on the land? It is to get people to think about God. At present, most are doing this, but think that God is punishing them for their lack of faith in Him, which is not the case. God wants to turn their hearts to Him and understand He is in control, not this rubbish called climate change. He has brought this drought on, not climate change. It is also to use the farmers in the bigger plan to punish those that have and still try to take the land from the farmers for their own benefit and are using their God-given powers to force farmers to sell their farms to them at a substantially reduced prices.'

Tim said, 'now that you mention it, that is right. The banks are forcing farmers to sell, and most of the farms are being acquired by overseas Chinese buyers. The banks act as agents of these investors. That explains why we cannot get politicians to build dams to keep the waters and stop the droughts. It is to their benefits not to do so until their mates have acquired all the strategic parcels of farmland. Then they will declare a large infrastructure program to stop droughts, and their friends will benefit.'

Peter said, 'That is spot on. So what are you going to call the music festival?'

Tim paused for a moment and stared at Alice. Alice looked at Tim and tried to help him out of this predicament, but could not think of an answer.

Tim said, 'We will call it the Miracle Musical Festival.' Alice said, 'I like that.'

Tim said, 'I am glad to hear it, because it will take a miraculous person to get it off the ground, and I don't have the time to devote to the project on a full-time basis.'

Alice said, 'It would be a shame to not at least explore the possibility of having the festival. I am sure if we all pitched in, we could make it work. We could all ask the Lord to deliver another miracle and make it rain.'

Helen asked, 'On the first day or second?'

Alice replied, 'The second day, of course. We want the festival to take place first, don't we?'

Peter said, 'I would prefer the first day myself. Then we wouldn't have to listen to the loud music.'

Alice said, 'I guess it will be up to Mum, Tim, and myself to do most of the arrangements. Otherwise, we will have the symphony orchestras playing Brahms instead of the music most young people enjoy.'

Peter said, 'Even Queen went opera. Remember "Bohemian Rhapsody"? That was a hit.'

Alice said, 'Looks like I will have to take over the running of the festival.'

Helen replied, 'You can't. We are busy doing the deliveries and helping the families around this area. Tim is talking about holding it west of here, some three hours away. You cannot go down there and arrange it. No, it can't be done.'

Alice said, 'Well, either it gets held here or I have to go west and arrange it at Rayleigh.'

Helen said, 'You can't go on your own. There is nowhere for you to live and to be away from us for so many months. Well, I won't hear of it.'

Alice said, 'Mum, I am cured. I must do something now that I can do so. The good Lord has made me well to enable me to do good and get on with life, not to just follow you around all day.'

Helen said, 'I won't hear of it. A young girl on her own in a strange town with a minister we just met. No, it is too dangerous.'

Peter said, 'You will have to let her go someday.'

Helen said, 'You stay out of this. She is my daughter, not yours.'

Tim said, 'Please, I didn't mean to cause you all to fight between yourselves. I just thought it was a good idea and I could get your cooperation in turning it into a reality, not to get you arguing between yourselves.'

Helen said, 'Sorry, Tim, it is not your fault. It is a good idea. The sudden thought of losing by daughter was something I never thought about, and, yes, she can decide. I will have to give up a large part of myself, as she is still my baby.

Both Helen and Alice burst into tears and hugged each other, while Peter and Tim looked on.

Tim said, 'You can work on the initial plan while living here, and we should all meet at Rayleigh in two weeks' time to complete the plan, and after that, we can get moving.'

Helen asked, 'Is there any place we can set up a base in Rayleigh?'

Tim replied, 'Yes, there are several farms near town where people have walked off to find work in the city. You can set up in one of these. I will contact the owners and get permission.'

Helen said, 'That is all right when we are all together but, is there anywhere where Alice can stay if we have to leave her? We don't want her on her own at night in a farmhouse.'

Tim replied, 'She can stay with me and my sister at our house. There are enough bedrooms for everyone, and someone will always be close by, as our house is near the church.'

Helen said, 'We will all put our heads together and come up with a plan and a timeline and see you in two weeks' time in Rayleigh, when we can go over the plan and bed it down.'

All agreed to the plan, but Peter still believed there would be trouble if Alice left Helen to concentrate on organising the festival.

Tim and Alice went for a walk downtown to discuss some ideas. Helen (the mother hen) stayed brooding, as she sensed there was something developing between Alice and Tim, and she still had not gotten over the possibility of losing her daughter.

CHAPTER 13

M IKE ELLIOTT SAT IS HIS office staring at the far wall. He was
not happy over the fact that one of the Chinese dairy producers
had just outbid his company for the country's largest dairy company.
There were six dairy farms up for sale. The government made certain
stipulations through its Foreign Review Board as to employment, etc.,
but everyone knew that none of these were going to be met, nor will
anyone police these requirements.

Elliott picked up the phone and got his secretary to ring the
minister for Primary Production. Within a minute, the call came
through. 'Minister, I pay you a lot of money to ensure we succeed in
what we go after. Why didn't you block the Chinese acquisition based
on national grounds?'

The minister said, 'Simply, the Chinese would protest this with the
prime minister, and we could have a Royal Commission established to
investigate the industry. You know the farm gate price is absurd and
puts the locals out of business. If we have a Royal Commission, this will
expose what we are trying to achieve and would be counterproductive
to your goals. I had no choice but to go along with the majority. 'The
next lot of dairy farms that will go up for sale will be forced by the
banks. There will be eight of the largest farms and most likely will be
the end of the dairy industry in this country.

After this, all dairy products will have to be imported into the
country, and no doubt at a higher price and will be of a poorer quality.
They will have to buy from us, as there will be no other supplier. The

Chinese will export to their own country and do not intend to sell back here. The farmers can never re-establish a dairy industry in this country, as all the expertise will have gone elsewhere. There will be no one to operate the farms except the people you fly in on work visas, which the government has agreed to allow you to do.'

Elliott asked, 'who owns these farms?'

The minister replied, 'It doesn't matter. I will force them to sell within a couple of months, as we design our relief package to ensure they don't get a cent from the government. We have promised a lot, but to get the benefits, they will have to have the best accounting and legal firms working for them. Most of the farmers are on their knees already and could not afford legal aid, let alone the best in the industry. Most are reducing the size of their herds and cannot upgrade their equipment, as the banks will not lend them more money. As soon as you are ready, we will get the banks to foreclose and auction off the farms.'

Elliott said, 'No, we don't want that to happen, as other countries may buy in and outbid us, as did the Chinese. Get the banks to foreclose and sell to us the highest bidder.'

The minister said, 'Other companies can claim that they would have paid more for the farms, leaving us to fight public opinion.'

Elliott said, 'We will claim they had the chance to put in their price, and we outbid them on a private tender. No one is going to care after the sale has been declared. I will call our contacts in the banks to start the ball rolling on the force sales.'

' The minister said, 'You better wait until I talk to other members of the government to ensure they are on our side.'

Elliott said, I pay them enough to make sure they are.'

Elliott hung up the phone and asked his secretary to get him the chairman of the country's largest bank.

Elliott said, 'Jim, I understand you control the accounts of the last eight dairy farmers' in the country.'

Jim McCarthy replied, 'I will have to check to see if they all bank with us. Why do you ask?'

Elliott said, 'I want you to confirm if you hold mortgages over all the farms, and if you do, set a date when you foreclose on their loans.'

McCarthy said, 'We can't do that if they are not in arrears. It would create an outcry if we did that.'

Elliott replied, 'Not if they are behind in their repayments. Those that are not behind, you can call up the debt on the pretext that you cannot see them being able to make repayments in the future considering the drought, the cost of bringing in fodder for the animals, and being able to make a profit in a rising cost environment. People will accept that.'

McCarthy said, 'Yes, they might fall for the lies, but it will make our bank look as if we are a greedy, unethical mob of crooks, and we do not want that image.'

Elliott said, 'You're joking. The average person out there with their few cents won't care, and the wealthy knows what is happening. Also, the five million dollars we will put your way no doubt will go some ways to addressing the stigma.'

McCarthy asked, 'when will the money be paid into my account?'

Elliott replied, 'once we have the farms.' McCarthy said, 'Agreed.'

Elliott went about his business and held several meetings throughout the day. After lunch, he received a phone call from McCarthy.

McCarthy said, 'You were asking whether we had all the dairy farmers' accounts. We have seven of them, not the eight, and the eighth is the largest.'

Elliott asked, 'whom do they bank with?'

McCarthy replied, 'one of the regional banks. We have enquired with them under the pretext of a credit check and found that they do not have any mortgage and are well financially. The farm gate price has not affected them so much, as they are exporting a good portion of their milk produce to other countries.'

Elliott said, 'We will have to find out who they are selling to, locally and overseas and stop their exports so the local supermarket price will be all that they can get, and overtime they will be forced out of business like the others were.'

McCarthy asked, 'Are you interested in agriculture, grazing beef or sheep farming?'

Elliott said, 'Why, have you got any decent farms coming up for sale?'

McCarthy replied, 'With the drought, there will soon be a lot coming on the market. They are selling their herds, as they cannot keep paying the increasing price for fodder. They cannot maintain their breeding stock, and a lot have already gone broke.'

Elliott said, 'Keep me informed. If we can buy them out at the right price and pick up a profit once the government declares they are building a dam. Why not?'

'But we are interested in the gas underground, not the vegetables on top.' McCarthy said, 'We will foreclose on the seven dairy farmers we have on our books, and you can handle the eighth yourself.'

Elliott concluded the telephone call and went out to attend another meeting.

CHAPTER 14

HELEN, ALICE, AND PETER COMPLETED their plan for the concert and prepared themselves for their journey to Rayleigh. Tim had advised them they could stay at a farm some forty minutes from town and gave them directions on how to get there. They packed their bags and loaded up the station wagon and trailer, and set off for the long journey. They finally got there and settled into the farmhouse.

The house was spacious and well-kept, and everything was clean. Tim drove out to meet them, estimating their arrival time. After having something to eat, everyone settled down to discuss what was planned.

Alice said, 'We all agreed on the concert being held in about three months' time over the long weekend. It will be called the Miracle Concert, and the theme will be "Pray for Rain—a Miracle".'

Helen said, 'We will ask the government for help in providing police to control the crowds, support medical staff, drug control, and the radio stations to publicise the event. We will ask artists willing to donate their time to call us, and we will schedule them in as performers. The problem will be, where are we going to hold the event?'

Tim replied, 'That's easy. We will hold it at our showground. it has a stage and is equipped for broadcasting and already has toilet facilities for a large crowd of people. Whoever wants to camp out can do so in the nearby paddocks. I think we should have a look at the facilities tomorrow, so we are all familiar with them. That is one reason I said we should hold the concert here. I also have several friends in the city television stations who will be glad to help broadcast the event and pay us for the rights. As for the administration of the event, I think we should hand this over to one of the larger charities, as they have the structure that can control the collection of donations and paying for incidentals as part relating to the event.'

Peter said, 'Yes, I agree, and they can establish the criteria as to how they are going to distribute the proceeds to the farmers. This hasn't been handled well in the past.'

Tim stayed for a while talking to Alice and asked if she cared to stay overnight with him and his sister, and the other two could meet up with them the next morning. Tim advised he had a christening to do that evening and would appreciate some help, as there were expected to be many people attending. Alice agreed and packed a bag and went off with Tim to Rayleigh. Helen was not pleased, but knew she could not object, as it would lead to another argument.

Peter said, 'It looks like those two have hit it off.'

Helen replied, 'Yes, I hope Alice is all right by herself.'

Peter said, 'It is only one night.'

Helen said, 'I don't know. I think Tim has ideas that are going to extend beyond just one night.'

Tim and Alice arrived at Tim's place, and Alice was introduced to Tim's sister, Mary. Both girls got acquainted, and Mary asked to be involved in the planning for the concert. In the course of the conversation, they agreed she would accompany them to the showground tomorrow; but as she was intending to move to the city, it was felt that it would be inappropriate for her to get involved in the finer details and planning of the concert.

Tim then took Alice to the church, and all set things up for the christening that evening. They agreed Mary would attend to the Bible readings, while Alice would hand out the program to those who come to the christening and greet them at the door. Flower arrangements were placed in the church, and everyone assisted with a general clean-up, and soon the guests were arriving.

The church soon filled up with guests, and Tim began the ceremony, with Alice assisting him. Within an hour, it was all over, and the baby christened, and all left the church. Another hour was taken up by putting everything away and locking up, and the three agreed they would go out for hamburgers, as no one felt like cooking. After their meal, they sat around for an hour watching a show on television while chatting between themselves and then had an early night and go to bed.

The next morning, Alice accompanied Tim to see how some farmers were making out and to check as to why some of them have not been seen in church over the last couple of weeks. Again, it came down to lack of faith in Jesus and the thought that this drought was some form of punishment towards them and brought on by God. It took more convincing on Tim's and Alice's part to turn people's thinking around that it was not punishment but the Lord asking people to have faith in Him in bad times. Most came around after it was explained to them, but there were some that could not be convinced and walked away from their faith. Those that needed help were asked to call into town to collect provisions, or they planned to deliver some provisions to them the next day. They knew this could be done, as Peter was coming with a full trailer load and that the trailer was replenished overnight through God's grace.

After taking the time to visit some farmers, Tim and Alice headed back to town to meet up with Helen and Peter, who were early and were already waiting for them at the showground.

Helen asked, 'Alice, how did you go with your overnight session? Did you get homesick and miss us?'

Alice replied, 'Mum, we didn't get time for that. Since arriving, we had a christening to attend to, and this morning, we headed out to some farmers who needed help. We came across many people who were going to give up their faith because of the drought. They are convinced that it's God's way of punishing them.'

Peter said, 'Yes, we have come across those, too. We should ask everyone that comes to the festival to pray for rain in three days' time.'

Alice asked, 'why three days?'

Peter replied, 'To give everyone time to get home and not find themselves stranded because of the wet conditions.'

Everyone burst out into laughter, even though the gesture was not taken lightly.

Tim said, 'That will be a good idea. We will incorporate it into our planning, when we will ask everyone to pray for rain.'

Tim gave everyone a tour of the showground and stage and the facilities that were on site, such as stalls and toilets. Everyone agreed that this would be the right venue for the festival. After walking around for a couple of hours, they all headed back to Tim's house and sat down for a drink while the team of volunteers unloaded Peter's trailer.

Helen asked, 'Tim, what does the mayor say about the festival? Is he in support of it?'

Tim replied, 'Very much so. He believes it will reduce or stop the suiciding rate, as people will come to find help and will seek those who will hear them and help them get the mental support they need. I gave him an assurance we will have the support services here for those who want to discuss their problems with qualified people. It will allow not only their family to be entertained but also for them to get back on their feet.'

Alice said, 'Well, here is the plan. The festival is to be held in three months' time on the long weekend. Our local member will seek government help regard policing, health, drug control, and look after the application for a permit to stage the festival. This is already under way, and we should get an answer within a fortnight. Once we get the right to stage the festival, we will write to the radio and television stations, seeking their support and to ask artists to register their interest. If we get enough, we will stage the festival. If we do not get any interest from recognised acts, then we will have to call the festival off, agreed?'

Everyone agreed with the plan, and after a quick meal, Peter, Helen, and Alice began their long drive home.

The next day, Alice received confirmation from her State Member that the government will support the effort and would donate the cost of providing the security and policing of the festival.

Alice wrote to the radio and television stations in each state requesting their support and for them to broadcast that the festival was looking for acts to play over the long weekend and any band or artist interested were to contact her.

In the first week, one or two acts phoned advising their willingness to donate their time to the festival, but, overall, it looked like they had misjudged the support they thought they would be getting. But after the second week, they got a deluge of enquiries from local and overseas artists and, by the fourth week, had to turn people away, as they had more than enough named acts that would draw in a crowd of fifty thousand, which they were hoping for.

Over the next few weeks, Alice formalised the acts and confirmed they were appearing with their agents on a pro bono basis. Then gave the list to Mary, who was returning to Sydney for work. Mary decided, with several sponsors and the radio and television stations, to schedule the acts in a logical order to ensure they flowed on seamlessly and without clashes. They did this at no charge to the festival.

Once the scheduling had been completed, the stations advertised the festival, naming the acts that were performing over the three days, and that all performances were free of charge to the festival.

Over the three months, Alice and Tim worked closely together so much that it became apparent that they had formed a relationship, which became obvious to all. Helen was becoming objectionable, and it was apparent that she was concerned about Alice staying over with Tim for days on end to complete the schedules for the festival.

Tim sensed Helen was getting objectionable and asked for his father's advice. His father, Paul Curtis, drove to Rayleigh to speak to his son and meet Alice, who was still there.

Paul Curtis turned up midweek and was happy to see that most of the plans for the festival had been completed and hoped that they could attract the crowd they were planning on. He advised he would attend the festival to give spiritual help to those who sort it.

In a private moment, Tim said to his father that he intended to ask Alice to marry him and asked how he should go about it, knowing how Helen would take it. Paul could not advise Tim other than for him to pray a lot before raising the matter with Helen and recommended he ask Alice first before raising it with Helen, a point Tim had overlooked. After staying the night, Paul awoke early and got off before dawn, leaving the two to make their own arrangements.

After about two days of trying to find the right time, Tim, who agonised over the best approach he should take, finally found the courage and proposed to Alice. She was going to stretch her acceptance out but could see he was in a state of anxiety and was ready to have a heart attack, so she accepted his proposal without drawing her response out, with both ending up in a passionate, lengthy embrace. Alice raised how Helen would take to the news and agreed that no matter how it would be put to her, she would take the news badly, and it was therefore agreed not to tell Helen until after the festival.

CHAPTER 15

PAUL CURTIS WAS MAKING GOOD time driving home to Castle Hill. He was thinking about what Tim had told him about Helen and remembered her as a friendly person with a great personality. He recalled she had turned up with a trailer of food just at the right time. Many of his congregation did not have any money or provisions to feed their family. Helen's contribution saved many from starving, and some from suiciding. He decided to drop in to say hello and see if he could stretch the friendship and arrange for another drop-off of food and provisions, as many in Castle Hill were down to their last provision and had received no relief from the government.

Paul drove for another hour and finally parked outside the church Helen had described to him. He went inside and sat down in one pew to rest for a minute and to say a brief prayer. Helen walked past him to the altar, where she was cleaning up and setting flower arrangements. She did not recognise Paul, as she was concentrating on the flowers she was carrying. As she passed Paul, he recognised her and said her name, 'Helen.' She turned around and saw him sitting in the pew but did not remember his name.

Paul asked, 'Helen, don't you remember me?'

Helen replied, 'Of course I do. How are you? What brings you to our church? I am glad you remember me. It has been some time.'

Paul said, 'Yes, it has been about two months since you came to drop off some provisions at Castle Hill.'

The penny dropped with Helen once Paul said, 'Dropped off some provisions. She remembered Castle Hill and the minister there.'

Helen said, 'Paul, you must excuse me for a minute. I will have to get these flowers in the vase. They came up with one of our drivers who was delivering fodder. He was kind enough to donate the flowers to the church.'

Helen arranged the flowers and, when she had completed her work, returned to Paul.

Helen asked, 'well, Paul, is this a social visit, or are you here on a mission?'

Paul replied, 'Both, I would say. I was driving from Rayleigh and dropped in to tell you that Alice is all right and well and working hard on finalising the festival with Tim, and to see if I could ask for another handout of provisions, as I have a lot of starving families in Castle Hill who need your help.'

Helen said, 'Paul, I think we should speak to Peter and see what we can do to help them. Would you like to come to the house, and I will get you a cold drink and we can talk?'

Helen led the way, and Paul followed her into the house. She went into the study where Peter was seated and speaking on the telephone, discussing a mental health issue with a farmer whom he got to know. Helen and Paul sat down and waited for Peter to finish his telephone call. Peter concluded the conversation by agreeing to come out to the farm the next day to see how he could help the family. When he completed his telephone call, he stood up and approached Paul and Helen.

Helen said, 'Peter, this is Paul Curtis, the minister at Castle Hill whom I spoke to you about some two months ago. He has come from Rayleigh and is headed back home and decided to drop in to say Alice is doing well, and Paul would like some help from us, as a lot of farmers in his area are running out of basic provisions.'

Peter said, 'nice to meet you, Paul. We could arrange for a trailer load to be delivered to you in a week. I unfortunately cannot spend a day driving to Castle Hill and back before then, as I have our own farmers to deal with who are being screwed by the banks.'

Paul asked, 'is it possible I can take a trailer, load up with me and return the trailer in a week?'

Peter replied, 'If you can tow a trailer. Have you got the connections?'

Paul said, 'Yes, and I am an experienced driver, towing caravans and trailers in my days.'

Helen said, 'Paul, didn't you say you also had a lot of commitments in Castle Hill? How are you going to distribute the provisions if you are going to be church bound?'

Paul replied, 'I will have to put off some of my commitments and do a distribution run to those who don't have a vehicle or can't come into town.'

Helen said, 'Maybe I should come up with you and give you a hand for a few days or a week. What do you think, Peter?'

Paul replied, 'Oh, no, I would not like to drag you from your husband. It wouldn't be fair of me to do so.'

Helen said, 'Husband? Paul, Peter is my brother. Alice is my daughter from my previous marriage. My husband died when Alice was very young, and we have been supported by Peter. Husband? No thanks!'

Paul immediately got this sparkle in his eye and a smile on his face.

Peter asked, 'Paul, is there any place safe that Helen can stay at Castle Hill?'

Paul replied, 'Yes, she can stay at my house, or if you prefer, you can stay with one woman from the church on one of the farms.'

Peter said, 'Well, I don't think anyone can trust a minister after what we hear on the television.'

Helen said, 'Peter, you shouldn't say that. I am sure I will be safe at Paul's house as long as I don't have to do all the washing up and ironing that no doubt he has left.'

Paul said, 'My house is clean, and I assure you I am not a molester of children or women or a fornicator. There are no pots and pans in the sink and no ironing to be done. I will make sure you are left alone.'

Helen said, 'Peter can hook up the trailer while I pack a bag for the trip.'

Peter directed Paul to drive his car to the barn and hook the trailer up to Paul's vehicle. It was tarped and packed full. Both men then headed back into the house to wait for Helen, who after fifteen minutes, came out with a packed bag.

Helen said, 'well, I am ready if you are.'

Paul put out his hand to Peter, and both men walked out, leaving Helen to carry her own bag. They took it from her and placed it in the Ute. Helen gave Peter a kiss and a hug and got into the utility. Paul said goodbye, got into the Ute, and drove off. They drove north for three hours with the dust being churned up by the Ute. Everything was dry, and only a few animals could be seen. They did not bother stopping, as there was no place to stop, and they both had bottled water with them. They finally reached Castle Hill and drove through the town to the church, where some folks had assembled to see if they could get some provisions.

As Paul pulled up, some of those waiting came up to him, and after a few minutes of conversation, he untightened the straps on the trailer and handed over some provisions to those waiting. After about an hour, those waiting had gotten what they came for and drove off to their homes and families grateful for the handout, which was more than the government was giving.

Paul and Helen re-tarped the trailer and went inside his house. Helen could see the house was clean. Paul took Helen to the spare room and put her bag beside her bed. He then took her on a tour, showing her where the bathroom, kitchen, and laundry were, and then left her to unpack her things. He went into the kitchen and got himself a cold soft drink and took out some sausages and salad for dinner. He prepared the salad when Helen came in and took over. They had their dinner, and Paul went into his study to attend to some work.

After about fifteen minutes, Helen had all the dishes washed and put away and sat down to read a book when there was a knock at the front door. She knew Paul was in his study and would not hear the knock, so she got up and went to the door and opened it. There was a man and a woman standing at the door, and they asked if they could come in. Helen asked them to wait, and she went and got Paul, who came out to see who the people were. He recognised them and asked them to come on in.

Paul said, 'Mary, this a friend of mine who has graciously agreed to help me for a few days to deliver some provisions to the outlying farms. Helen, this is Mary Holster and her husband, Jim.'

Helen shook their hands and was about to go out when they said what they had come for was not private and she should not go on their accord. She then took them to the living room, and they all sat down.

Paul asked, 'what brings you here?'

Mary replied, 'Our daughter, Ruby, whom you know, is in terrible shape, and our local doctor believes she hasn't much time left. Her condition is deteriorating. We would ask you to bless her and ask the Lord to look after her. She is crippled and wheelchair bound, and her spine cannot support her body anymore. They say she will pass on, as she will not be able to breathe once her back gives way. No one can help her, and we do not have money for specialist treatment. We can only try to let her pass without pain.'

Helen asked, 'where is she?'

Mary replied, 'in our van outside. We only wanted to have a quick visit, so we left her there.'

Helen said, 'I am going out to see her.'

Helen went out and opened Mary's van door and could see Ruby was in a bad way. She clasped Ruby's hand and bowed her head in prayer for her. A reflection immediately startled her in the opposite rear window of an old man in white, whom she knew too well to be Jesus Christ. She did not know what to do and asked for wisdom as to what the Lord wanted her to do. She asked the Lord to cure Ruby, and as she prayed, a white light appeared and the old man came into the van and placed his hands on Ruby as Helen prayed.

After about a minute, Helen realised the old man was no longer present, and she concluded her prayer. She noticed Ruby was trying to get out of her wheelchair, which was strapped to the van. She untied Ruby and manoeuvred her wheelchair out of the van. At that time, Mr and Mrs Holster came out of the house with Paul. They came up to Helen and said, 'What are you doing? We did not want her out of the van. She is a problem to handle. You should have left her there.' Ruby was still trying to get out of the wheelchair, and Helen was unstrapping her to the displeasure of the Holsters, who were raising their voices and pushed Helen away.

Helen freed Ruby, who, to the amazement of the Holsters, stood up and put her hands out to greet her parents. She tried to speak and, at the beginning, slurred her words and progressively made herself understood by hand motions and broken speech.

Mary said, 'This can't be. What miracle has taken place? She could not sit up, let alone stand by herself. Look at her now. Her back seems to support her own body as she moves around slowly.'

Helen said, 'The Lord has cured her. She will take a week or more to get her strength back into her muscles and will later be able to help you on the farm when the rain comes.'

Mary said, 'I don't understand how this could happen.' Helen replied, 'Why worry about those things? Say a pray toGod thanking Him for his miracle.'

Mary said, 'Helen, get real. Miracles do not happen. They are just stories made up by people who want you to believe in mystical things, not real things. They are a magician's outcome to promote his trade. Something happened, but it was no miracle, and I, for one, will not be thanking the Lord, but I will get to the bottom of what happened.'

Mr Holster put the wheelchair in the van and Ruby in the back seat, and both Mr and Mrs Holster got in the van, and they drove off to their farm.

Paul said, 'You better come on in and tell me what happened, as I know Ruby couldn't walk before and she was very ill when you walked out to see her.'

Helen said, 'Let's go on inside.'

Helen told Paul what had happened when Peter came home, and the first miracle took place with Alice and how it happened, and the appearance of the old man dressed in white, whom Helen believes was Jesus. She made it clear that without His presence, nothing could be done, and no miracle would occur. They were all in His name. She then briefly described the miracles she remembered, and that Ruby was the first one she did on her own under the directive of the gracious old man.

Paul did not believe her and declared she was stretching the truth regarding the prior miracles, but acknowledged that he could not come up with an explanation as to how Ruby was cured of her condition. The conversation continued, increasing in volume until finally Helen accused Paul of not believing in God. Paul was taken aback by the accusation. Him being a minister of the church, of course, he believed in God. He thought he did.

Helen said, 'Paul, you are a fraud. You do not believe in Jesus Christ, yet you remain as a minister of His church. You are a social worker, not a minister of religion.'

Paul said, 'I believe in Christ, but don't accept what you have told me about the miracles. They do not happen on this earth. They are based on Middle eastern superstitions, sorcery, and not on an act of God.'

Helen said, 'Even though you witnessed what had happened to Ruby, you still don't believe in Christ's work and they say show me a sign and we will believe.'

Paul replied, 'All I saw was she was acting as a normal person and not as a disabled. I never saw who cured her or how it was done.'

Helen said, 'well, I hope someday you get to see a miracle being performed, but I doubt you will believe even after you see a miracle, as you have little faith in Christ.'

Paul said, 'Let's leave it there, as I think we have different opinions regarding God and faith.' With that, Paul stood up and walked out to his study, leaving Helen on her own. Helen knew her week was just about up and was glad when the next day Paul decided to drive her back home. Helen knew she had overstayed her welcome.

The next day, they set off at about ten and arrived at about two in the afternoon. Peter was home and took the trailer into the barn and, after chatting with Paul for a while, left Helen and Paul to attend to the needs of a local farmer. Helen chatted with Paul for a while until he drove back home. Helen gave him a sandwich he could eat on the way with a drink, and he set off, intending to arrive home before sunset.

After Paul had left, Helen settled down into her usual routine and was glad to be home. After a while, Peter came in and asked how she liked her stay at Castle Hill.

Helen said, 'It was all right, except I performed a miracle on my own on one local who had been crippled all her life. She was cured and could stand and begin talking to her parents, at their amazement, yet they said they did not think this to be a miracle but an act of sorcery.'

Peter said, 'Not a miracle? An act of sorcery? You would have to be joking.'

Helen said, 'Not only the parents, but when I told Paul, he didn't believe it was a miracle, and we argued about that point to the degree where I accused him of not believing in Jesus Christ.'

Peter asked, 'I guess that went down well?'

Helen replied, 'no, it didn't. But it is obvious he does not have faith in Christ.'

Peter asked, 'whom does he have faith in?' Helen replied, 'In himself, most probably.'

Peter said, 'Don't worry about it. The next delivery to Castle Hill won't be made for another few weeks, and if you won't make it, I will make the delivery.'

Helen said, 'We will see.'

Peter and Helen went about their business and did not discuss Paul and his beliefs again that day. The next day, they both went to visit outlying farms and to drop off provisions off, which were well received. They returned home late and had a quick dinner comprising salad and some cold meats that were cooked a day before. The next day was a Sunday. They held a service for the farmers, and as usual, the church was packed. Peter advised everyone of the festival to be held at Rayleigh and asked everyone to pray for the rain. A few farmers stayed back to collect some provisions and to advise Peter that the banks had made a move on their farms and had advised them they had thirty days to pay up their mortgage or their farms would be repossessed and auctioned. Peter arranged to see them on Monday to discuss what they should do.

On Monday, Peter went off to see the farmers who had received notices from the bank, while Helen stayed home to clean the church and to attend to the emails received from Alice regarding the pending festival at Rayleigh. She was concerned about Alice's continual favourable expressions regarding Tim and could see from the correspondence that Alice and Tim were in a relationship. She decided to talk to Peter about Alice when he came home.

Peter came home late, as he had gone to several outlying farms and was concerned as to what the banks were doing in repossessing the farms. He called Vince Marconi to find out what was happening.

Vince knew all about what the banks were doing and advised Peter as to their intentions and that it was supported by the politicians who stood to profit from the immoral acts of the banks and the gas companies who were waiting to enter the farms to drill for gas.

Vince said, 'Peter, you better stay out of this one, as the banks are determined to take possession of the farms and sell them to their influential friends. They do not care about the farmers or morals, only their bonuses they stand to make. They will come after you if you try to stop them. Remember, they have the money and political clout to knock you out of the ring if you try to interfere with their plans.'

Peter said, 'Vince, one farmer affected is your son. Are you going to allow them to run over him after all the work he has put into his farm?'

Vince replied, 'Well, I might help him, but I can't interfere with the others. These people are too powerful and would end up putting me away on a framed-up charge just to shut me up.'

Peter asked, 'What about going public?'

Vince replied, 'And who do you think owns the news services and radio stations? The same people who are going to buy up the farms. It is clear these poor kids do not have any support and will end up losing everything they have, and the banks don't care about them or what it will do to them or their families. It will take a miracle to get the farmers out of this one.'

Peter said, 'Well, I better start praying.'

Vince said, 'Good luck. A lot of good that will do.'

with that, Vince ended the conversation and hung up the phone.

Peter sat back thinking about what he could do and concluded nothing. It was beyond him, and Vince was right—the power and wealth that these people had were beyond him. Even if he went and threatened a few of them, it would not force the others to act ethically. The moral fibre of the people in the banks was the issue here, and no amount of head butting would change this. Peter prayed for the Lord's guidance and help in coming up with an answer, as the problem was too big for him to resolve or force the banks to change their ways.

Helen came into Peter's office and sat down and told Peter about her concern with Alice. Peter pointed out Alice was of age and could make up her own mind. Helen did not agree and felt that Alice was still pure and innocent and should not contemplate a relationship.

She was too immature. Peter thought differently and, after a few minutes, ended up in an argument with Helen, as he felt Alice had a right to decide what she wanted to do with her life, which contradicted Helen's thoughts that Alice should remain with her for at least a few more years. After a few more minutes of arguing, Helen stormed out of Peter's office and went into the lounge room to think about what she should do. While brooding about Alice, there was a knock at the front door, and Helen got up to answer it. She opened the door and was dumbfounded to see Paul Curtis standing there with a bunch of flowers, which he handed to Helen.

Helen said, 'That's very nice of you. What brings you back so soon?'

Paul replied, 'I had a phone call from Tim, and I am off to see him and wondered if you want to take the trip down to Rayleigh?'

Helen said, 'Yes, I would like to go down and see Alice and see what is happening with the festival. If you give me a few minutes, I will just pack a bag and tell Peter where I am off to.'

Peter, hearing Helen talking, came out to see who was there. He greeted Paul with a handshake and ushered him into the lounge room. He got Paul a cold drink, and both men settled down to talk. Before Peter said a word, Helen came in and informed Peter that they were off to Rayleigh, as Tim wanted to discuss something about the festival. Peter, who was glad to get rid of both, stood up and took Helen's bag to the car. Both Helen and Paul walked out, followed by Peter, and, within a few minutes, drove off to Peter's delight. Peter knew that there would be problems between Alice and Helen if she refused to allow Alice to run her own life.

CHAPTER 16

P
ETER'S PRAYERS HAD NOT PRODUCED rain or a grand plan as to
how he was to stop the banks from repossessing the farms or the
politicians from blatantly lying to the public.

In his pre-prison days, Peter used to know several of the gang
bosses in various countries and influential politicians and sought
their support to persuade the local banks not to foreclose on the local
farmers. He still had his contact register and telephoned several of his
former contacts, who were surprised to hear from him considering
they had heard about his demise in prison. Most asked a lot of
questions to make sure he was the same person and not a plant by
someone in the FBI or police. Eventually, they came around and
agreed that he was who he said he was and were glad to hear from
him and that he was alive.

The conversations Peter had were lengthy, and most of his
contacts said they would see what they could do to stem the tide of
influence. One of the more powerful bosses, who had a similar thing
done to his father many years ago that drove his father to suicide,
agreed to get his attorney onto it and to pull some strings to get some
international objection towards the banks. He arranged for one of
the larger news organisations to follow up as to what was being done
to the drought-affected farmers and arranged for the matter to be
raised at the international court by serving the banks with legal
documents declaring their practice and intentions to foreclose to be
immoral and unlawful. The intention here was to get the matter raised

internationally and to have a wide audience condemn the practices and actions of the banks.

What started off as a possibility gained momentum, and within a few weeks, the news became the main discussion point worldwide, including the United Nations.

The heat was put on the government to act in defence of the drought-affected farmers, leaving the politicians no course of action but to order a Royal Commission into the practices of the banks and their exploitation of the farmers.

The banks who were arranging the sale of the farms for the benefit of the politicians and several wealthy families were caught out by surprise and tried to declare they were influenced by the politicians and others and stood to gain by their action. But, of course, the politicians denied ever having anything to do with this matter, and the influence of opinion forced many of the executives of the banks to resign their positions in disgrace and leave their employment with substantial bonuses. Several executives declared they would appear before the Royal Commission and had evidence to prove some politicians and wealthy businesspeople were at the cause of the bank's action and stood to benefit from the purchase of the farms at fire-sale prices and exploitation for natural gas.

The executives who were willing to appear before the Royal Commission and refused to take the blame found themselves discredited, while others mysteriously committed suicide or just disappeared without a trace. Those that appeared took the approach that they were acting in the best interest of the farmer, who could never repay their loans and would never sell their property because of family heritage reasons. They, in fact, were doing them a favour and allowing them to begin a fresh start.

This argument fell apart when it was revealed that the difference between the loan amount and the sale price, (which was always below the loan amount) was carried on by the farmer as a personal loan and most times could never be repaid by the farmer to the bank. The bank who forced the sale did not forgo or write the amount off.

Even if the farmer never missed a mortgage repayment, the bank still repossessed their property and sold it at a substantially reduced price, leaving the farmer with a huge debt to repay to the bank, which they could never do, forcing them to declare themselves bankrupt and allowing the bank to gain a tax benefit from the write-down of the loan.

The Royal Commission did not accept the mediocre reasoning given to them by potential purchases of these properties and, by methodical research, found the original purpose of forcing the farmers off their properties was to drill for natural gas to fulfil future contracts that had been entered, and that the people concerned had already committed themselves to buy drilling rigs to drill and cap potential wells.

What the farmers did not know was that preliminary exploration had been done over previous years and that this area was known to be the richest area for coal seam gas, natural gas, and fracking. They had already spent millions of dollars on exploration and on capital equipment. A sea port was being built miles away on the coast, which was to turn the natural gas into LPG for export and that the plant, which was nearing completion, could take large tankers to China, India, and Japan, which were the main markets for LPG.

Funds derived from selling forward contracts were used to purchase equipment for the LPG conversion plant and the rigs to drill for the natural gas. The forward contracts were especially drafted by lawyers in America who had expertise in these resources and gave the seller of the resource very little right to withdraw from the contracts and had severe penalties written into them should the seller not fulfil the contract both as to volume and price.

They set the volume over a period, and they established the price at a fixed sum in United States dollars (USD). However, if the purchasers could acquire LPG at a lower price at the time of shipment, then the lower price would prevail, and not the forward price. The seller agreed to these terms, as there were no other large-scale explorations taking place and the price struck as the forward price was the lowest prevailing in the western world.

The Royal Commission had exposed these dealings and, because of the refusal of allowing the sale of the properties to proceed, had placed these companies who entered the forward contracts in financial risky position.

The Royal Commission dragged on with further evidence being uncovered that the government was implicated in this matter. The key aspect here was, why hadn't any dams or pipelines been allowed as a major project, since there were no less than thirty-five enquiries being held over a thirty-year period in this infrastructure?

The Royal Commission kept asking as to why the government continually came up with schemes that would in the long run cost more than to build dams or pipe the water to the drought-affected centres.

No matter how many times it asked, it could not get a logical, conclusive answer from any minister.

CHAPTER 17

Paul decided not to go straight to Tim's house, but to the showground to see what progress had been made and whether the facilities were in place. He pulled up, and both he and Helen got out of the car and began walking towards the main stage. As they turned to go in, Helen noticed Tim and Alice standing in an entranceway, embraced in what seemed to be a long-drawn-out kiss.

Helen immediately rushed up to them and yelled, 'What do you think you are doing? Surely you could find a more appropriate place.'

Alice and Tim broke their kiss and froze, staring at Helen, who had red in her eyes and was foaming at the mouth and had her hands waving above her head with her fist closed.

Alice said, 'Mum, we weren't expecting to see you here. We just got engaged and were giving each other a celebratory kiss. Look at my engagement ring.' with that, Alice put out her hand to show Helen.

Helen knew what she wanted to say, but froze and was taken aback by the events. After staring at Alice's ring and saying nothing, she said, 'nice,' turned, and walked away, followed by Paul. They drove to the local motel and could book two rooms and took their cases in to refresh. After about half an hour, Paul knocked on Helen's door and was led in.

Paul asked, 'What would you like to eat this evening? We were to have dinner with Tim and Alice, but I have cancelled that. Alice was upset, but I said you were not feeling well.'

Helen said, 'Well, that's no lie after what we saw and were told.'

Paul said, 'I think you will have to meet with them both, like it or not.'

Helen replied, 'Yes, I know, but I never expected to see what I witnessed today.'

Paul asked, 'What are you going to do about it? We are only here today and back home tomorrow.'

Helen said, 'I could not face them both today and would like to go home first thing tomorrow. I need time to think about what we saw. Otherwise, I will say the wrong thing, and that will lead to world war three.'

Paul asked, 'What do you want for dinner?'

Helen replied, 'Nothing for me. You said you had planned dinner with Tim this afternoon. You should keep the appointment. Make my apology, and I will catch up with them next time.'

Paul said, 'All right. I will not be late, and we should plan on an early start home tomorrow.'

Paul left Helen, closing her door behind him, and went into his own room to freshen up. After changing his shirt, Paul gathered his things and drove to Tim's house. He rang the doorbell, and Alice came to the door and opened it and peered at the absence of Helen.

Alice asked, 'Where is Mum?'

Paul replied, 'She was not feeling well and stayed at the motel and get an early start tomorrow.'

Alice said, 'Motel? What motel? You were going to stay with us here, remember?'

Paul replied, 'Yes, but, unfortunately, the events took Helen by surprise, and she needs time to think about you two. After we left you, we booked into the motel down the street for the night.' With that, Alice burst into tears and stormed off into her room. Tim came to the door and saw his father there and asked him into the lounge room.

Tim asked, 'Where is Alice? We were going to go out and have dinner.'

Paul explained to Tim what had just happened, and Tim went to get Alice. He knocked on her door, but there was no answer. He knocked again and was told, 'Come on in,' and entered Alice's room.

Tim asked, 'What's up? We are going to dinner, remember?' Alice replied, 'Mum's not coming, and I don't feel well, as she has upset me.

You go with your dad and have a meal. If I want something, I will get a snack out of the fridge.' Tim said, 'All right, but not happy.'

Tim walked out of Alice's room, closing the door behind him, and went into the lounge room where his father was waiting.

Tim said, 'Looks like it will be just us two. Alice doesn't feel up to it.'

Both men walked off to the restaurant. They had their meal and discussed the festival, and Tim advised his father that they intend to marry two months after the festival. They had their meal and, after some talk, went home to have an early night. Paul dropped Tim off at his home and drove off to the motel.

The next morning, both Paul and Helen got up early, had breakfast, and set off for home, first to drop Helen off and to pick up another trailer of provisions, and second, to head off home to Castle Hill.

Paul arrived at Helen's place at about eleven and was greeted by Peter. He took Paul into the lounge room and gave him a cold drink, which was very appreciated. Helen went to her room and stayed there while both men sat and talked. Paul advised Peter as to what had happened, and that Helen was not her usual self after the display from Tim and Alice. After about half an hour, Paul headed off home and drove his car into the barn so it could be coupled up to the trailer. The coupling was checked, and Paul headed off to Castle Hill.

The journey to Castle Hill was stressful for Paul, as the road was dry and there were a lot of dust storms, making the road hard to see, forcing Paul to slow down. He arrived two hours later than expected and put the trailer and utility into his barn and decided to distribute the provisions tomorrow. He then went into his house and straight to bed.

Paul awoke at about two in the morning in a pool of sweat, noticing he could not raise his arms and was very dizzy and had lost all coordination. He reached over to the telephone near his bed and dialled emergency. An ambulance came immediately, and because the front door was not locked, they could get inside the house and search for him until they located him in bed.

The paramedics immediately checked his vital signs and were able to conclude that he had a stroke. They gave him the clot-dissolving medicine necessary in these cases and placed him on a stretcher and took him to the ambulance. They locked his front door behind them and drove to the hospital. At the hospital, they noticed that his left side was paralysed, including his arm and foot.

In the morning, they took Paul into a ward, and administration came around to take his details and to see if he would eventually have to go to a nursing home or rehabilitation centre. At Paul's request, Tim was notified of his condition and was noted as next of kin.

Tim told Alice, who immediately telephoned Helen.

Alice said, 'Mum, some bad news. Tim's dad had a stroke last night and is currently in hospital. He has lost movement of his left arm, left side, and left leg and foot and slurs when he speaks.'

Helen said, 'My god, it is my fault. We should not have let him make that long drive home in one day. I should have been more caring and considerate.'

Alice said, 'It is not your fault. We are preparing to drive to Castle Hill tomorrow. Do you want us to collect you on the way?'

Helen asked, 'When will you be driving back?' Alice replied, 'Same day or the next day.'

Helen said, 'Let me speak to Peter, and I will ring you back in ten minutes.'

Alice replied, 'All right.'

Helen ended the call and went to speak to Peter in his study. She told him what had happened, and that she blames herself for what had happened to Paul in that she should have been more considerate of others instead of concentrating on her own emotions. Peter tried to calm her down, but she kept raving on and finally said that Tim and Alice were driving to Castle Hill tomorrow and would call in to collect her. Before Peter could say anything, she said she was going with them and had dialled Alice's number and told her to call in and collect her en route to Castle Hill.

The next day, at about ten in the morning, Tim and Alice drove to the church and gave Peter a warm welcome. Alice hugged her mother, and Tim gave her a kiss and Peter a handshake. After a few minutes of pleasantries and a cold drink, all three got into their car and began their long journey to Castle Hill, arriving there at four in the afternoon.

The group considered they would best stay at Paul's house and should freshen up first and go to the hospital in an hour's time. Everyone relaxed, washed, and changed their shirts and, at five, drove to the hospital. They eventually found Paul with his face twisted, his hand claw shaped, his left side twisted, his right foot sticking out at right angles to what it should be, and his left leg twisted, which would prevent him from walking.

They spoke to the doctors, who advised that the paramedics had not administered the clot-blocking medication within the prescribed time, as all indications were the stroke happened while Paul was sleeping, and it was not until he woke, he knew something was wrong. However, it was early days and too early to set a rehabilitation plan, as some of his muscles may revert to their former positions and support the weight of his body. They made sure he was comfortable, and he knew they had visited. His mind was losing memory, and at one time, he had to ask Tim who he was, which upset Tim.

After the visit, they went to a hamburger place and had hamburgers and chips with a Coke each. They then went back to Paul's place, and Alice burst into tears on reflection of how Paul looked. Helen was quiet, just staring into space, and Tim was not sure what to say. After watching television for an hour, they all decided to go and have an early night, and everyone went to their bedrooms.

At about midnight, there was a loud knock at the front door, and Tim was awakened. He went to the front door in his pyjamas and opened it just to have a torch shine in his eyes.

The police said, 'Police here. Are you Tim Curtis?' Tim replied, 'Yes. what is this all about?'

By this time, Alice and Helen had gotten up and were standing behind the door.

The police said, 'Your father, Paul Curtis—he has had another stroke, and the hospital has asked us to advise you, as they don't expect him to make it through the night.'

Tim said, 'I will get dressed and drive to the hospital immediately. Thank you for coming and telling us.'

The police turned and went back to their car. Tim closed the front door and went back to his room to dress. When he came out,

Alice and Helen were waiting for him, already dressed and ready to accompany him.

Tim said, 'You might as well go back to bed, as we can do nothing for him.'

Helen replied, 'You're wrong. We can pray for his speedy recovery and for the Lord's help through this terrible time.'

They got together and said a prayer for Paul, asking for the Lord's help. At the conclusion, they got in Tim's car and drove to the hospital.

The three approached Paul and noticed he was bent in every direction, making his body seem to be a replica of what Ruby looked like, with very little recognition of the different limbs. The doctors approached Tim and told him this last stroke had weakened Paul's heart and that he could not survive a third.

Tim prayed over his father and, after staying a further fifteen minutes, left to go back to bed.

Considering the condition Paul was in, Tim decided not to go home the next day but stay until Paul's condition had stabilised. They got to Paul's home and went to their rooms.

The next morning, everyone got up early and, after showering and having breakfast, set off to the hospital to check on Paul's condition.

They arrived shortly after the doctors had completed a thorough examination of Paul, and they were ushered into a conference room to be told that Paul's condition would only improve marginally over time, and he would be disfigured and bedridden for the rest of his life. They could not operate on him, as the stroke had rendered him extensively disfigured. They intended to monitor him in intensive care for the next two weeks so they could ensure he does not have a third stroke. He would be kept in a coma for the next week and then slowly brought out of the coma. 'There is likely going to be a third stroke, as the heart has been damaged and is not functioning as it should. Because of the disfiguration, Paul's body is not functioning as it should, with certain areas not receiving the correct volume of blood and a reduced air supply. This will cause further need to thin his blood to improve his circulation, which could cause bleeding complications. It is an exercise where we must weigh up the benefits against the risks. We believe the family should prepare themselves for further complications, or another stroke, which he will not survive.'

Everyone was in a sombre mood, and no one asked any questions. The doctors walked out, leaving the three in the room. After a few minutes, they got up and went to see Paul in the ICU. He was still on his side and being forced to breathe with the aid of oxygen. They stood there, and Tim said a prayer, and after a few minutes, all walked to the car, and they drove off to Paul's home.

After having coffee, Tim decided they should start their long journey to Rayleigh, as he had commitments the next day that he could not put off, and Alice had to complete schedules for the festival, which was to happen in just a few weeks' time.

Tim said, 'There is nothing we can do for the next few days, so we better go home and attend to the commitments there. Helen, we will drop you back home.'

Helen replied, 'No, I won't go with you. I will stay and try to attend to the distribution of provisions to the farmers who are expecting Paul. Also, I can visit him daily and attend to any of the needs the locals may have of the church. I have spoken to Peter, who suggested I stay, and I agree with his thinking.

When you leave, I will take a trip north to the two farms up there, which I noticed Paul was going to drop off provisions to the families, as soon as we could get a trailer load to him.'

Alice said, 'Mum, I would prefer you didn't. If you break down, there are a lot of miles between stations, and anything could happen.'

Helen said, 'As Peter reminded me, that type of thinking will get us nowhere, and we have the best security one could have accompanied me.'

Alice asked, 'Who, Roxy the blue heeler?' Helen replied, 'No, God, the true healer!' Alice said, 'Maybe I should stay with you.'

Helen said, 'The festival is in a few weeks' time. Are you sure you can spend the time or put it off for the next long weekend?'

Alice replied, 'No, I guess I can't.'

Tim said, 'I will drive Dad's wagon out of the barn for you. Hang on, last time Dad picked up provisions from you, he distributed some when he came home and said he went the next day and distributed the rest to some farmers. So, the trailer should be empty, and we do not have to worry about you driving on your own, as there is nothing to distribute.'

Helen said, 'You must be mistaken. The trailer is full, and here is your father's schedule for distribution of any future loads. Why argue with me? Bring the wagon and trailer to the front of the house, and you will see the trailer is full.'

Tim went to the barn, and, sure enough, the trailer was packed to the brim with provisions, as Helen had said. Tim stood there, trying to figure out how the trailer could be full. Eventually, he got in the wagon and drove it to the front of the house where both Alice and Helen were standing. Helen knew that the good Lord would fill the trailer as He promised and that He would look after her on her journey.

Tim said, 'I don't believe it, but the trailer is full, and I am sure we cannot get you to change your mind, so we will get our things and be on our way.'

They all went inside, and Tim came out with his bag, followed by Alice. They secured both bags in the back seat, and they went back inside to get their lunch and water, which Helen had made for them.

Helen said, 'I know this is not the right time to mention it, but congratulations on your engagement from me and Peter, and I hope you have a wonderful life together. I was upset when you told me first. I needed time to realise Alice would not be with me forever and that the good Lord had a plan for her. Otherwise, He would not have cured her.'

They hugged each other, and Alice cried. Tim and Alice got in their car and, with a few waves and kisses, drove off to Rayleigh.

Helen went inside and got her lunch, water, and bag and placed it in her car. She locked the front door of the house and went back to the utility and drove off to make her deliveries. She drove north first, along a sealed road and then a dry track for about three hours and finally could see the homestead and a bloom of dry dust.

She drove to the front, where there were about twenty people waiting on the veranda out of the sun. As soon as she got out of the utility, she was surrounded by people asking why she had come to their station. She advised them that Paul had a stroke, and that she was trying to distribute provisions to as many stations as possible that he had listed as the ones who need help. This station was marked urgent!

Everyone was ecstatic, and all helped her to remove the tarpaulin and distributed the trailer contents. Before Helen could say something, more people arrived; a steady stream of folks all came from nowhere all helped themselves to the provisions. Within thirty minutes, the trailer was empty.

Helen realised she could not drop off provisions to the next station, as nothing was left. She did not expect that there were so many farmers in need and that none could receive government help, even though, in theory, they were entitled to it. All took only what they needed, making sure they did not deprive another family of provisions. Everyone knew that all the families in the area were doing it tough, so no one took an advantage over others. They took what they needed and drove off to their farms, leaving Helen to recover the trailer and tie down the tarpaulin.

The owners of the homestead invited Helen in and gave her a cold drink and a piece of lemon cake, which she was happy to consume. After finishing the drink, she thanked them and drove home.

After driving for an hour, she needed to make a toilet stop, as she had drunk a lot of water at the homestead, which, even though it was boiled, still had a lot of chemicals in it, and the cake most probably was a few days old as her insides were exploding and needed to be calmed down.

She pulled over off the track behind a small hilly patch and removed her shorts and underwear and got in a crouching position. Before she could get down all the way, the first explosion of the volcano took place, followed by two more mighty earth-shattering eruptions with rock and liquid pouring out, and then the monsoon rain, which seemed endless.

She stayed in this position for a minute and then realised she had forgotten the toilet paper, which was somewhere in the wagon. She slid back and forth on the burnt ground for a few seconds and then stood up and felt relieved that she got through that without loss of life or, worse, an embarrassment.

As she walked to the car, she could smell what she knew to be her deposit but thought that it was high in volume and therefore high in odour. As she walked to the car, she looked down and saw that she had soiled the backs of her legs, her socks, and shoes, and this was the source of the smell.

She got to the car and ransacked it but could not find a roll of toilet paper. She grabbed her bag and looked through it for a packet of tissues but could not find any, not even a single tissue. She remembered she had some old rags in the trailer and moved to untie one of the side straps. As she loosened the strap, she noticed the trailer had replenished itself and the provisions had covered the rags. She would have to unload the trailer to get to the rags.

Helen decided cleanliness was more important than modesty, so she wiped herself down with her underpants. She moved to the cabin of the vehicle and reached for her bottle of water. It was two-thirds empty, with little water left for a quick wash.

She started taking her shoes and socks off and then standing up, washing at the crevice of her backside and then her cheeks, with her underwear being used as a washcloth. She then washed the back of her legs and found there was no more water left. The rest of her legs she rubbed with dry dust. When she pulled her socks out of her shoes, she realised they were covered in poo. She put on her shorts and decided she could not take her socks with her, so she dug a hole and buried them, along with her underwear. She rubbed her shoes in the dry sand and got off what she could and put them back on without the socks. She rubbed her hands in the dry dust and thought, *Maybe I could get a bottle of water from the trailer.* She untied one rope but could not get the knot loose, so gave up.

Helen walked around to the driver's side of the wagon, thinking to herself, *Typical man's wagon. No toilet paper or tissues anywhere.* She stood there and could still smell as if she had shitted herself. She thought *it must be the wind blowing in the wrong direction.* She got into the wagon and headed off to the second station north.

En route to the station, she thought, *I would have thought God would have lent a hand back there or provided some water, but, no, you seem to be on your own at times of need.* Yet she knew He was there, as the trailer had been replenished, but she was still left with no water, tissues, or toilet paper. Unbelievable, a God that could perform miracles but refused to help in matters of emergency even when she thought she was doing his work.

After a further two hour's drive, she arrived at the homestead and drove up to the front main building and was greeted by the owner who had been expecting Paul for the last four days.

She advised them of Paul's stroke and that she was deputising for him while he was in hospital. While they were talking, people came out from everywhere, and soon she had a crowd around her, who hurried away from her after thanking her for coming.

One farmer who came out to help moved away from her, quickly advising she smelt of shit, which embarrassed her to no end, as she had nowhere to go.

The owners of the station got some men to unload the provisions and to take their portion inside and went and got Helen a drink and a slice of homemade cake. Helen thought to herself, *not again. I don't have water or toilet paper if this happens again.* But she could not refuse their hospitality and so ate the cake and drank the water that was offered. Within a half an hour, the trailer was empty, and the tarpaulins tied up and anchored. The owners thanked her for delivering the provisions and immediately went into the main house, leaving Helen standing outside with the wind blowing up her shorts.

Helen was quite embarrassed, thinking the least they could have offered was to ask her inside while they unloaded the trailer. She walked around to the driver's side, got in, and drove off south. Destination: home.

About midway, Helen felt sick and pulled her wagon over. She got out just in time as she spewed up the cake she ate. She made sure the spew went on the ground and not on her shoes. She stood upright, but the spewing started again and again, until ten minutes later, she was reaching but nothing was coming up. She looked at her shoes and could see nothing on them and thought, *I did it right this time.*

As Helen stood there, she wondered why there was a sick smell about her. She checked her shorts, and they appeared to have avoided any spray. She checked in the side wagon mirrors to see if there was anything on her face, and there was none. As she looked down her shirt, she could see she had spewed down her shirt and it was all over the front. She took the shirt off, but she did not have enough water to wash it with. She thought *I might as well take everything off and drive home naked.*

She rolled the shirt up and put it under the tarp in the trailer. Standing there in her bra, she presented a great sight. She got in the wagon and began driving home when she got another urge to spew. She pulled off the road and just got out of the wagon when she let loose, and the spew mostly ended up on her shoes, and as she was looking down, a second eruption occurred and then a third came out however, this time, she didn't stay bent over but tried to straighten up with the last lot of spew going over her bra and stomach.

She removed her bra and with sand tried to clean herself up as best as she could. She refused to drive without a bra, so she put it back on whether it stunk. She got back into the wagon and began the long journey back home.

As she approached the residence, she could see people waiting outside, even though there was a sign saying she would not be back until tomorrow. She was not prepared to confront anyone in her present condition, as no doubt people would talk about her being a loose woman or one with a drinking problem.

Helen drove on and out of town and pulled up off the main road and waited an hour. It was getting dark, and she thought whoever was there would go. She was not feeling well and had vertigo. She drove past the church, but there were still two cars parked there, so she drove on past the town and pulled off the main road again. It was getting dark, so she waited half an hour. She got out of her car and spewed on the ground, this time missing her bra or their contents. She was dizzy and was losing coordination. She sat in the car for another fifteen minutes and then drove home again. This time, no cars, so she pulled outside the entrance and went inside.

Helen quickly checked no one had entered unexpectantly and then pulled the blinds and went into the bathroom and immediately had a shower. She got out and went to her room and dressed. As soon as she had pulled up her shorts, there was a knock at the front door. She went to answer it, and there were two men standing there asking for Paul. She advised them he had a stroke and was in hospital.

Man 1 said, 'We come to get some provisions.'

Helen replied, 'Didn't you read? We won't have any until tomorrow.'

Man 1 said, 'Yes, but we thought we could get in first before everyone else came. So, you better give us what you have.' Helen said, 'I don't have any provisions, and you better go away, or I will call the police.'

Man 1 said, 'There are no police around here, lady. We just robbed the petrol station, and no one cares.'

Helen tried to close the front door, but the man kicked it, sending Helen flying to the floor. The men immediately entered the house but were momentarily occupied trying to make their minds up as to where to go. They did not see the police pull up outside and run in. The police quickly handcuffed the men and took them back to the station. Helen got up off the floor and noticed she was bleeding from the elbow. She got a Band-Aid and stuck it on to stop the bleeding. Her arm was sore and so was her hip where she landed on.

After resting a moment, Helen reversed the trailer into the barn so the trailer would replenish itself, as promised by the Lord. She uncoupled the trailer and placed two thick towels over the seat and drove the wagon into the barn. She took a rag from the barn, immersed one under a tap, and washed down the driver's seat, drying the seat with the other. She took her shoes and shirt from under the tarp, washed the shoes, and let them hang to dry. The shirt and rags she took inside and washed them together with her bra and shorts.

The next morning, Helen caught the bus to the hospital to see if there had been any improvements to Paul's condition. She spoke to the doctors, who advised there were none and that they would be bring him out of the induced coma in the next few days. She sat there staring at Paul's disfigured body, which was not that dissimilar to Alice's or Ruby's, and thinking about what he thought of God in his present condition. If he did not believe in miracles when they happened in Ruby's case; he must by now have totally lost faith in God. She sat there for about fifteen minutes and then got up and went home.

As she approached Paul's home, she noticed people gathered outside the church, waiting. Most were well dressed and had modern cars, not old utilities, and when she enquired what they were there for, she was told to get some provisions, as they were free. She asked where the people came from and found out that they were townspeople, not farm people, and that most could afford to buy their own groceries but, because they were being given away free, took part in the distribution. Most did not care about the farmers or that they had nothing to buy their groceries with all that they were concerned with was making a quick profit in not having to buy groceries for themselves that week.

Helen did not open the barn. She made them wait a couple of hours and gave them nothing. She went in and made herself lunch and sat down, thinking about what she should tell Peter and Alice about her trip. She decided not to mention the diarrhoea or the spewing, but to tell Peter about the profiteering that was going on and about Paul's condition.

Helen phoned Peter, and they agreed she would stay there until they knew what was happening with Paul, who was still in a coma. She advised him of the people lining up outside the church for provisions who really did not deserve help but did not tell him about the other mishaps, which she knew she could never live down.

CHAPTER 18

ONE WEEK TO GO BEFORE the festival goes live worldwide. Most artists have been given temporary accommodation over the three days in caravans and mobile homes that have been donated for that purpose. The artists performing on the first day will fly back home that day or to a major centre for flight connections. Those who choose to come in early for that night's entertainment or next morning's performance could choose to stay in one of the caravans or mobiles, and it was agreed that the artist would have a picture taken with the owner of the mobile so the owner could brag as to who slept in their caravan or mobile to promote future business.

Tensions were running high, as some artists wanted preference, while others refused to follow a less recognised act. others wanted to be supported by an orchestra, not just a band, while others refused to have an orchestra if they're to support other acts performing later that day.

A tent city had been established on a farm nearby, and they could use this over the three days to house anyone who will pay. All farmers coming in off the land were entitled to enter freely. Others would be charged a fee with all funds going to the relief foundation.

Television crews from all different stations around the world had come in and were setting up their cameras. The performance at the festival would be televised by a consortium, and all other stations would link into the network, beaming the performance to every country across the world.

They declared that the money generated by the festival would be approximately US$1.4 billion.

Added toilets were brought in to cater for an estimated crowd of one hundred thousand people, and all food outlets increased their quantity of snacks and hot foods such as pies and sausage and cabbage rolls.

The drug squad set themselves up with sniffer dogs and were prepared for a hectic couple of days.

The ambulance set up for emergencies, and the care flight helicopter was sent in to help transport critical cases to major town medical hospitals. Drug overdoses were declared to be the chief concern here. As usual, the group for drug testing was out in force, declaring it should be introduced, yet the majority were against this, as there should be no illicit drug taking, and no amount of testing would not stop the drug user from experimenting.

Alice was completing all her schedules, and the charities were in place to crunch the numbers and ensure the farmers got their fair share of the proceeds.

Helen stayed at Castle Hill rather than go to Rayleigh for the festival, which did not please Alice. Helen said she would no doubt get a better view of the acts on television rather than at the back of the stadium.

Peter also decided not to go to the festival, declaring rock was not his type of music. He did not want someone recognising him and forcing him back in prison or televising his picture.

CHAPTER 19

Paul was brought out of his coma slowly over a week and was transferred to a ward where he could be monitored. They placed him in a bed with a television and he could view the festival as it broadcasted worldwide.

Helen came into the ward and sat alongside Paul, who was motionless yet breathing. He could make sounds, but could not make himself understood. He stared at Helen and made several sounds, getting her attention.

Helen asked, 'Paul, do you know where you are? Grunt once for yes and twice for no.'

Paul grunted twice.

Helen asked, 'Do you remember what happened to you?' Paul grunted twice.

Helen said, 'Paul, you went to Rayleigh to see Tim, and I came with you. After you dropped me off home at Bungarby, you went on to Castle Hill. That night, you had a severe stroke, and it partially paralysed you. You cannot use your arm or leg and cannot stand or sit up in a chair. While you were recovering in hospital, you had a second stroke, which has left you twisted and unrecognisable, owing to the damage done to your legs, arms, body, and face, all twisted out of shape. The doctors have declared they cannot correct your situation, as they are too extensive and many and doubt you will ever get back to your usual shape. The way you are at present is how you will remain for the rest of your life. Tim would be here except he has the festival to run with Alice and a church in Rayleigh to administer to.'

Paul grunted, and Helen understood he had a question to ask, but could not do so. Helen asked, 'You want to ask a question, don't you, Paul?' Paul grunted once.

Helen said, 'I will ask the questions, and you can decide which one you wanted answered. One grunt for yes and two for no.'

Helen asked, 'Has it got something to do with religion?' Paul grunted once.

Helen stopped for a minute when the prayer for rain was announced. 'Ladies and Gentlemen, my name is Tim Curtis. I am the minister at Rayleigh. Any of you who feel the need to connect with Christ and don't know how to do so may come to my service, which is held daily, and speak to me directly, and I will be more than happy to set you on the right path. Today is the first day of our festival, and on each of the three days, we will pray to the Lord to send us rain in three days after the festival ends. The reason we say three days after the festival is to ensure you all get home safely and don't get bogged down or swept out to sea, owing to the volume of water we are praying for.'

The crowd burst into spontaneous laughter.

Tim said a pray for rain, and all were quiet while they delivered the prayer, after which there was a spontaneous 'Amen', and the festival continued.

Helen asked, 'Do you remember Tim?' Paul gave out a grunt.

Helen went through several questions through a two-hour session, but was ordered to leave Paul to allow him to rest. She returned that evening and continued asking questions until over two days she believed she had the questions he wanted answered.

Helen said, 'First, I don't think Peter would ask the Lord to miraculously cure you because you are a non-believer. What you are saying is "Do the miracle, and that will make me believe." It never does. The Pharisees saw Jesus raise Lazarus but still found excuses not to accept the miracle as a genuine sign. You will be the same, and I doubt anything will change your mind of Christ. You lack faith, which is the key criteria. You just do not believe in Jesus Christ or have faith in him.'

'The second question, yes, you are in a slightly worse position than Ruby, and, yes, she is doing well, and her parents are true believers in Jesus Christ.'

'The third question is medical science able to operate, or try to fix your deformity? The answer is no, as the complications are too severe and extensive.'

'At present, doctors say you will remain as you are for the rest of your life.'

Helen could see tears running down Paul's face, and she wept with him, realising he now lives with no hope and no God that he believes in. The belief in himself has gone, as he can do nothing, not even go to the toilet or feed himself. He understands he is in prison in the body he lives in.

CHAPTER 20

D AY ONE OF THE FESTIVAL saw a lot of the top international acts appearing, with many clearly showing their best to an international audience. Most attendees appreciated their appearances and applauded loudly.

The police arrested thirty people trying to sell drugs of various types, and some were only teenagers. They found stashed in garbage cans and other containers approximately three thousand tablets of amphetamines.

There were twenty arrests for theft where wallets or items of personal belongings were stolen and later found in the possession of others.

There were six drug overdoses of various types, which were rushed to hospital, and from these, three people died, all under the age of twenty-three.

Three people were taken to hospital with suspected heartaches, and further examinations proved two had had a heartache, and the third subsequently had a stroke while in hospital under observation.

The second day was like the first, and the third day being the last day had double the number of overdoses, with six people dying from overdosing.

On the last day, they again asked all to pray for rain in three days' time, and the Bureau of Meteorology spokesperson dampened this to some extent declaring they can't see a cloud in sight for the whole of this month and that in their opinion there will be no rain for the next two months.

The last bands to play on day three were local bands who could drive in and perform and then drive out. They did not need accommodation, and therefore, most of the caravans and mobile homes could be removed on day three.

On the last day the acts finished early, allowing the electricians to remove the loudspeakers which were installed to ensure all the bands could be heard. By the end of day three, most of the crowd had disbursed and gone home, and all the emergency units had packed up and were preparing to leave.

Early indications were that the festival had earned $1.1 billion; however, the police were brought in, as a good portion of the money had been unaccounted for, and three senior members of the charities responsible for handling the finances had disappeared along with the missing money. There was no insurance taken out against theft, as this was considered not a possibility, as all employees of the charities were security checked by the police beforehand.

CHAPTER 21

TIM AND ALICE SAT IN their lounge room, pleased with the festival and the amount received from donations and takings. They debated whether the police will trace the $1 billion that was transferred to unnamed bank accounts in Morocco and what had happened to the rest of the funds. They were concerned that the farmers would again get nothing, owing to the greed of a few.

Throughout the day, they received telephone calls and visitors complimenting them on the festival, declaring, 'The farmers should be all right now after all that money raised for them.' Of course, most did not know of the theft and that, unless the money was found, the farmers would again end up with nothing.

Tim had his church services to attend to and the demands of his parishioners. Alice had nothing to occupy herself with now that the festival was over. A couple of jobs were offered to her to manage other musical festivals, but these were mostly overseas, which meant she would be away from her family for at least half of the year.

Tim could see that she was looking to do some work and took her with him when visiting parishioners, especially the outlying cattle stations. She enjoyed talking to the farmers and their families and making sure they were mentally stable and not depressed, as many were.

After about a week, Alice went back home to Bungarby to help Peter, as Helen was in Castle Hill attending to Paul. Tim was not available to make the drive for another week, so arrangements were made for Peter to drive down to Rayleigh with a trailer load of provisions, and he would call in once he had made his deliveries and would pick up Alice.

Peter left early so he could do his drops and still have time to collect Alice. At about three in the afternoon, he made his last drop-off and drove into Rayleigh to Tim's house. Alice greeted him and was thrilled to see him. Tim was not home, and she did not know what time he would get in, so the arrangements were for Alice to leave whenever and not wait for him.

Peter had a cold drink and walked around a bit and then took Alice's bag and placed it on the trailer. After a few minutes of standing around, they decided to be on their way. Alice closed the door behind them, and both set off home. On the way, the conversation was mainly about Helen, Paul, and what had transpired. However, Peter noticed there was not even a word about Tim and the wedding, which was to take place in two months' time.

They arrived home just as it was getting dark. Peter drove the trailer into the barn and went into the house. He carried Alice's case into her room and placed it on her bed. Alice began unpacking and putting all her dirty washing in a pile to be dealt with the next day.

Peter, after washing up, went to the kitchen and prepared a salad for dinner and began grilling sausages. By the time they cooked, Alice came into the kitchen, and both sat down and had their meal.

Peter and Alice decided to drive up to Castle Hill the next day to catch up with Helen and, if necessary, bring her home, as there was little she could do for Paul. There were also several farmers en route who had asked for help, so they would drop off some provisions on the way.

The next morning, they headed out to Castle Hill and, after making four drop-offs, reached the hospital at about three thirty. They went to the ward Helen had advised them of and saw her sitting near Paul, who was asleep. They approached Paul's bed and noticed how his body had become disfigured and agreed that he could never regain his former stamina. As they approached, Helen got up and gave Alice a big hug and kiss and gave the same to Peter. They moved away from Paul's bed.

Peter asked, 'Any change?'

Helen replied, 'No. They have decided they can't do any more for him here and are planning to send Paul to a nursing home. The problem is none of the nursing homes will take him because he needs 24/7 care, which they cannot provide. He is a problem for them, which they do not know how to handle, as this is a hospital and not a rehabilitation centre or nursing home. Where he ends up will not be good. To some extent, it reminds me of what I went through with Alice before her miraculous cure.'

Peter said, 'You can't help him any more than what you have, so maybe it would be better for you to come home with us and allow the hospital to do what they think best.'

Helen said, 'Think best is to push Paul out to wherever is most convenient and not what is best for him. No, I cannot let that happen to him. He deserves better than that. Besides, the people here deserve to have a church and someone preaching the word of God. Who would do it if I was not around? We also have farmers to look after and provide for, and this takes time to make the trips to their stations and talk to them to see what their mental health is like. What has happened to the Royal Commission?'

Peter said, 'I agree that all these things must be attended to, but you can't do this on your own. It is too dangerous. As for the Royal Commission. they are due to hand down their report in a week.'

Alice said, 'I could stay with Mum and give her a hand.'

Helen asked, 'But what about your wedding? Won't you have to be working on that?'

Alice replied, 'The wedding is going to be basic and straightforward, with sandwiches and tea after the ceremony. Nothing prestigious.'

Helen said, 'Well, I could use the help and company, as it is lonely on your own.'

Peter asked, 'But you don't have a bag with you, so how can you stay here?'

Alice replied, 'I never thought of that. What about I come home with you today, and next week when you do your run, you drop me off, bag and all?'

Peter said, 'OK. Let us leave it at that. Remember, the rains will come tomorrow, which is three days after the festival.'

Helen said, 'Fat chance of that. The weather forecast is for record temperatures, and there is not a cloud in sight except for a tornado, which is miles away and not going anywhere where we are.'

Peter said, 'I have prayed to the Lord for the rain, and I believe it will come.'

They decided to leave Paul and make their way back home, dropping Helen off first at Paul's home.

CHAPTER 22

T HE GOVERNMENT HAD MADE GESTURES to hand over relief funds to the farmers during droughts, but these were never taken up, as to qualify for them would require enormous effort by the farmers and would strain their limited resources in acquiring expertise to take care of the red tape. The government knew this and apparently was quite willing to use these grants as a political point-scoring exercise, knowing that it would be impossible for the farmers to take up the grant and that this would not affect their debt levels. Also, it was a government department that evaluated the farmer's application and not an independent body, and they could reject the application without giving a reason. If they had to build a dam or other structure like piping the water to the centre, then this would require expenditure, which they weren't, willing to make at this point in time as it didn't meet their personal plans. As to what would be best for the country, well, this did not come into the equation. Again, if they waited long enough, they would own the farms' rights to the gas and get appreciation in property values owing to the property being made drought-proof.

The Royal Commission explored all these questions and took evidence from contributors all over the country, delaying action regarding the acquisition of the farms. Other countries realised that they, too, could capitalise on the world shortage of LPG and began exploring for this resource and rare minerals. Amongst the leaders were the United States of America, which found extensive areas of natural gas and developed their own LPG plant and ports to export their resource.

As more and more gas was discovered, additional countries entered the forward markets, and the price of LPG tumbled substantially, resulting in those who had committed themselves to the earlier contracts to lose substantially, and if ever allowed to begin production, they would have to produce more to cover the loss in selling price for LPG. This would not be easy, as other counties were exporting their discovered gas and filling any demands that arose. Along with the discovery of gas came a new discovery of oil, and this forced the price of petrol down to where major producers held emergency meetings in Ciro to agree on production targets.

The firms who found themselves wound up in the banking scandal tried to seek government help, which normally would be passed onto them discreetly. However, the government, realising that they were being watched, declined, forcing these individuals and firms to fight for their existence in court. Many contracts were found to be guaranteed by their sole director and major shareholder, which meant that they would eventually lose all that they had accumulated, including their private assets and wealth, unless things improved. Many farmers declared it could not happen soon enough to those vultures.

The Royal Commission tabled its report, which was highly critical of the government in that, in the commission's opinion, there was an intention to secure a benefit for certain unknown individuals rather than the country. The commission made it clear it could not find out why no dams had been built to safeguard against drought. Especially when the government knew that in a few years' time, there would be another drought around the corner and more subsidies and grants would be needed to be provided to protect our primary producers.

In relation to the dairy industry, the commission declared that it was obvious the government allowed the destruction of this industry intending to decimate it, to ensure all of our dairy products were imported from overseas rather than the country being self-sufficient. The commission declared the government was deciding on behalf of influential organisations that stood to profit rather than the country overall. In relation to the banks, the commission declared they acted unconscionable and in their own interest. The contract entered by the farmers were unfair because they were structured intending to give the banks an unfair advantage over the farmers. The right to call in the mortgage, even though all repayments had been met, was a prime example of this.

The right to sell the farm without an auction was another. The commission declared all these clauses within the contract were unfair and therefore void, rendering the contracts unworkable and preventing the banks from taking legal action against the farmers. In short, the banks handed over money to the farmers but could not use the mortgage document or loan document to begin litigation against the farmer. All that they could do was to recover a debt, which was unsecured.

The banks lost respect, and shareholders were not happy with their actions. The directors and boards did not care, as they had been well paid over the years and could resign their positions with large payouts, ensuring they were better off than any of the farmers.

Many executives of the banks were not as lucky as their CEOs or board members and found they were on the nose when they tried to find jobs outside of the banking industry and lost a lot of money in litigation being brought against them, forcing them to declare themselves bankrupt. The financial stress tore their families apart, and some even suicided, as they could not face a world without the political power and wealth that they had spent a lifetime securing.

CHAPTER 23

WELL, IT IS DAY THREE and not a drop of rain. The radio station declared, 'where is the rainmaker, the one we all prayed to? I guess He is not willing to cooperate and answer our prayers, or is it that this proves that there is no God and we have all been wasting our time in having faith and praying for something He is incapable of delivering? Either way, nothing and not a cloud insight. I guess Tim Curtis, the minister at the festival, might have an answer. We will try to get him on the line if we can locate him. No doubt he has taken advise and has gone into hiding. No, I understand he is on the line.'

The commentator said, 'Minister, your prayers don't seem to be answered, and it seems the whole festival was a scam to not only rob the farmers of donations but also to pull the carpet from under them, in that there is no hope of them getting back on their feet. No rain, Minister. will it rain soon or never? You're close to God, so tell us.'

Tim said, 'Thanks for having me on. While I appreciate you must spice up your program to keep your ratings up, I take umbrage at your suggestion that I would be in hiding.'

The commentator said, 'Well, Minister, where is the rain you promised?'

Tim replied, 'It seems stretching the truth is part of the course here for your program. The truth does not matter. You and your listeners well know we asked everyone to pray for rain on the third day, and today is the third day. It has not finished yet, just started. I would ask your listeners who agree with me to phone your station and register their protest at your dishonesty and endeavour to belittle the Christian faith and in particular, Christ. My understanding is this is not the first time you have done this. It seems you have a private battle against Christ. Maybe you can enlighten us as to what this is, so we can all help you get over your problem.'

The commentator said, 'Well, we know we won't be getting any calls. Thanks for your time, Minister, but the proof is out there. No rain.'

With that, the commentator cut Tim off. As for protest calls, only a handful of listeners bothered telephoning in and complaining at the blatant dishonesty of the commentator. He was right where religion is concerned—only a handful would support the church; the others would not care about God or the church.

Throughout the day, the commentator persisted in mocking Tim and the prayer for rain with half-hourly updates as to the number of clouds that could be seen and reports from the Department of Meteorology as to any satellite coverage of clouds. Continual reports stated there was none, and the commentator made it clear that it was a hoax, and so is God.

The radio station asked the Department of Meteorology about cloud coverage in the area, but not about other developments that may bring rain.

Out in the Pacific, there was a hurricane developing, which most meteorologists declared would either fizz out or head north and burn itself out. However, it did contrary to the experts' predictions.

The hurricane picked up intensity while over the ocean, sucking up an enormous amount of water and building in intensity still unobserved. It then moved left towards land mass and started at the tip of the drought-stricken area. It had speed and mass, and as it moved inland and down south, it dumped an enormous amount of water on the parched land.

The radio station was still broadcasting 'No rain' and it is most unlikely to happen when it was hit by the hurricane. The building that housed the station was demolished completely, and the hurricane took the commentator up as it passed over. His body was never recovered. It could be said his conflict with Christ was resolved or it had just begun.

Peter sat on his veranda looking at the parched land and radiated heat from the ground. Alice came out with a glass of cold water when, suddenly, the heavens opened, and the entire area received a deluge of rain, which continued for hours afterwards.

Peter said, 'Our prayers have been answered. Call your mum and make sure she is all right.'

Alice grabbed her mobile and rang her mother. Alice asked, 'Mum, are you all right with this rain?'

Helen replied, 'Yes. It hit with a vengeance. I was listening to some smart radio commentator who was trying to make a name for himself at the expense of the church when the rain came with a fury and vengeance. Boy, I bet he will find it hard to wipe the stupid look off his face.'

Alice asked, 'Is there any damage to the house?'

Helen replied, 'No, it is all right. Nothing has fallen off.' Alice asked, 'Any change in Paul?'

Helen replied, 'No, he is much the same, except they have found him a bed in a nursing home and intend to shift him there in the next few days. I tried to protest, but they will not listen to me, and it seems that is where he is going to end up unless a miracle happens.'

Alice said, 'I will call Tim and advise him. Love you.'

Alice rang Tim, and after several goes, gave up. It seemed their transmission station was knocked out and there was no mobile connection.

Peter said, 'what did your mum say?'

Alice replied, 'She is alright. They are going to move Paul to a nursing home in the next few days. I tried to call Tim, but the transmission station has been damaged, and I can't get through.'

Peter said, 'Then ring him on the landline?'

Alice said, 'I never thought of that. They still exist, don't they?'

Alice went into the house and rang Tim's home number.

Finally, after a lengthy period, Tim answered.

He confirmed that all was all right and there were no injuries. He advised Alice that the radio station in the town was demolished with not a stone left on top of each other. The broadcaster still has not been found, presumably taken out to sea with the hurricane as it moved off the coast back towards the Pacific. All areas received a lot of rain, and they topped up all dams and creeks and, in some cases, these were overflowing. It had just stopped raining, and many farmers had made artificial dams on their properties, keeping as much water as they could. Some were talking about the type of crop they were going to sow, while others were looking to restock their herds.

Alice asked, 'How many have come forth and given thanks openly to God for the rain?'

Tim replied, 'None. Sorry, one person, me.' Both burst out laughing.

Tim said, 'I am going to hold a service tonight to give thanks to the Lord for hearing our prayers. Not sure how many will come, but I would advertise it if we had a radio station.'

Alice said, 'I am not sure how many will know about it, but we have advised our local station we will hold a service at seven to give thanks to the Lord for the rain, and Mum is doing the same in Castle Hill. I will ring the radio station and ask them to broadcast that you are also holding a service at seven.'

Tim said, 'That would be great. Thanks.'

Alice said, 'Mum is looking after your father, and she said they are going to move him to a nursing home, and she can't prevent it from happening.'

Tim said, 'I am not sure what I can do to stop it. If she wants me to ring and protest, I am more than happy to do so, but I know these people. Once they have made up their minds, it is very hard to persuade them otherwise.'

Alice said, 'I will tell Mum, as I am going up there to give her a hand and some support. I think, under the circumstances, we should postpone our wedding until we can see what is going to happen to your father.'

Tim said, 'Let us leave it at present and see what happens in the next week or two. I want to drive to Castle Hill and see Dad and bring Mary up with me soon, and we can talk about it then.'

Alice replied, 'OK. I love you. Bye.'

With that, Alice hung up the telephone and went out and told Peter that Tim intended to drive up soon to see his father. After a week, the roads dried up, and the creeks settled down and became passable. Peter made another trip to Castle Hill to restock some farmers who had run out of food and didn't have the money to buy provisions. In many of these cases, the primary bread earner had walked off the land and tried to get a job in a factory to earn money to feed their family. However, if they had to go to the city or away from their homestead, the rent that they had to pay left them little for food for themselves, let alone to send back home so the rest of the family could be fed. More and more tried, but found it hard to support themselves and their family. The isolation and being in a new geographic area led a lot into depression and suicide. Many that tried to get help found no one cared, and while everyone had jumped on the bandwagon to support the farmer, it was purely for the publicity rather than to provide legitimate help. When it came to providing a helping hand, it was not there. Many mouthed the words but did little to provide practical help.

CHAPTER 24

PETER PULLED UP OUTSIDE PAUL'S residence, and both he and Alice walked up to the house and rang the doorbell. Helen came out and embraced them both, and they all went into the house. Helen had prepared a meal for them and insisted on Peter staying the night and driving home the next morning, which he agreed to do, as it was late and he was tired. They had several deliveries to make and were held back by joining the search to find a lost farmer who had walked away from the homestead with no provisions or water and had been missing for three days. They found him stumbling across his paddock delirious, not knowing where he was. There is little doubt that he had dementia and depression. A helicopter was ordered, and they took him to the local hospital in a dehydrated condition.

They had their dinner and chatted for a while about various things and then went to bed. Peter wanted an early start to drive home, and the two girls set off to see Paul and then make a trip to some farmers a couple of hours away.

The next morning, Peter had breakfast and set off to drive home. The girls drove to the hospital to see Paul, who had developed a fever and could not be taken to the nursing home as planned until they brought the fever under control. The girls went and attend to their deliveries and come back that evening.

They drove south of Castle Hill for about two hours and stopped at a farmhouse, which Paul had noted as needing help, and knocked on the door. A lady answered, telling them her husband was not home.

After explaining who they were and that they were there to make a food drop, the lady's attitude changed. She arranged for her boys to help de-tarp the trailer and to take what provisions they needed, which they did. Once the job was completed, they said their goodbyes and were just ready to get into their wagon when the lady came out with two cold drinks and cakes wrapped for their journey. They thanked her and settled into the wagon and drove off.

As they were heading for the second stop, Helen noticed Alice eating the cake and drinking the water given to her. She immediately stopped and got out and grabbed the cakes from Alice's hands and the drink (water from the bore) and threw them onto the ground.

Alice asked, 'why did you do that? I was enjoying the cake.' Helen replied, 'Because it will make you sick.'

Alice said, 'Rubbish. I'll just finish my cake. There isn't much left of it.'

With that, Alice scooped the cake up from the ground and gulped it down. She washed her hands with her drink. And both got back into the wagon. About half an hour later, Alice yelled out, 'Mum, stop the car! I have to get out.'

She stopped the car, and Alice got out, not knowing where to go. She stood there frozen and then suddenly let loose from the rear and could not stop for a minute.

Alice said, 'oh, no, I just shitted in my pants.'

Helen could not stop laughing at Alice, who had poo running down the back of her legs onto her shoes.

She said, 'You will have to take your shorts off and underpants, shoes, and socks off so I can wash them.'

Helen went into the wagon to get her emergency pack, which she now carried with her every time she went on the road for deliveries. She searched at the rear and could not find it. She checked the trailer, but it could not be seen.

Helen asked, 'Alice, did you see a blue bag in the back of the wagon?'

Alice replied, 'Yes, I took it into the house for you. Why?'

Helen said, 'That bag had the water we needed to wash the shit from the back of your legs and shorts, that's why. Now we only have my drink to clean you up with, which won't be enough to wash the shit out of your underpants and shorts, let alone your shoes and socks.'

Alice said, 'What are we going to do? We have one more drop-off to do, and I'm naked with poo all over me.'

Helen asked, 'Do you want my cake?'

Both burst out laughing and decided they would have to go home and make the second run the next day. They took a piece of plastic from one pack and wrapped it around Alice's vital parts as if it was a modern dress. The soiled shoes and clothing were placed in a bag and tied down on the trailer, and they set off for home.

After three hours, they arrived home and parked the wagon in the barn. The plan was for Helen to go in and unlock the back door, and Alice would come out of the wagon and enter the house from the rear. Just as they were ready to exit the vehicle, Tim appeared in the barn with his sister, Mary.

Tim stuck his head into the passenger's side and immediately withdrew himself and said, 'who shitted themselves?'

Alice pushed the door open and, with the plastic wrapped around her, stormed off to the house, leaving Helen, Mary, and Tim standing in the barn.

Helen said, 'we had an accident en route to one farm, which, as you can see, left Alice in an embarrassing situation after you turned up on the scene. Why are you here? We weren't expecting you.' Tim replied, 'Dad's condition deteriorated, and the hospital tried to contact you. Since they could not reach you, they rang me. I tried to call Alice, but she did not answer because she was with you, and both were out of mobile range. They think his increased body temperature has something to do with the way his body is bent over, preventing circulation and causing infections and his organs to slow down. Eventually, they will close down. They do not believe he has much time left.'

Helen said, 'I better call Peter and let him know.'

Helen rang Peter, who was planning to call in after dropping off some provisions. She gave him the address of the station they missed, and he said he would do the drop-off on his way.

Alice had a shower and, after dressing, went to the trailer and took out her dirty clothing and shoes and went back into the laundry and washed everything spotless. She then came out to speak with the group. No one dared to ask what had happened, as they knew it was something Alice would prefer to forget. They decided to visit Paul at the hospital and then go to McDonald's and have an early night.

They went to the hospital and found Paul in a bad way. Everyone, including the doctors, expected him to pass on that night or the next day. Nothing could help him now other than to keep him out of pain on oxygen and try to lower his temperature with antibiotics.

They left Paul and went to have their McDonald's, except Alice, who did not want to have any food. They then went back home and after watching a bit of television, went to bed.

Peter was awakened during the night with a premonition. The Lord appeared to him and said he is to perform another miracle in the name of the Lord and that the Lord will be with him, and then nothing. Peter, on this occasion, did not know who the benefactor was, when, and where. He did not start challenging God, as he knew he would be told these things when God was ready.

The next morning, Peter drove from Bungarby out towards Castle Hill and distributed provisions to those farmers in need. Many had not received help for months and were desperate, and all appreciated the helping hand. Some were talking about grass coming over their barren land and the possibility of restocking their herds. Peter knew this was only talk, as the government would not come up with the grants or would make it so difficult that the farmer would never get a cent. He felt that there was a sinister motive behind this attitude. But he also knew that the only way they stood to make a dollar was to restock and export their produce. This was the thing the government was praising, but behind the scene, it was doing its best to prevent the farmers getting back on their feet.

He delivered all that he had and finally made his way to Paul's house, where Helen and the other three were waiting for him.

Peter had a shower and got himself ready to go to the hospital to see Paul. They took two cars, and Helen led the way. Once there, they walked to the ward where Paul was lying, but before reaching Paul's bed, they were intercepted by Paul's doctor, who advised them he was not responding to antibiotics and there was a good possibility he would not make it through the night. The doctor wanted permission to take Paul off life support and let him pass naturally.

Tim at first said no, but Mary asked the doctor whether Paul could still pull through. The doctor said 'No, no chance and there was a significant possibility he may have a last stroke, which will kill him.' With that, they agreed to take Paul off life support.

The doctors asked them to wait fifteen minutes before seeing Paul, which would allow them to take him off life support. They waited and then entered where Paul lay.

Peter moved to the head of the bed and Tim and Mary were on the left and Alice and Helen were on the right of Paul's bed. As Peter approached Paul's bed, he heard the Lord say, 'I command you,' and Peter knew God was going to do what medical science could not do—cure Paul physically.

Peter asked if they could wrap the screens around the bed for some privacy, which the nurses did. The ward Paul was in was the Palliative Care Ward, where old people were brought to die.

Tim said a prayer over his father, and everyone stared at Paul, thinking nothing can help him. Alice knew better, as she once had been in a similar situation and the Lord saved her. She was praying for the Lord to save Paul. Helen knew of the Lord's powers and did not believe He would do nothing to save His minister, especially with Peter present. Mary wanted to go, as she was upset to see her father in that condition. He looked worse than she first imagined and could barely look at him, a grotesque figure, nothing what her father used to be like.

Peter looked up and placed his hands on Paul's head, and as soon as he did this, Helen and Alice knew the Lord was present and would cure Paul. They had faith in the Lord.

Tim was ready to object, but something made him say nothing. As soon as Peter prayed, a white light appeared, and an old man stood there near him who placed his hands on top of Peter's hands just as Peter said, 'I ask for Paul to be cured in the name of the Father, Jesus Christ.' The light stayed on for a minute, and Peter then stopped his prayer. Alice and Helen were smiling as if to say, 'Success.' Tim and Mary were looking at Peter, ready to say, 'What in the hell do you think you are doing? We don't believe in miracles, nor do they happen these days. Stop the masquerading.'

Slowly, the monitors picked up activity as Paul moved his arms and then his legs. He began straightening up his body, and his face turned and fell back into shape. Doctors came running into his section and asked the visitors to move out into the waiting room.

They witnessed Paul's body untwining itself and straighten up, and after about fifteen minutes, when the miracle process seemed to have ended, Paul swung his feet around and stepped onto the floor at the amazement of the doctors and nurses, who insisted he stayed in bed. It was inconceivable to them that someone who had been considered close to death could suddenly stand and walk fifteen minutes later. They left Paul for a minute, who walked to the waiting room where everyone went to at the insistence of the doctors. He plodded down the hall in a shuffle motion and found the waiting room at the end of the ward. Everyone hugged and kissed him, and he particularly thanked Helen for visiting him every day, whom he refused to let go of and kept her in a big hug. He thanked Peter and understood what Helen had told him previously about the miracles that were performed and thanked God for His miracle. Tim was still trying to come to terms with what had transpired and found it difficult to accept what he saw, as he had no faith in God coming to his father's rescue. He was thinking, *There is one thing in believing in God's powers, but another in God doing what you pray for.*

The doctors ordered Paul back to his bed, as they wanted blood samples to see what he had taken to correct his condition. Paul said goodbye to his family and asked when they will come again. Helen said she would come tomorrow with some clothes, and they all kissed him and left him to the insistence of the doctors that he get back into bed.

The doctors were of the opinion that Paul had taken something that reversed his condition and were determined to understand what cured him. They ordered not only blood samples but also CT scans of his whole body to see if there was some implant. For the rest of the day and into the next; tests were ordered, but all came up showing Paul to be normal and no reason for his dramatic change in stature and health. He kept telling them it was in answer to his prayers and that it was a miracle performed by Jesus Christ, but no one would accept this as the genuine answer. All that they could say was that he should stop saying that otherwise, he would end up in the psychiatric ward instead of a nursing home. 'Miracles don't happen. They are read about in the bible but never happen in real life.'

The next day, Helen arrived at the hospital at about ten o'clock with Alice. Tim was holding a service at the church, and Mary was helping him. The girls gave Paul a big hug and sat down near his bed. He advised them that after twelve hours of tests, they could not conclude how he could miraculously be cured and told him they would place him in the psychiatric ward if he kept telling everyone that Jesus Christ cured him.

Helen said, 'Well, Paul, are you able to go home today, since they wanted to get rid of you the other day saying they needed the bed?'

Paul said, 'I will ask them.'

Paul went to the head doctor and asked whether they could release him from the hospital. The doctor said no at first and then changed his mind, as he could not think of any more test that could be done to assist them to draw a conclusion. They decided Paul could be discharged and, if necessary, could come back for re-examination. It would be better that he was out of sight than there, continually showing himself as a walking miracle. A newspaper reporter might get wind of the story, and the hospital would find it difficult to explain his sudden change in health. They may even refer to him as *Lazarus.* They would no doubt describe it as a miracle despite what the doctors said, and that wouldn't be much, as they didn't know or accept what had cured Paul.

Paul promptly pulled the screen around him and got dressed. After they handed his discharge papers to him, he left the hospital with the girls and accompanied them home.

Everyone was waiting for him, except Peter, who had to go back home to attend to church services of his own.

They held a welcome home celebration for Paul. Tim and Mary were leaving the following morning, taking Alice home on their way. Helen would stay back to attend to the church services and distribute the food provisions until Paul got his strength back.

The next morning, everyone made their way back home, and they dropped Alice off en route. Peter was not home, as he was making a delivery of supplies to farmers in need. He finally came home at about four in the afternoon, tired and hungry.

Alice attended to some post-festival matters and noted that the three executives who stole the money were arrested, but the whereabouts of the money were still unknown.

Tim had a heavy week of engagements in Rayleigh. There were several suicides, and therefore had to attend to several funerals and asked Alice if she would assist, as Mary had gone back to the city. He drove to collect her the next morning, and they immediately headed back to Rayleigh.

Paul and Helen got on well over the weeks that followed, and it came time for Helen to leave, as it was considered Paul had regained his former strength and stamina and could now do what he was doing before his stroke.

On the day before Helen was due to go home, Paul proposed marriage to her, which was not unexpected. Helen accepted, as she knew he was the man for her. Paul knew Helen visited him every day when he was in hospital and was the closest one to him, and he wanted them to be together for the rest of their lives.

Helen wanted to tell Peter first, as he has always been close to her and looked after her. The wedding was to be in two months' time and was to be held in Castle Hill. Paul would ask his friend from the city to attend to the service.

They planned, Peter would call in on one of his trips close to Castle Hill and collect Helen and drive her home, which he did some days later. Helen said nothing while they were driving, not sure how Peter would take the news. When they got home, she went to her room to freshen up, and then made them dinner. Over dinner, she told Peter that Paul had proposed and that she had accepted. She understood with Alice and now her getting married that Peter would be left on his own, but, hopefully, he would also meet a girl and settle down.

Peter knew this was coming and told Helen he wished her and Paul the best. No doubt she would move to Castle Hill and living there, which she acknowledged would be the case.

Peter was asked to be the best man, which he agreed to, and to walk Helen down the aisle in the ceremony.

Helen then telephoned Alice and told her the good news. Alice was thrilled and immediately told Tim, who suggested they have a twin wedding to save costs. Alice told her mum, who agreed that would be great, and Peter could walk both the girls down the aisle.

Everything was set for the wedding, and there was to be a small party afterwards comprising sandwiches and finger foods. The venue was booked, and all set in stone for the big day.

CHAPTER 25

THE DAY BEFORE THE WEDDING, Peter was packing his clothes and getting ready to drive to Castle Hill.

There was a knock at the door, which Peter went to answer. Standing on the other side were two police officers with two more near the police car.

The police asked, 'is your name Peter Edwards?'

Peter, having to think for a moment as to what his name was, said, 'No, Marlow—yes, I mean Edwards. Why?'

The police said, 'We have a warrant for your arrest for burglary and assault that happened three years ago. We have been after you for some time, Mr Edwards.'

Peter glanced at his watch, which showed the exact day and time he had left jail twelve months ago as Peter Marlow. The Lord had said that he would release him from jail for twelve months and he would return thereafter from where he came. The only difference was he had changed his name and thought that he would get away from going back to jail, but this might have been his plan, but not God's.

Twelve months to the day, to the minute.

With that, Peter was placed in the police car and taken to the station and locked up in the cell for court appearance the next day.

After Peter settled down in his cell, he remembered the weddings were on today and he could not make the ceremony. He tried to telephone Helen, but the police would only allow him one telephone call, and that was to his lawyer, who was in the city. They agreed the lawyer would appear on a conference call and have the matter deferred to the city so he could handle the representation. This would also mean, if granted, they would transfer Peter to the city for trial.

Peter was at a disadvantage, as he did not know what Peter Edwards had gotten up to before he died and did not know how Edwards died. The only thing he knew was that Edward's body was never found, and his death had never been officially recoded with the government department that handles the recording of deaths. Peter's matter was set before a judge and, the next day, was brought before the court. His solicitor was on the conference line, following the proceedings.

Peter was asked to stand and state his name. Peter stood up and said, 'Peter Marlow,' but then realised his error and said, 'Edwards.' The judge looked at him but said nothing.

The judge asked Peter how did he plead, and Peter was ready to give an answer when his solicitor interrupted and advised the judge that Peter was arrested on a warrant that had listed a different charge to the one the judge had asked Peter to advise on, and, therefore, he could not enter a plea until the actual charge was known, and since this was not known at the time of arrest, then Peter should not have been arrested on the charge noted. The judge agreed that there was a conflict and ordered Peter back to his cell until the prosecutor could find out the correct charge.

Later that day, Peter was brought back before the judge and advised he was arrested for theft of several expensive automobiles, robbery of several petrol stations and small food outlets, and assault.

After discussing the matter with his solicitor, he was advised that the police had as evidence CCT footage of Edwards (who looked like Peter) doing the robberies and assaults, and, therefore, he should plead guilty, as he would receive a discount on his sentence if he entered an early plea.

Peter entered a guilty plea and received a sentence of five years with a non-parole period of three years, which was the exact time of his previous sentence before he was released from jail. They returned him to the exact jail that he had been previously released from.

CHAPTER 26

THE DAY BEFORE THE WEDDINGS, and things were hectic, with Tim and Alice turning up at Castle Hill about midday. Everyone was all excited and took part in a champagne lunch, and all waited for the best man to arrive, who was going to walk the brides down the aisle.

Everyone had a lengthy lunch, and the champagne flowed freely, and they exchanged gossips about family and friends. After about three o'clock, they all went and had a nap, as they had all drunk considerably more than what they were used to and were getting merry, slurring their words. Also, it was noticed that Peter had not turned up, and they did not want to appear drunk when he did. So off they went to their rooms. Unfortunately, they all slept through the night and got up early the next morning.

Helen made several telephone calls to Peter, but he was not answering his telephone or his house telephone. Everyone had breakfast, and the girls went off to have their hair done, which they promptly did. They left it to Tim to track down Peter.

No matter how much he tried, Tim could get no one that could say where Peter was. At about eleven o'clock, all four were concerned about Peter, for it was unusual for him not to turn up at such an important function. Even the police at Bungarby did not know what had happened to Peter and went to the church and his home to search for him. They noted his belongings were still there and advised Tim, who told Helen.

Helen was concerned that Peter had broken down on his way to Castle Hill and asked the police to check the roads to see if he had. The police at Bungarby advised that Peter's car was still parked in the barn, which meant that he had not driven to make a drop off of provisions at any of the farms.

Tim could not call the wedding off just because Peter was missing, so he went to the church and asked the elder to act in substitution for Peter and to walk the girls down the aisle. The elder agreed, so everything was back on track, all except the whereabouts of Peter.

The local police at Bungarby were asked to check their records, and after an hour of searching, they found out that Peter had been arrested and taken into custody and was due to appear in court to enter a plea the day of the wedding. They telephoned Tim just as the men were getting dressed and advised him about what had happened. Tim decided that there was no use in telling the girls, so he kept the information to himself and continued preparing for the wedding.

The girls got dressed, and each had a friend to help. Their outfits were basic, nothing flashy, and the wedding dresses were borrowed from folks that heard they were getting married and who were glad to lend a hand. While the girls did not know many people in the town, a lot knew Paul and were turning up to see who he was going to marry.

Some close friends of Tim were going to turn up, but unfortunately, with the cost of petrol and the low-income farmers were receiving, they just couldn't afford to come to the wedding.

The wedding was scheduled for five, and a large crowd turned up to see the brides and their grooms. A minister from one of the other churches in another county was asked to perform the ceremonies, and at five, the grooms entered the church to wait for their brides.

The brides waited fifteen minutes and then entered the church. Since the residence was close by, they walked to the entrance. Not quite your spectacular entrance, but good enough for the guests and girls.

At the entrance, they were met by the church elder in his suit, tie, and well-polished farm boots, all well dressed for the occasion, and all three waited until the music started before proceeding down the aisle. They took their time as the church was packed, as this was considered an important event by the community, and all were welcomed and came into town to celebrate the occasion.

Most stood as the girls passed by, and some thought it was a miracle that their minister, who some had seen in hospital resembling a 'motor accident victim', now stood on his own feet and was going to be married to his carer.

The girls walked down the aisle and to the front of the church and were handed over to their partners. The elder went and sat down in the pew with his wife, who gave him a kiss of approval. The minister stepped forward and began the ceremony. After half an hour, the rings were produced, and each couple said their vows and placed the wedding ring on their partner's finger and, soon after that, they were pronounced man and wife.

All those attended were asked not to throw rice or confetti, as it would require someone to clean up the mess. They invited all to take part in some finger food and an outdoor barbecue. Helen and Alice estimated they would cater for about fifty people, but over three hundred turned up for the wedding. Since there was no live entertainment, the crowd made their own music. Whoever could play a musical instrument went to the front and played. The brides and grooms were the first to dance and thereafter, all took to the dance floor.

Helen could not stop thinking about Peter throughout the ceremony and knew that something had gone wrong, and he was in trouble needing help. She put on a brave face but could not keep her feelings from showing, and Paul knew she was worried.

Helen was concerned that they would not have enough food to feed the crowd that turned up. She and Paul went over to the table where the finger pies, rolls, and sandwiches were and noticed that a crowd of people had swarmed onto the table containing the food, and after they had got their plates filled, they moved on to the beer and soft drinks, which were in buckets of ice that were provided by the publican of the local pub. Anyone who wanted a draught beer could go to the pub and buy a schooner, and many did while carrying their plate of finger foods.

Paul and Helen approached the table and were expecting to see it bare. To their surprise, there was the same quantity of food there waiting to be consumed as when they started. They realised the Lord was replenishing the table to ensure all that came could be fed. It was the Sermon on the Mount, repeated without the fish. While they stood there, many more came with their children and filled their plates with food. Possibly they thought they should go to the wedding to get food, which was not available at their farm.

Helen went off to tell Alice what she saw and finally caught up with her, talking to a farmer who was wishing her and Tim all the best for the future and declaring the food was the best he had eaten for a long time. Finally, Alice and Tim broke away from the crowd and headed to a quiet corner to have a few words.

Tim told Helen that he had received word from Bungarby police Peter was arrested on a warrant for theft and assault on the day before the wedding and taken into custody. He was brought before the court on the day of the wedding and had entered a guilty plea and was sentenced to five years in prison with a three-year non-parole period. He currently was on his way to a maximum-security prison where they would assess which jail he was to be sent to.

Helen, on hearing the news, just about fainted, and Tim had to grab hold of her to stop her from falling. He sat her on a chair, and Alice quickly got a glass of water and gave her some to sip. Paul, seeing her collapse, came over quickly to find out what had happened. Tim told his father of what he knew and the bad news about Peter. Paul could not believe that Peter, of all people, would be arrested on those charges and kept saying that the next day they were going to clear Peter's name, not knowing the history of what had transpired.

Helen asked Tim to keep the information confidential and not to mention it to anyone; if anyone asked to say they were still trying to find out what had happened to him. Helen regained her composure and, with Paul, Alice, and Tim, mingled with the crowd, who were enjoying themselves thoroughly.

At about six, the crowd showed no sign of breaking up to go home, and some, unfortunately, had a lot to drink and were in no condition to drive home. They would have to rely on their wives, daughters, or sons to attend to that formality; otherwise, they would have to sleep it off outside town and begin the journey the next day with a hangover.

Most of the crowd were unaware of the sudden accumulation of cloud coming in from the west, and it was not long before it rained, bringing everyone out into the streets dancing for joy. This was the second time it had rained in the area, and most people thanked the Lord for His gift. Helen and Alice, like most, stood outside soaking up the rain, which brought relief from the dry, searing conditions. After an hour of rain, the novelty of getting wet wore off, and most people decided to call it a day and head off home. Most came and paid their respects and wished the married couple well, while others just packed up and headed off home. The married couple walked home, deciding to clean up the next day. They all thanked God for His grace and gifts in replenishing the food and drink and causing it to rain.

Now married, the couples could sleep together, and it was not long before they consummated their marriages, and they were truly man and wife.

The next morning, they cleaned up the church and the hall where the food and drinks were located and donated leftover food to those in need, and the drinks were handed over to the publican of the local pub, as he was the provider of the ice and all the glasses for the wine and beer.

Helen made some enquiries as to Peter's whereabouts and decided to go to where he was being held to find out what was happening. She realised the Lord had always said that after one year, he would be returned to jail to finish his sentence. Initially, he was released to show him the power of the Lord and to let him see what this world offered compared to what the Lord could provide, which was priceless and not able to be bought.

Tim and Alice decided to leave for Rayleigh and headed off early, as it was a long drive to get home.

CHAPTER 27

T HEY SENT PETER TO A jail some forty kilometres from the city to
serve out his sentence. The township comprising an approximate
population of about thirty-five thousand people. As usual, they placed
Peter in a two-man cell, and his roommate tried to dominate him by
getting stuck into Peter at the first opportunity. He unfortunately did
not know Peter's true background, and Peter could disarm him and
send him to the hospital for about a month with multiple injuries.
The exercise yard saw similar treatment, with some men trying to
tell Peter what he could and could not do, and how to divide up his
money from working in the prison factory.

Helen turned up at the jail to see Peter without an appointment
and insisted on seeing him. She was initially refused, but after advising
that she would speak to the radio station about prisoners' treatment,
they allowed her ten minutes to see Peter. He was brought up from
his cell in chains and was placed behind glass. She could not touch
him and could only speak to him through a telephone.

She asked how he was and could see that he had been in several
fights as he bruised knuckles and had several cuts on his face.

She was concerned about his safety and wondered what the benefit
was of letting him out of prison for a year just to throw him back into
jail. Peter advised her not to be bitter about his return to jail and it was
God's will and is part of his plan. What he had experienced in the year
he was out of prison was more than he could have in a lifetime. He
understood what the Lord can provide as compared to Satan, whom

he followed previously and who urged and encouraged him to follow the ways of this world. He advised Helen that his sentence was the same as before, irrespective of whether he was Edwards or Marlow. The sentence was neither shorter nor longer.

Helen advised Peter what happened at the wedding and that they planned on fifty people attending and ended up with three hundred more. She advised him they could feed the cast of 'thousand with a few fishes and loaves of bread,' and neither the food nor the drink ran out, and to cap things off, they had rain, which lasted for five hours. Peter was amazed at the miracles the Lord gave them and was sure that their marriages were blessed in heaven. As to what was going to happen to him, he did not know what God's had planned for him but knew one day he would be put down if left in jail. He thought maybe that was the divine plan.

Helen's ten minutes were up in jail, and she gave Peter a kiss on the telephone and left him in tears. She decided to drive back to Bungarby and stay the night and attend to any outstanding matters, as some farmers needed provisions. Peter's wagon was in the barn connected to the trailer, which was full, so there was nothing stopping her from doing the deliveries.

Helen arrived at Bungarby late and went to their residence and made some dinner and had an early night. The next morning, she headed off to make her deliveries and came back to Bungarby at about four. She intended to make more deliveries tomorrow and drive thereafter to Castle Hill.

Peter settled into his routine and was again placed on the gang to repair roads and community services. He was outside the community hospital working with a gang of ten when they heard a bridge had collapsed and there was a bus full of children from the local primary school on board, and the bus was going to slide off the bridge down a ravine, which would mean all the children would perish. The gang leader asked which of his men would help if possible. Two men, including Peter, volunteered. The team leader telephoned the police and said he had two men willing to help in the rescue of the children. The police sent a car to collect them, and before they knew it, they were on the bridge.

Peter knew from looking at the situation that time was not on his side. Children under eight want to move around, and they would not understand the danger they were in. The other prisoner, who was in for ten years, said he couldn't do anything to help and bolted back to the police car, saying it was a suicide mission.

The warden from the prison, who had two children on the bus, turned up with his third son. They quickly called the children's mother, and she turned up, telling her husband to do something.

The bus lurched sideways, and it was obvious the bus and children would not survive much longer.

Peter said a prayer asking for the Lord's strength and guidance. He then moved to the front of the bus and noticed that the driver was unconscious but breathing. He used a crowbar he had with him to force the door open, ensuring he did not slip to his death while working.

By this time, television crews had set up their cameras and were filming the rescue live throughout the country.

Peter opened the door far enough to order the children on the leaning side to move one by one over to the other side, which they did under instruction. It was clear they were worried, and some cried out for their mothers.

As time went by, more and more parents arrived at the scene, wanting answers as to why one jailbird was the only one saving their children. The police tried to calm them down and advised that more people on the bus will force it to roll down and over the bridge.

After all the children moved to the opposite side of the bus, Peter stepped in slowly and made his way to the back of the bus. He hit the back window with his crowbar, sending the rear screen flying onto the road, and then, one by one, ordered the children to walk slowly towards him. He picked the child up and initially dropped the child on the road outside the bus with instruction that they were to turn and walk towards their mothers on the entry to the bridge. After about two children were dropped, another person ran up to the bus and took the children from Peter. Then a third person came to help and a fourth. They took all the children off the bus one by one. The only person left on the bus were the driver and Peter.

Peter walked slowly towards the front of the bus and put his arms around the driver, who was still breathing. He could see the paramedics had brought a bed up to about ten feet from the bus. Slowly, he pulled the driver to the rear of the bus and lifted him out of the window and into the hands of the paramedics waiting on the other side. Unfortunately, with the shift in weight, the bus leaned further over the bridge and, in a split second, rolled on its side.

Peter, knowing what was going to happen, immediately leapt from the rear of the bus straight onto the road, knocking himself unconscious. The bus continued its way down the ravine and broke up in pieces as it hit large rocks and trees on its way down.

They rushed Peter to the hospital with a severe head wound and put into a coma to help prevent brain damage.

After a week, they brought Peter out of the induced coma. He had a swollen head with bruises and stayed in hospital for a further week and was then sent back to prison with instructions to rest for the next two weeks.

CHAPTER 28

ALICE AND TIM WERE HAVING a well-deserved rest at their home in Rayleigh watching a movie when a news flash came on television about some trapped children in a bus, and only one person was sent in to save the thirty children and one driver from certain death.

They stayed glued to the television until the live camera fixed on Peter, and Alice immediately recognised her uncle and ran to the telephone to call her mother.

Alice said, 'Mum, Peter is on the news trying to rescue a busload of children whose bus had just tried to cross a collapsed bridge.'

Helen quickly switched the news on in horror and found all channels had the story, and all declared there was no way in the world those children could get out. It was certain they would all be killed.

Helen saw the story unravel and how Peter rescued the children and then the driver and his last leap to safety as the bus rolled down the ravine. She saw him hit the road with his head smashing on the road and was sickened to see him lying in a pool of blood for at least ten minutes before anyone attended to him and took him to hospital. They considered him to be a prisoner from jail and therefore he didn't count. No one had to worry about him. Well, he counted as a brother to Helen. She immediately went and packed a bag and told Paul she was heading off to the hospital to make sure Peter got the care he deserved.

After hours of travelling, Helen arrived at the hospital that was shown on television, but no one would listen to her or allow her to see Peter, and despite her pleas, they sent Peter back to prison after a week in a dangerous state. Even though Peter had saved the warden's children, he did not receive any special treatment, and the warden did not even go up to Peter to thank him for what he did for his family in saving the children.

At the end, Helen could do nothing but return to Castle Hill.

Peter's heroic rescue received worldwide coverage, and he was praised for his courage, but authorities back home had a different view and refused to let him go on parole or reduce his sentence. In fact, they had a different view of what should happen to Peter, and so did some of Peter's old mates, who now were running some of his former establishments and dealing in drugs and prostitution. They, too, wanted Peter out of the way permanently, as he may want to reclaim what they had taken from him while he was in jail.

Vince Marconi was also listening to the news when the story broke about Peter saving the children. He saw the situation he was in and had respect for what Peter had done but knew that others would see the face and recognise the man as Peter Marlow, onetime boss of the whole crime syndicate, and knew that they would try to get rid of Peter while he was in jail and unable to defend himself because of his injury.

Vince arranged for some of his men at the jail to protect Peter around the clock, with two men being in Peter's cell. The warden, not knowing of these plans, arranged for the police to leave Peter's cell door unlocked one night with the intent that someone would slip in and cut Peter's throat.

The men in the cell found out about the plan.

When the door of the cell was unlocked, they immediately shifted Peter to sick bay and grabbed hold of the warden's nephew, tied him up, gagged him, and laid him in Peter's bed. His nephew was in prison on a seven-year sentence for drug-related crimes.

Sure enough, as expected, shortly after the last call for lights out, someone slipped into Peter's cell and cut the throat of the person lying in Peter's bed. As soon as they heard the person enter the cell, they locked the door behind him. As soon as the person yelled out, 'Guard, guard!' he was let out, but his cellmate was bleeding. On further examination, it was found that he had his throat cut and that there could only be one person who could have done that, being the other person who was locked up in the cell.

The warden wanted to know how Peter got out of the cell and how his nephew was placed in his bed. No one, of course, knew anything about the incident, and the warden had to go to his sister and tell her that her son was dead despite his assurance that he would protect him.

Peter was found in the infirmary with the relevant papers signed by the doctor, declaring he had a fever and could not be left in his cell. He needed urgent medical attention, as his head wound was getting infected.

To ensure Peter's safety, he had to be away from the prison, elsewhere, where those who wanted to kill him would find this difficult to arrange. They agreed Peter would stay in hospital until he got his strength back and, for the next three years, would study theology at a university in another state. They forged papers to transfer Peter to another prison and to allow him to attend university to undertake studies in theology. He could work in the library on his days off and could stay on campus during the semester to attend lectures and do his assignments.

For three years, Peter attended lectures at the university and graduated with a degree in theology. He then enrolled in a course to become a minister and once graduated, was ordained as one.

Peter's sentence had now reached the stage where he could apply to be released and was granted release on strict parole conditions, which he had to meet over the next two years.

Peter understood that there was no minister at Bungarby. no one had moved into his place while he was in prison, and during his imprisonment, Helen and Paul tried to fill in for him as best they could.

He also owed a lot to Vince Marconi for his help in protecting him from the gang who tried to kill him when he was in hospital and in jail and for the transfer, allowing him to study to become a minister.

As soon as they released him from jail, Peter paid Vince a visit to thank him personally for all his help and protection.

Vince knew Peter was a changed man; however, he would not accept his preaching about a God and the greater fortunes that lie after death. To Vince, what you have here is all that you are getting, and while he did not entirely dismiss what Peter said, he wanted proof before accepting a God that you could not see and communicate with.

Peter knew Vince to be an honest man with principles. Like many, he did not believe in God because of the wars, hatred, diseases, and misery inflicted on mankind these days throughout the world. To Vince, if there was a God, He would set things straight, fix things now, immediately. What Vince refused to accept was that all these things will happen at the Second Coming and not now. It is an assurance from God that He will fix things when He returns. The requirement by God now is for mankind to gain faith in God and not to abandon the faith when things go wrong or move in a direction that is not to their liking. The purpose for mankind on the earth now is to get this solid rock- hard faith in God and not the shallow, shifting sand-like faith that most show these days. Vince could not be convinced of this.

A few months after release from prison, Peter changed his name back to his original name, Marlow, and made his way back to Bungarby. He found most people did not know what had happened to him and thought he had left to go to university to get his degree and become a minister. They did not know he was in jail. Most did not know of his heroic rescue of the children. Peter noted God had blessed the farmers with regular rain, enabling most to build up their herds and those that wanted to seed a crop.

The banks had received a poor judgement from the Royal Commission and were forced to renegotiate their loans with the farmers. The politicians who moved to gain the farms at substantially reduced prices found themselves voted out of office and therefore could not directly influence or manipulate the decision-making process and could not do as they had planned. With the rain, the farmers could generate an income and pay off their loans to the banks and prevent future foreclosures.

Peter made his way back to the Bungarby and was surprised that things had not changed there. The town could not appoint a minister to the church, as no one really wanted a life in a regional area. The residence attached was the same as he had left it, and his clothes still hung from the same closet he left them in. Peter went to the barn, and his car was still there, attached to the trailer. Helen had used it over the years to distribute provisions to farmers who had no means to buy food, but other than on those occasions, they left it in the barn. Peter noticed the trailer had replenished itself and was full, as if they had taken nothing from it.

He went back into the house and made himself something to eat and then telephoned Helen to tell her he was home. She was thrilled to hear from him and that he had been released from jail and had graduated as a minister. She advised him what had happened in his absence and that some rain had fallen, allowing farmers to begin to either sow crops or build up their herds. She also advised him that Alice and Tim were expecting their second child in the next few days, and she and Paul would drive to Rayleigh once advised of the birth, and they would drop into Bungarby on their way to Rayleigh.

Peter settled in as minister of the church. In all the years he spent at university and in jail, he did not see the old man once, nor was he asked to perform a miracle on anyone. He assumed things had changed, and he was not required to attend to God's needs other than as a minister. He remembered what he witnessed before he went back to prison, and the miracles performed in God's name. He assumed that was now over and he had to look after his congregation and look after the farmers.

Peter went out and met the farmers on their properties and discuss their needs and, over the months, noted that most accepted the rains and what it brought, but few gave thanks to God for His mercy in bringing the rains and breaking the drought. Most accepted the gift and took it as something they had a right to and expected it from God. God was required to perform for them while they had no obligation to God. He made the covenant, not them.

Some of the local farmers and their wives had rejected God because of the drought and, by their actions, showed the shallow faith they had in God from the start. He was a God to do as they commanded, otherwise they would reject him outright. They rejected him as if God was their creation and not the other way around. Peter tried to argue against their view, but found they would not listen or care for what he had to say. It was their way or not at all. They didn't have time for

God, who was expected to provide for their needs. Some understood what Peter was saying and accepted the drought was God's way of demonstrating to them the faith they had in Him and that they had failed in that they, too, rejected God but now sought repentance and forgiveness and acceptance of God.

Peter continued preaching God's mercy and love for his people.

CHAPTER 29

ACROSS THE OTHER SIDE OF the globe, a wealthy man looked at his daughter, six years of age. She could not walk or stand, as she had multiple sclerosis, and the doctors did not give her a chance of living beyond ten.

Standing by her side as she lay in bed, he remembered reading about a person across the other side of the world that had performed miraculous things in God's name and wondered whether he should try to seek this person out and see if they would help his daughter. He would pay them handsomely, assuring the willingness to cooperate. He thought about it while at work. As time went by, he got his people to find out what they could about the miracles and gave them a week to come up with a report. In the meantime, he would concentrate on making more money, which he was good at.

The week flew past quickly, and he assembled his small group of researchers, and they advised him of Peter's whereabouts and that there had been unproven reports of people being miraculously cured of illnesses, which could not be explained by doctors. They cited Paul's illness and his unexplained cure as the last example.

The wealthy businessman was Richard Fellows, who was reputed to be worth a few billion dollars and was very influential with politicians and the rich and famous around the world. He found early in life that money always was the persuasive force, and when that failed, political force did the trick.

Mr Fellows took his daughter to Bungarby with support staff, as he was sure he could negotiate a deal with Peter, as most churches needed funds, and money was always the persuasive element in any negotiation.

Bungarby was not a large regional town with city hotels. To Richard's horror, he could not find suitable accommodation, so he sent his assistant out to see what she could find. She came back with a farm with large acreage being on the market close to town. The occupants were forced out by the banks, who refused to proceed with their forced sale after the Royal Commission, as the repercussions would have been horrendous. The family moved to the city for work and to educate their children, who were a year off attending university, and listed the property for sale at $5 million.

Richard Fellows went to see the property and noticed it was empty but furnished and liveable. It was a sturdy property with four bedrooms, a study, a large barn, and the house had wrap-around verandas. He tried to negotiate a reduced price over the telephone, but the owners were not interested. Their price was $5 million or nothing. Fellows agreed to pay the price if it included the furniture, tractor, and everything left on the property. The owners agreed, as they did not want to come back to get rid of furniture and other items. It was also agreed that Fellows could take immediate occupation of the property, and he could have an early settlement date.

Fellows moved his family and support staff into the farmhouse while he was trying to decide for his daughter. That week, he sent back his support team, as they were no longer needed now the matter of accommodation was settled. His lawyer would take care of the acquisition, and $5 million was not a large sum for Fellows to pay.

On Sunday, he went to church with his wife, Sue, and met Peter for the first time. He met with him after the service and went home and, with his wife and nurse, came back with his daughter to see Peter. He advised Peter that he had purchased a farm close to town and may settle in the area when he retires. Peter knew of the purchase, as the family who sold the farm to Fellows had informed him, they would not be returning to the area after they sold their farm. They had enough of the dishonesty and lies from the politicians and their refusal to support the farmers and make the area drought-proof. Fellows said, 'You certainly gave a wonderful sermon this morning.

Faith in God is a critical aspect of man's life. My daughter, as you can see, is very ill and cannot support her own body and, unless something is done, will not have much time left on this earth. I understand you can perform miracles and cure people with severe ailments. I would ask you to cure my daughter. She has suffered all her life and deserves to be healed.'

Peter looked at his daughter, Beth, and could see she was in a bad way. While he was concentrating on her, he could hear God speaking to him, saying, 'You shall not cure Beth.'

He stood up and approached Mr Fellows and said, 'Unfortunately, you're not a believer in Jesus Christ. He is the only one that can cure a person or make good the wrongs of this world. I am, like you, a man and do not have the power to do the things that you have requested. Since you do not believe in Jesus, I can do nothing for either you or Beth.'

Fellows said, 'I will make it worth your while. Name your price and I will pay it. Heavens only knows I have been all around the world trying to get the best doctors to cure my daughter, but all take my money, but none has done a thing for her. Leeches, every one of them.'

Sue Fellows said, 'You're right, my husband is not a Christian, but I am, and that is one problem we have with our marriage. My husband believes in himself and his money, not in God. I believe in God and ask that you help me and Beth, as no one will. We have two other children who idolise Beth, and I have brought them up in the Christian faith. My husband is the only one that does not believe. It is not right for Beth to be punished for my husband's ideology of self and money. We have argued for a long time about this, and it is splitting the family apart. He denies God's existence and doesn't have faith in the Lord. We ask for your help so we can show him that the things he believes in are temporary things and will not give him what the Lord promises. By denying us, you are saying your belief amounts to nothing. We are not putting the Lord to the test but ask that He show Richard how wrong he is for our sake.'

Peter knew what Sue was saying was right, and Richard would walk away saying it was all a fraud and no truth in Christ. He bowed his head and prayed to God for wisdom, as Beth has done nothing wrong, and her mother and the rest of her family were Christians relying on the Lord and having faith in Him to help the family. The Lord answered him, agreeing he may cure Beth in His name. Before Peter could say anything, Richard stood up and said, 'Look, if it helps, just name your price and I will pay it.'

Peter replied, 'Richard, I don't think you quite get it. The grace of God has given the money you have to you. You may be struck down immediately by a heart attack or a car while crossing the road, and you end up with nothing. Most of your wealth is tied up in assets, which are valued on today's basis. But if there was a depression, you could lose the lot or most of what you have. You have been given these resources to show you what a fool you really are, that all you believe in is yourself and money. Neither will last beyond this world, and God has given them to you, yet you believe you have earned them. You go around as if you are a brilliant person, gifted, thinking you have gained all this wealth, which can be taken from you just as quick as it was given to you. Look at Beth. You have all the money anyone could ever want, yet you cannot find a doctor who can cure her. What good is your money?'

Fellows said, 'Look, I will make it worthwhile if you cure Beth. The farm we are buying, I will give it to you with all that is there if you cure Beth.'

Peter said, 'The answer remains the same. For Sue and the children who have faith in the Lord, He will not refuse you in time. As for your proposal, I will not accept the farm or anything you offer me. I am sorry, but I cannot help you until you believe in God.'

Fellows said, 'So what you are saying to me is that you will do nothing for Beth while I have wealth. Is that the case?'

Peter replied, 'No. You can have wealth, as this is not the issue here. What is at issue is what you do with your wealth. Do you use it for yourself or for God's good? It is not whether you are wealthy or poor. It is whether you have faith in Jesus Christ that is the issue. If you had faith in Christ, you would use your intelligence and expertise for His good and help His people. You do not do these things. All you do is use it for yourself and steal from others to gain more. I am sorry, I will not help you.'

Sue said, 'We have faith in the Lord and keep our faith. We know He will cure Beth in His good time.'

Peter said, 'Your husband reminds me of the Pharisees that kept saying, "Show us a sign." The Lord raised Lazarus, and they saw what He had done, and they kept saying, "Show us a sign." At his crucifixion, they kept saying, "If You are the Son of God, come down from the cross so we can see You can perform miracles, and we will believe You," but they never would. You, Richard, are the same. "Just cure Beth and I will believe," which you will never do.'

Richard said, 'You're right, no matter what you do, I would not accept as being the act of God and would brush it off, as I deny God. I guess I will never find Him and will travel on my own for the rest of my life. Thank you for your time. We won't bother you again.'

With that, Richard, Sue, and the nurse with Beth in a wheelchair made their way out and drove off to their farm.

Peter was not sure he handled the matter adequately or convincingly. Being Sunday, he still had a last service to perform and felt he let the Lord down in not curing Beth. So, he began preparing for it. After the last service was completed, he packed up all the Bibles and closed the church and went home for a reasonably early night.

The next morning, Peter was surprised to see Richard Fellows in the church, who advised him that shortly after they arrived home, Beth died in her sleep. He noticed she was not breathing when he checked on her at midnight and called the ambulance helicopter and police. Nothing could be done for her.

Peter was upset and, to some extent, blamed himself for not curing Beth in God's name as he could do so. To some extent, he shared the grief that the parents felt and prayed for the Lord to take care of her in heaven.

Richard and his family buried Beth at the farm and packed up and went back home. Peter prayed to the Lord to find out why Beth was taken, and the Lord responded by advising him that while she slept, He decided Beth had done what she should do on earth and was recalled back home to heaven. Richard was not bitter about Beth's death and, over a period, understood that God's favours cannot be bought. He continued running his business until three years later he was struck down by a stroke and was paralysed down his left side. He lost his speech and mobility and, after a further year, died a multimillionaire, still not accepting God. His wife, Sue, sold her husband's business and moved back to the farm at Bungarby, where her daughter was buried, and lived there having faith in the Lord.

All that mattered to Richard was to gain more wealth. There was never enough. The family was a status symbol, which he had little time for. The purpose of why he was born on this earth did not matter, as he was going to run his life and not the Lord. He was going to decide what was to be done, not God. He was born into this world and would live by its rules, not try to please God or strive to find his purpose in life. He didn't care what happened after death. His wealth did not buy him eternal life, nor did it make him happy when he was alive. One wonders the purpose of it all.

CHAPTER 30

Peter was determined to see Edna and John and provide them with provisions. He promised to make the trip some days ago, but too many things stopped him from making the long journey to their farm.

He hooked up the trailer and took his bag containing water and some food and drove off, heading north. The farm was four hours from Bungarby, requiring Peter to dodge sandpits and a section of the road that had opened because of the intense heat. Peter drove non-stop to the farm and was welcomed by John, who told him they were getting worried, as they had run out of provisions and feed for their small herd of cows, which they were trying to keep for breeding.

He went into the house, and the children all welcomed him, but John seemed uneasy and looked worried about something.

Peter asked, 'John, is everything all right? You seem on edge and look worried.'

John said, 'Come on outside so we can talk.'

Peter asked, 'Where is Edna? I would like to say hallo.'

John replied, 'That's the problem. She doesn't want to come out of her room until you leave.'

Peter asked, 'But why? What have I done? I just arrived.'

John replied, 'It is not what you have done but whom you represent.'

Peter said, 'Represent? I don't represent anyone.'

John said, 'You do. You, as a minister, represent Christ and preach His word. What Edna is saying is that God wants us to have faith in

Him, but He makes things very hard to where He will force us either to starve or leave our farm as we can't afford to pay for necessities. The children are starving, and no one cares about us, not even God. our prayers are not being answered. We ask for rain, and we get a few drops, and then we are back to where we were. God knows that what He gave us would not allow us to get back on our feet. We can't even get feed for our cows and will have to shoot them in the next few days.'

Peter said, 'That's why I am here to offload provisions to carry you over for at least a month. If you give me a hand, we can bring the provisions into the house and the feed in the barn.'

John replied, 'Sure, no problem, and we appreciate your help, but it is only a short-term solution, isn't it?'

Peter said, 'No, not if you have faith in God. We do not know His plan and can only have faith because what will be the outcome of all this misery will be to your benefit and not your detriment. Remember, you will only be able to judge your faith in Christ when you hit rock bottom. You can't judge it when you're doing all right.'

John said, 'Yes, I guess you're right.'

Peter asked, 'Before we unload, can I see Edna?'

John replied, 'I don't think so, Peter. She has a personal problem to take care of and needs a bit of privacy to get it right in her mind.'

Peter said, 'John you have been beating around the bush as to Edna since I arrived. What is her problem? I may help her come to terms with whatever is troubling her.'

John replied, 'I don't think so, Peter. As you know, Edna is pregnant with another child. We have decided it would not be fair to bring another child into this world with the problems that are facing us now. We are broke and will end up losing our farm. There is no prospect of rain or ongoing rain that will break this drought. We cannot even feed our three children, let alone think of another mouth that we will have to feed. We have decided to terminate Edna's pregnancy, and she will have it done tomorrow. She is worried as to how this will happen and thinks that it is the wrong thing to do. But we have no option. We cannot feed another mouth; let alone the children we have. God has made it clear we will end up in debt without a roof over our heads and it will take us a long time to get out of the hole He has dug for us.'

Peter said, 'You can't end the pregnancy. You will kill a living child. It is against God's laws.'

John said, 'Then why doesn't He help us instead of belting us about the head time after time? No, we are right on this one, Peter. We have both discussed it and agree it is the only thing to do. We have no option. We either abort the child or let it starve after birth. Edna will not be able to breastfeed the baby, and we can't afford to buy formula. We are broke and would starve except for your generosity in giving us some provisions.'

Peter said, 'It is not my generosity. The provisions come from God.'

John replied, 'I don't think so. He is not that generous or concerned about our welfare. We know who God is looking after. They are the rich and famous. He does not care for peasants like us. He supports the people who don't deserve help and crucifies people like us who need His help.'

Peter said, 'You have got it wrong, John. I better see Edna and get her straightened out, because if she is thinking your way, then the devil certainly has misled both of you, and you will both end up declaring him king and your ruler.'

John said, 'No, Peter, no matter what you say, we have made up our minds and we are going ahead with the abortion. We have waited a long time and prayed a lot asking for the Lord's intervention and help, and we have got nothing but more kicks in the teeth, and it is clear the Lord has turned His back on us and doesn't care for us, nor will He do anything to help us. He is more concerned about giving another lottery win to a rich person or help them take care of some minor problem, not the life-and- death issues He has placed us in.'

'Sorry, but can we get on with unloading the trailer? Edna made it clear she did not want to talk to you about our decision, as there is little doubt you will see it differently from how we see it. The thing you must understand is that we have lived through this and have asked God for help. It is God's decision not to help us. We are not good enough for Him. We are not the type of sinners and people He wants to tolerate. Remember Peter, when Jesus went into a new place, He always stayed in the house of the wealthy, never with the poor.'

Peter asked, 'Where did you get that idea from?'

John said, 'Well, tell me where in the Bible it says Jesus stayed at a poor man's house.'

Peter replied, 'Well, offhand, I don't recall any passage that says He did. But the Bible is not a hotel register, you know.'

Both men got into Peter's Ute and drove off to the barn, where they offloaded feed for the animals, bottled water, and petrol for the generators. They then drove back to the house where they offloaded the consumables and water for general consumption.

John said, 'I am sorry, Peter, I can't even offer you a cold drink, as we don't have any.'

Peter replied, 'No worries. I understand, but I do want to discuss the issues you have raised with both you and Edna. You are wrong about the Lord and you thinking you are being persecuted.'

John said, 'We are, Peter. Just look around. Have a look in our fridge, pantry, and cupboards. We couldn't even offer you a cold drink on this hot day. We have had to sell most of our cattle and shoot the rest. All we have left are a few heads of cattle that we tried to keep for breeding, and they will have to be shot, as we cannot afford to cart them to the sale yard. We are like Job. The only difference is the Lord finally reversed His condition and reinstated Job to a better position than what he was before Satan took everything he had. We do not question the existence of God but have concluded He will not help us. He seeks to support the people that do not believe in Him. He is like a politician chasing after electoral votes. He supports them, hoping they will change their mind and follow Him. He has decided they count not people like us. Just look at the facts that are before you, Peter, and you must draw the same conclusions.'

Peter replied, 'No, I don't agree. Just let me sit down with Edna and yourself, and we can discuss these issues, and there are a lot you have raised.'

John said, 'No, Peter. We have discussed this for a long time and said many prayers, but they make no difference to our situation. We are right, and Edna does not want to go over it anymore. It is too upsetting. Jesus says in the Bible, "Ask in My name, and you shall receive." Lies—that is all that it is. You can ask until the cows come home, and you will get nothing. Not even a breadcrumb. We must act now rather than hope that the Lord will help us. He will not. He has done nothing for us other than give us another kick in the teeth. I am sorry I cannot offer you dinner before you go on your long journey. We have nothing except what you have kindly given us. The government talks about help but gives none. The publicity is just to help their re-election prospects. They do not intend to give the farmers one cent of help. Just enter a talk fest thinking people will believe they are doing something. The average person knows it is rubbish and lies. I am sorry I was the one to have told you about our situation. We kept it confidential and thought you would turn up after the abortion and Edna would not feel guilty about terminating her pregnancy. Unfortunately, things don't turn out the way you hope they would.'

Peter said, 'I will be on my way. If you and Edna want to discuss the things you have raised, you can either ring me or come to Bungarby and talk to me. I urge you to reconsider your decision to end the pregnancy. If you can't feed the baby or circumstances prevent you from taking care of the child, then there are a lot of families or couples out there who can't have children and would love to adopt your child. You really need to think this thing out rather than come up with a decision that will haunt you for the rest of your life.'

John replied, 'Thanks, Peter. We appreciate your concern and that you have come out here with provisions and feed for the cattle. We really appreciate your help.'

Peter said, 'Before I go, I would like you to join in with me to say a prayer to the Lord.'

John replied, 'I would prefer not to, Peter. Our prayers have not been answered, and I feel it is only a waste of time.'

Peter said, 'Have it your way. I will include you in my prayers when I get home.'

With that, Peter got into his Ute and drove off back home.

The journey was long, and he was glad he had water with him and some sandwiches. He could not stop thinking about what Paul had said to him and that both had rejected the Lord—a decision that they did not make on the spur of the moment. There was little doubt that their faith in the Lord had reached rock bottom and they were allowing Satan to dictate what they were to do from now on.

After driving for four hours, Peter arrived home tired and parked the Ute and trailer in the barn, and entered his house. He had a quick shower, and after a cold drink, made himself some dinner. He sat up and watched some television and then went to bed.

The next morning, he drove to a farm south of Bungarby to deliver some provisions some three hours' drive away. As usual, the Lord replenished the provisions, and the trailer was stacked to the brim with provisions, water, and feed for the animals.

Peter headed off early, as he wanted to get back home at a reasonable hour. He drove non-stop to the farm and drove right up to the farmhouse. He noticed everything was dry and only patches of green shoots appeared after the rain. There were no visible animals around in the paddocks and no sign of anyone. Peter went up to the front door and knocked, but no answer. He walked around the back and noticed the door was unlocked, which was not unusual in these areas. He let himself in and went from room to room but could find no one around. He went back into the kitchen and looked in the fridge. There was no food there, and they switched the fridge off. He went outside and got into his car and drove to the barn at the rear of the homestead and got out of his Ute. He walked towards the barn when he heard a shot fired from a rifle. He crouched down momentarily and decided that the shot came from the barn and was not meant for him. He hurried to the barn and entered from an open door.

As Peter walked in, he noticed Sam and her two children were sitting on a bale of hay. She was holding them tightly, and they were crying. Sam's husband, Don, was standing some ten metres away from them with a rifle pointed at them. It seems he was going to shoot them and had missed killing one of them just a moment ago, as the rifle moved upwards when fired.

Peter walked in and could see this was a very dangerous situation and froze momentarily as Don pointed the rifle at him.

Peter asked, 'Don, what are you doing? Put the rifle down before you kill someone, or is that the intention?'

Don replied, 'Minister, please go out. We do not need you here. This is hard enough as it is.'

Peter said, 'What do you mean you don't need me here? You are going to commit suicide and you say you do not need me here. Put the rifle down and let's talk about what has driven you to do this act. Kids, come here and help me unpack the trailer. It is full of food and water. Come on.'

Peter was determined to get the kids away from Don's sight and to reduce the tension so some reasoning could prevail. The kids immediately broke free from their mother's grip and ran outside to inspect the trailer. Don lowered the rifle, and Sam came up to Don and said, 'what on earth were we doing?'

Both walked over to Peter and just stared at him, not knowing what to say.

Don said, 'Peter, leave and let us get on with what we have to do.'

Peter said, 'Let you kill your children and then yourself?'

Don said, 'We started with our cattle and now have to finish the job. No one has helped us feed our animals or find water for them, leaving us no option but to shoot them. We reared them up from calves and knew them all by names. They were like family, and we loved every one of them. It was either let them starve or shoot them, so we waited, hoping our prayers would be answered, but God ignored our pleas and prayers and did nothing to help. He just sat back and waited until we had no option but to shoot them. One by one, we had to kill our family, and so there is no difference in the situation between them and us. We prayed, but as usual, our prayers were never answered. God is not interested in people like us from struggle street. He helps the rich and famous get richer and grow in wealth and political strength and pees on people the likes of us.'

Peter replied, 'That is not true. God loves you and will help you. Give Him time.'

Don said, 'Time is something we don't have. We are ruined by the drought, and the government has used us as pawns in a chess game, making promises it knew it would not fulfil. Grants—what a joke. You must fill in a hundred-page document before they will consider whether you are eligible for a grant. None of the bureaucrats have ever come out this way and do not know how bad things are. Nor do they care. They have a good job and earn high salaries, so why should they care for some poor bastard in the country trying to overcome drought and hunger? They believe we should be eradicated and not be a burden on the country. You know the government could stop droughts by building dams and piping the water from the north, but they refuse to make this country drought-proof. why? Where is the logic in that, and God sits in judgement and comes down on us while supporting them who would not care for Him or have faith in Him?'

Peter said, 'That's the crux of the argument. God has given you the opportunity to test your faith in Him. It is not a test like a school exam but a test, so you are the judge, not Him. You judge whether you have faith in God. To determine whether and to what extent you have faith in God, you must face difficult situations. It is no use having you on top of the world with a lot of money, for your faith will be in your money, not in God. But if you are forced down to the pits and you cannot fall any further, then you can judge whether you have faith in God.'

'It is not for God to make the call. It is for you to decide. Things got bad for you, and over time, got worse. Instead of having faith in Jesus, you decided, since things were not going your way, that you will give up God and take things in your own hands. You said, "God is not doing what I expect of Him, so we will switch over to Satan and worship him." He did not want you, as you were a throwback from Jesus, so he convinced you that Jesus was not the answer and that the only way out of this mess was to kill yourself. By shooting yourself, you affirmed you have no faith in God and did not want eternal life, which He offered to you. Also, you wanted to be with Satan for a thousand years and not Jesus. By you killing yourself, you can never accept Christ and would be tied to Satan forever. Once dead, he would not have to worry about you coming to your senses, as it would be too late.'

Don replied, 'It is too late for us. We have killed all our animals and have no food to feed the children. We have no money, and it is unlikely we will ever see any of the money donated or grants given by the government. We either take the matter into our hands or starve to death.'

Peter said, 'Well, that's rubbish. I am here with a lot of provisions that will see you over for a month or two. We do not know how long the drought is going to last, and it could end the next day or month. Who knows? Trust God, who sent me to you with these goods. Put the gun down and help me and the kids to unpack the trailer.'

Everyone went outside and unpacked the trailer. They brought the feed and water into the barn and took the provisions inside the house.

Peter asked, 'well, Don, what are you going to do when I leave? Try the same thing again?'

Don replied, 'Nothing has changed. We are still struggling and have nothing to look forward to.'

Peter said, 'So what you are saying is Satan has the answer and not God. Is that the case?'

Don said, 'We are not supporting Satan. Just doing what we think is right.'

Peter said, 'Can't you see Satan is pushing you to commit suicide? You either believe in Christ or in Satan. There is no alternative. One or the other. Take your pick. The Lord has saved you today because He loves you and asks you to have faith in Him. He will deliver you out of this drought, or mess, as you put it. You have been down to the pits and have said you have faith in God. Ask Him for forgiveness and rest on Him to save you and bring you out of this misery. Otherwise, you will be confronted with the same problem, and I am sure you will kill yourself the next time around. You need God's strength, and the only way you are going to get it is to ask for His help, and no matter what transpires, have faith in Him even when it seems you are facing the impossible.'

As they were talking, they heard some noise outside, and everyone went out to investigate what was making it. There were five cows and one steer with some calves that came up to the property looking for food. They could smell the feed in the barn and headed that way. Don ran and closed the barn door to prevent them from entering.

Don said, 'These are not our animals. They are in better condition than ours, and we had to shoot our animals, which I did this morning.'

Don, Sam, and Peter went amongst the herd and noticed that none were branded.

Sam asked, 'whom do they belong to?'

Don replied, 'No one, so we can lay claim to them. We will keep them, and if no one claims them, we will look after them as if they are ours. I will open the barn and give them some feed and water you brought over in the trailer.'

Peter said, 'A gift from God. Possibly you can ask for His forgiveness and mercy and have faith in Him. How many animals did you have to kill?'

Don replied, 'exactly the same that came to us.'

Peter said, 'I better be going home. I think you should be all right. Promise me you will come and see me if there are any thoughts of killing yourself again. I will try to get some medical help for you and drop back again in about two months with more provisions.'

Peter gave Sam a kiss and shook Don's hand, gave the kids a kiss, and drove off for home, thanking the Lord for His mercy.

CHAPTER 31

PETER WAS IN HIS STUDY preparing for Sunday's sermon when he heard a knock on the front door. He went to the door and was surprised to see John and Edna standing there.

Peter said, 'Well, this is a pleasant surprise. Where are the children?'

John replied, 'We dropped them at their cousin's farm on the way in. They can play with my brother's children while we sort some things out.'

Peter said, 'Come on in. Can I get you a cold drink or something?'

John replied, 'We feel we don't deserve one, as we couldn't give you one when you called in on us.'

Peter said, 'Don't be silly. I will get you a Coke.' Peter went out and brought back two bottles of Coke and handed them to John and Edna.

Peter asked, 'Well, what is the purpose of your visit? You're still alive, so you haven't come to collect your tickets for your flight to heaven.'

John replied, 'No. We are still thinking the right thing to do is to have an abortion, as what we said to you still applies. We do not think God will help us and is only a God for the rich and famous and not for the poor like us. One less mouth to feed would be a help to us.'

Peter said, 'Edna, John has been doing the talking so far. What do you think about having an abortion? It is your body and not his, and the slogans tell us that the women may do what they want with their bodies.'

Edna replied, 'Yes, it is my body, but I am concerned that what we want to do is for our convenience may not be what God wants from us.'

John said, 'Who cares what God wants? He doesn't care about us. We should do what is best for us and not listen to this rubbish.'

Peter said, 'John, the answer to your outburst is for you to say, "Satan, get behind me," for Satan is leading you, but hasn't quite convinced Edna as to what she should do. Both of you have failed to understand God and His purpose. Satan is here to give you whatever you want to convince you to jump ship and go with him. The more followers he gets, the longer he stays around before being sent to purgatory for a thousand years. You commented at the farm that God must like the rich and famous, for they thrive and get richer, whereas you seem to have grief and never get on your feet.'

'I am sure if you approached the so-called rich and famous, you would find that they know of Jesus but do not believe in Him, have no faith in Him, and do not require His help or presence. They are doing fine and are quite happy on this earth. The problem here is that they have forgotten or do not care as to why they have been placed on the earth. It is not to get rich or enjoy your days until death. It is to gain faith in Jesus, and the only way you can do this is by experiencing the lows of life. If you were rich and lost one hundred thousand dollars, you would say, "So what? I will get this back in a month.'

'But if you are poor, you would have lost everything, and the only thing you can do is have faith in God that He has done this for a genuine reason and that you will come out of this situation not only stronger in your faith but also better than you were when you had the one hundred thousand dollars. In your case, it is obvious the Lord has used the farmers to teach those wealthy investors a lesson. Many have lost their entire fortune when they associated themselves with the politicians and banks. In your case, the Lord has asked you to have faith in Him, but you have none and decided it was you're way or what Satan was telling you rather than have faith in God.

'To have an abortion is a convenient way of terminating a life. The baby that lives within you has a heartbeat and is alive. It is God's creation. To end the pregnancy is to end that life, and while the laws of the state allow it, God's laws do not. He is the Creator, and He has given you a life to take care of. You kill that life, and you will be answerable to God. They say a woman's body is hers and for her to decide. I say to you, yes, but within the realm of God's law—the God who created you and has placed you on this earth to serve Him. This is a test of faith in the Lord. If you believe in Him and have faith in Him, then do as He commands of you. Yes, it may be difficult for a while, but you have proven to yourself that you have faith in God and refuse to listen to Satan. Satan makes it easy for you so he can win you over. God allows you to decide.'

John said, 'well, we have made up our minds, and we are going to abort the pregnancy.'

Edna replied, 'no, we haven't. You say these things because you do not believe in God. You never believed in God. That is part of our problem in that you really are an Antichrist, a sheep in the devil's clothing. You say you believe in God, but you do not. You mouth the words to be accepted, but the first time there is trouble, you blame it on God and declare how bad He is or why He doesn't do something about the problem. You have no faith in God and never, ever had faith in Him. It is always God's fault. No, I am not giving up this child. You can live with your parents or leave us and the children, but I will not give up my baby.'

John said, 'we can't afford the baby, don't you understand?'

Peter said, 'That is just lies, John. I can put you in touch with some charities that will look after you during these hard times, and, of course, I have been helping with food and fodder. By the way, how are the cattle you kept?'

John replied, 'I shot them shortly after you left.'

Peter asked, 'why? They looked healthy, and you had the feed to look after them.'

John replied, 'I thought about it and decided we should kill them now and did so.'

Edna said, 'He has changed since the drought and won't see reason. I am scared what is going to happen to us in the future as I grow more and more in my faith while John rejects the Lord. I do not know what will happen to us. I fear he will do something to us to hurt the Lord.'

Peter said, 'if that is the case, maybe you should stay in town for a while until John decides what he intends to do spiritually. The spirit is the driving force in these cases. Most people will not acknowledge this because they do not want to accept the premise that we are on this earth to serve God, not ourselves. This somehow gets turned around, and when God refuses them, they serve Satan, as he is more than obliging in providing for your worldly needs. They forget you are on this earth to find faith in God so you can serve Him in the future. You are not here on a holiday. Those who don't see it keep telling you it is your life and you can do what you want with it. They forget to say, "And steal it from the Creator, for He put you here.'

Edna asked, 'Where can the kids stay to allow Don to decide?' Peter replied, 'We have several families who can take you in or widowers who have big houses and would love the company.'

Edna said, 'I will stay in town for a while to allow John to decide as to what he wants to do. The kids can stay with his brother for now, as we said they can have a week with their cousins. I would feel scared if the children and I went back to the farm right now. John can leave us for a week or two and then come back so we can discuss the matter further.'

John, 'Well, if that is what you want, I will leave you here and the kids at my brother's farm. I will come and pick you up in a week, and we can collect the children on our way back home.'

Peter said, 'No problem. It will give you time to think things out. Can I get you another drink?'

John replied, 'No thanks. I will be on my way. I will ring you towards the end of the week and tell you what day I will pick you up.'

With that, John got up and went to his Ute and drove off.

Peter made a telephone call, and shortly after, a middle-aged woman came and introduced herself to Edna. They went to her car and drove off.

The next day, Peter was in his kitchen listening to the news and heard that there was a fatal accident two hours from Bungarby along the main highway where a fully laden truck bringing in much-needed fodder for the animals clipped a Ute being driven at high speed. The truck was not damaged, but the Ute veered off the road into a gully and rolled about four times before stopping. The only person in the vehicle was the driver who died at the scene.

Peter telephoned the police to see if they had identified the driver, and they advised it was John. He advised the police of the whereabouts of John's wife and went personally to tell her the bad news.

CHAPTER 32

THE EMERGENCY ROOM SIREN SOUNDED 'emergency one', and nurses and doctors were running to the bed that had the red probe blaring. A doctor immediately yelled out, 'Cardiac arrest!' and he quickly grabbed the defibrillator that was close by.

There was a man in the bed showing no life, and the graph indicators on his monitor showed a straight line. The doctor tore the man's shirt open and yelled out, 'All clear!' The doctor placed the pads on the man's chest and sent a shock through his body. The monitor showed no reaction. He yelled out, 'Second charge, all clear!' and again sent a shock through the man's body. This time, the man showed signs of his heart beating with the monitor coming back to normal. The man started to breathe and come around with his chest showing movement.

The doctor said, 'Mr Marconi, can you hear me?'

Vince replied, 'Yes, I am all right. You should have let me go. It does not matter whether it is the heart or the cancer that kills me. Either is going to get me, no matter what you try to do to keep me alive. It's just a matter of time.'

Vince's men breathed a sigh of relief when they heard their boss's voice.

Vince said, 'Joe, shoot the next nurse or doctor that revives me, understand?'

The men smiled but were not willing to follow that order.

As everyone stood down, there was a skirmish at the end of the hall. You could hear someone yelling, 'Get away from me! I will stab anyone that comes near me!' Vince signalled Joe to go down and settle the problem. Joe could see a person in a hospital gown with a pair of scissors in his hands, threatening the hospital staff and two police officers standing about twenty feet away from him with their guns drawn, ready to shoot the person. Joe walked up to the person, who yelled out, 'Don't come any closer or I will kill you!' Joe could see the person was off his rocker. He walked up to him and, before the person could swing his scissors, gave him a punch to his face, which rendered him unconscious. The man fell to the floor, and the nurses ran up to him to see if he was dead.

Joe said, 'He is still breathing. He will be all right. He might have a headache for a while. Handcuff him to a bed to stop him from repeating this performance.'

A male nurse picked the man up and carried him to his bed, and the police handcuffed him to the bed to ensure he did not get out and threaten anyone else. Joe went back to Vince and sat down.

A doctor came in and thanked Joe for handling the situation and preventing his death, as the police were determined to shoot if the man lunged at them.

Vince was told he had to stay in hospital until they could stabilise his condition. This would mean hospitalisation for a week. They made plans to move Vince into a private room for security reasons and that two of his men would be on duty around the clock to ensure nothing happened to him.

As the days went, Vince's condition became worse, as the cancer was eating away at his body, and he only had a few days to go. Joe telephoned Peter and told him about Vince's condition and that he was terminal with cancer.

Peter drove to the city to see Vince before he died. He collected some clothing and his travel bag and headed off. He was going to telephone Ryan and tell him about his father but decided not to. If Vince had not done it when he could have, then it was not Peter's place to interfere.

It was a long drive to the city, and Peter booked into a hotel. He got some sleep, and the next morning, headed off to see Vince. Joe had told Peter what hospital and room number Vince was in, so there was no difficulty in finding him. As soon as he stepped into the room, two men grabbed Peter and searched him for weapons and asked him why he was there. He advised them he was an old friend and wanted to pay his respects. They let him enter the room.

Peter moved closer to Vince, who was flat on his back and breathing poorly. It seems the cancer had damaged his lungs and his liver. It had gone throughout his body. The doctors said there was no hope he would pull through.

As Peter stood there, he noticed the white light appearing near Vince. The Lord appeared and said to Peter, 'Pray over him, for he has done as I have commanded of him. I have promised to look after him.'

Peter put his hands on Vince's head, and the Lord put His hands over Peter's. Peter prayed to the Lord, asking to cure Vince of his illness and forgive Vince of his sins. As he was praying, he noticed the Lord had left Vince and that the two bodyguards were at the base of Vince's bed looking as to what was happening.

Peter stopped praying and stepped back, and sat down. Shortly afterwards, a nurse came in to awaken Vince to take some medicine. Vince sat up, to her astonishment, and she immediately called for the duty doctor, who came immediately.

Vince sat up and then moved to get out of bed. The doctor stopped him and said he can't, as he could not stand. Vince stood up, to the doctor's amazement. Vince walked up and down, holding on to the rail of the bed for support. The doctor immediately rang for support, and a more senior doctor came trying to urge Vince to get back into bed before he collapses.

Vince said, 'Doctor, there is nothing wrong with me. I am all right and most probably will go home today.'

The doctor said, 'That is impossible. You have final stage cancer and have just had a heart attack. You shouldn't be standing, let alone walking up and down.'

Vince replied, 'There is nothing wrong with me. I am cured.' The doctor said, 'Don't be silly. Nothing on this earth could cure you. You will die shortly, so you have to get back into bed.'

Vince asked, 'Do you want to check me out before I walk out of here?'

The doctor said, 'You are being silly and unreasonable. We have all the CT scans we need to diagnose your condition.'

Vince replied, 'well, the good Lord has just cured me, so be quick, check me out, as I want to go home.'

The doctors quickly sent Vince off for CT scans and ultrasound examination and, after a few hours, could find nothing wrong with him. They refused to accept it was a miracle but could not explain what had happened. Vince booked himself out of the hospital and went home.

At the hospital while waiting for the doctors, Vince thanked Peter profusely for coming and curing him and now understood what Peter had said many years ago that people with a lot of money could not buy the gifts God can provide.

Vince believed in God from that moment on and had faith in the Lord. He went back home and found that other gang land bosses were moving in to take over his empire. He sold his house, and no longer took part in underworld activities. He would seek a more peaceful life, relying on the Lord for guidance and would help those whom he felt needed his support. He moved to Bungarby with Peter and stayed there for a while, resting and trying to come to terms with what had happened to him.

After a week, he went with Peter to some farms and helped with the deliveries. Vince was not someone that just sat home doing nothing. He went out with Peter and two of his men to a property west of Bungarby. The land was dry and needed more rain if it were to get out of drought. After driving for a couple of hours, they came to the homestead and got out and knocked on the door. Tanya Smith opened the door and welcomed Peter. She said her husband was out checking on the herd they had, as there was no water or feed for them, and the grant promised by the government never materialised. She was happy they could get some help, as they had run out of provisions and had no food left to feed the family. Both parents have had little to eat over the last two days, and what they had, they kept for the kids, hoping some charity would assist them, but none could.

She directed Peter to take the trailer to the barn and to offload the fodder and water and to bring the provisions in the house. Once they completed all their work, they were ready to go but decided to check on Tanya's husband, Rod, to see if he was all right. He had been gone a long time, and there was no message from him on the two-way radio. They tried to contact him, but there was no reply.

They got some directions from Tanya as to where he may be and headed in the direction she had last saw him driving. After driving for half an hour, they could see a small herd of cattle near a dead tree and a Ute parked nearby. They got out and walked slowly towards the Ute, and as they got closer, they could see the cattle were starving and had no water. In the Ute was Rod staring at them, motionless, just breathing but not moving. They tried to get him to say something, but he just stared at the heard saying nothing, not even blinking. They radioed the flying doctor service and discussed what they had found with the base doctor, who sent out a helicopter to pick him up and take him to the hospital to check him out. They waited for the helicopter and assisted, putting Rod on a stretcher and into the helicopter. They decided not to kill all the herd but to drive those that seem able to walk slowly closer to the homestead and feed them and allow them to gain some weight. The other animals they shot, as they could not walk the distance.

They finally made it to the homestead, to the surprise of Tanya, who was concerned with what they told her about her husband. She could not go to the hospital, as she had four children to look after. Peter said he would keep her informed and come and pick her up and take her to the hospital.

They fed and watered the animals and left out some fodder for them to eat. Out of twenty heads, they could save four. They were forced to shoot the others.

They drove to Bungarby with little said. It was noticeable that Vince and the men got a shock as to the condition of the land, the herd, and that Tanya had no food to feed her children. They also concluded the government had failed the farming community and did not care, and still making promises it did not intend to keep.

After a couple of hours' drive, they drove into Bungarby tired and hungry, and all went to wash up and have a cold drink. Peter phoned the hospital to check on Rod and found out that the doctors believe he had a severe case of depression requiring hospitalisation until they can get him to recognise where he was and who he was. They may have to resort to shock treatment but will try first with medication. The doctors believe Rod had suffered a mental meltdown when he had to shoot his animals. They had to get his brain to unwind and come back to reality; otherwise, he will stay as a zombie for the rest of his life. Another farming casualty.

Peter made a salad for the men and barbecued some sausages. They cooked all within twenty minutes, and the men sat down to have their dinner. Once completed, they sat around talking for about an hour about whether what happened today was normal and were assured this was the case, as a lot of families have been pushed to their limits and many couldn't take much more of the drought. You could see the concern on Vince's face, and today's occurrence would show the fragile condition most families were in. After a while, everyone headed off to their rooms to get a good night's sleep.

The next morning, Peter rose first and prepared the Ute and trailer for another delivery. The others were still asleep, so he did not want to bother them. It was a farm close by and was about an hour out of town. He had just backed his water and medical items into his bag when Vince appeared and asked where he was going. He mentioned he had to restock provisions for a widower about an hour out of town.

Vince said, 'Peter, you pick up the supplies and we will be ready when you come back.'

Peter said, 'I don't need to collect the supplies. Anyhow, the trailer is packed and ready to go.'

Peter could see that Vince wanted to be part of the effort, so he told him he packed a couple of extra sandwiches if he wanted to go with him. The boys were still asleep, so there would not be any escort on this trip. Vince took a rifle with him and got into the passenger seat, and they drove off. They left a note on the kitchen table saying, 'Back in three hours.'

They drove off, and after a half an hour, Vince asked questions.

Vince asked, 'How were you able to purchase the supplies and load the trailer up so quickly? There does not seem to be any shop or warehouse you can restock around here, and what did you do for money? One load would have cost you a couple of hundreds of dollars. A load every day will set you broke.'

Peter replied, 'I don't restock or purchase supplies. The Lord does that for me overnight. I put the trailer in the barn each night, and He replenishes the trailer. I always have a full trailer of supplies enabling me to help those who need help and hopefully believe in the Lord.'

Vince said, 'That is unbelievable. No wonder you kept saying to me that what is happening, I would not understand. I still find my situation hard to accept. One minute I was dying, the next cured completely and being in the presence of God.'

They drove on for a while and reached their destination. After the usual welcome and introductions, the owner, a widow, advised that she could not cope with looking after the farm and the animals while trying to school her children. She has bought a house in the city and allow her children the opportunity of proper schooling and a normal life.

One of her children, who was to sit for their final exams at the end of the year, wants to be a vet and will need to go to university, and she didn't want to be away from him since her husband died. Vince did not ask how he died, but was very interested in her intentions.

Vince asked Margaret what she wanted for the property, and her asking price sounded reasonable. He said he was interested in buying the property from her and would arrange for someone to contact her regarding a contract.

After they had their discussion, they all went outside to offload the trailer and help feed the cattle that were left on the property. Once they finished, they said their goodbyes and drove off.

Peter asked, 'Are you serious about buying the farm?'

Vince replied, 'Yes. it seems large enough for what I want and is in good condition. There are enough rooms for me and the boys, and when the rains come, it should be a profitable enterprise. The price seems fair, and it is close to town. The house seems in good condition, and, overall, the property doesn't seem to be run-down.'

Peter said, 'Well, that's good. At least I can drop in now and then.'

Vince said, 'Always welcome.' they drove back home and parked the trailer in the barn. The boys were up and annoyed that Vince went anywhere without them; someone might still try to kill him.

Vince immediately telephoned his attorney and arranged for him to purchase the property.

A couple of farmers came around to see if they could get some provisions, and Vince sent them off to the barn with a couple of his men to help restock them. The men entered the barn, and to the surprise of Vince's men, the trailer was full. They loaded up the men's Utes with supplies and helped them tie down their loads. They then rushed back to Vince to ask how they could restock the trailer before driving it back to the barn. Vince advised them it was an act of God, but none of them accepted what he said or could believe it.

For dinner, the men barbecued some chickens and had a relaxed time chatting. The one thing that was unanimous was that all agreed that life out in the country was far more relaxing than they experienced in the city.

That night, Peter received dreamed that he was to leave Bungarby and to move to the city and take up a position there replacing a minister who had left the church. Vince was to continue delivering the groceries and feed those in need and support the church when possible.

The next morning, Peter told Vince of his dream. Vince also received the same message and knew that Peter was about to leave. Both men now thought they understood why Vince was spared. Peter made his last delivery that day and, the next day, made his way to the airport and boarded the plane to the city. The dream advised Peter that the Lord was not pleased with what was happening to His church in the city and described it as like the scenes at Sodom and Gomorrah. He will destroy those that use His church for their benefit and not for the benefit of the Lord and His people.

Peter caught a taxi from the airport and was soon at the administration block of the church. It was a large church with what seemed a set of housing units set at the back? The church was modern and large and on first appearances, could seat two hundred parishioners or more.

Peter's instructions were to say he had come as instructed to fill the vacant position and to hand over a letter confirming his appointment. He went to the office and asked to see the Archdeacon and was told to be seated.

After a few minutes, the archdeacon appeared and asked what Peter wanted.

Peter replied, 'I am here, Archdeacon, to fill the vacancy.'

The Archdeacon said, 'I don't remember interviewing you or advising you we will accept your application.'

Peter asked, 'Archdeacon, is this not your name that appears in this letter?'

The Archdeacon read the letter and looked at Peter and said, 'My apology. My memory is not what it used to be. I unfortunately forget what I have done. Yes, it seems I have appointed you and no doubt want to settle in. I will get my assistant to take you to your accommodations, and we will talk after you have settled in. I will also introduce you to the other ministers.'

The assistant took Peter to the unit block at the rear of the church and then to a modern two-bedroom unit.

The assistant said, 'You should forgive the archdeacon for not remembering you. His dementia is no doubt getting worse, and it seems he has forgotten your appointment. Lately he has been under pressure and has forgotten you were coming. Please call me if you require anything. Freshen up and make your way back to the archdeacon's office. The archdeacon has the hour unallocated in his diary. No doubt he did this when he wrote to you.'

Peter freshened up and made his way back to the administration block. The archdeacon was waiting for him, and they took a tour of the church and halls attached to the church. Peter was introduced to the senior minister, who was surprised to hear of Peter's appointment and was annoyed that he was not informed of this sooner. Peter was introduced to all the other ministers, who seemed on edge and surprised when advised of Peter's appointment. After the tour, they went back to the archdeacon's office and were met by the senior minister, John Clements, and another minister. They chatted, and it was agreed that Peter would have the rest of the day off and would take up his duties as a minister the next day. He was expected to be available to advise parishioners on religious matters and to hold a mass on Sunday and was allocated the time of 7:30 a.m. After chatting for a while, the group broke up, and Peter walked out of the room and continued walking towards the city.

Peter walked around for about an hour and remembered many of the sites and buildings, as he had been in the city some years ago when he owned and ran some brothels, nightclubs, and a protection racket. He walked past his old headquarters and noticed things had changed.

He passed the entertainment precinct and remembered there was a coffee shop down the road and headed towards it. He entered there and ordered a coffee and toast and sat back, staring out of the window. He wondered why the Lord had directed him here and what was the relation to the comment 'Sodom and Gomorrah'.

After his coffee was delivered to his table, he read the newspaper that was left there by the previous person when he was interrupted by two men in suits standing near his table. He stared at them, wondering where he had seen them before. They stared at Peter, and one of them said, 'Don't you remember me?'

Peter replied, 'Sorry, you look familiar, but I have been out of town for some years and just can't put a name to the face.'

The men introduced themselves to Peter as Detective Frank Jessop and Brien Ramous.

Frank said, 'I don't blame you, Peter, for not owning up to knowing us. We were in uniform before when you looked after us. We have been promoted and are straight. No more on the take. What are you doing back in town? You're not getting back in with the mob, are you?'

Peter replied, 'No, God forbid. I am a minister at St Nicholas and have the day off to look around town and to relax.'

Frank said, 'we knew we could always trust you in those days. You went to jail and died there according to the police records.' Peter replied, 'Yes, there were several attempts on my life, but the good Lord looked after me, and as you can see, I am still alive.'

Frank asked, 'what made you go into ministry? Not the money, I am sure?'

Peter replied, 'No, money would never do it. I had the lot, no doubt you will remember. It was a few miracles that turned me to God and made me become a minister. Possibly you should come to my sermons on Sunday at seven thirty in the morning. I am sure I can convince both of you to give away your current jobs and follow God.'

Frank said, 'No, I am not a religious person and don't believe in that stuff. If there was a God, there would not be all this crime. However, you may be useful to us, as it seems the church is involved in some dirty schemes with the mob, which we cannot pinpoint. We have picked up some minor players, but never the big boys. Stooges in our office tip the big boys off, and by the time we get there, they put everything away, and no one knows anything.'

Peter asked, 'what are you saying? The mob is involved with the church?'

Frank replied, 'Pornography is one area that the church is involved in. The other is preparing young teenagers for the sex industry or for private clients.'

Peter said, 'Are you sure?'

Frank replied, 'Positive, but we can never get a lead as to when and who is doing it. The boys on the internet tell us the mob controlled it in association with the church.'

Peter said, 'I will keep my eyes open and let you know if I hear anything.'

Frank said, 'Here are our business cards. You can call us anytime to discuss anything you see or give us a name of who is involved.'

The three men shook hands, and the two detectives walked out of the café, leaving Peter.

Peter knew someone had tipped the detectives off, and they wanted to know what Peter knew and to make sure when he finds out what is happening that they are there to make sure it doesn't go any further than them. Possibly if he telephoned them to report anything, they would be the ones who would come around and make sure he disappears, a hot party with an early cremation. Peter got the picture quickly and could see why the Lord was determined to get rid of the sinful act and those involved and why he was selected. Not too many people would have Peter's experience or expertise to do the job. He had a lifetime of training..

Peter paid his bill and walked back to the church to take another look at the facilities and halls to see what he could find out.

He went into the church and sat in one of the pews and prayed for enlightenment and guidance. There were a few people seated, and he sat there for about fifteen minutes. He then went to check out the halls and found one had a video camera in a back room and lights and screen. He was interrupted by one minister who came in and asked what he was doing there. He explained he was new and was just familiarising himself with the facilities. He was told to mind his own business if he wanted to fit in with the rest of the ministry. Peter went out to make sure there was no trouble.

The next day, Peter was rostered to attend to several ministry duties. He did a morning mass and saw some parishioners who sought guidance on various matters that were troubling them. One of them was David Barlow, a young man, early thirties, who was depressed and found life would never give him a fair break. Things always seemed to go wrong, and when he tried to confront the problem, he always got a kick in the guts for his effort. He advised Peter that God doesn't seem ever to be around, and there was no purpose to his life. He was a failure and has accepted this. It was getting him down and stopping him from having faith. 'How can you believe in a God that won't help or assist you and set you on the right path?' Peter pondered on the problem for a moment, trying to evaluate where David was coming from. While he was thinking, a couple of other young people that were around came over and asked if they could sit in on the discussion, as they also had the same problem and could never seem to get on their feet.

Peter said, 'well, one thing that has come out so far is that it seems that you, David, are not alone with this problem, even though you thought it was something that only you were experiencing. The other people, who now seem to have increased in numbers, also experience similar problems, maybe not to the same degree that you have.'

'Let us start from the beginning. Most people have the problem you describe because they are not really Christians and do not believe in Jesus Christ. They know of Jesus and, while things are going all right, say they believe in Him, but they believe in themselves and not Jesus. They take the lead and expect Jesus to follow. They have forgotten, Jesus put you on this earth and not the other way around.'

'Why are you here? To serve the Lord and not for Him to serve you. Those that have faith go through a process that tells them what degree of faith they have. The process is called trials and is hard on the soul because to gain genuine faith, you must experience trauma, fear, rejection, and things a normal person would not experience because they do not believe in Jesus and do not experience trials. If you do not believe in Jesus, there is no need to be tested. You might as well go about enjoying your life and having a real good time on this earth. The problem is that the music stops at death, and so does the good time. Christ went forty days and nights in the desert to be tested. He did not have a lifetime on this earth as we have. He had a brief period but was tested whether He had faith in His Father.'

'The spirit that tested Him was Lucifer, the same that tests you.'

'Modern men and women have the world to be tested in and not the desert. They are tested as you are in your environment and not sent to the desert or Siberia to be tested. The testing starts small and, over many years, ends up with a major event that usually is soul searching, like the loss of a loved one, a child, or parent in extreme situation.'

'Jesus was exhausted, and the devil offered Him the world. All He had to do was kneel before him. Jesus refused, as the world was not the devils to offer, but God's. The devil will come to you and make you an offer that will be very tempting. You, too, must decide whether to kneel before him and declare him king, or reject what he offers and have faith in Jesus.'

'Part of your problem, from what I can gather, is "Why am I always finding myself yoked with misery and problems when my friends are enjoying themselves and seem to be free from these problems?" The answer is you have accepted Jesus Christ as your Saviour, and you confirm faith in Him. The problems are to show you how much faith you really have in Him.

'Most people have very little faith in Jesus, and as soon as things do not go their way, they say, "Well, that proves there isn't a God," and walk away from the Lord. They then align themselves with the alternative ruler of this world named Satan and, over time, are persuaded to kneel before him and declare him king. They have forgotten why they are here and that they are to serve God, not themselves or Satan.'

'I think, David, you are experiencing a conflict of the soul. Each of you will, in time, be tested. The trials start off small and are climaxed with something that will be personal and cause you to question whether there is a God. It will show the faith you have in the Lord. Remember that God will never leave you to go through these trials on your own and is always there with you, even if you do not sense His presence. You must remember that it is His world, and you are here to serve Him. You are to be trained for the future, and the first stage is to train you to have faith in God. You are periodically tested so you can judge the degree of faith you have in Him.'

'Depression is an illness that a doctor should diagnose and treat. However, most times, the problem is spiritual and can be helped by understanding what is happening to you and why is it happening.'

'David, in your case, things most probably have gone wrong, and you most probably have become depressed and we're questioning, "Why me, Lord?". What you should have done is pray to the Lord and ask for His wisdom and understanding as to what is happening and for Him to lead you away from the problem. I am sure you did neither. You most probably said, "I can fix the problem this way," instead of asking the Lord for guidance and help. As the problems compounded, you became alone and confused as to what was happening and depressed as to why.'

'Seek God's guidance and have faith, He will stand by you and lead you out of trouble. Remember, the main thing you are being trained to have on this earth is faith in Jesus Christ. The problems and heart-wrenching things that will happen to you are designed to show you whether you really have faith in Jesus or if you are just mouthing the words.'

'Your thinking should not be as to why God is not supporting you, but for you to understand that it is His world and not yours, and you are here to do His work and not for Him to do yours. He already knows what has happened to you and is dealing with it. You are here to do His work and not the other way around. It is not why this is happening to you, but it is happening to the Lord while you are employed in his service,

and it is up to Him to resolve and not you. It is His problem, not yours, so let Him fix it.

'What you were saying is that "It is my problem, and why isn't He willing to assist me to fix it?" not the other way around.

'Any questions?'

Some shook their heads, while others stood contemplating their situation. As the group broke up, Peter could see that some had questions but did not want to ask in the presence of a group. David came up to Peter and thanked him for advising him and said he would return after thinking about what they said.

As there were no further duties Peter had to attend to, he took a short walk around the surrounds of the church. As he was walking along the eastern side of the church boundary, he noticed that there was a school for infants and a day care centre, which seemed attached to the church. He went into one classroom and saw that it had young boys and girls of various ages between three and six years. He stepped out of the room and walked on to another room and saw that this room contained older children. He moved on and ended up in the day care centre, where there were infants up to three years of age being looked after. He thought this was great, and the church was progressive in providing such facilities to the community.

He stepped out of the building and noticed there was a final building that was attached to the classrooms and wondered what they used it for. He went up to it, and it was closed but not locked. He opened the door and looked in and noticed there were several cameras and backdrop scenes hanging from the ceiling and spotlights on tripods. He thought this was strange, but as no one was around, he did not bother asking what they used the equipment for. He made his way back to the church and attended to the last Mass for the day.

It was late, and Peter walked back to the day care centre to see if they were still open and wanted to be present when the children's parents came to collect them. He walked through the day care centre and noticed this time that the photographic room was open. He opened the door and saw two ministers and undressed infants being photographed. The third minister was taking pictures and videos of the scene.

As soon as he walked in, he was confronted by another minister, who said, 'what do you want?'

Peter said, 'I am new here and just came to see what you are doing here.'

The first minister, John Clements, said, 'None of your business. Get out if you know what is good for you. You're not required here.'

Two of the ministers confronted Peter and pushed him out of the room and slammed the door behind him. Peter realised they were photographing the children before their parents came to collect them. He knew it was not for identification purpose.

CHAPTER 33

IT WAS PETER'S DAY OFF and he walked into town and do some shopping. It was a busy week with new routines, environment to get used to, and people to meet. He came to town with only a few things and therefore needed to buy a few personal items and some shirts. He strolled down to the shopping centre and, on his way, noticed that he was being followed by a black Mercedes with two men in the vehicle. He didn't let on that he had observed them trailing him and gave them the slip by walking through an arcade as if he was looking in the window for clothing. He looked to see if they were still following him and sure enough, he spotted one man. He decided to see what this was about, so he went into a men's shop and stood near the door so the man could see him. The man entered the shop, looking to see if he could spot Peter. Peter, being behind the door, grabbed the man from behind and said, 'Now, why don't you tell me why you are trailing me?'

The man tried to wrench his way out of Peter's grip, and Peter noticed he had a gun under his coat. He tightened his grip on the man, but the man still tried to wrestle out of the hold. Peter, not wanting to make a scene, gave the man a hit to his head, rendering him unconscious. The man fell to the floor behind a carousel containing men's trousers where no one would see him. Peter walked out of the shop and back to the street to see if the other person was sitting in the car. Sure enough, he was. Peter went to the back of the car and around to the driver's side and hit the man in the head, rendering him unconscious. He walked on, not wanting to be seen with them. He attended to his purchase and walked back to his room.

The next day, he was back at his routine when three men came into his office. Two of them grabbed his hands; the other one hit Peter's midsection, forcing him to bend over. They grabbed him and threw him into his chair. A fourth man then came in and introduced himself as Marcus Devilo, the head of the syndicate that runs the area for the mob, and that they understood Peter was snooping around the other day, asking what was going on with the photograph of children. They were there to convince Peter that it was none of his business, and if he stuck his nose into their affairs, he would regret it and possibly end up dead.

To make sure he understood the message, they were going to arrange for him to have a holiday in the hospital to give him some time to think about his position and the consequence of him interfering. With that, Marcus moved away from Peter, but before he could, Peter grabbed him and pulled the gun from under Marcus's coat and put it to Marcus's head. The other two gorillas moved forward but stopped when they saw their boss with the gun to his head.

Peter said, 'Move and you will bury your boss. Now, let us get this straight. You think you can come in here and roughen me up to teach me a lesson, don't you?' As Peter was speaking, one man made a move towards Peter, and Peter, out of reflex, shot him in the shoulder, and the man fell to the floor bleeding. No one came because of the gunfire noise, as everyone thought it was Peter who was shot, never thinking it could be one of the gangsters.

Peter pushed Marcus forward, and he stumbled over the man on the floor. 'Let us find out what is going on here. Since you seem to be the big shot here, Marcus, why don't you tell me?' Marcus replied, 'We have an arrangement with the church that new children that are taken in, are photographed and filmed, and the pictures are sold worldwide by our syndicate. The church gets twenty-five percent of the take. The church gets to keep all the fees paid for the child-minding facilities, and we donate one hundred thousand dollars for renovations each year. Everyone down from the Archdeacon agrees with agreement, and it is to all our benefit. We don't need some smart minister to derail a good set-up that took years to establish.'

Peter asked, 'Whose idea was it? The mob?'

Marcus replied, 'No, it was Rick's, who helped to set it up and convince the ministry to assist in the production of the pictures of the children and the filming of them.'

Peter asked, 'Does it stop just at pornography?'

Marcus replied, 'No. Some of the children are orphans or under the care of the church. They are sometimes sold to buyers who want to have sex with children, and we also facilitate selling young teenagers to wealthy buyers who use them as sex slaves or for their private purposes. We normally take them, drug them, and ship them to another country where they bring in good money. We have the police on the take, so they list the kids as missing persons and don't take the matter any further, always saying the parents are at fault for the children running away from home.'

Peter said, 'So the church is involved in this grubby business right up to its eyeballs, and what you are saying is they were the instigator of the entire plan.'

Marcus replied, 'They couldn't get it off the ground without our help, and we couldn't get the pornography and young talent without their help. They alert us to any potential teenager that will bring in good money, and we take it from there.'

Peter asked, 'So you were scared that I would spill the beans and tell the police?'

Marcus replied, 'No. we have the police working for us and pay them to keep us informed of anyone finding out about our scheme. That person finds themselves at the bottom of the ocean quickly. We normally do not give warnings. That is why the scheme has been running smoothly for several years. Rick felt you would fall into line if we gave you a good working over, unlike the previous minister.'

Peter asked, 'what happened to him?'

Marcus replied, 'He accepted the plan but recently got religious and went to the police. We had to take care of him before he made trouble. Each of the ministers gets a share of the profits and is happy to be part of the scheme. They make more money this way than what they could as a minister. They hold their jobs down while making substantially more. Each of them owns real estate, cars, and investments that they would normally not have. Who says religion doesn't pay?'

Peter said, 'So I am to keep my mouth shut or you will fix it I disappear.'

Marcus said, 'You got it. The next time we meet, we won't be so pleasant.'

Marcus got the man that was shot to his feet and, with the others, helped him out to their waiting car. Peter stood there for a moment with the gun in his hand and put it in his desk drawer, as he could hear someone coming.

John Clements, the senior minister, came in and was amazed to see Peter still standing. There was little doubt that he knew what was going to happen and was surprised to see Peter in one piece.

John said, 'You are all right, I see.'

Peter replied, 'Yes. The boys came to have a chat about your enterprise and to tell me I should fall into line, or I will end up as the previous minister.'

John said, 'Well, I didn't have anything to do with that.'

Peter said, 'Yes, you did. You pulled the trigger by telling him to phone the police, knowing the cops were in on your scheme.'

John said, 'Get smart. If you play along in a few months, you will afford your own unit in the city rather than living near the church. You will be looked after and have more money than you could make as a minister. It is your choice, but these people will not let you or anyone else disrupt their operation. You either fall into line or end up dead. It is your choice.'

Peter asked, 'what about your faith in God?'

John said, 'You must be joking, aren't you? He wouldn't give you the type of money we make.'

Peter asked, 'What about the promise of eternal life? Surely this would be worth more to a man like you than the money you earn from the gang.'

John replied, 'I will take the money and have a good life here. I am sure I can talk to God into letting me into heaven when the time comes.'

Peter said, 'You will never get the chance to bargain with Him. You know you will end up in hell along with your king Lucifer.'

John said, 'At least he gives you the material things you need for a good life on earth.'

Peter said, 'He wouldn't care about you. All he wants is for you to stop believing in God and start believing in him.'

John replied, 'Who cares? I believe in myself and will do what I think is right for me. Keep your mouth shut or you will end up the same way as your predecessor.'

With that, John walked out of Peter's office, leaving him to ponder what he should do.

Peter went back to his room and did nothing for a few days, just in case his telephone was bugged and they again came after him.

A week later, Peter went into town to make a telephone call to Vince. He went and purchased a prepaid mobile and went to a café for coffee. He checked he was not being followed and then rang Vince.

After some small talk, Peter told Vince what he found out, and the threats made against him. Vince knew of the scheme, but not the church's involvement. They agreed Vince would meet Peter in a week's time at one of Vince's old nightclubs. They had set aside a private room so the men could speak freely without being overheard by the mob.

Vince left a few men at his farm to look after the distribution of supplies and made his way to the city a few days before he was to meet with Peter. Some of Vince's old team were contacted, and they were asked to attend the meeting.

Peter turned up as planned and made sure they did not follow him. Everyone greeted each other as old friends and told stories about the good days when it was easier to do business. Eventually, the group quietened down, and Peter took centre stage and described what he had learnt. Most of the men present knew of the pornography and slave trade but did not know from where it originated.

After about an hour of discussion, the consensus was 'to let sleeping dogs lie' and do nothing. Most could not see what the problem was. Yes, it was illegal, but it had been going on for years, and it entitled the mob to the profits of their venture. Also, the mob was operating from several countries, sending the sex slaves to any destination where the right money was paid. To touch the locals would certainly bring the wrath of the overseas crime bosses on their heads, and there would be no place they could hide to prevent certain death.

The group ended up having lunch and finally going their separate ways.

Vince and Peter stayed back, not convinced that nothing could be done and knew they had to do something, as that was why they were each saved. They agreed Peter would move into Vince's city apartment so both men could watch out for each other. They would also contact senior officers of the police force who they knew well and who they could trust, as it was considered those being paid off currently were junior to middle-ranking officers and not those in senior positions.

In Vince's and Peter's day, it was the senior people that were bought and not the men on the ground. These days, the mob believes it is more productive to pay off the junior ranks rather than the senior-ranking people in the police and courts.

Peter went to his unit and packed his bag and moved into Vince's apartment as planned. The two apartments on either side of Vince's were also owned by him and were maned by his men around the clock.

As Peter was moving out of his unit, John saw him exiting and asked where he was going.

Peter said, 'I don't want to be around here, so I am moving into another unit away from your dirty enterprise.'

With that, John grabbed Peter by the collar of his shirt, ready to punch him in the guts. Peter quickly lifted his bag to take the force of the punch and threw a punch at John, which hit him right in the face, knocking him out. He stepped over John and continued his way to Vince's apartment.

John did not know of Peter's background and thought he was like the rest of the ministry, unable to defend himself. To Peter, this was second nature to knock a person off their pegs and finish it with a kick to the head. But being a minister, he did not follow through with the final flow.

They arranged a meeting in a private room at one of Vince's nightclubs. The police were not told what the meeting was about; just a get-together to meet old friends. They arrived, and Peter and Vince welcomed them and invited them to help themselves to some drinks and snacks. After a while, one invitee named Jim Bishop said, 'Vince, you always threw a good party, and this is nice, but why don't you tell us the real reason you asked us here?'

Vince replied, 'I better leave it to Peter, as he has a better insight as to what we will be discussing.'

Peter took a big gulp of his scotch and then described what he knew about the pornography and slave business and how it was being protected locally.

Peter said, 'We want to know whether you will help us bust this racket. I am sure no one will support the kidnapping of teenagers and forcing them into becoming sex slaves in brothels or for private wealthy individuals. We know what happens to them when they get older. It could be your son or daughter. So, we want your help to stop this racket and, if possible, put those responsible behind bars.'

Jim said, 'My daughter went missing some five years ago, and no one knows where she has gone. She was walking home from school on a Tuesday when she disappeared. It has always been on my mind that she was kidnapped and sent overseas as a sex slave. My wife, till this day, still cannot get over her disappearance. You can count me in.'

One by one, each agreed to support the cause as best as they could. They referred to themselves as 'the Brotherhood' and not to mention to anyone what they were up to. All agreed that the mob would have contacts worldwide, and any mention of them doing something about stopping the trade would mean certain death.

They agreed that each would seek their counterpart overseas and, if they could trust them, would try to get them onside. Only those that could be trusted were to be contacted. It was agreed to meet in two weeks' time to discuss where they stood. Everyone made their way out, and Vince and Peter went back to their apartment, not sure whether the problem was too big for them to handle.

Peter went back to his routine the next day. The only thing different was he carried a gun with him just in case it was needed. He was midway through his day when he heard that the daughter of one of his parishioners had gone missing. The family did not go to his sermon, but to John Clements and advised him of her disappearance.

Their daughter was about fourteen years of age and very attractive. Peter knew it was no coincidence, and that the parents would never see the daughter again unless some miracle happened. He prayed for the Lord's guidance, as he was not having much luck on his own. The day ended, and he went back to his unit. Vince and the boys were getting ready to go out to dinner, so he joined them. At dinner, Peter told everyone of the missing girl and that she was taken yesterday on her way home. No one had any ideas as to how they were going to get a lead on the missing girl. They finished dinner and went back to their apartments.

The next day, Peter went to the school where the missing girl vanished and asked the principal to see the CTTV takes from when school broke up. It amazed him that the police had not approached the school to view the images. He sat down and, sure enough, after watching for fifteen minutes, could see that a car pulled up and a man jumped out and injected her and she collapsed. They put her in the back seat of the car, and it drove off. All took just a few seconds. He took a copy of the disc and went back to work. He called Vince and told him to meet him at the cafe near the church in an hour.

Vince was seated when Peter walked into the café.

Vince looked up and said, 'what's up?'

Peter said, 'I have a copy of the CCTV showing the girl was kidnapped and bundled into a car after she left school. The police have not bothered reviewing the footage. I need your help to get the number plate of the car as it is being driven away and who owns the vehicle. I intend to pay them a visit.'

With that, Peter handed the disc to Vince, and both men stood up and walked out of the café. Peter went back to work and completed his day early. He went to his apartment, and Vince was waiting for him with the information. The vehicle was registered to a company owned by the mob, and the registered office was in the industrial precinct.

Vince and Peter decided to take a trip out there with some boys to scout out as to the layout of the factory. They drove to the area and parked some distance away. They walked to the factory and found it to be of medium size, with an office complex attached. They entered the factory, staying clear, and did not see anyone. In the factory were several forklifts and two shipping containers. From the outside, there was nothing different from normal containers; but when they looked in, they could see they padded the containers to make sure no one injured themselves. They knew they were onto something, but where were they hiding the girls?

As they were standing looking into the containers, one worker spotted them and wanted to know why they were there.

Peter replied, 'We had to make the last inspection to make sure everything was ready for the shipment. You know Marcus would not appreciate the cargo being damaged or not arriving in one piece.'

The workman said, 'Yeah, I guess so. You looked like you were looking for something.'

Peter replied, 'No, just checking to make sure everything was ready to be shipped out.'

The workman said, 'Yeah, no worries. The girls will be here tonight, and we will ship them out and on the high seas by tomorrow morning.'

Peter said, 'Thanks.'

With that, Peter and Vince left, and the other boys made their way out of the factory without being seen. They walked to the car and drove off to Vince's apartment. There, they contemplated what to do. There was no use in calling the police, as they were part of the problem. They would have to handle the matter themselves. But how?

Peter, as usual, said a brief prayer asking for God's help. A plan then came to him.

Peter said, 'What if we get the girls out and allow the containers to be delivered to the wharf and loaded on the ship? Everyone will think everything was going to plan.'

Vince replied, 'Yes, but it would mean we would have to get the girls out while they were being loaded into the shipping containers, and no doubt in a drugged condition. They will have the place guarded, and they will surely spot us as we move up to the factory and the containers.'

Peter said, 'no, not if we were there already. How many men have you got?'

Vince replied, 'I can have twenty here in ten minutes.'

Peter said, 'Get them, and make sure their faces are covered and they are armed with automatic rifles.'

In fifteen minutes, Vince had twenty extra men plus his six that always guarded him. They assembled in Vince's unit.

Peter outlined the plan and cautioned the men not to shoot unless necessary. As soon as gunfire starts, everyone was to make their own way out and back to the apartment. They set off to the factory, assembling some distance away. It was dark, so they had surprise on their side. They moved into the factory and hid away from the containers and waited. They divided the team up, and each group went to their designated spot and waited. At about eight o'clock, some men arrived, and ten minutes later, a van arrived with several cars and other men. They took the girls out of the van and placed them near the containers, ready to be loaded up. A man appeared with a bag that contained some bottles and syringes. They intended to drug the girls and carry them into the container for shipment to an overseas port.

Armed men who were patrolling the parameters surrounded the factory. The girls knew they would never see their family again and were frightened and crying. They lifted two of the girls into the containers, and one man took a syringe and began filling it up from a bottle. At that point, Peter moved in with his group of men, telling them to put their guns down and move away from the girls. They did what they were instructed to do, and Peter grabbed the syringe and stabbed the first man, emptying the syringe into him. He immediately fell to the ground. Peter's men lifted him up into the container and, one by one, gave each of those working for Marcus a syringe full of what was in the vials.

When all of them were knocked out, they instructed the girls to get back into the bus and lie flat on the floor. They were told they were being rescued and would be returned to their parents soon.

They sensed they were being helped and cooperated. The door of the container was closed, and Peter and his men took their face masks off and took up positions as if they were Marcus's men. The doors were opened, and the driver of the semitrailer came in and stepped into the truck's cabin and started the engine. He drove out and down the highway, followed by the bus with the girls and the rest of Vince's men in it. Once clear, Vince's men were let out, and the girls were driven to the church and untied and told to wait in the church for their parents.

Peter and Vince spoke to each of the girls and cautioned them about going to the police or telling anyone about their ordeal. They were never to say who rescued them other than a group of men with guns and face masks.

Peter and Vince phoned the girls' parents, using the name of one of the ministers that were involved in the conspiracy, telling them they could come and collect their daughters. The parents rushed to the church and were grateful to see their daughters alive.

There was food and water in the container, ensuring the occupants arrived alive.

When the doors were opened at their destination, the mob expected to see young girls, not aged men, and ordered the execution of those that were in the containers.

Word got back to Marcus that his bosses were not pleased as to what had happened. They wanted to know what had happened to the girls. They ordered Marcus to find out or they would replace him as head of that region. He sent men to speak to the parents of the girls and were told they received a phone call from the minister whom they named telling them their daughter was at the church and could be collected.

Marcus stormed into John's office, demanding an answer. John, of course, could not provide one. Marcus left, and over the next two weeks, each of the ministers at St Nicholas, except Peter, disappeared, never to be heard of again. They sent the Archdeacon by this time to a nursing home, as his dementia had worsened, and he could not remember who he was. The police were called in to investigate what had happened to the ministers, but could not provide an answer.

According to Peter, they aligned themselves with Satan and joined him sooner than they expected.

The Archdeacon, even though he was an ill man, came back to work and promoted Peter to the position of senior minister, as there was no one left in the ministry. Peter sourced out five other ministers to join the church and assist in the ministry's work. They re-established the church as a centre for Christian learning.

The Archdeacon had his moments and, some days, could remember, while on other days found it difficult to remember what had happened in prior days.

Marcus tried to re-establish the same scheme that existed with John, but Peter would not have a bar of it. His bosses were getting annoyed that he could not set up the same operation that existed as before. Finally, Marcus was recalled to the overseas headquarters and never heard of again. The operation still exists, but not with the church's involvement.

Vince considered this was becoming too much for him and went back to the farm at Bungarby, thinking that Peter would soon join him. But God had other plans for Peter.

Peter moved back into the church unit.

CHAPTER 34

PETER HAD JUST COMPLETED MASS and went to his office to attend
to some correspondences when he received a phone call from the
Archdeacon's office asking whether he could come to His Reverence's
office immediately. He politely said no, but no matter how many times
he tried not to say no, His Reverence's secretary insisted, and before
Peter knew it, His Reverence's driver was in Peter's office taking his
briefcase and escorting him to the car.

Before Peter could wink, he was standing in front of the
Archdeacon, whom he barely knew.

The Archdeacon said, 'Peter, I had accepted an invitation some
time ago to attend the World Spiritual Organisation's (WSO) annual
conference in Spain. I unfortunately cannot go, as I have a few problems
with my health, as you know. These conferences are very important, as
they set the agenda for the next three years as to where the world churches
will head. We are not speaking at the conference but attending there
merely as an observer. There will be several eminent and highly qualified
speakers who will present papers at the conference, and there will be a
vote taken if the committee is asked to decide on any matters. I have the
conference papers but have not read them. I want you to go in my place.'

Peter was flabbergasted to think of all people the Archdeacon
could have chosen, he decided on him as being the right man to send.

Peter asked, 'Archdeacon, why me? There are several ministers in
the diocese that you could choose, and most would be better qualified
to attend than me.'

The Archdeacon replied, 'not so. They have qualifications but no experience. You are street-wise and will see through the facade that will be presented and act accordingly. The qualified ministers will be persuaded to follow like sheep, whereas you will act as the Lord directs. I know you are in His favour, and therefore I have selected you above all others to act in my place. I warn you I have been told that there will be an attempt to persuade the conference to water down the Bible in some sections to align it with the "worldly view" rather than the Creator's.'

Peter said, 'So, therefore, this is going to be more than a talk fest and could become political and allow the minority to have their way.'

The Archdeacon replied, 'Yes, unless we stop it.' Peter asked, 'How? You said we are not speaking.'

The Archdeacon replied, 'we are not one of the scheduled speakers. However, at the conference, a name is selected at random to speak and present an alternative view. Normally the speaker selected is ill prepared and says nothing or makes a fool of themselves, which is expected.'

Peter said, 'So there is no need for me to speak unless selected, which gives me a one-in-a-thousand chance of not being selected, right?'

The Archdeacon replied, right, but I had a dream where I was directed to send you in my place, so if I were you, I would prepare myself, as I believe the Lord will want you to speak for Him. it is just a gut feeling, but I believe your number will be chosen.'

Peter said, 'I wouldn't know what to say, and who would listen to me, without academic recognition or qualification?'

The Archdeacon replied, 'I agree, but you can only pray and do your best. You fly off tomorrow to Spain. I will ensure someone fills your post here temporarily.'

Peter stayed with the Archdeacon for about ten minutes and left with his blessing. He went to his unit and packed a bag, had dinner, and went to bed to get a good night's sleep.

The next morning, Peter headed off to the airport where he booked in and was on a plane for Spain, travelling first class. He arrived at the airport and was immediately escorted to the hotel by security men, who seem to be all over the place. Soldiers were outside the hotel where the delegates were staying and on every corner for several blocks from the town centre.

Peter was shown to his room and was advised of the registration procedure for the conference. He freshened up and went to the main auditorium and went through registering, which took about an hour. They gave him copies of the speaker's papers and he decide to have dinner in his room and review some papers.

To Peter's horror, the first speaker was advocating altering the Bible to allow same-sex marriage and homosexuality to be accepted and not be rejected by the church. The more he read, the more he was convinced that the speaker in reality had a different God than Jesus Christ and had rewritten sections of the Bible and wanted the majority to accept his god and "word" rather than follow what the Bible currently said.

It was late that night after Peter had finished reading the papers from the first speaker. He got some sleep but kept waking up thinking about what he had read and what he could do about it. He thought other members would raise an objection, and this would lead them to a debate or consensus.

The next morning, Peter went downstairs early to have breakfast to avoid the crowd. Like him, there were several members that also had the same idea. He gave his details to the concierge and went in and helped himself to a plate of bacon, eggs, and orange juice. He sat at a table by himself, away from others who seemed important, but within ten minutes, three other members joined him and started a conversation with him.

None had read the speakers' papers and were out enjoying the town last night rather than preparing themselves for today's session. To them, this was a time to enjoy themselves rather than preventing a catastrophe. Peter quizzed them as to their attitude towards changing verses of the Bible. All would not care and thought it was a good idea to modernise the Bible to bring it up to date with modern thinking. What came out of the conversation was that, to them, religion was a good secure job, and if more people attended church because of fewer restrictions, then that would be great, as more money would be raised for a multitude of projects such as replacing old church buildings. Of course, they mentioned nothing about feeding or educating the poor.

They all finished breakfast and went to their rooms to freshen up and meet in the main hall afterwards, where the presentations were being made. Peter did not have any intentions to meet with them, as his view of the Bible was that it should remain as is and not be altered. It was the word of God, the Creator, and should stay that way. He knew that if their view became paramount amongst the delegates, then he had a fight on his hands, and like Moses, he would need Aaron to present his argument against change.

Peter collected his papers and reviewed his notes and walked to the auditorium. He was approached by one lady, who registered him and gave him a name tag and directed him to his seat, where he prepared himself for the presentation.

After about fifteen minutes, the auditorium become quite full and deafening with the noise of those talking while waiting for the presentation to start. Eventually, the president of the WSO came to the centre of the stage and adjusted the microphone and spoke. He welcomed all the delegates and outlined the agenda for the weeklong conference. He then advised that, as was customary with the WSO, there would be one further speaker at the end of the conference who will be drawn randomly from all the delegates to make an ad hoc presentation if he wished to. In the past, most delegates had not accepted the offer, but some had made representations, which had been adopted by the WSO. The president then introduced the first speaker, who was, it seems, well known in various countries of the world and was highly credentialed. He outlined the paper the speaker was to present and then introduced the speaker. There was an applause, and then everyone settled down to hear what the speaker had to say.

The presentation went for one hour and fifteen minutes. The argument of the paper being presented was the need to adopt modernity or die a quick death. Religion should either modernise its thinking, attitudes, and teachings or would be instinct like the dinosaurs within the next fifty years. The speaker went on and gave statistics of religion dwindling in the western world and, if unaddressed, would result in no one following the Bible. He gave examples of instances throughout the world where legislators made laws that opposed the Bible's teachings, and in the main, these were supported by the country's population and not by the orthodox religions. The prime examples covered were the same-sex marriages and homosexuality. Other contentious issues that were also becoming state laws were the right to euthanasia and abortion.

The speaker's main argument was 'the individual's right of choice' and presented a case where the Bible did not give the individual a choice but was dogmatic in its teachings on these and other subjects, hence the need for the state to legislate what is acceptable as viewed by the majority in a democratic society. There now exists a gap that is widening between the state and religion, which necessitates religion being modernised to bring its thinking and teachings in line with the state. To do nothing or allow things to remain as they are would be a recipe for disaster and annihilation of religion as we have known it.

The speaker concluded his presentation urging delegates to vote for the modernising of the Bible and adoption of the recommendations that other speakers will be making.

Other speakers were then invited to make their presentations throughout the day, with lunch and several shorter breaks taken to ensure everyone stayed awake. The presentations went on for four days, and except for several technical papers, most of the speakers were advocating changing the Bible to 'bring it up to modern-day thinking'.

On the fourth day, after the morning tea break, the MC moved back to centre stage and advised the meeting that as part of their custom, a speaker would be selected by a lottery to speak in support or against the previous speakers' position. They also had the right to raise issues that had not been raised by previous speakers but could not speak about these in depth.

A number was selected and read out, and sure enough, as predicted, it was Peter's number.

The MC said, 'would delegate number 7777 please come to the stage?'

Peter was momentarily stunned to hear his number called out and remembered the Archdeacon saying that there must be a reason for him to have been selected and that he thought his number would be read out. He was right.

Peter thought he could be a ghost at the WSO conference, as he had very few credentials to his name and was not well known. He was out of his comfort zone. Whatever he said would not be supported by the academics. However, if it was God's desire for him to make a fool of himself, then so shall it be. As he walked to the stage, the shock of his number being called wore off, and reality dawned on him. He did not agree with the position taken by the previous speakers,

and their opinions and demands were not referenced to any works other than their views and the views of the minority that they represented. They also were trying to make a name for themselves by taking what they thought to be the populous view. Peter thought most Christians would see it his way, so why should he kneel before those who were advocating change? He should, contrary to the intentions of the WSO, put an argument forward for following the Bible as it stood rather than a changed populous Bible crafted by men who now consider themselves greater than God, a position that was taken by Lucifer. He was going to move a motion that the status remain unaltered, and the motions recommended by the previous eminent speakers be rejected.

Peter finally moved to centre stage and stood at the podium looking at the audience, stunned, not knowing what to say. He could see the members of the WSO waiting for him to say a few words and then get himself off the stage quickly, as others had done in previous years. He looked up again at the audience, but this time saw the image of the old man in a blaze of white light facing him and showing for him to proceed. He gained confidence, as he knew God would not let him make a fool of himself or make errors that would embarrass himself, God, and the church.

Peter said, 'Mr President, members of the WSO, previous speakers who presented their papers advocating change, and those that tabled academic papers and delegates at this conference. My apology if I missed someone out. This is the first time they have asked me to speak at such a large gathering, and while it is not evident (stuttering), I am nervous. 'Those that presented papers to this conference had a common theme, and all were in support of modernity and change. All advocated changes to the Bible, as they believe it's necessary to bring the Bible up to date and address modern thinking. Some have said that they have already done this and teach this to their congregation. Regrettably, none have said they have disclosed these changes to their congregation and are misleading them when preaching the word of God.

'To change the Bible is to say that you refuse to follow the word of God and have come up with a new version dictated by man, not a revised version, as there is only one who can revise the Bible, and that is God. This Bible you have updated or altered its interpretation is according to your beliefs, and not that of God's. In fact, not only have you rewritten the Bible but also you replaced the one and only God with yourself to ensure popularity with the state.'

'If you can persuade enough people with similar views to those you hold, then you can get the state to legislate your view, and it becomes law. So, the Bible, over time, changes dramatically from what God gave us, and the state becomes the new god, and the wealthy become the manipulators or phantom gods, as votes can be gotten by persuasion and money. The wealthy will operate or manipulate behind the scenes to ensure you never get back to where you came from, and Lucifer would have achieved what he could not by trying to overthrow God in heaven—namely, the control of mankind by replacing God's word with his own.'

'How many times have you picked up the newspaper and read about the sinful dealings of politicians and bureaucrats and even the church? Those that advocate change to the Bible are, in my opinion, Antichrists. Cast your minds back to their speeches. In their presentation, not once was the word "God" spoken, nor even mentioned. Not one had mentioned Jesus Christ. Why? Because they refuse to acknowledge Him to be the Creator, Lord, and King. He has given them the right to decide whether they will follow Him and have faith in Him or follow the alternative named Lucifer. There are only two ways to go, not three or forty or a hundred ways, only two, and they have chosen self and not God's way. They therefore have chosen Lucifer while still earning a living from the Lord's church and preaching wrong interpretation of the Bible and the word of God. Is there a need to change the Bible as currently it prevents them dictating to us and making ethical policies to suit themselves? We need the word of God to stop them from corrupting our lives with their sinful views and interpretations. Their intentions are contrary to the way God has planned and designed life for us, and it is clear they want control.'

'Mankind was put on this earth to do God's work, to gain faith in the Lord. Most have decided not to follow God and insist on doing as they please. Do not get me wrong, this is their prerogative, as we have given them a free will to decide and have adopted a materialistic life instead of believing in God.'

'Those advocating changes to the Bible are saying they want to control religion and not religion as God meant it, but as they advocate it. They want a new religion and a new god. They have already built the golden calf and require your contribution of gold to complete their task.

'I, for one, reject their plan, as we have the word of God. if it does not suit you to adopt God's way, then don't try to get the majority to follow you, for your way is unworthy and untruthful. It is a good recipe for a lifelong period in hell with your king Lucifer. To follow God and believe in Him is an assurance of independence, a life of truth, and an internal life.'

'To present this deception to this conference under the disguise of modernity is to mislead the population. Why not be truthful and say we are ministers of a new religion and have resigned from the one that follows the Bible? The reason is that they want to keep their jobs, and it could backfire on them, leaving them with a new religion that no one wants, and deny them a good income stream as wages and publication royalties.'

'Lucifer knows that if given a choice between the modern version and the current historic version, most people will take the historic version, as its principles come from God and not man, and these principles have been tested over time and found to be faultless. They have been in place for the last three thousand years and are still applicable today as they were then. To adopt modernity would mean changes according to mankind, and more so according to the rich, who will end up persuading people to change their principles and view of life, to reflect what the rich and influential consider it should be, and not the word of God.'

'Lucifer tried to get the average person to change their view of God but failed. He now tries a different path—that of putting Antichrists amid God's church to muddy the preaching water and make sure the message that is getting through is confused and disrupted. He makes some ministers abandon God and take up his cause, persuading them that materialism is the way of this world and discredits others by declaring them to be rapists or involved in pornography or other illicit trade. He corrupts the church within and discredits it by persuading ministers to adopt his cause and not God's.

'I believe those advocating changes to the Bible have already changed their way of worship and teachings and should have the moral strength to leave the ministry and set up a new religion, for to stay as they have is only to prevent the public from readily seeing them for what they are—wolves in sheep clothing. They still want to earn an income representing Christ when they do not believe in Him or intend to preach the truth about Him or the Bible. They are there to mislead and spread the lies that their king Lucifer directs them to do.

'I urge all those here to reject the recommendation and to support Christ as He has requested and as He stands before you here at this conference.'

With that, Peter lifted the Bible he had with him above his head.

Immediately, the assembly burst into spontaneous applause, so much so that the committee declared the vote to reject the proposal, as unanimously defeated.

Peter moved from the stage and was congratulated by people in the audience, and it took him an hour to get to his room, where he kneeled down and prayed to God for His support and directing him as to what he should say. He did not think it wise to have dinner in the restaurant, as he had made some enemies, and therefore ordered a light meal to be delivered to his room.

After completing his meal, Peter thought he might as well inspect the sites, as he was flying back the next morning and had to be at the airport by seven in the morning to check in.

He slipped out of the hotel and walked down the main street, and eventually he came past a nightclub, and while looking in the window, noticed in the reflection that two men across the road were looking at him. As he stopped, they crossed the road, so he moved on and noticed they were following him.

He went inside one of the department stores, and they followed him as he moved from department to department. They kept their distance, no doubt waiting for him to be alone without a crowd of people around. He gave them the slip, so he went into the gents, and, sure enough, they eventually followed him. One stood at the entrance to make sure no one came in, while the other approached Peter and said, 'You made a fool out of the speakers at the conference, which is not the right thing to do. We are here to make sure you fall into line and, in the future, support the cause, or we will send you to your God sooner than you expected.' With that, the man threw a punch at Peter, who moved away, forcing the man to punch one of the handbasin, possibly breaking his hand. At the same time, Peter grabbed the man and kneed him midsection and, as he went down, slammed his head on the hand basin, knocking him unconscious. His friend, seeing what had happened, ran to the entrance to get out.

Peter left the toilet block and made his way back to his hotel room. He locked the door and braced a chair up against it to make sure no one picked the lock and got in while he slept. He had a shower and packed his bags, ready for a quick departure in the morning, and placed the bags standing upright just in case someone got in during the night. The sound of the bags flipping over would alert him to any danger.

Nothing happened during the night, except Peter was awakened at four in the morning and quickly prepared himself for a long flight home. He ordered a light breakfast and packed his last things and took his bags downstairs and booked out. He boarded the bus to the airport and, once there, checked his baggage in and went and sat in the departure lounge. After about ten minutes, a man came and sat near him to talk to him. 'You roughened up one of my men yesterday.'

Peter asked, 'is he still alive?'

The stranger replied, 'Yes, but will be in hospital for a few weeks undergoing surgery on his head and arm.'

Peter asked, 'why were they sent after me?'

The stranger replied, 'You roughened the feathers of some very influential people from the Dominium Group who always get their way, particularly the chairman, James Coelicola.'

Peter said, 'I have never heard of them. So, what are they going to do now—blow the airplane out of the sky?'

The stranger replied, 'Possibly in the future, but not now. I suggest you fall into line with these people, or they will kill you. They preach forgiveness but are the most unforgiving lot you could meet. Do not underestimate them, as they have contacts all over the world, and they will either persuade you to come across to their side, buy you off, or eliminate you. This is a warning: do not cross them again. I give you a personal warning to be careful, as you have caused them embarrassment and have delayed their plans. They now intend to make you out as a drug addict or get you involved in pornography or prostitution, declaring that no one can accept your word or dedication, as you do one thing and preach another.'

With that, the stranger got up and left Peter on his own, leaving an envelope on the seat near him. Peter immediately realised that it most probably contained pictures of children and got up and moved out of the lounge to the opposite corner and waited.

An elderly woman came into the lounge and sat where Peter was sitting before. Sure enough, the police arrived. Being tipped off, they went to the seat where the envelope was and opened it, and there were pictures of very young children undressed and a hand around their genitals. They looked at the elderly woman and asked her if she knew anything about the pictures. She said no. The envelope was there when she sat down, assuming whoever owned it would eventually come and collect it. They left with the envelope.

Peter came back into the lounge, which was at this point crowded and jammed with people wanting to board their flight. He noticed a somewhat distinguished-looking man standing by himself with his ticket half hanging out of his pocket. Peter walked up to the man and bumped into him, slightly pulling the ticket out from his pocket while dropping his ticket on the ground near the man. He moved away and noted the man had an allocated seat near to his.

The call came through to board the plane, and Peter went to the seat shown on his ticket, assisted by the steward. He placed his hand baggage in the compartment above him and sat down in his seat, which was a window seat, which he also selected. The man moved into Peter's seat, unaware that the tickets had been switched.

When the flight was an hour in the air, complimentary drinks were served, and the man in Peter's seat took a Chardonnay. Peter took an orange juice. The man had a second and, after about fifteen minutes, took on the appearance of being drunk.

At that time, a young lady with a very short skirt sat near him, and she moved closer to him and placed his hand between her legs while hugging him. A flash went off, and they took several pictures of the planned incident. The woman abruptly got up and moved away, leaving the man to sleep off whatever was placed in his Chardonnay. The crew knew what was happening, as they did not disturb the man until they arrived at their destination. They woke him up and helped him to his feet. All the passengers left the plane, and so did Peter. He passed a news stall and saw the headline 'Minister Found with Prostitute on Plane.' The story declared he was rowdy, and it took several of the crew to quiet him down before the alcohol took effect and he fell into a deep sleep.

Reporters were waiting to get the man's story as he came out of the aeroplane. As he appeared, the cameras rolled, and the flashes exploded, with pictures taken of him in a somewhat confused state with a painful expression.

He walked out of the plane to questions from the reporters as to what this would do to his cleric position and how the Archdeacon and church would view his transgression. The man, of course, knew nothing about what was being reported and was not a minister of the church. He was, in fact, a member of the United Nations sent to find out what was happening to the indigenous people and how the country was looking after their welfare.

Once the man got wind of what was reported, he reported back to the UN, who recalled him to answer questions as to what had happened.

CHAPTER 35

PETER LEFT THE AIRPORT AND went back to his unit and made an appointment to see the Archdeacon to report back to him.

The Archdeacon was glad to see Peter and welcomed him warmly when he arrived at his office. He had received several reports of what had happened at the conference and a transcript of Peter's speech.

The Archdeacon said, 'I support you in what you said. However, you have upset those in the Dominium Group, I am told, who will now try to bring you down and embarrass you before you can cause further damage to them or disrupt their plans.'

Peter said, 'Dominium Group? I have never met them, heard of them, or gotten involved with them. Who are they?'

The Archdeacon said, 'I really don't know much about them other than they are a sect that goes back to pre-Christ days. Some say that the head of the group, James Coelicola, is Lucifer, and the group comprises men who are extremely wealthy and, through their wealth, have gained power and influence. In Jesus's day, the Pharisee or Sadducees were part of this sect. This is one reason they refused to accept Jesus, as He was preaching things that would bring their world to a halt. They could not allow Him to go on and disrupt their lives.

'These days, it is said that they run the governments of the world and manipulate elections to get what they desire. People think they are in a democracy, but the reality is this group determines who wins elections in which countries throughout the world. They also decide who will be appointed to positions of influence, such as judges and heads of churches. They comprise wealthy people and members of the church, and no one knows who they are or how many make up their sect. You must be very wealth to join them, and once one of their members decides on a course of action, he has the full support of all the other members of the group. As people die off, they invited new members in to join the order.'

Peter said, 'That can't really be the case, surely. We elect people to Parliament, not some unknown order or sect.'

The Archdeacon replied, 'That is what you think, but the reality is that they persuade the way you vote by influencing your judgement through television and media, by internet and direct mail, or by cash handouts through governments. They will spend whatever it takes to get whom they support across the line. If that is not enough, the opposing person may find himself discredited by being with a prostitute or tied up with pornography or whatever it takes to discredit them, or they will get at their family or their parents, or the person may find he has a sudden accident or winds up dead.'

Peter asked, 'How can you get at them if you don't know who they are?'

The Archdeacon replied, 'You can't. They run the show and have the power and wealth to do what they please. The law cannot stop them. They decide what is going to happen in every country throughout the world. They keep the wars going for their benefit and nations in poverty to ensure they control their raw materials and land. What you did with the farmers and getting support for a Royal Commission did not go down well with them, as they were the ones who were telling the banks what to do. They were also preventing the government from deciding about building dams, as it was not in their interest to have a dam built. Why do you think the government has been delaying building a dam, especially when interest rates are so low? It would be the right time to borrow the money and start building, but the Dominium Group has decided otherwise, and the government makes excuses to try not to look as if they are idiots. They can't come out and say anything. Otherwise, if they did, we would have a new leader the very next day.'

Peter asked, 'How do you know all this?'

The Archdeacon replied, 'How do you think I became archdeacon? I have been told to warn you that your life will be in danger if you pursue this line of thinking and not support their cause of altering the Bible to suit their purpose. From a population point of view, altering the Truth of the Bible makes no difference to the average person. They would not care or even know the ramifications of that action. Most have never read the Bible. I sent you to the conference hoping that your number would not be selected, but it seems a higher power had different ideas. He may decide to rock their boat or remove some of them from office.'

Peter said, 'Yes, I am sure He will clarify that He will not allow the Bible to be diluted, nor for another God to be substituted on this earth in place of Him. There will be no more golden calf. You know, Archdeacon, they may have Lucifer as their leader, but all their money and influence cannot match the power of our Lord. You may have bowed before them, but I will not. Lucifer tried to get Jesus to bow before him when Jesus was in the desert going through His trials, and even then, hungry and near exhaustion, He refused to.'

The Archdeacon said, 'Then I can only hope you take care, as I have been instructed to remove you from your position and declare to the news and press that it was with regret that I was forced to end your service owing to several complaints from some parents about their children. You will be tried by the press, and everyone will find you to be a sex offender even though no action will be brought against you.'

Peter said, 'God, who created the world and mankind, will not allow you or the Dominium Group to falsely accuse me. You preach religion, but you're nothing but a stooge for Lucifer. Tell your master that it is God who decides when their time is up and not Lucifer, and He may have already nominated the time they will depart from this earth.'

With that, Peter walked out of the Archdeacon's office and walked to his unit. As he walked in, Vince was standing in the lounge room.

Peter asked, 'What on earth brings you here? I thought nothing would pull you away from Bungarby and the good life.'

Vince replied, 'It's good to see you, old friend, especially in one piece. I was instructed in a dream to come and give you support, as it seems you have roughened some feathers at the WSO.'

Peter said, 'Yes, as they were voting on the right to alter certain passages of the Bible to water down God's word. I unfortunately was selected from all the delegates to present the ultimate argument, and my view was carried by the majority, and their motions were defeated.'

Vince said, 'I hope you realise you will be dealing with the Dominium Group, and I have not known them not to have their way. Even when I was running my business, I would not cut across them, as they have the power and wealth to ensure they get their way.'

Peter said, 'They won't this time.'

Vince poured out a scotch for Peter and himself and handed a glass to Peter.

Peter said, 'Thanks. Cheers.'

Both men downed their drink just when there was a knock at the front door. Peter went to the front door and looked through the spyhole to see who was there and noticed the Archdeacon standing at the front door in street clothing. He opened the door and let him in looking quite surprised. Vince moved closer to the Archdeacon, and Peter introduced Vince to him.

Peter said, 'Archdeacon, I am surprised to see you, and especially in a casual outfit. What brings you here?

The Archdeacon replied, 'I couldn't talk freely in my office, as the room is bugged and all my conversations are listened to, so to discuss anything, I have to go away where no one can hear me. I advise you that you will be stood down, but that has not been officially done, which gives us some breathing space to figure out what we should do about your predicament.'

Vince asked, 'what do you mean?'

The Archdeacon replied, 'I was instructed to either get Peter to fall into line with the Dominium Group's intentions to change the Bible or to dismiss him from his position on a cooked-up charge of child molesting and allow the press to have a field day with his reputation.'

Vince said, 'But you have fired him, haven't you?'

The Archdeacon replied, 'I haven't officially. I wonder whether we can stall them, as like you, I believe the Bible should not be altered and God's word should be available to everyone and not some substituted words that alter the true meaning of the Bible and to misrepresent the truth.'

Peter said, 'Archdeacon, I thought you were in support of these men and against me and wouldn't care whether the Bible was altered.'

The Archdeacon said, 'Many years ago, when I was a junior minister, I met a young girl and fell in love, and we got married. I had total faith in Jesus, and life was reasonable. We tried to start a family but could not and believed, given time, the Lord would bless us with a child or two. However, as time went on, my wife could not conceive, and she remained childless. We were thinking of adopting a child, but waited to see if the Lord would allow my wife to fall pregnant. We both worked hard at our jobs. My wife was a pharmacist and worked at a pharmacy in the city. We lived out of town, and both had to rely on public transport to get to work.'

'I was approached by two men one morning advising me to discontinue my objection to abortion, which was the topic of the day at that time and woman's right to decide whether they had an abortion. This is the same argument that is still being discussed today.

'I said I had no intention of dropping my opposition to abortion and that I intended to raise my objection whenever the opportunity arose. I was intending to go on the morning television programs and do radio to get my view across to the public.

'Again, I was approached and told that I would regret my opposition to abortion, as they were intending to act and not just warn me. I told them they could do nothing to me that would change my mind and that I had total faith in God to protect me from anything they intended to do. They left, and I was never approached again.

'Two days later, a junky walked into my wife's pharmacy and pulled out a gun and demanded to be given heroin. My wife tried to convince the man that she had none, as heroin was not a drug sold in pharmacies. As she was talking to him, he pointed the gun right at her and shot her right through the heart. He then left. The police were called, and after an hour, came to investigate. The ambulance was called but never turned up, saying I gave them a wrong address. Alongside my wife's body was a picture of her that the assassin had, and on the back of the picture was her address and the words 'contract amount $20,000'. They had a contract out on my wife owing to my objection to abortion.'

'Over the months, I tried to understand why God had allowed my wife to be shot dead. I was objecting to abortion as a minister on his behalf, and I thought He would protect us, but that was not the case. I lost faith in God and changed my stand on abortion and fell into line with what the Dominium Group wanted.'

'The Archdeacon at that time, died in a car accident. He was driving along the freeway with a minister and his wife when a petrol tanker jumped lanes and smashed straight into them, killing all the occupants of the vehicle. I was promoted to the position of archdeacon with no opposition and have remained Archdeacon since.'

'About two months after my promotion, I was at home going through some papers when I stumbled on the autopsy report on my wife. I was going to throw it in the garbage tin but read it. The report said my wife died from a bullet shot by an unknown person trying to rob the pharmacy. It also said my wife had been suffering from cancer, which had moved throughout her body and that she would have died within weeks had not the gunman shot her.'

'God was looking after us both. I am still alive, and my wife is with the Lord. She did not suffer as she would have if the gunman did not shoot her dead. The report said that the type of cancer she had did not reveal itself until the person was a few weeks from death, and the person would experience excruciating pain, which would require high doses of morphine. I lost faith in God thinking He had abandoned both of us, but He took my wife to heaven before she experienced the worst aspect of the cancer and kept me alive even though I lost faith in Him and turned against Him, joining Satan's camp.'

'I have asked forgiveness every day since and, like Peter in the Bible, find it hard to find a place to hide my shame in not trusting in the Lord. Every time I hear a cock crow, I remember my lack of faith in the Lord. This time, I will not abandon Him or lose faith in Him. I played the part they wanted me to play to give us time to come up with a plan so we can turn things in God's favour even though He doesn't need our help. I can still show my support and faith in Him.'

Peter said, 'I agree you should seem to be on their side. Unfortunately, both Vince and I come from the background, where their dirty work is not handled by the person who wants it done. They go out to the underworld and buy the services, so it is an independent person who is unrelated to them who contracted to do the dirty work for them.'

'What we must do is come up with a plan that will tilt the advantage in our favour and not theirs, something that will delay their intention to a more favourable time, for there is no doubt that they will eventually get their way when enough people support Satan and not the Christian faith.'

'We will have to think about it, but one thing is for certain — they will send the reporters after you Archdeacon, to see what you are going to say about me and whether I am to be dismissed. If you declare you support me, then I am a man in line for an accident, as they cannot have someone in my position going against them.'

'What you should say is the matter is being considered by church leaders and I will make an announcement after their deliberation. It is not up to a single minister to decide these important issues. It is for the church leaders to decide. The minister was expressing his personal views only, and it is contrary to the view of others and modern-day thinking.' The Archdeacon said, 'That is good. Yes, I will stick to that line. If they ask if you have been dismissed, I will ask them how many times they have been fired for expressing their own opinion. We will see how many stones they have cast and which one thinks they haven't sinned.'

With that, the Archdeacon got up and was escorted to the door and left.

CHAPTER 36

THE ARCHDEACON ATTENDED HIS DUTIES and was not available for the next two days to see reporters, but as predicted, the reporters were sent out to find out what had happened and where the Archdeacon's stood on the matter. He stated exactly what they had agreed to and left it at that. The reporters pressed him for a more definitive answer, and he turned the tables on them to advise what they would do in this situation. They were not prepared to answer the question, and therefore, he was not prepared to continue the interview and refused to take any more questions.

Peter resumed to his normal routine and attended to Mass and his other duties. Most of his congregation made it clear that they supported him, but there were a good 40 percent that came forward and advised Peter that they supported the motion to change the Bible. Peter asked them, 'Therefore, you are in support of changing God, aren't you?' Some would not agree to that, but most agreed that if required, they would be in favour of this happening, as, in their opinion, the current one was not doing a good job or supporting them. He asked why they attend church. They replied, 'it is the acceptable thing to do on Sundays.' They had to show they were Christians.

Peter was on the alert, and Vince had sent some of his men to act as bodyguard for the Archdeacon, while he and the rest of his team stayed close to Peter.

On Monday, Peter received a call from the hospital saying that there had been a car accident and that the driver was near death and asking for a minister. He wanted to relate to God before he died. Peter went off to the hospital, accompanied by Vince and two of his men.

They parked their car and went to the information desk to find out which room the patient was in. They were given his name over the phone and the room he was in, but wanted to check out the information. The information desk confirmed the patient's name and the ward and room number he was in. Peter and the men headed off to the ward, but somehow the sign hanging from the ceiling was damaged and showed the ward in the opposite direction. They started walking towards what they thought was the ward when they heard a colossal bang coming from a room in the opposite direction. They turned around and headed toward the gunfire and were prevented from entering the room.

A cleaner was shot in the arm by someone who immediately fled after shooting him. Police were called, but after half an hour had passed, they still hadn't turned up.

Peter and the men headed back to their car but were stopped by maintenance who noticed the sign was pointing in the opposite direction and had to use a lifting chair to reach the sign to turn it around. Once they had completed the job, the men could move on.

On their way back to their car, they passed the children's ward and were stopped by a young man who recognised Peter as being a minister of their local church. He asked Peter if he would pray over his young daughter, who was very ill and not expected to live through the night. Vince decided to check this one out, as the first call turned out to be a set-up. Vince accompanied the young man to the room where his daughter lay and checked out the room and found it was legitimate and not a set-up. The men waited outside while Peter entered the room.

The young mother immediately recognised Peter and thanked him for coming. She said to Peter she was not sure why God would want to take her daughter from her but understood that as she had a multitude of problems from birth and doctors didn't seem to know how to handle the problems, that God was taking her back home away from the suffering.

A nurse came into the room as they entered and checked the drips feeding into the young girl's arm.

Peter, upon entering the room, noticed a white light in the room and the old man standing at the head of the girl's bed and knew why he was brought to the hospital.

Peter moved to the head of the bed and placed his hands on the young girl's head. He noticed the old man had likewise placed his hands on top of Peter's. The nurse stopped for the moment, allowing Peter to say his prayer.

Peter, to the astonishment of the parents, started his prayer to the Lord, asking for His divine intervention to cure the young girl who was one of the Lord's children. He ended his prayer by thanking the Lord for His presence and help and, in the name of the Father, the Lord's cure of her illness.

The parents looked at Peter as if to say, 'You are mad. She will not be cured. Your prayer, like all the others they had made, will go unanswered. There is a god by myth, not by fact.'

While they said they had faith in God, it was obvious it was not genuine faith. The Lord used this occasion to show them His miraculous powers and cure their daughter and to see if they would trust Him from this day forth.

The nurse stood there looking at Peter, and it was obvious that she was thinking, *you must be mad. The best doctors in town cannot cure this girl, and you think your invisible God will.* You could see she was expecting someone to walk through the door and begin curing the girl. She believed what she could see and touch—material things only.

Peter, after saying his prayer and looking at them, stepped back and moved from the bed and walked out of the room, leaving them there. He and Vince made their way back to the car and drove off to their unit.

On Sunday Mass, Peter noticed the young couple with their daughter sitting in the pew. After the service, they came up to Peter and thanked him for the miracle.

Peter said, 'You are thanking the wrong person. All I did was what you asked me to do, and that was to pray for your daughter, which I did. You should give thanks to God, who was willing to cure your daughter, not me. I can not make miracles, but He has. It is just a pity you did not have faith in Him to cure your daughter.'

The mother replied, 'No. We thought the Lord would take her from us to stop her from suffering. It is a miracle. Even the doctors could not explain how someone who was so sick could be cured so quickly of all her ailments. Look at her. She hasn't a worry in the world now, yet a few days ago, she was near death.' The couple left with their daughter skipping down the street.

Peter went back to his work and began preparing for the next Mass.

CHAPTER 37

VINCE HAD LEFT PETER TO return to Bungarby with his men, as there seemed to be no further attempts on Peter's life.

Peter was dozing off in his chair in front of the television when he woke up quickly hearing the reporter say that a vote will be taken soon on legalising euthanasia, the right to a premature death at the designation of a person.

This matter had been debated in Parliament, and it was agreed that a vote would not be forced along party lines, but each member was to vote according to his or her conscience.

This was contrary to the teachings of the Bible, and before too much time had passed, Peter was before news cameras and on radio and television preaching the Bible and that euthanasia was contrary to God's teachings.

Most of the population made it clear that they believe the individual had the right to decide when they were to die and not a God that they did not believe in. In fact, suicide is the right of everyone. Their argument was that the individual should be able to die with ease and with the help of others.

Peter made it clear at all the places that gave him the opportunity to speak that individuals did not have a say as to when they were to be born, so they shouldn't have a say as to when they were to die. It is God's decision alone and not mans.

For authority, Peter referred to the Bible. The true Bible that had not been watered down to suit some or from which some had intentionally misinterpreted.

Some ministers came out in opposition to Peter and declared that they were for euthanasia and that they should update the Bible to reflect modern views.

Peter noted these ministers were not following the original Bible, but a version written or changed to suit their own desires. He also stated that, most likely, they not only wanted to change the Bible but also had already changed their god. They were working for the opposition, Lucifer, and undermining the teaching of God and the church. They were worshipping a god they had created for themselves rather than Jesus Christ.

To prove his point, he asked these parishioners to think back and answer the question, "Have your ministers ever in their sermons referred to God or Jesus Christ? No doubt the answer would be no. Have they ever referred to the Holy Spirit? No. in fact, they intentionally mislead their congregation as to what the Bible says. They do not want to preach the Truth as directed by Jesus, but still want to earn money as a minister of the church while still trying to destroy the Christian faith and belief in God. They never come to the defence of the church or the teachings of Christ, but look for the opportunity to bring the church down or to spread lies about religion, Christ, and the church."

"As to when a person departs from this earth is God's prerogative, not that of mans."

Peter's criticism of and opposition to euthanasia was reported widely and in many countries throughout the world.

His criticism gained momentum and was raised at the board meeting of the Dominium Group.

Euthanasia is one of the principal policies of the Dominium Group, as they need to be established this before branching off to other areas. Their intention is to eliminate the disabled and, maybe later, older adults. All those that are a cost or burden on society or those who oppose the principles of the Dominium Group should be eliminated. If this was done, then fewer taxes would need to be paid to governments, allowing greater wealth to be accumulated. Why should people earn money to pay for those who cannot fend for themselves? To declare we are a better society if we look after those less privileged than ourselves is contrary to the principles of the Dominium Group, who believes no one should have to look after their fellow man or love their neighbour.

The Dominium Group also took these principals through the second world war when they assisted Germany to murder Jews in the gas chambers. They recalled, God wanted Israel to be his people, and fear that he may again take this view. They, therefore, had tried over time to eliminate the Jews. Again, if euthanasia laws were in place, what would prevent them from passing laws to euthanize an entire race of people? All they would have to do is convince a nation that this was in their best interest, and it would be the law. You only needed the majority to agree, and this could be arranged by some payment scheme for the individual's vote.

There would be no end to their ability to eliminate the undesirables. Deserted mothers and children who had to be paid a pension would eventually also fall under these laws, as these people were a burden on society, as were the disabled, according to the Dominium Group.

It was agreed at the meeting that Peter should be eliminated, as he has become too vocal in his opposition to euthanasia and to abortion, two key principles supported by the Dominium Group. The religious members of the group also noted that the Archdeacon had not dismissed Peter and had not done what they ordered him to do. They considered he was not up to the task and that they would need a new archdeacon to run the church. There was also a notation made that Vince Marconi was seen with Peter and could present an opposition to the Dominium Group in the future, once Peter and the Archdeacon were eliminated. It was agreed that he, too, should follow the fate of the other two.

The chairman of the meeting noted that, in the past, they had to crucify Christ along with two thieves who were elements of the underworld. Now they again have an archdeacon and two former criminals who ran brothels and nightclubs and earned their money from extortion and bribery. They gave the order to eliminate the three.

CHAPTER 38

V INCE WAS BACK ON HIS farm when he received a telephone call from a friend in the underworld who advised him that a contract had been put out on him and two other religious ministers for immediate extermination.

Vince concluded the conversation and immediately phoned Peter and advised him of the situation and that he was returning to the unit to ensure they all stayed together and were alive.

Peter telephoned the Archdeacon and informed him of the contracts and advised him to be extremely careful, especially in open spaces. The Archdeacon said he was not scared, nor felt intimidated or threatened. He realised that with his failing memory that he would not be much of a loss if killed, but Peter and Vince were different, as they actively served the Lord. He concluded his discussion with Peter by saying, 'It shall be done as God wills it.'

The Dominium Group stayed in America longer than they had expected, formulating their policy on major events throughout the world. The matter of Brexit took more time than originally planned, and it was agreed two of their members would visit the prime minister in England and advise him of their requirements as to Scotland and Ireland and as to their schedule of England's departure from the European Union.

They agreed that two of their members would fly immediately to England and would report back to the group in a month's time. It was also agreed that they would first fly to Australia and meet with the prime minister to advise of the group's requirements regarding the bushfire relief packages before flying to London. They flew to Canberra, Australia, and discreetly met with the prime minister at his residence, where a heated discussion was had about farm relief and infrastructure.

The prime minister declared that the group's policies were making his government look like fools in that they seemed inactive and directionless. They, the government, would have to do something; otherwise, the people will lose faith in his government and vote them out at the next election.

The group pointed out that it was they who decided which way the election went and not the voters. Also, they reminded the prime minister that there had been a revolving door lately of Prime Ministers being voted out of office, and he would join them if he did not toe the line as they had directed.

They held discussions with the Australian government regarding bushfire relief, budget surplus, and Indonesia. The government was again advised that it should not agree to the building of any new dams or the piping of water from the north to the centre of Australia. The group was adamant that they did not want this to occur, as they had other plans for the centre of Australia to become either a nuclear dumping area or a missile testing range for military hardware. They would decide on economic grounds as it affected the wealth of most of its members. They did not care what benefits would be derived by farmers and the nation. What only interested them was what effect it had on their wealth.

The meeting ended abruptly, as they had to board a flight to Sydney and connect to an international flight to London.

They got to the airport late but telephoned ahead for the flight to be delayed for take-off. Those passengers that were waiting to board their flight were told that a minor maintenance problem was encountered that would delay their flight by about thirty minutes. They got to the airport and boarded their domestic flight to Sydney, and could connect with their flight to London via Singapore.

They boarded their flight and settled down, knowing that a meeting would be arranged by the chairman of the group and that their job was to seek assurance from the prime minister that their demands would be implemented. They knew the prime minister would not want to have another election, as they just had one, which they won convincingly. The opposition leader would not agree to their demands and lost the election, forcing him to resign and a new leader appointed. They had already nominated who the new leader was to be, and allowed the democratic process to be followed, so legitimacy was seen to have happened. Their nominated person would finally be voted in and do as instructed.

The plane was cruising along at thirty-five thousand feet flying over Iran when, suddenly, an almighty explosion occurred in the fuselage's midsection, ripping the plane into two. Bodies were sucked out of the plane along with hand baggage and plane seats. The two sections of the fuselage spun spirally on fire and finally crashed to earth, leaving two separate sections in deep holes.

An hour later, reporters were on the scene stating there were no survivors, declaring it was a tragedy caused by mechanical fault of the plane. Footage of the incident showed someone had fired a missile at the commercial airline. The Iranians were forced by public pressure to confirm their military thought it was an American spy drone flying over their territory and they were determined to destroy it. They declared it was an accident.

The chairman of the Dominium Group, upon hearing of the incident, authorised America to place further sanctions on Iran for its destruction of innocent lives and especially two of its members.

The group held an emergency meeting in New York, agreeing to replace the Iranian general that authorised the shooting down of the plane and dispatching a further two members to London to speak to the prime minister regarding Brexit. It was further agreed that the chairman would approach two billionaires that came to the group's attention some months earlier, to see if they were interested in joining their group and to evaluate whether they could be trusted to keep secret the group's identity.

CHAPTER 39

THE ARCHDEACON WAS ATTENDING MASS in St Nicholas. There was a full church, and two other ministers assisted him. He sat down as one minister rose and walked over to the centre stage and placed his Bible on the lectern and began reading a section of the Bible. The congregation were listening attentively as to what was being said.

Unknown to the congregation, a large van stopped outside of the church and waited. It stood in a no-parking zone, but the driver did not care that he was illegally standing there. The front of the church was a no-parking zone to allow a hearse to offload coffins for a funeral or to collect them after a service for burial.

There were six men inside the van, all dressed in military garments with automatic rifles and ammunition belts over their shoulders. They were there to shoot the Archdeacon and some of his congregation, so it did not look like an assignation but a terrorist killing of innocent church parishioners. They waited for a moment to ensure that the Mass was well and truly on its way.

As they sat there, they could hear singing from the church and felt their van shake, thinking it had to do with the singing. Suddenly, their van was hoisted up, and with water sprouting everywhere around them, they were tossed into the air van, and all, and ended up landing on their roof, with the van crushed by the sudden impact.

The occupants of the church rushed out and could see an enormous hole in the ground with water sprouting from the centre of the hole, with dirt and rocks being tossed into the air and landing some distance down the street. The van was resting on its roof with no sign of any survivors.

One parishioner rang for the police, who turned up within minutes of receiving the phone call. They called for police rescue, who also turned up promptly, and they cut a hole in the van's rear door. They pulled out several men dressed in military uniform with high-powered rifles attached to their chests. The men were rendered unconscious by the van being thrown onto its roof. The police called the Defence Department, who knew nothing about the men but agreed to investigate the matter to see why they were there. Military police arrived quickly on the scene and took possession of the rifles and ammunition and noted there were hand grenades in the van. For safety reasons, the military police also took these.

The Water Board turned up and located the master switch and, with some effort, turned the water off. They arranged for a crew to work to repair the burst pipe, which carried the city water to a distribution station. The pipe was a large concrete pressure pipe and would require heavy machinery to dig it out and replace it with a new one. The team would have to work a full ten hours to repair the damage to the pipe and road.

The men, once rendered unarmed, were taken by ambulance to hospital for examination with a police escort and military police backup. After being medically examined and treated for concussion, they were placed in cells at the local police station. The vehicle was compounded and held for examination, and it was noted that it was registered with the defence force.

The men appeared before the court, and they were represented by lawyers who immediately asked for bail, which was refused. The prosecutor argued the men were thought to be terrorists, as they were armed in military-style outfits, yet not part of the defence force, and were carrying powerful weapons. Documents found at the scene showed the Archdeacon was to be killed along with his parishioners, which is what a terrorist group would do. The military police also objected to their release, as there was no sign of who they were and where they came from. The men were not cooperating with authorities and refused to answer questions asked of them. The van was from an army base but was not reported missing, which shows they were assisted by personnel in the military.

The Archdeacon could see what the intention of the men were and thanked God for protecting him and the congregation from the murderous actions of the men. It was God who used the damaged pipe to his advantage in preventing the men from carrying out their plan.

CHAPTER 40

ETER AND VINCE WERE AT the hospital paying their respects to an
old friend (who was part of their gang in the old days) who was
in palliative care, dying from cancer. The doctors had advised them
that their friend only had a few days left before death.

They were reminiscing about the good old days and how life was
easier than, compared to now, with the high-tech computer and whizz-
kids scamming and defrauding online.

Their friend said he had several friends visit him over the last
week, and a few had mentioned that Peter and Vince they had upset
the Dominium Group, and because of this, they had contracts taken
out on them. Their friend warned them to be very careful, as one of
their own men was informing the group about their movements and
was receiving a considerable sum of money to do this.

Their friend had been a member of the underworld for most of
his life and, like most people in the family, only knew about money,
and tried to get as much of it as he could during his lifetime.

Peter sat there thinking what a waste of a life securing vast amounts
of wealth through lying and cheating, and he could not take a cent
with him. A good life on earth will now end up in a thousand years
in hell with his master, Lucifer.

The two stayed for a while and then left their friend after doctors
advised them to leave as their friend was too tired and needed his rest.

They walked down the corridor and were confronted by a member
of their congregation asking Peter to say a prayer over his wife who

had breast cancer, which was diagnosed that day when she collapsed at home and was brought into hospital by ambulance. The women had three children; the oldest, fifteen, and the youngest, four.

Her husband was in shock and kept saying to Peter, 'How can God do this to us? What have we done to be punished like this?' His wife was trying to stop him from being silly, yet he took it that God was punishing him for something through his wife's illness, and he could not understand why. He kept repeating, "What have they done to have her taken from him?"

Peter tried to reason with the man, but he was too emotional, and asked him to come and see him at the church tomorrow and they would talk, or if that was not convenient, when his wife came out of the hospital.

She thanked Peter, and he and Vince stepped out of the room and continued their walk to their car.

Vince stayed close to Peter, knowing that they will attempt to collect on the contract that was put out by the Dominium Group. Vince was always armed, and so was Peter, and both men made sure they took extra care when crossing the street or at major intersections.

Peter and Vince stopped off and get a bite to eat on their way home and pulled into a restaurant, with Vince's men following them in another vehicle. They walked through the restaurant to the fresco settings outside under the umbrellas and ordered a quick meal of chicken and chips when they noticed a van pull up outside and a second vehicle pull up behind it.

They realised that this may be an attempt on their lives, so Vince signalled for the men to spread out around the two vehicles to make sure that they were not directly in the line of fire. The men moved away from the restaurant near the vehicles but were still on the footpath and not on the road, ready to draw their guns should it be needed.

No one came out of the vehicles, which made the men suspicious as to what was happening. The men stood waiting when they noticed the road opened, and the vehicles sank into a hole, which seemed to get bigger by the minute.

The men in the vehicles sat there for a few minutes, not realising what was happening to the road below their vehicles. As they sank further, they realised that something was not going to plan. Then the hole opened further, dragging them deeper and deeper into the hole.

They tried to open the doors of the vehicle but could not, as by that time they were too deep in the hole and sinking further and further in. They tried to open their windows, but the engine was off and, therefore, the electrical windows would not work.

One man inside pulled out his gun and shot through the window, causing it to shatter. He tried to get out but got stuck as the vehicle sank further and further into the hole until finally both vehicles sank so deep that they could not be seen, and even the roof of the vehicles was below the surface.

The whole thing took everyone by surprise, even Peter and Vince, who came out of the restaurant to see for themselves as to what was happening. Eventually, someone called the police, who turned up within minutes of receiving the call. They in turn called in their rescue squad, who responded quickly but could do nothing to help, as they could not understand what had happened to that section of the road, which by now had spread to both sides, forcing police to block entry to the area.

The hole became bigger and deeper, opening a large crevice that ended up deeper as time went on. Engineers were brought in and geologists from the university, who described this as a sinkhole and declared it too dangerous to rescue the men until the mud was pumped out of the hole.

Over the next fortnight, a team of men pumped out the liquid mud and transported it to a landfill in one of the open cut mines. The men eventually could scale down to where the two vehicles were and, with an aid of a large crane, could pull the vehicles out of the sinkhole. The mud had penetrated the van, suffocating all the occupants comprising six men. Each was dressed in suits and carried firearms, and some had automatic machine guns.

The occupants of the second vehicle also suffocated, and it was noted they also had weapons and wore suits, showing they were part of a professional group out to eliminate someone but did not get the chance to do so.

The police, who took the names of those present and witnessed the catastrophe, believed that the men were tipped off by someone in Vince's group as to the location of Peter and Vince and were there to kill the two men. It was an act of God that they were prevented from fulfilling their contract.

Peter and Vince thanked the Lord for His protection and mercy and knew He was ensuring their safety.

CHAPTER 41

THE DOMINIUM GROUP ARRANGED FOR its members to meet in Singapore to discuss several issues and to be briefed as to what had happened about the elimination of the three who had contracts placed on them.

They were briefed as to the meeting with the British prime minister and his win at the election recently held. They also were advised of the Brexit intended timetable and agreed to allow the devised plan to take its course.

They were advised of the European Union and its stand on Britain leaving the Eu and the consequence this may have on their fortunes. It was agreed that by Britain leaving the Eu, they would benefit substantially in the long run and that the course established by them should be followed. They noted the strength of the Sterling currency since the election and the effect this had on their individual wealth.

They were briefed as to what had happened regarding the attempt to eliminate the three whom they had issued contracts on. They were advised of the events that transpired in trying to kill each of the three and that it was felt that they had divine protection and that anyone who tried to take their lives will themselves be killed. This caused the chairman to become furious, and he started to rant and rave abuses against those believing divine power and God. He made it clear he wanted them dead, and this was to be done before the next meeting no matter how many resources it took. On this earth, it was as he commanded and not God, so these three were to be eliminated to prove who was in charge.

The meeting continued for another hour where members discussed what was happening in the Soviet Union and China and noted China still refused to cooperate with the group. Attempts to buy their way with influential people in authority were confronted with their head of the Asian area being arrested and shot as traitors of the state in trying to buy information from members of the Congress. They considered the benefit of sending in a team of assassins to bring in a new leader to control the People's Congress, but waited a while to see what they agreed to accept. China would not stand in their way of world dominance.

The Soviets also would not cooperate with the Dominium Group, and it was considered a lesson should be taught to them; possibly damage to their gas pipeline to Europe would be required to prove who was in control.

It was finally decided that while that would damage the Soviets economically, it wouldn't do the trick, and, therefore, they needed something that would draw world attention onto the Soviet Union and cause nations to not to trade or have any dealings with the Soviets. A plan was conceived and put into action.

Three weeks later, the world was horrified to hear that a Russian missile had shot down a commercial airline over Hungary, killing all passengers and crew.

The Russian parliament was horrified and in disbelief that anyone in the Russian hierarchy would allow such an act. The president denied he had anything to do with it and that it was an unfortunate act in that the commercial airline was taken to be a military aeroplane spying on the terrain. During the investigation, certain men in the military were implicated and found to have fled with substantial sums of money.

The world did not believe the Soviet president had nothing to do with the grounding of the airline, and sanctions were put on the Soviet Union for its total disregard for the life of others.

The Soviets learnt their lesson and fell into line, agreeing with the decision of the Dominium Group.

The Chinese refused to buckle at the knees and made it clear they would not be intimidated by the Dominium Group and would arrest any of their members found trying to buy their way or blackmail any of its officials.

CHAPTER 42

PETER KNEW THE DOMINIUM GROUP would not leave him alone, but still went about his business to ensure his duty as a minister was not affected by them. He believed in God and therefore, did not fear the group.

He had learnt to have faith in the Lord, and it would be the Lord's decision when he was to leave this earth and not the Dominium Group's decision.

That morning, he walked to the café, as he had been housebound for a while and wanted a bit of space and fresh air. He felt he needed a coffee and to get some exercises. He walked past a girl who was facing down the street as to not allow Peter to see her totally, face on. As he passed her, she immediately confronted him, holding a knife in her hand, demanding his mobile phone and wallet. He advised her he had neither on him, but she did not believe him. She again threatened him and demanded he hand over his wallet or she would put the knife into him. At that point, another young girl came up to assist her, and she was also armed with a knife, and both were determined to get something from Peter. He again said all that he had with him was enough to buy a cup of coffee. They did not believe him, and with that, one of them made a lunge at Peter, trying to stick the knife into his torso.

Peter immediately reacted by grabbing the first girl's arm and punching her straight in the face, sending her to the ground. The second girl also made a lunge at Peter, and again he put a boot straight into her gut, sending her flying. He walked up to them and disarmed both and grabbed them by the neck and dragged them to a bench nearby and prompted them up on the bench. Both girls tried to make a run for it, and Peter immediately hit them, forcing them to fall unconscious on the ground.

He sat them on the bench again, and as they came to, he asked them questions about themselves. They tried to rob him so they could get money for drugs. This and prostitution were the ways the girls fed their habits. They have been on the streets for the last three years, abandoned by their family, who were also drug addicts. While the girls were talking to Peter, two other girls came up to them and asked if they were all right. They were signalling for them to make a run for it, but the two stayed, so the others stayed to help them if this was required.

The girls seemed to have a low opinion of themselves, and society had made it clear that they should be locked up in jail rather than helped. Society made them feel abandoned, and so they moved to a life that they could control and foster, as this to them was all that life could offer.

Peter talked to them and found out that the girls were a tough breed and could defend themselves when in a pack, which is how they normally operate. Another two girls joined the group, which would mean that Peter would have a difficult time defending himself against eight girls who were armed with knives. He thought the best way to prevent himself from being injured was to convince some girls to move back into society.

Peter asked, 'Are any of you girls Christians? Do any of you believe in God?'

The first girl replied, 'Are you joking? We all have heard of God, and some believed in Him in the past, but look at us. Do you really think God would want to know us? We have nothing other than what we steal. With the money, we buy drugs to blank out from our minds that we are worthless on this earth and must live this way until death. We are not rich, nor are we educated. Most of us can't even read or write. Most of us in our own way have prayed for help, but we got nothing from God, just the continuation of the same.'

Peter said, 'Girls, I am a minister at St Nicholas. I would like to extend a handout to you girls and ask that you come to my church today at four o'clock, and we can talk about your situation. I will arrange for a soup kitchen to be there, and we have facilities where you can shower and get fresh clothes from one of our charities. The only thing you will have to do is listen to one of my sermons, as I will try to clarify some misgivings you have raised and set the records straight. So can we say we have a deal?'

The first girl discussed it with the others, and they all agreed to go, as they were going to have a meal, which a lot of them hadn't had for a while. Some were interested in showering and getting out of their dirty clothes.

Peter left the girls and walked back to the church when one girl yelled out to him, 'not that way! They will be waiting for you.'

Peter asked, 'Who will be waiting for me?'

The girl replied, 'You were being followed by two men in a car when you came here. We know these men, and they are hit men. It looks as if you are a target. Go the long way around and you will avoid them.'

Peter said, 'Thank you.'

Peter walked back to the church, checking to see if they followed him. He immediately called his group of church workers, who were willing to help, and several charities who made clothing available should the girls take the offer of a shower and change of clothes.

At four o'clock, Peter was in his church, and a group of ten girls came in and were immediately introduced to the helpers and were given a meal, and some took the offer, having a shower and change of clothes. As time went by, more girls came, and the group swelled to twenty-five, stretching the resources of the charities and workers that were there to help.

After everyone had dinner, shower, and got a change of clothes, they settled down in the pews of the church to hear what Peter had to say.

Peter said, 'I want to address some issues some of you raised this morning. To answer your questions, I must go back to the beginning of Creation. Originally, God created angels with their full powers given to them by God from the start. Angels were created complete and did not grow to maturity but stayed the way they were created. Some of these angels wanted a different life to the one God had planned for them, and they sinned against God. Their leader was Lucifer, and they wanted to replace the Creator with either Lucifer himself or an alternative creation of theirs. God would not agree with them and ended up booting them out of heaven, and they took occupancy on earth where Lucifer now rules.'

'God created the heavens and earth. He also created mankind. The difference now is that He has not created mankind with all the features he will eventually secure and all the powers that he will eventually gain over several lifetimes. Here on earth, it is intended that mankind earns what God has offered him as outlined in the bible.

'The concept now adopted by God is that you will have to earn the powers He can give you, and only those souls who show they believe in Him and have faith in Him will develop and go on to the next life and further training.'

'Like angels, we will never be given mystical powers, but will have to call upon God and do things in His name. We will never be a God or achieve what He has but will do what He can do only in His name.'

'The first thing to note is that you can do nothing by yourself. Yes, you can construct and build things, but out of materials supplied by the Lord. We use His raw minerals out of the earth to make steel and timber from His forests to make houses and furniture, but we do not make these raw materials. It is God who provides these basic raw materials along with the sun and rain so we can do the things we desire.'

'Mankind, in his stupidity, believes in his own greatness without realising or recognising that what we have achieved is to use God's knowledge, which is given to us along with His natural wealth, which He created.'

'Jesus often said you can move mountains if you have faith, but as mankind, we know the reality is we cannot do these things except in the name of the Father. Jesus Himself did nothing on this earth. He was not a magician. He did not heal the blind or heal the sick in His own right. He did it in "the name of the Father", and like Him, if you were to do something or ask for something, it can only be given or done in the name of the Father.'

'So, we are placed on this earth under God's direction to serve Him, while He trains us to have faith in Him. You are given a life and expected to seek His support to strive and achieve what He has planned for you. It is He who directs whether you are to be a teacher, a lawyer, or a sheet metal worker.'

'Unfortunately, most people do not realise this or seek God's help in doing what He wants of them. They are their own person and go about doing what they want to achieve, not what God has planned for them. Some develop an internal conflict and end up not liking the job they are in. Others go for the money, the material things of this world, and leave God out of their lives. Without God, you are like a ship without a rudder and drift endlessly until death, and then you leave this world with nothing.'

'If you do not seek God's help in achieving what He has in mind for you, then you will sell yourself short, as you will not achieve your full potential.'

'Those that believe in God go through a lifetime of training, which is emotional and heartbreaking at times. The first and foremost thing that you are taught is to have faith in God. This is the first lifetime lesson and the only one that is to be passed on to us on this earth and in this lifetime.'

'To show you how much faith you have in God, He puts you through a series of tests called trials, starting from small trials to eventually a heartbreaking trail. As you go through life, the trials become harder to accept, and most people question the existence of Christ or God or question the word of God or the Truth of the Bible.'

'The Bible tells you the hardships that Christians had gone through and will go through. Yet, mankind still questions the actions of God when something goes wrong. For instance, should one of you girls die through someone defending themselves when you attack them, you will immediately say God did not protect her and therefore He is not looking after her. Yet it may be God's way of saying her time was up and she is being recalled back home, but because you as a group would have lost one of your own, you will turn against God rather than saying, 'I don't understand why her life was taken but have faith in God that He has taken the best course of action and done what the

Lord desires.' God will always act in your best interest. It sometimes takes a bit of patience before God's plan is revealed to you.'

'The last test in a Christian's life is soul-searching, and you can only accept what God has done by reflecting on other trials you have experienced and calling upon the faith you have in God. If this faith is weak and built on sand, then you will at this moment reject Christ and, like Peter, question or deny Jesus. If it is on solid rock, you will be hurt, but accept the fact that God may do what He has done, and it is not up to you to question his judgement.'

'Throughout your trials, you may reject God and take the position of Lucifer. You can reject eternal life, which God offers you, and take up the life that most have taken up in this world based on 'me' and 'materialism'. Here, most strive for an alternative God based on splendid houses and furniture, modern cars, and large bank accounts. If the individual has them, the way they were acquired is irrelevant. For most, these are the only things that count in life, not a God that they cannot physically see, even though He stands in front of them. These people tend to look down on the poor and needy and feel they should be able to achieve the things they have gained or achieved in their lifetime — namely, follow corrupt and dishonest ways that suit their needs.'

'To sum up, girls, you have been placed on this earth to serve God and gain faith in Him. What you get for this is not a big house or car but the promise of eternal life and can walk with Him, which brings joy to your spirit and a sense of purpose to your life on this earth. Currently, most of you have been forced out of your homes by parents to live a life that you seek to change but cannot owing to the lack of opportunity. I would ask you to consider what God offers and accept Him as your Lord and allow Him to use you for His purpose and not for what Satan has in mind for you.'

'Those of you who want to leave the streets and start a new life, then to you I say it will not be easy, but it will be rewarding. We have people, as you can see, that can help you and try to put you back on your feet. We have a group of young people like yourselves that have had it tough that can act as mentors for you and help you in trying to get back on your feet. We will put you with families who will try to support you in getting a job or be trained to fill one and to help you back into a Christian community.'

'To those who want to stay on the streets, we have rehab facilities that you can avail yourself of, and we can offer you a hot meal in the afternoon and somewhere to shower and wash your clothes. We also can offer help should you want to talk to me or any of the other social worker here that you have met today.'

The group broke up with some girls leaving immediately, while others came to God and asked for the church's help to get their lives back on track.

CHAPTER 43

EASTER WAS APPROACHING, AND THE Archdeacon decided he would officiate at St Nicholas on Good Friday, as his church was being renovated and would be closed that month. He contacted Peter and advised him he will officiate over the service on Good Friday and Peter would assist him. This was a busy period, and it was good to get some help, especially from someone as senior as the Archdeacon.

Peter thought about it and rang the Archdeacon, advising that his church at St Nicholas could only hold a third of the congregation that the Archdeacon's church held and that a lot of patrons would miss out on such an important day. He recommended the service be held outdoors, allowing a crowd of, say, five thousand to attend. They discussed the idea and the venue, and they agreed the Archdeacon would consider the suggestion and come back to Peter in a day or two.

The Archdeacon called in his senior ministers and asked their opinion of the proposal, and everyone agreed it would be a great idea, allowing a pageantry of the Crucifixion to take place and Christ's washing of the feet. The Department of Meteorology was contacted to see what the forecast for Good Friday was, and it was found to be dry and cool. It was agreed that all the ministers would attend and assist the Archdeacon in the service to ensure it was a memorable one.

The Dominium Group heard of the Archdeacon's plans and agreed that it would be an opportune time to take out all three at the one time. It would prove who was running the show, and that Lucifer had the resources to ensure they carried the directives out without delay and hindrance.

The Group, through their contacts, found out that there were two ministers who held different views from that held by the Archdeacon, and they preached against God's word.

They set up a meeting with the ministers and agreed to ensure one of them would become Archdeacon and the other his deputy, and each would receive substantial payment if they cooperated with the Group. They agreed they would pass on to the Group the details of what and when things were to happen, and the Group would decide how the three were to be dealt with.

First, the Archdeacon or Peter would have to seek council approval to allow the grounds of the sports auditorium to be used, and a fee agreed upon. The police had to be contacted to ensure they managed the crowds, and the parking was orderly. The audio equipment had to be managed to ensure the service and they could hear prayers. All was arranged, and a detailed itinerary was sent back to the Dominium Group by their spies, the two ministers.

As agreed, the ministers were to be paid three hundred thousand dollars each once they disclosed the detailed itinerary. From there, it would be possible to work out where the Archdeacon and Peter would be on Good Friday.

The Dominium Group, upon getting the itinerary, immediately called a meeting of their team that was to handle the assassinations. The two options were to either plant a bomb under the stage, set to go off remotely, or have them shot by long-range shooters. The bomb idea was not totally supported, as some of the Dominium Group's own contacts were going to be there, and they may be on stage at that time when the bomb goes off, which would kill them as well as the targets.

It was agreed the best way would be to assassinate them by using sharpshooters from a building or a rooftop, and this would leave no misunderstanding that the Group always took care of those who want to oppose them. They sought the best shooters and paid them to do the job. They were brought in and given whatever they needed. They established the plan that as soon as they made the hit, the sharpshooter would, with in an hour of the killings, be flown out of the country on a commercial flight.

All was revealed to the sharpshooters, including the identification of the garments that were to be worn by the Archdeacon, Peter, and the various other ministers that would be on stage.

The Easter service was publicised extensively, and a replica was made of the cross, and large screens were installed to enable the congregation to view what was happening from several strategic points.

The big day came, and Peter and the other ministers were ready, as was the Archdeacon, who had come a day earlier and lived at the church in his private quarters. The plan was for Peter and the Archdeacon to be driven to the grounds by a hired car, and both would change into their ceremonial garments once there.

The garments and all the outfits were to be brought over by the two ministers who were to assist the Archdeacon. These were the same ones who sold the information to the Dominion Group and were promised the Archdeacon's job should something happen to the Archdeacon.

The day called for several Masses to be held to enable as many people as possible to receive the Lord's blessing. There were to be three sessions throughout the day, the first starting at ten in the morning.

There was a long-standing principle within the church that Good Friday was a special day, and if for whatever reason the ceremony was disrupted by something happening to those who were to officiate over the ceremony, then the next two most senior ministers would step up and fill in for those who could not attend.

Peter and the Archdeacon got into their hired car, which was chauffeur driven, as parking was not guaranteed at the grounds, and they did not want to lose time trying to find a parking place and miss the ceremony.

As they were driving through a tree-shrouded street, a large wind blew up, toppling a tree right on the bonnet of their car and stopping traffic from getting through. Frantic residences, seeing what had happened, rang the police and ambulance, fearing someone might have been killed under the tree.

The police arrived, followed by the rescue squad, and all got to work with their chainsaws, cutting the tree from the car's bonnet, trying to see if anyone had been injured. After about ten minutes, they could move the logs cut from the tree and pile them on the footpath. The paramedics opened the door of the vehicle and found that a large branch had crushed through the roof of the vehicle, killing the driver, and hitting both the Archdeacon and Peter in the head. Both were bleeding from the forehead, and the Archdeacon's leg was broken, partly impaled by a branch.

They pulled the men out of the car unconscious and placed them in separate ambulances, and rushed them to hospital for X-ray and examination. The driver was finally freed after his body was cut out of the tree that landed on him.

At the showground, the ministers were waiting for the Archdeacon and Peter and were unaware as to what had happened to them. As the time drew near, it became apparent that something had gone wrong, and the substitution principle was to apply. The two ministers removed their garments and were assisted to put on the robes that the Archdeacon and Peter would have worn in the ceremony.

The ceremony began five minutes later with the deep emotional re-enactment of the walk by Jesus carrying his cross until they reached the stage, which was to substitute for Golgotha or Calvary.

Some ministers dressed in traditional robes to represent the Pharisees, while others were dressed as Roman soldiers, and were traditional Jewish men and women. The two ministers, in substitute for those injured, played out their part, and all was proceeding well when suddenly, two enormous bangs rang out, and the two ministers fell to the stage. No one moved, as they thought this was part of the ceremony until someone ran onto the stage and kneeled over the ministers lying on the stage and yelled out, 'They have been shot!' Police that were on hand in the area immediately ran to where the men laid. They turned the men over and were astonished to see that they shot each through the head.

They kept the Archdeacon and Peter in hospital for three days and allowed them to go home once they carried out the last tests. They were told on the second day as to what had happened at the pageantry but could not understand why the two ministers were shot dead. Vince, who had heard what had happened, came to watch guard over the two men, fearing there might be a second attempt on their lives.

He was told through a good source that the other two ministers had sold out the Archdeacon and Peter and, for their cooperation, were promised promotions, but he did not understand why the Group had eliminated them. He told the Archdeacon and Peter what he knew, and they could pin it down to God's justice for an act of portrayal by Judas.

The three left the hospital and went to Vince's apartment, saying a prayer to God, thanking Him for looking after them.

CHAPTER 44

THE DOMINIUM GROUP HELD ITS meeting in Geneva, and the first thing on the agenda was China and the lack of success in gaining a foothold there. It was agreed that they should change the government there, and since the election had recently been held, there was only one way to do this, and that was by elimination.

The second thing on the agenda was the elimination of Peter and the Archdeacon. They congratulated their men for their efforts and moved on to the next matter on the agenda.

About an hour later, they were advised that the shooters had shot the wrong men at the Easter Pageantry, and, in fact, they had shot the men that were feeding them information behind the Archdeacon's back, the ones they had paid off.

The chairman was furious and looked at those attending the meeting in disbelief. 'Are you all a bunch of f—— fools? You kill the men who provided us with the information that no one else would, and the ones we wanted eliminated are still alive. Can no one attend to a simple job? Now, no one will provide us with information for fear we are going to kill them so they don't get to claim the money.'

The chairman walked out of the room but was blocked by another man standing in front of the door. Someone that just appeared out of nowhere. The chairman looked worried, staring at the man in the doorway.

The chairman said, 'What are you doing here? You said men had a free choice on this earth and could do whatever they chose to do.

They are following me and want nothing to do with you. I am king on this earth, not you. I decide what happens on earth.'

God said, 'You are as corrupt now as you were when I threw you out of heaven onto this earth. Over the centuries, I allowed you to sift mankind to see which ones had faith in me and which should follow you to a life in hell. You did not create this world, I did, and it is not yours, nor the people created yours. If they choose to follow you, then that is their right, which I have given them. They will, at the end of time, join you in hell.'

'The day of my coming is near. You have witnessed the earthquakes throughout the world, the fires as noted recently in California, Turkey, New Zealand, and Australia and other countries. Share markets have collapsed around the world, reducing your wealth. Diseases never known to mankind have manifested themselves and spread to all countries on this earth. These are the signs I have told you in the Bible are the beginning of the end.

'Your men, sit in judgement and think you rule the world through your wealth. You buy influence and bribe those who have bowed before your chairman, Lucifer. You and they will soon see death and will be judged as your chairman was. None of you will see the sun rise again, and your wealth will be of little benefit to you in the future life.

'I will save those that I have protected, and your men will join you in hell.'

They looked, and there was no one there.

The men got worried, especially the fact that they were told they would not see the sun rise again. The chairman assured them they were well protected, and this was an idle threat, which he could take care of, as he controlled this earth. He was the supreme ruler here, not God.

Suddenly, through the midst of the beaming sun came a great burst of lightning that hit the building where they were meeting. The roof flew off. The large glass panels in the front shattered with an explosive force, and the table where they were sitting split in half, splintering to the floor, causing everyone to jump to their feet to prevent being pushed under the debris. Then a further explosion occurred from pipes leaking gas, and flames roared through the insides of the building, scorching all those inside. Some tried to run to the front door, but it was locked from the inside, and the heat prevented anyone from undoing the lock. Some tried and screamed as they burned their hands to the bone. Everything inside the building was on fire, and the fire consumed all occupants inside, except one.

As the flames consumed the members of the Dominium Group, one figure walked out of the building with ease, unscorched and uninjured, by walking through a wall. Once clear of the building, he turned and looked at it for a minute, seeing it was engulfed in flames, and then walked to his car and drove off, leaving all those behind, as he knew he would see them next in hell. Their lives had ended.

Lucifer was determined to prove his point that he ruled the earth and not God and that he was to say what was to happen on earth. He was determined to prove his point by taking control of the assassination of the three men himself. He could not leave it to others, as they were incapable of confronting God and would, if they knew the truth, turn and follow Jesus rather than support Lucifer's army.

He decided it was a simple plan that was needed — namely, confront them and kill them—and if witnesses were there, the men who did it would be arrested and put on trial. If no one saw the incident, then they would walk away from it.

Lucifer flew to his headquarters and sought and hired the men necessary to do the killing. Money was no problem, as he had billions stashed away and could afford whatever the price was. He decided a team of five was all that was needed and got a team of killers who had spent time in jail for their crimes.

He made it clear what he wanted and was not prepared to accept excuses. He knew the men chosen could do the job and could see they were corrupt and would do anything for money.

It was decided the first person to be eliminated was Peter, as he would be the easiest to locate. They knew his routine in church, so it would be easy to shoot him either as he walked to the church or while he was attending to Mass. The plan was for the killing to take place the next morning. The men assured their boss that he did not have to be present, as they could quite handle the job on their own, without a nursemaid.

CHAPTER 45

THE GIRLS IN THE STREET knew something was going on, as they heard some hired guns were brought in from out of town and they were staying at a B & B outside of town. The place was a prestigious house with a pool, a high wrought-iron fence, and garages that could cater to five cars.

The men wore suits, which showed they were highly paid for the work they did. The girls saw they had guns under their jackets, which showed they were not the type that could be messed around with. The girls followed them to see where they went to. That evening, the men went to an expensive restaurant and, after a few drinks, talked about the job and kept referring to the minister going to heaven on a one-way trip. This was relayed to the girls by the waitresses at the restaurant, and a picture emerged as to what they intended to do. The minister was Peter, and they were here to kill him, possibly tomorrow at Mass.

This was the girls' territory, and no one could come in and do what they wanted to do without their approval. The girls decided it was useless to get the police involved, as no doubt they have been paid off to turn a blind eye as to what the men intended on doing. A plan was agreed to, where they decided the best way to stop the thugs was to eliminate them one by one.

The girls went to the local vet surgery and discreetly borrowed the vet's rifle and tranquilliser darts. One girl was positioned on the roof of the building opposite the church, while another shooter was positioned on another building next to the first shooter. Each of the shooters had a spotter, who was there to look out for anyone that may try to disrupt their plans. They armed each with a gun and had a bag of ammunition.

The plan called for four of the girls to be present while dressed in short skirts, and their job was to stand at the entrance to the church and hold back each of the men so the shooter could fix on their target and shoot a dart into them. The tranquilizers used were to take immediate effect, and the girls doubled the dose to ensure the men did not wake up quickly.

There were five other girls positioned near the church to drag the men away so they could be dealt with later. They positioned other girls in strategic positions near the church to ensure that should all fail; they were to shoot the men before they got into the church. The next morning, the girls positioned themselves as planned and waited. At ten in the morning, two cars pulled up outside the church, and the five men got out. They looked around and saw that no one was around. They opened the boot of their cars and took out rifles and walked up to the church.

Two of the girls moved up to the men, who stopped in their tracks staring at them in their short skirts. The shooters took aim and fired. Two men fell to the ground unnoticed by the other three men. Two other girls moved to distract the other men, but one of them was not interested and continued towards the church. The shooters shot at the two, that stayed to look at the girls. It hit one, while the other moved and avoided the dart. He realised the girls were there to set the men up for a shot and immediately grabbed one girl and held her in front of him while walking backwards towards the church. The other man saw what was happening and grabbed the remaining girl and used her as a shield. The girls hidden away realised the girls were in danger and that the men would not hesitate to shoot them if it would help them. They moved in with guns drawn.

One girl brought the first man down and shot him in the leg, causing him to fall while still holding onto his shield. He drew his gun and put it to the head of the girl he was holding. A shot rang out, and the man fell to the ground, bleeding from the chest. The second man also drew his gun and shot the girl that was being used as hostage, and she fell to the ground bleeding. Two more shots rang out, and the second man fell to the ground, motionless. The last man momentarily stood with his gun drawn. A last shot rang out from the shooter on the roof, and the man fell to the ground. The girls quickly grabbed each of the men and dragged them out of sight into an alley.

Peter finished Mass a few minutes later than usual and walked out of the church to say goodbye to his congregation. He looked around and could see nothing unusual, but was certain he had heard a shot being fired. He got involved in a conversation with one parishioner for about five minutes and then went back inside the church to attend to some duties.

The girls knew they could not leave the men free to go, as they would come back with reinforcements and take them all out. They decided they had to be disposed of, and this was to be done quickly, as they would soon wake up from being sedated. The bodies were searched, and the men's wallets and guns were taken from them before they were loaded into a utility and driven away. With the cars the men came in, the girls drove them near the centre of town and left them there so the hired operators could recover them. They locked the cars and took the keys with them, dumping them into a garbage bin as they passed by one.

The men were taken to a warehouse, given a further dose of tranquiliser, and loaded into a container, which was then loaded on a vessel, which was due to leave port that day. It was arranged for the container to be dumped overboard when the vessel was out on the high seas.

The girls got the men's ID and bank account numbers from their wallets and hacked into their accounts. Each had been paid $1 million for their involvement. All the funds were transferred out of their accounts by several transfers, which could not be traced, leaving fifty dollars in each of their accounts to ensure the accounts were not prematurely closed.

The licences in the wallets were marked with a red cross across their face and were bundled together and sent to the headquarters of the Dominium Group, which, once received, would be a clear sign the men were dead.

The girls sent some of the money to St Nicholas Church to ensure the church continued its good work for the girls on the street, in providing a soup kitchen and a place where they can shower and discuss their problems with community workers. The balance of the money the girls passed on to charities who had, over the years, helped them or would take up their cause when necessary.

CHAPTER 46

THE CHAIRMAN OF THE DOMINIUM Group sat at his desk looking at the list of prospective members he was going to invite to join his prestigious group. His mind moved from the list to wondering what had happened to Peter and why his men were taking so long to do a simple job. His secretary came into his office with the morning mail and placed it on his desk and left.

The chairman looked through the mail and noticed a bundle of cards. He unwrapped them and removed the elastic band that was holding them together. He opened the bundle and read the names on the licence and realised his men were dead and would see him in hell where they could tell him what happened.

He thought to himself how such a simple task could take so long to perform. All he wanted was three people dead. It has never taken this long in the past, so why is it taking so long now? In the past, he merely directed what he wanted done, and there was always someone who would do the job, especially where a lot of money was involved. Why, suddenly, were things going wrong? They have always worked out in the past, even three thousand years ago, when he arranged for Able to be killed. He never had problems with Cane.

He would try again, but this time would start with the killing of the Archdeacon. It was not possible to kill Vince discreetly, as he had good men always around him with guns. In his case, it would be a shoot-out along the highway with possibly a grenade being thrown into the car.

In the Archdeacon's case, he should be shot by a sharpshooter with no problems. The chairman consulted who was available and made the arrangements with payment this time, to be made after confirmation of the death of the Archdeacon. The arrangements were made, and the man dispatched to attend to the contract quickly. The person chosen was a professional and came at a high price.

The shooter arrived at the city where the Archdeacon lived and found out the Archdeacon's routine. He spent a week going over the Archdeacon's calendar and routine, which he put together from public news, and decided the best shot would be as the Archdeacon drove into work in the morning. He was always early, at about eight, and driven in a chauffeur-driven car. The Archdeacon always sat behind the driver's seat and attended to work while being driven in. The shooter decided to do it the next day from a nearby building.

The shooter positioned himself early to ensure he was not seen and was ready should the Archdeacon himself was slightly early. He sat peering through binoculars to see if the Archdeacon was coming. After an hour, he spotted the Archdeacon's car approaching and took his rifle and placed it in position as to where he was going to make the shot. The car drew nearer, and he was ready when a pigeon flew over and landed on the barrel of his rifle. He shook the bird off and refocused the rifle, ready to take the shot. The pigeon flew back and landed on the end of the barrel of the rifle, facing the shooter with his tail over the barrel. The shooter shook the rifle to get the bird off, which he succeeded, but as soon as he looked through the scope, he could only see a white blur. The shooter thought the rifle was out of focus and dialled up and down to get the rifle to focus, but nothing worked. He then pulled the rifle in and saw the bird had crapped on the end of the scope, preventing him from seeing clearly. He would have to abort today's effort and try again tomorrow when he will have his pistol with him so he could shoot the bird if it came back.

The next morning, the shooter was in position with his pistol and a silencer attached to the pistol so he could shoot the bird if it came close to him. He checked his equipment, and everything was ready.

The Archdeacon's vehicle approached, and the shooter took his rifle and focused on the archdeacon so he could deliver the fatal shot.

As the Archdeacon's vehicle approached, a bee flew onto the sights, preventing the shooter from seeing the Archdeacon clearly. He tried to brush the bee away, but it refused to move until he hit it and it fell dead to the ground. As he bent down to see what had happened to the bee, he noticed he was leaning over a wasp nest, and what he thought was a bee was, in fact, a wasp. The wasps flew out of the nest and landed on the shooter, stinging him around the head and on his arms. He got up and tried to brush them off, but there were too many, and he was struggling to keep them from his face.

As he was trying to fight them off, he lost his balance and toppled over the lip of the roof and fell three stories to the ground, severing his spinal cord and dying where he lay. Police were called and could see where he had fallen. After investigating the roof, they could find the shooter's rifle and put together that he was trying to kill someone, possibly the Archdeacon.

The police reported the incidence to the Archdeacon, who immediately declared it to be an act of God and prayed for the Lord's protection in the name of the Father.

The chairman was at home listening to the news when it was reported that a hit man had fallen to his death, presumably trying to fulfill a contract on the Archdeacon's life. He stared at the television, not believing what he had heard. 'Idiots, all of them are idiots.' If the job is to be done, then the chairman will have to attend to this himself.

CHAPTER 47

P ETER WAS ASLEEP AND HAD a dream. There was a child born at the local hospital to Christian parents who had faith. The child was to fulfill an important role in society in the future and was therefore of need, as he had been borne with multiple problems regarding his spine, heart, and lungs. Doctors had advised the parents that there was no way the child could survive, as the complications were too many and complex, and to correct one may cause premature death.

The parents at the time of the pregnancy were encouraged to have an abortion as imaging showed the baby was not healthy and would be born with complications that would prevent it from living a normal life and the condition, he was in would reduce its life span.

The parents had prayed for the Lord's help and made it clear that the Lord's will, would prevail. They understood the child was a gift from God and that He had the right to bring him home to heaven anytime He chose.

Peter was commanded to go to the hospital and pray over the child in the parents' presence, so they knew the Lord had heard their prayers and had acted.

He got up in the morning and had his usual breakfast and showered and prepared himself for a busy day. He caught the bus to the children's hospital and asked for administration for the ward and room number of the child. He went to the child's room, but when he opened the door, there were many people there. A nurse came up to him and said, 'You can only stay for fifteen minutes, as the child is very ill and expected to die within the next hour. We would like the parents only to be present when the child dies.'

Peter thought it was rather ridiculous to say the time of expected death when, in reality, no one knew when this was about to happen. Yet the Lord said they expected the child to die shortly, as he had several major complications that were beyond the doctor's ability to cure.

Peter moved to the head of the child's bed near the parents, who remembered Peter. Several of the relatives were chatting between themselves about the stock market, while other relatives were discussing the health of some aunt whom they thought should pop off before the child did.

They thought it was wrong that the old lingered on while such a young child was taken from the parents. He spoke to the parents, asking their permission to pray over their child. They were thrilled to see him and apologised for the crowd in the room and the fact that most who were there did not believe in Jesus, as taken from their conversation.

The nurse was attending to the child's drip at the same time a doctor walked into the room. He checked on the monitors and said to the nurse to increase the dose of one medication, as the child was developing low blood pressure.

Peter prayed over the child as the doctor was staring at the monitor and ordering the increase in the medication. Peter noticed a bright white light shone in the room and that the old man was there and he moved up to where Peter was standing and rested his hands on the child.

The monitors immediately showed an improvement, so much so that both the doctor and nurse stood staring at the screens, not believing what they were seeing. Nothing had been done by them, and no increase in medication was administered while they stood there, so what had caused the child to improve mystified them? As Peter continued praying, the child's condition improved, and the parents noticed this and immediately sensed that it could only have come from their prayers being answered and from divine intervention. Doctors had given up and said they could do no more for the child and had told the parents that their child would die shortly.

The parents prayed to God for His help to save the life of their child. After about ten minutes, Peter noticed the old man was no longer in the room and ended his prayer. He withdrew his hands from the child's head and stood there momentarily and walked out of the room as all stared at him. As he moved out, one relative said to his wife, 'A lot that will do for the baby.' His wife told him to be quiet, and as Peter moved out, he gave him a dirty stare; no doubt another Christian that had no faith.

The doctor noticed the monitors were showing the baby was registering normal signs and felt that this was because of faulty equipment. They asked everyone to leave the room so they could change over the monitors and reconnect the baby up to the new monitor. They did not believe what they were seeing, and the nurse went out to get additional medical backup. The parents knew it was not faulty equipment, but their prayers were answered and that the grace of God would save their baby.

Peter walked out of the room and made his way out of the hospital when he noticed the old man sitting on a bench outside a waiting room. He sat near the old man, who, after a few minutes, talked to Peter. He advised him that Satan would do all that was within his power to kill or destroy his reputation and the reputation of the other two that he, Satan, had tried to kill. Peter was to warn the others to take care and was to take care himself, as Lucifer could be deceitful as well as a murderer and was determined to show his authority. Peter looked up and noticed a nurse looking at him and asking if he was all right. 'Who were you speaking to? Do you often speak to yourself? There is no one sitting near you, sir.' Peter replied, 'I am a minister, and I was talking to God. That's not a crime, is it?'

The nurse said, 'No, I guess not, but it is unusual for people to talk to God. Maybe you should see a psychiatrist.'

Peter asked, 'Don't you believe in God?'

The nurse replied, 'I have never met Him, let alone spoken to Him.'

Peter asked, 'Haven't you prayed to Him?'

The nurse replied, 'I used to, but that did no good. My prayers were never answered, which proved to me it was all a great hoax. Now, how often have you seen God?'

Peter said, 'Of late, about once a week. Why?'

The nurse said, 'You should come with me, sir, and see a doctor about your friend God and the discussions you have with Him.'

The nurse took Peter by his arm and escorted him down the hall. Peter resisted, and she yelled out for help. Before Peter could blink, there were about four people around him, ensuring he went quietly to the psychiatric ward to see a doctor.

As he was being accompanied to the ward, an emergency call came over the speaker, and all those around him left quickly, as the call was a code red, which meant all available were to attend. The nurse that first spoke with Peter sat him down in a waiting room and told him to wait for her, as she had to attend the code red alert. She ran off, leaving Peter.

Peter was not sure what to do. Should he go to the psychiatric ward and try to convince them of the existence of God, or should he decide this was one of Lucifer's schemes to have him locked up and put out of action? He considered it was a plot to get him isolated and locked up so he could no longer spread the word freely. He could take the opportunity to get away and did just that.

Peter went straight home and, after a quick scotch, wondered about what had happened. They considered him a nutcase for talking to God and were going to lock him up in hospital for telling people he believed in God and spoke to Him. He thought how many people were like that nurse, and will the future be a situation where to speak of God will result in persecution of Christians and castration of the individual?

He decided to speak about God and the reluctance of Christians to do so openly.

On Sunday, after they read prayers, he entered the pulpit and began his sermon.

Peter said, 'During the week, I had cause to go to hospital to pray for one of our parishioner's children who was very ill and who, I may say, made a miraculous recovery, which confused the men of science. While there, I went out of the room to get some privacy and to give thanks to God for His mercy. While praying, a nurse saw me and was ready to escort me to the psychiatric ward of the hospital, asking me when I see God and how often I enter conversation with Him. All these, according to the nurse, are the first signs of madness.'

'My experience has led me to think about those of you who come to church and about your own lives. Do you speak to others about your faith? Do you believe it is your responsibility to spread the word of God, or is it just my responsibility because I am a minister? Do you find it uncomfortable to speak to your friends or mates about God? Or do you feel embarrassed talking about Him? Are you scared they will think you are a wimp, someone who cannot stand on your own feet and needs the help of God, an invisible spirit from another world?'

'The feelings you feel about Christ and reluctance you show of spreading the word are not reciprocated by Jesus. He boasts about you and tells everyone you are the greatest. So much so that even Lucifer stands up and takes notice of you and goes out of his way to prove God wrong. God has total faith in you and stands back and lets you run the show. What do you do when that happens? This is an important question.'

'Most people are shy and therefore do not want to get into conversation about their beliefs. They consider them private and therefore never speak about Jesus to others or even declare whether they believe in God. That is their business and no concern of their friends or neighbours.'

'Other people believe they are not sufficiently equipped to get into a discussion about Jesus Christ and do nothing about answering the questions, setting the record straight or correcting the wrongs or abuses made against God. They consider it is someone else's responsibility to take up the cause and not theirs. They think God came to them rather than they went to seek God, and therefore they do not have to stand deputised by God on this earth. It is His problem to spread the word and not theirs. He is the powerful one and not them.'

'Those that do not fit into the two categories do not want to offend their mates by talking about God, even if it means their mates will end up in hell. When you do this, you have forgotten the reason God has placed you on this earth. Not for your joy and happiness, but to serve Him.'

'In this instance, the person is serving themselves and not God and is saying they are, in fact, more important than God. They lack the faith in God and do not believe that God will assist them to pass on the message and therefore do not speak up in defence of God or to pass on His message.'

'There is a good percentage of Christians that believe their duty rests on initiating the conversation and mention the good Lord. It is then up to God to do the rest. Whether the person asks a difficult question or does not want to discuss religion is irrelevant. All you must do is to make the first approach and then pass it over to Jesus to do the rest.'

'So, the question revolves around your obligation as a Christian to God, to spread the word, or is it God's responsibility bearing in mind we were placed on this earth to serve Him?'

'The key aspect regarding the so-called Christian is his love of God. If the Christian goes to church to look ethical and for appearance's sake, he will not stand up for God and take the discussion forward to the non-Christian.'

'If the Christian has love in his heart for Christ, he will consider he has a responsibility to others outside the church and to those who do not have the faith. If God's love is working in your life, it will cause you to act on His behalf and in His name. If the love exists for Christ, we will not be unduly obsessed with our own struggles with life and problems Lucifer has given us, but will help other people in their effort to know God.'

'We read God said to Isaiah, "Whom shall I send and who shall go for us?" and this is still the case today. God deals through His creation, mankind, and does not debate with him what ought to be done or not done. He relies on us to make the initial approach and, once this is made, will then take over and assist that person on his journey to eternal life.'

'Unfortunately, most times, Christians do not care sufficiently about Jesus to raise the issue when it deserves to be raised or object to the character assassination of Christ when it happens. Most are there to be quiet and not to defend, in their eyes, the indefensible.'

'A fact that must be pointed out is that no person in the New Testament came to faith other than through the agency of a human being. God worked through mankind to achieve His purpose. For instance, the Ethiopian. God sent an angel to tell Phillip to go to the Ethiopian and proclaim the Gospel to that man. Then there was the Philippian jailer. He allowed Paul and Silas to be incarcerated and be a witness and finally proclaim the Gospel to that man, bringing him to faith. There was Cornelius, a man searching for God, and it was Simon Peter who articulated the Gospel to him.'

'Once we have proclaimed the Gospel, our work is done. The rest is up to the Holy Spirit. We are not expected or called to lead people to Christ because we, as mankind, are incapable of doing so. You cannot save anybody yourself. our brief is declare the facts and truth as advised in the Bible. It is then God's responsibility to do what He wills with that person. We are responsible for "faithful proclamation". It is up to God to save the person, not us.'

'You should remember, God is not looking for those with ability. He is looking for availability. He will help you in your effort, but you must make the first move and support His word.'

CHAPTER 48

LUCIFER WAS DETERMINED TO PUT the three out of action. Since killing them did not work, he decided to do what was necessary to disgrace them. He knew everyone on earth would do anything for money. Most times, it was more important than religion. It was why mankind works, and when the opportunity presents itself, takes it from others. Even the rich and famous seem never to have enough money. So, initially, he would try to ensure that the amount of money was enough, first, to get their attention and, second, for them to take the money and then be accused of taking it from the church or from donations, causing them to lose credibility.

First, it would be necessary for someone to approach Peter and the Archdeacon and donate a substantial amount to the church. Second, it would need someone to steal the money for their benefit and accuse Peter and the Archdeacon of taking the money. To put the plan into action, it would be necessary to find out details about their bank accounts, and after that, it would be easy.

James Coelicola encouraged a rich developer to donate to Peter's church in the belief that by making such a donation, he would secure a place in heaven when he died. The developer had gone to a funeral, and he knew the deceased was an outright crook, but he donated money to the church. At his funeral,

the minister could not control himself from declaring what a great person the deceased was and that he would no doubt be in heaven owing to the generous donations he had made to the church and the community. The developer was convinced he should do the same and therefore approached Peter, intending to donate a large sum to the church for renovations.

Peter declined because he did not know the developer and all renovations were to be handled through the Archdeacon's office. The man insisted, so Peter arranged for him to meet the Archdeacon and discuss the donation with him. The meeting was arranged and held, and the Archdeacon was very keen to get the donation, as there were several churches in the parish that needed renovating.

The Archdeacon arranged for the developer to meet with the head of finances to sort out the arrangements. To ensure transparency, a separate account was opened, and the account details passed onto the developer. Unfortunately, the department head at the church was a gambler and had lost a lot of money betting on horse races and the outcome of football games. The person would go to every race meeting he could and bet heavily, thinking his luck must change soon and he would win big. He would attend football games and again bet heavily and, like most gamblers, kept losing.

Lucifer made sure the person lost a fortune to ensure he would only have one option, and that was to steal the money from the donations. The department head knew that it would be only a matter of time when his debts became public knowledge, so he had to do something quickly. He was told by the bookies to pay up his debts or he would suffer a fatal accident. His bookmakers would not wait forever to get paid. He kept phoning the developer, asking when he intended to make the donation and if there was anything he could do to assist him in expediting the payment. The calls became annoying to the developer, and he spoke to Peter to see if what he was told before was true.

He made an appointment to take Peter out to dinner and would find the truth about whether he could buy his way to heaven.

An average restaurant was selected, and both men turned up on time. During the meal, the developer asked the question, and Peter replied, 'No, you cannot get to heaven by your deeds. You can give all your money to the charities or the church, and still, this would not guarantee eternal life. The only way to have eternal life is to have faith in Jesus Christ. You cannot trash Jesus' teachings and then spend up big to buy your way to heaven to recompense. You should accept what Jesus said in that the path to heaven is very narrow.'

The developer finally realised that he had been wrongly advised and had been misled by those who were only interested in his money and not his soul or in Jesus. He decided not to make the donation as planned but still help the poor and needy and to seek God, as he realised his wealth was the Lord's resource and not his own. He had stewardship of it, and one day he would have to account for what he had done with the resources he was privileged to have had control over.

The developer advised the Archdeacon's office that he would not be making the donation as planned but would support charitable organisations directly by helping the poor. The head of the finance department had no option but to declare himself bankrupt and resigned from his position. Lucifer was not happy, as he thought he may discredit both men by this scheme, but never mind, there will be another opportunity. Lucifer did not give up easily, if at all.

Lucifer decided that there was another way of discrediting the men by giving them a fortune and allowing them to see the benefit of having money. He planned on the two winning the lotto prize, which stood at $650 million, a record prize. on the night of the draw, the numbers were selected, and the next day, it was revealed that the Archdeacon and a minister of his church had won the prize, and since the ticket was purchased online, they would not have to produce their ticket. The prize was to be distributed within a week and would be paid to their nominated bank accounts.

The Archdeacon and Peter were contacted by the Lotto, and it was confirmed they were the prize winners, and they would pay directly the money into their account. Neither said anything to the organiser or to the press.

Peter met with the Archdeacon to discuss the situation and what they should do. Both agreed that it would be wonderful to have $300 million each, but both men had money in the past, and while life was pleasant, it could not buy the things offered by the Lord such as eternal life. They in the past found out what could be done with money and knew of the limitations it presented. Yes, great things could be done with the money, but both knew that they were being set up, as neither had taken out a ticket in Lotto. It was agreed to make a declaration that neither had a ticket and, therefore, a mistake had been made.

The declaration was made, and the press had a field day declaring the whole thing to be a sham. Management declared they would seek the services of consultants and get to the bottom of what had happened. This they did and after making a final investigation, could only say that some unknown person had bought the ticket in their names as a gift. After much deliberation, the organisers reran Lotto for that week and gave the prize to three other participants. The three subsequently were found to have spent the money on themselves and not for the good of their fellow man.

Coelicola (Lucifer) was furious, as he considered all mankind would want more money, and his experience was that men would sell their souls for 'thirty pieces of silver'. He was prepared to give them $330 million each, and they rejected his offering, which was more money than what they could earn in their lifetime. Lucifer could not understand their rejection. This only happened once before to him, and that was three thousand years ago, when he offered the world to Jesus and He turned him down. All that Jesus had to do was bow before him and the world would be His, but Jesus refused to, as the world is His.

Coelicola tried to keep that incident quiet, as he did not want the world to hear about him being rejected, but, somehow, it ended up in the Bible and broadcasted around the world. He did not want this rejection being told around the world, as people may decide not to sin or refuse to become corrupt and reject wealth or greed and turn against him and follow Jesus.

He would have to think about what to do next to ensure they eliminated the three.

CHAPTER 49

A COUPLE OF MONTHS HAD PASSED, and Lucifer was looking through a short list of people he considered worthy to approach and invite to become board members of the Dominium Group. The world was not being managed as it had previously, as all members had died at the hands of God and stood to be judged by Him. At the end of time, they will join Coelicola in hell, but if he has his way, it wouldn't be too soon, as God could not assemble His team of faithful followers to replace the angels who were expelled from heaven and took occupancy on earth.

The more people who lose faith in Jesus or just don't want to give up their material assets for exchange or belief in eternal life, means the less will support God or follow Him, which will mean more time before the end of the world. If he, Lucifer, can prevent God getting the quantum of followers he needs, then he will accumulate an army of followers who will support him and not God, and he will overthrow God and prevent judgement and retribution taking place for a long period or from ever happening.

He still held dominance over the world, so he still ruled the parliaments and government of each of the countries of the world. It was not what people wanted, but what he Lucifer decided. However, without his team, parliaments were making decisions that were good for the people rather than what Lucifer wanted. He will have to establish his order worldwide again and soon; otherwise, people may revert to Christianity and believe in God.

Lucifer had decided to meet with several potential applicants throughout the month in various countries, so until that happened, he would have time to establish his scheme to discredit the Archdeacon and Peter. As for Vince, he knew it would be of no use to apply the same tactics to him, as he had no standing in the community. The only way to get rid of him would be to kill him, and that could be done after they took the other two care of.

To kill the Archdeacon and Peter would be to act against God's directive, but Lucifer never worried about God's will even though he knew God's word should not be challenged. Yet why do this if there was a way to discredit them and God and have believers move from their belief to deciding against the faith?

The usual course of events where a person was tinkering on the edge of not being sure of God's existence or whether they should have faith in God, was to cause an accident to occur, which, in nine out of ten cases, would cause the relatives and sometimes the person themselves, if they weren't killed, to question the good intentions of God or His existence. How often have you heard, 'If there is a God, why does He allow this to happen, or why didn't He prevent this person from being killed or hurt? No, there is no God. only fools believe there is a God.'

Lucifer decided to arrange for an accident to occur where he would take a life to make sure it got personal and made a deep impact on the person. He decided to concentrate on the Archdeacon and then would switch his sight onto Peter.

The Archdeacon had a sister who, like her brother, believed in God. Her name was Joy. She was not a deeply religious person, but from childhood was brought up to go to church on Sundays and believe in God. She said her prayers each night, or what she could remember of them, as she raced through them, and like most people, she thought herself to be a Christian even though she remembered God only when she went to church. On all other occasions, she made her own decisions until next Sunday. She had a daughter who was disabled in that she had trouble at birth and was wheelchair bound for the rest of her life. She could do nothing for herself, as, intellectually and physically, she was incapable. Despite all the problems her daughter presented, Joy still loved her and was never far from her. Her husband died of leukemia when he was in his late thirties, leaving Joy to raise her daughter by herself. The Archdeacon helped whenever he could and prayed over the girl often.

Lucifer decided to kill Joy, which would then leave the Archdeacon to question God's good intention and would force the Archdeacon to step aside to look after his niece. He would put doubt in the Archdeacon's mind and could get his own man appointed to the vacant position. The Archdeacon would, over time, question God's good intentions and eventually lose faith in Him and kneel before Lucifer to seek his good fortunes.

Joy had a routine of taking her daughter to the local hospital once a month for a check-up and to have tests done if they were necessary. Sometimes she stayed overnight, but mostly she is in and back home in a day. That day, Joy was driving to the hospital and was about half an hour away from the hospital when she felt ill and wanted to throw up. She pulled over to the side of the road and quickly got out of her car and stepped onto the sidewalk. She vomited out and, after a minute, went to the boot of the car and took out a bottle of water she kept just in case her daughter was car sick. She washed down the footpath and, as she was doing this, noticed an entourage comprising three vehicles with consulate flags flowing and police escort passing her by with flashing lights. As they passed her, a car pulled out from the footpath, hitting the first car, causing the second car to slam into the first and third car into the second car.

Within minutes, police and ambulances were on the scene. Joy decided that she could not get through the accident, so she went home and try to go to the hospital another day. She settled her daughter down inside her home and switched the television on to see if the accident was reported, and it was. One of the world's wealthiest people was driving in the entourage with consulate officials, and he had suffered a heart attack following the accident and died at the scene.

Lucifer was furious, as the person who died at the accident was on top of his list for selection as a board member for the Dominium Group. How could this happen as he was in control? Despite this setback, he was determined to cause grief to the Archdeacon—to have him either dead or lose faith in God. He would try again, but this time, he was determined not to fail.

Two weeks passed, and Joy was home looking after her daughter, who was progressively getting worse. She had a high fever and was refusing to eat. Her body was aching from some virus, which seemed resistant to antibiotics and other medications that doctors had prescribed. Nothing seemed to work. Joy finally took her daughter to hospital and called for an ambulance. They admitted her with respiratory problems and a high fever. Blood tests revealed nothing abnormal, nor could they pinpoint the cause of her condition. The Archdeacon, who had been in touch with his sister from the start about his niece, knew something was wrong. The doctors could not advise him as to the cause, and she was not responding to medication, which clearly showed it was not a viral problem. He called Peter and explained the situation over the phone and asked him to meet him at the hospital.

Peter turned up as promised, but the Archdeacon was delayed. Peter sought directions from hospital administration and, after walking through what seemed miles of corridors, eventually came across Joy's daughter's room. He went inside and was immediately confronted by Joy, who calmed down once he advised her of his name and that he was a minister and a friend of her brother, the Archdeacon.

Joy told Peter what had happened two weeks ago with her and the witnessing of the road accident, which she was sure was meant for her and her daughter, and since then, her daughter had become ill, and her condition got dramatically worse as if an evil spirit was directing this trouble onto her. At that time, the Archdeacon walked in and greeted Peter and asked whether an exorcism was in order, as he too believed that unseen spirits were at the heart of this matter.

Peter was as confused as was the Archdeacon and said, 'If you believe an exorcism was in order, then why don't you do one? I have never performed one and would not know where to start. My recommendation would be to pray and ask the Lord for His help and guidance.'

Joy said, 'A lot of good that will do. My experience is when you need the Lord, He is never there. You men of religion cannot do a thing. You are as useless as the doctors.'

The Archdeacon said, 'You have said enough for us to see that you have no faith in God. When things get tough, the majority tend to drop their bundle and run. I do not share your feelings and will leave it to God to guide us as to what we should do.'

Peter moved to the head of the bed where Joy's daughter lay. As he approached her, she became agitated and restless, waving her hands around to prevent him from touching her. He knew that there was a spirit within her causing the problem and knew that the only way he could address the problem was in the name of the Father.

He told the Archdeacon to hold her down as best as he could and for Joy to assist her brother. He went to the head of the bed just as a nurse and doctor walked in to check on her condition. They said they were none the wiser as to how to treat her condition and stood there while she was being held down. Peter placed his hands on her head and prayed. He glanced partly up to see the old man was standing with him and was placing his hands on the head of the child. All those present could see the image of the old man.

Peter asked in the name of the Father for the evil spirit to be removed from Joy's daughter, and immediately, everyone sensed a movement of an invisible body race out of the room. Joy's daughter became calm as Peter continued to pray for the Lord to heal her from her condition. Peter looked up and saw that the old man had left, and all were looking at him as to see whether they would witness a miracle. The doctors were asking who was the old man that was in the room, how he came to be there, but no one answered them.

Joy's daughter moved around in the bed as if she was trying to get up, so Peter let her go, and so did the others. She swung her legs over the bed and stepped out on the floor, to the total surprise of the doctors and nurses.

Peter knew Joy's daughter was going to be all right and was to make a full recovery, not just recover from the virus. He left the room to allow the Archdeacon and his sister, doctors, and nurses to come to terms with the miracle done by God.

CHAPTER 50

THE CHURCH HAD, FOR CENTURIES, been infiltrated by Antichrists loyal to Lucifer. Their primary intentions were to create disruption and embarrassment to the church and to the true believers and to leave the church in a situation of disbelief and to show that the word of God was immaterial, false, and not applicable to this world.

If you can't defeat them, then join them and create an image that is contrary to the word of God, creating disbelief and an impression that Christians are not people of faith but shysters seeking respect from the word of God while acting out an entirely different life.

Lucifer knew that pornography was rampant in the ministry with ministers over the years being brought before governing bodies to explain their molestation of young boys and girls in their care. Many had been accused, but few were brought to justice on charges. Many were just moved to another position rather than prosecuted or stood down. Lucifer encouraged these activities, as it discredited the church and the word of Jesus Christ. Many would look at what was happening in the church and lose faith, asking how the Lord could allow this to happen. Unfortunately, they considered these acts as failings of the church rather than failings of men.

Within the Archdeacon's ministry, there were several ministers that gained pleasure from viewing pornography and producing pictures and films of naked young children and selling these on the dark web for monetary gain. Archdeacon had been informed of this activity but could not get the evidence to accuse anyone of the act.

The minsters concerned were careful to cover their tracks but knew it would only be time before they would be caught out and dismissed. They devised a plan to implicate the Archdeacon and to blackmail him into sanctioning their activity for their silence.

The plan was to film some activity showing the testicles of some young boys being handled by a person in ceremonial garments that normally are worn by the Archdeacon. This would be filmed and transferred onto the Archdeacon's computer, and emails would be sent to prospective buyers of the material from the Archdeacon's computer, again confirming his involvement.

The Archdeacon was scheduled to go to the police academy in a week's time to bless the new recruits. Parents would drop off their children into the day care centre before going to work, so this would be an ideal time to attend to the devised plan, as time was not on their side.

The Archdeacon arranged for the police commissioner and some of his senior officers to call in the morning to collect him so they could all go down to the academy in the official bus. That morning, an officer noted the roster showed for the Archdeacon to be collected that morning, so he did this on his way to work. He did not advise anyone that he was going to pick up the Archdeacon; he decided to just do it, as he did not think it was a big thing. That morning, he called at the Archdeacon's office, and both men walked down to the police car and drove to the police headquarters to connect with the official bus.

With the Archdeacon out of the way, the ministers set themselves up to film their hideous crime. One of them, who was the same height as the Archdeacon put on the archdeacon's official garments and moved to where the children were playing. Some children were made naked, and the filming begun.

The chief of police, who did not know that one of his officers had already collected the Archdeacon and was driving him to head office, called into the Archdeacon's office and see if he would want a lift. He got out of his car, and the other two officers that were with him also did the same, as they had never been to the Archdeacon's office, nor were they religious. The three walked into the building and caught the lift to the seventh floor. The commissioner, who knew the Archdeacon well, led the way, and the other two officers followed.

They walked into the main office, but no one was there. They could hear voices, so headed to the office where the voices were coming from, assuming the Archdeacon would be there. They pushed the door open and entered the scene of an official licking the testicles of a young boy while others were filming the act. The police immediately knew something was wrong and demanded that all remain in the room until they understood what was happening. Eventually, the commissioner phoned the Archdeacon, and he was driven back to his office to take charge of the erotic scene.

After lengthy questioning, the plot was revealed to the police and the reason one of them dressed up and tried to imitate the Archdeacon. The ministers were arrested and taken to the police station to stand trial on several charges.

It was concluded at the trial that the Archdeacon did not know of the pornography racket operating out of his office and that the pornography was being sold on the black web for monetary gain.

To say the least, Lucifer was not happy that his scheme didn't come off, although he inflicted a lot of embarrassments on to the church, and because of this, some parishioners lost faith in the church. As for the three ministers taken into police custody, Coelicola (Lucifer) did not care about them, as there were many other ministers within the church that earned a living from the church but did not believe in Jesus Christ, and he would use then in the future.

CHAPTER 51

T HE CHAIRMAN SAT AT THE head of the boardroom table staring at
his new directors, the wealthiest men in the world, and, according
to their chairman, James Coelicola, (Lucifer) the most powerful.

The chairman said, 'You have accepted your appointment for
the sole purpose of gaining more wealth, knowing we control the
governments of the world and dominate the decision-making process.
Should there be resistance or opposition to our control, then we, as
a group, will take care of it, as we are not willing to share our power
and wealth with others. The world is dominated by our policies, and
unknown to the majority, we control the world's countries, their
economies, and their resources through their parliaments. Should
there be resistance, then we will take care of it and replace individuals
and governments if necessary to ensure our will dominates.

'I have begun the spread of a disease, which we established in
China, and intend to spread it to all counties of the world. The purpose
of this virus is to disrupt the economies of the world, to cause prices of
major assets to decline sharply, and to eliminate the aging population
and eradicate the ill, infirmed, and degenerates.

'By introducing such a virus, the believers will seek God's help,
but this will not be forthcoming, as the virus will be man made and
not a creation from heaven. The elderly will plead for God's help, but
because He allows mankind to have a free will, which gives them the
freedom of making their own decisions, then He will not assist them
to eradicate this virus. Man made the virus, so man must overcome it.'

'Knowing this will happen soon, all assets held such as shares and real estate are to be sold at their highest price, as these can be bought back at a fraction of their original price when the world economies crash, and industries become insolvent and individuals bankrupt. Soon, most will not be able to pay their mortgages or put food on the table to feed their families.'

'A world recession will occur and possibly another depression, which will take years to overcome. The world as it now stands will change, and many will die from the virus, leaving us to buy the best assets available and control the economies of the world.'

'You each have been allocated a geographic area to control, and each knowing what is on the horizon must divest yourselves of assets, so you are able to be in a position in the future to acquire major industries and companies that are essential to mankind's livelihood and existence. By controlling these, we will control the world and its population, allowing mankind to think it lives in a democratic world, but in reality, a world controlled by us.'

'The virus that has been unleashed is highly contagious and will spread rapidly once it takes hold. None of you are to associate with groups or persons after two months have passed, as the virus may claim your lives as well as mankind's. After two months, you are to attend to your business by telephone, emails, and the internet and quarantine yourself to ensure you do not contract the virus. Each of you has been provided with an antidote for the virus, but you should not be seen in public after the virus has taken hold and the dead mount up throughout the world. Some countries will not treat the virus seriously, and they will pay a high price for their stupidity. Many families will be torn apart from this virus, leaving the healthy to be the survivors and the infirmed and aging amongst the dead.

'I have been informed that the three whom we have a contract out on are still alive. I will again see to their demise, so members will not have to worry about addressing old issues. They have been fortunate up till now, but their luck will shortly run out, and they will join those in the spiritual world.

'Ensure you control those in power and who have influence. Many will resist you, and it will be a legitimate way for you to eliminate them using the virus. Those who are appointed in their place must be loyal to us and our cause and accept direction from you. The public will not recognise what is happening and still believe they have a democracy.'

The board discussed several issues within specific countries, particularly drought and heatwaves that caused horrific fires in California and Australia. it was agreed that the opportunity was ripe to again have banks and commercial institutions foreclose on the farmers and to acquire their properties at basement prices. 'The Royal Commission was over in Australia, and the banks took the brunt of the criticism and were accused of impropriety; however, they were acting on our orders and therefore could not divulge who would benefit from their actions. Most thought they were working in the interest of their shareholders, which is what we planned and misleads the population into thinking. We will now move in and acquire the farms that strategically will be of benefit to us and which will increase in value when a dam policy is introduced in approximately a year's time.'

CHAPTER 52

FOLLOWING THE GREAT FLOOD, LUCIFER led mankind, who spoke a single language, westwards to the land of Shinar. There, they settled and built a city and a tower which was to be tall enough to reach the heaven. God observed what Lucifer was endeavouring to achieve through mankind and confounded their speech so they could no longer understand or communicate with each other and scattered them throughout the world, disrupting Lucifer's plans to control mankind and govern him. Using greed and easily gained assets was the primary means of persuasion used by Lucifer to get mankind's support and cooperation.

Since then, Lucifer has tried to control mankind through wars and economic downturns and have these appear to be an act of God so mankind would repeatedly ask, 'where is God, and why does He allow this to happen? Does God exist at all?'

Man has undertaken control of his environment and praises himself when things go well, but curse God when man's actions backfire and cause suffering to the individual or population. Faith is shallow in mankind, and most try to reap the rewards that are offered by Lucifer rather than following God.

Over the centuries, Lucifer has methodically worked in every country to again establish a single recognised language but, instead of trying to reach heaven, has established himself as king on the earth and in control of most of its population. The world has become global rather than viewed as a collection of individual countries as established by God. Travel is freely undertaken throughout the world. Trade is worldwide rather than within a single country, and economics and investments are made around the world.

The world is driven by the economies of each country, the acquisition of strategic assets, and greed has replaced God in many countries. Mankind no longer fears God and, most times, is disrespectful towards Him until the individual faces death and their last departure from this world.

Lucifer has become king of this world, and God, the church, and His religion are diminishing in the western world at dramatic speed.

Babel is established in conclaves throughout the world—in new York, Paris, England, and Germany, just to name a few major cities designed to control wealth and, therefore, power to control mankind.

The young have no thoughts about God, as they have been brought up in a materialistic society and clamour for more assets and wealth, as they realise that with money, they, too, can buy influence and have the power to attend to their needs. They, too, follow their king Lucifer to hell, but do not give this consideration unless it is too late.

The old have spirituality and believe in God knowing His teachings. Life experience has taught them the truth, and through trials, some have embraced His word. According to Lucifer, they that know the Truth must be disposed of to ensure there is less opposition to Dominium Group's plan to control governments and the world. The young have not been taught by their parents as their parents have not taken the time to find out about Jesus and what he really has tried to do through the cross. For them, materialism counts, and they do not stop to consider why they have been placed on earth.

CHAPTER 53

Peter had been called to the local hospital, where one of his parishioners was sitting in a waiting room. Her husband had been bashed repeatedly by a group of men who were on a drinking binge. Her husband, as a result, was fighting for his life. She had been told he had suffered extreme pain during the fight, as he could not adequately protect himself from the group, who all took pleasure in first punching him to the ground and then persistently kicking him in the groin and head until he lay motionless.

A motorist driving past captured the incident on his mobile phone and called the police. The men were arrested and would face a charge of manslaughter if not murder. They did not recall the instance after they sobered up. Each had a young family and was out with mates for a bit of recreation.

Susanne sat in the waiting room in a daze not believing her husband, sixty years old, was in a coma, near death, because of the actions of three animals that were allowed to roam the streets and didn't have the common decency to leave an older person alone. All her husband was doing at the time was standing at a bus stop waiting for a bus back home.

Susanne's daughter, Mary, turned up and rushed to her mother, crying and hugging her. She was shortly joined by her brother and his wife and their two children, whom they could not leave on their own at home. All sat in a sombre mood, waiting for some word.

Peter arrived and was greeted by Susanne, who was emotional and under pressure.

Susanne said, 'How could the Lord allow those animals to do this to Bill? He has hurt no one in his life and has always believed in God.'

Peter replied, 'Susanne, you must have faith that the Lord did not do this. It was those men acting freely that did this. They have the same free rights that you have, and, unfortunately, they used Bill as a punching bag. God does not stand in between men or direct what you should do. You have the free will to act according to your conscience, but the day of reckoning comes, and you will have to account for your actions. With freedom of will come the responsibility of ensuring you know how to use it wisely.'

Susanne said, 'That is a lot of rubbish. God, if He exists, should have stopped this. I have been going to church all my life for nothing. There is no God, and if there is, He doesn't care for us.'

A doctor stepped into the room just as Peter was about to answer Susanne.

The doctor said, 'Mrs Bates, I am sorry to advise you, your husband has passed away. We could not save him. His heart failed five minutes ago.'

Susanne asked, 'Can I see him?'

The doctor replied, 'Yes, but only for a few minutes.'

Susanne went in and saw Bill's bruised and battered body lying in bed with blood over the sheets and his head bandaged. She broke down and wept over his body, leaning over him and crying uncontrollably.

The other members of the family followed her in and were aghast to see what had been done to their father. The bruising around his head left him unrecognisable. All stood in unbelievable silence, just looking at their father and crying at the sight and recognising the pain he must have suffered at the hands of those three men.

Peter walked into the room and stood staring at Bill. He recognised the injury, as he had himself inflicted such brutal punishment on those that had opposed him when he was controlling organised crime in his area. He was taken aback by the extent of bruising Bill had suffered and remembered that this was not normal and only happened when a person was to be made an example of or intentionally beaten to death. He stood there for a few minutes and then left the family to mourn their dead father.

That evening, Mary, Susanne's daughter, rang and said they wanted to arrange the funeral and had ordered this through one of the local funeral parlours. The family wanted a simple ceremony at a chapel in the grounds of the cemetery and that they would like Peter to say a few words about their father, as he had known him for some time and their father had faith in God, even though they now don't.

Peter said, 'Mary, I am sorry, but I will not take part in such a ceremony. Your father was a Christian who believed in God and had gone through many trials and kept his faith in God. Yes, he was brutally murdered at the hands of three men, and no doubt they will pay bitterly for their actions. But your father would not just cast God off at the first instance of some catastrophic incident, as you are doing. He believed in God and had faith in Him and, because of that, will have eternal life, whereas the rest of you will be in hell with the rest of the disbelievers.'

With that, Mary hung up the telephone.

The next morning, Susanne, Mary, and her husband turned up at Peter's office asking to see him. The receptionist advised that he was tied up for an hour and would therefore not be available. He also had a busy day, so she did not think he could see them for long. They waited for about an hour and a half, and Peter came into his office and greeted them.

Susanne said, 'I understand you prefer not to speak at Bill's service at the chapel.'

Peter said, 'Your husband was not a heathen but a Christian, so he deserves a proper Christian burial, not a ceremony of recognition that you have arranged at the chapel.'

Mary said, 'well, the family has decided this is best, and, therefore, we will go ahead with or without you.'

Peter said, 'The family has decided nothing other than allowing you to have your way of being the sheep that they are. Who among you has stood up and said the only reason you are having this is because you feel God should have acted as Sir Lancelot and taken out His sword and killed those men? None.'

You sit there allowing Bill to have a service contrary to his beliefs because you have no faith in God. You come to church each Sunday praying and declaring your faith in God, but when the first trial happens, you drop your bundle and declare there is no God and Lucifer, who got into those men and persuaded them to do this, is king over you now. Go to him and enjoy your life on earth, for you will not be with Bill in heaven. You will have to excuse me. I have several parishioners to see and am running behind time.'

They all got up and walked out, leaving Peter.

Around midday, Peter received a telephone call from Susanne asking if they could again come and see him, as they had spiritual conflict and could not find peace. He thought about it and decided to see them if it was brief.

They all turned up with Susanne and went into Peter's office. Susanne said, 'Peter, thank you for seeing us. I would like you to arrange for a Christian service for Bill and for you to officiate. Bill often said to me that the Lord will test us, but I never thought it would be me and in such a dramatic way, nor so soon. You know, "Why me, Lord?'

Peter said, 'What about you? You have lost faith in the Lord, so why go through a masquerade? Just do what you want and get it over and done with. I will not try to reason with you or get you back to seeing my way. While I do not mean it, you can all go to hell, where you seem to want to end up.' Mary said, 'No, that is not right. Yes, we thought the Lord has abandoned us and didn't care for us, but we have had time to think about Dad and, while we do not understand why this has happened, realise that God has a plan and will use this catastrophe for our good. We really have faith in Him.'

Peter looked at his calendar and booked it in to the relief of the family.

CHAPTER 54

Peter stood at the pulpit, waiting a moment. Then said, 'We are here to say farewell to Bill, a person who, throughout the years, had faced adversity and had faith in the Lord knowing that he was here to serve the Lord and to trust Him, and when it was time for his departure and return home, that the Lord would arrange for this and be there to welcome him in heaven.'

'Bill was brutally murdered, and at the hospital, it was hard not to burst into tears at the sight of the man with a swollen face and blood-spilt sheets around him.'

'Mary asked why it could happen if there is a God, as the Bible tells us.'

'Surely there isn't, as He would have intervened and prevented this happening. Not so, for all mankind has been given the promise by God that they are free willed and can decide what they want to do and will be judged for their actions. 'When I was in hospital looking at Bill with his swollen face and blood-stained body, I remembered another occasion when something like this happened. It was before the Crucifixion when Pilate ordered that Jesus be whipped for His blasphemous declaration to the Pharisee that he would destroy the temple and build it in three days.'

'They used whips and steel blade implements that shredded the flesh off his body.'

'This was the Son of God, and yet God did not intervene in mankind's action when they bloodied the body beyond recognition of His only Son. They did not care about Him and, driven by Satan, intentionally and systematically went about killing Him. After they were stopped when He was near death, they put a crown on His head and mocked Him, saying, "King of the World" and bowed before Him. They then nailed Him to a cross and crucified Him. Still, God did not intervene and allowed mankind to do what it desired, even though they were driven by Satan. They stuck a spear into Jesus's side to make sure He was dead, another free choice allowed to mankind. They said, 'If you are God, come down from the cross and we will believe you." But these were lies. All the miracles He did before them were not enough. They still did not want to believe in Him.'

'We have the free right to put Jesus to death, and even today we still maintain that right, and many have done this in their minds and by their actions, daily crucifying Him and putting Him to death. God will not prevent you or anyone else doing this, as He gave you the right of choice without hindrance or interference, and you can do as they did—crucify Jesus anytime and as many times as you wish. Of course, this right ceases upon your death, and then you are called to account for your actions. The reality as to why you were placed on this earth than dawns upon you, and you realise you have made the wrong choice. The fun stops here, and you then get to experience hell for your stupidity and actions. It was you who went there. Not God sending you.'

'How was Jesus able to accomplish what He did? We know He took all our sins to the cross, and those who believe in Him and have faith in Him will never die but are promised eternal life.'

'Jesus did it, first, because he had faith in His Father. He knew God was capable of all things, including protecting and saving Him if He wanted to.'

God could have sent a legend of angels to defend Jesus if He wanted to intervene. But God made a promise to mankind, and even the death of His own Son could not make Him break that promise - the covenant.

'The other aspect was that Jesus was alone on the cross when God turned His face from Him, leaving Jesus on His own. No doubt this was a horrible time for Him and will be for those who do not want to know Him, for you too will experience this isolation and emptiness yourselves if you lack faith.'

'Until this point in time, Jesus was never alone. He always prayed to His Father and continually sought help and wisdom through His prayers. He did nothing in His own name but always in the name of the Father. He used God's power to perform miracles and called upon God, continually seeking guidance and wisdom. He never did things in His name or by His authority. It was by God and faith in God that made things happen.'

'There is little doubt that since Adam and eve, we are all doomed to death. We are all going to die. Some believe this to be a random act, while others believe that our entry on this earth and last departure is planned and up to God. I believe this is the case, and while Bill left this world in a most tragic circumstance, it was all under the control of Jesus, whom he had faith in.'

'Bill often prayed with me for God's help and guidance, and he was not a shallow believer, but one truly tested over time by many trials. Yes, he, too, heard the cock crow in his early days in denying Jesus, but over time came to believe in the Lord and trust in Him and was glad he found the faith and held on to it.'

'Those who find it hard to find an answer as to why this could happen will never come to the right conclusion.'

Those who say, 'Lord, I don't understand why you permitted this to happen, but I trust you, it is your will and under your control, and I will leave it to you to resolve, as I am not capable of doing so, will be those who have the faith and belief in Jesus Christ.'

'In these situations, the factor of time is important. God, over time, reveals His plan to mankind. You get an answer down the track as to why a tragedy happened. Time is needed to prove to you, not to God, whether you have the faith you think you have. The trial at which this is showed tends to be one involving a close family member, leaving many to question the Lord. I urge you in these times to hold on to your faith and do not discard it just because you are not given an immediate insight as to why something has happened and the purpose of it all.'

'It must be understood that God created you and anything that happens to you, or your loved ones, can only happen with his permission. If he rejects it, then it doesn't happen. If He agrees, then it happens. This is revealed in the story of Job.'

'As to why things happen. We are specifically not told. Why was Bill attached? The police can find this out. Why did God allow it to happen is what we do not know? However, as time goes by, we get to find out and the unique pieces of the puzzle come together.'

'Take the case of Joseph. He was sold by his brothers to merchants, and they considered him dead when they pocketed the money. Yet God allowed it to happen despite their intentions.'

'What transpired is that over time, he became the second highest authority in Egypt and fed them and their families during the years of drought and famine that hit the country. So, when tragedy hits, we can-not immediately expect the answer as to why but can only rely on our faith in Jesus to ease the pain and grief and have faith in Him to help us over time, to come to understand why this has happened.'

'Most times grief or an accident is a wake-up call by God to get our attention and to bring us back to Him. Remember, in his own situation, God brought good out of the death of his own son. Your grief has a purpose and will be overcome by God, if you allow Him.

'Let us pray. . .'

CHAPTER 55

THE VIRUS SPREAD OUT OF China rapidly, and, because of lack of facilities and hospital care, many were taken ill while others died of respiratory failure. The extent of the catastrophe was kept quiet by the authorities, who could not gather the workforce to control the epidemic. The death rate was in the millions, but this was kept a secret until the truth was exposed.

Travellers moving from place to place, took the virus with them, and the larger cities in China being business centres, near airports, where overseas visitors attend international conferences and exhibitions, aided the spread of the virus not only within China but also to the world at large.

Before the world realised it, there was a pandemic that was uncontrollable. Many countries tried to control the spread of the virus by shutting down regions or preventing or restricting the movement of their population. Most concluded that the only way to stop the virus was to inoculate their population.

Millions were affected throughout the world, and each country recorded many deaths. Trade and commerce were affected and so was assembly of individuals, including Christians on Sundays at churches, weddings and assembly at funerals, were prohibited.

The Dominium Group profited substantially from the spread of the virus in that stock exchanges throughout the world fell, allowing the board members to short sell and profit from such dealings. Also, the value of assets fell owing to initially lack of liquidity, which again allowed the Dominium Group to move in and acquire assets at fire-sale prices.

From a religious point of view, Lucifer spread the word that this virus was from God to punish mankind from lack of faith, and this was the first of many that God would bring down on mankind, as a punishment for lack of faith in Him.

Most countries introduced laws to prevent the gathering of people, including church gatherings. While modern technology was introduced to assist people to work from home and such, the church was slow or uninterested in rapidly introducing online services on Sundays, which most people thought was a good thing to have.

Travel globally was restricted, forcing airlines to cancel flights and mothball their fleet of aeroplanes and dismiss their employees or put them on unpaid leave.

With the world in turmoil, Lucifer decided his plan for the eradication of the sick and elderly could proceed without raising undue alarm. The virus intensified and became more potent, causing worldwide alerts for those over seventy and with ailments, to be extremely careful, as they would be in the high-risk category and could find themselves in hospital on ventilators and in intensive care wards. Many did not heed the warning and found themselves extremely ill, while others died of respiratory failure.

Lucifer increased the opposition to God, as this was a good time to point out to the faithful the failure of God in not intervening and saving the lives of His followers. It was likened to the Christians being thrown to the lions in the Colosseum.

The Antichrists imbedded in the church were influenced to raise doubts in people's minds as to where is God? Why doesn't he do something? Does He really exist or care, as we have not been given any answer to our prayers and there is no one out there listening to the cries of the poor and feeble asking God for help?

Even traditional countries such as Italy were experiencing high death toll from the virus, causing the aging population to have doubts whether God cared about His people.

The world experienced a shortage of medical masks and ventilators, and researchers scrambled to come up with a cure. Amongst the confusion and anxiety experienced by the nation's population, was an increase in alarming news as to each country's death toll, leading to anxiety amongst the population who thought that they would be next to contract the virus and die.

In this environment, very little was heard from the church on radio or television, leaving the true believer to think they were alone and that maybe God had abandoned them.

No leader stepped forward to assure Christians that God was still looking over them and they should pray for His support and grace. As usual, many earn their living as ministers and religious academics in universities, but none came forward to represent the Christian faith in this time of need.

Political leaders were falling over themselves to advise what they had implemented or were doing about the crisis, but none mentioned God or called for prayer in these desperate times.

No one will stick their necks out and go out on a limb, declaring that it was not God who had abandoned mankind, but mankind had abandoned God.

CHAPTER 56

PETER WAS NOT ONE OF the ministers who refused to mention God in his sermons and prayers over this period. Yet he noted that most ministers at the church were doing just that and that their attitude towards God had changed. They were allowing parishioners to think that same-sex marriages and homosexuality should be accepted by the church when they were not. Abortion was not permitted by the church, yet some ministers told parishioners as it is accepted by the state, so it was all right by the church. These same ministers also preached euthanasia was acceptable to the church, as the state had legalised it, and, therefore, the church could do nothing about it other than accept it.

It got to where Peter lodged an objection with the Archdeacon, who knew he would have a revolt on his hands if he allowed Peter to remain in his position.

Peter, likewise, was not happy with the course the church was taking. The church was being allowed to shed its traditional teachings as dictated in the Bible and adopt the worldview of things in its place, allowing the state to dictate what was acceptable as teachings rather than the Bible.

He received an email from his sister, Helen, who was living at Castle Hill, advising him that her husband, Paul, was rushed to hospital with suspected coronavirus (Covid-19) with respiratory complications and was in the hospital in the isolation ward. She emailed her daughter Alice, who was married to Paul's son Tim, to advise him of their troubles.

Peter tried to telephone Helen, but she was not answering her telephone or mobile, so he decided to see if he could take a few weeks off to go to either Bungarby or Castle Hill. He telephoned the Archdeacon's office but was told that the Archdeacon was home resting, as he too, had a bad cold and was advised not to see anyone but self-isolate until they could find out whether he had the common cold or had contracted Covid-19.

He spoke to a senior cleric who knew the situation that was developing with other ministers in the church and thought that it would be an opportunity for Peter to have some time off, allowing the conflict brewing within the church to be defused. He conceded to Peter's request for leave and granted him four weeks' leave with a request he move from the city and not to contact any of the other ministers who were trying to destroy the traditional church.

Peter went off to Bungarby first to see his old friend Vince and to chill out with him for a couple of days. He would then drive to Castle Hill to catch up with Helen. He predominately wanted to go to Bungarby, as he knew there was still no minister at the church and that the farmers were finding it hard to cope with the lack of facilities and support services and the outright theft of their farms by the Dominium Group and some politicians.

He called into a medical supply company and, with the support of several doctors at the local hospital, bought quantities of masks, gloves, disinfectants, and hand sanitisers. He loaded his utility up with as much as it could hold, including some supplies of antibiotics and other needed supplies. Unfortunately, the regional areas got very little support even though promises were made by the politicians who did not keep their word.

Early the next morning, he began the long drive to Bungarby. The authorities were alerted that he was carrying supplies for the local hospital and to allow him through, even though there was a lockdown in place. What he was doing was considered by the police as an essential service.

After three hours of driving, he stopped on the side of the road and stretched his legs and had something to eat before starting off again. He was determined not to stop at places where there would be crowds of people or where he could become infected. He had been tested before he left, and word had come through that he was clear of the virus.

After twelve hours of driving, he pulled up outside the church in Bungarby and parked his utility in the barn around the back. He unloaded his utility and went into the house to find that there was a note saying that food had been left for him in the fridge and that the place had been cleaned and made liveable by Vince and his men. He telephoned his old mate, who drove in and meet up with him.

Vince pulled up with his men in tow, and all went into the house, glad to see Peter. They brought their dinner with them and set themselves up in the dining room two meters apart to ensure they were observing the distancing rules.

The discussion mainly was around coronavirus and how it could become a pandemic and the plight of the farmers who were finding it difficult to survive in these circumstances.

Peter advised he intended to drive to Castle Hill the next morning to catch up with Helen. Vince knew of her husband contracting the virus and the seriousness of the situation.

Vince decided to join Peter on his trip to Castle Hill even though Peter insisted on making the trip by himself. Vince still knew that there was a contract out on their lives and was very mindful that someone may want to cash in on the bounty.

Vince and his two men made themselves home and took up residence in one of the spare bedrooms.

The next morning, after breakfast and after Peter held morning Mass at the church, they headed off to Castle Hill. Surprisingly, the church was near full, as many of the farmers' heard Peter was back in town and came to welcome him and advise him of their predicaments.

It was mid-morning before Peter and the group could head off on their four-hour trip to Castle Hill.

CHAPTER 57

THE ARCHDEACON LAY IN HOSPITAL in a contamination ward aided by a respirator. It was confirmed he had the virus and that his lungs could not function under the strain. His heart condition made things even worse in that his immune system was compromised and he could not cope.

The doctor came in to see if there had been any improvement. He checked the monitor, which showed blood pressure, pulse, and oxygen content. None were showing any improvement, and there was no cure available for this virus. He lay still. Nothing further could be done for him by the men of science, as they had depleted their bag of tricks.

The clergy sat outside the room in protective gear to make sure the Archdeacon was being looked after.

The hospital was working under extreme conditions in that an increase in cases had been recorded and there were not enough intensive care beds to cater to those that were admitted.

The decision as to who was looked after was based on the importance of the person and whether they could afford private health cover. All the beds in the public hospitals were full, and the government was trying to make makeshift hospitals in parks (tent cities) and large halls but found that they could not save many, as they did not have the equipment needed to support their breathing.

The Archdeacon's heart showed signs of being under strain, and a nurse was brought in to provide one-on-one care. As the evening progressed, the Archdeacon's condition became worse, and it was decided to give him an insulin injection. The attending doctor wrote the script out and handed it to the nurse to take down the pharmacy to have dispensed. The pharmacist at the time had just completed dispensing a script for another patient who suffered from blood clots. He completed this and put it aside and dispensed the insulin and once completed handed it to his assistant, who took it and the blood thinning medicine out to the area for collection.

At that time, there was an emergency, and a doctor ran in and grabbed the insulin held by the assistant and ran off to administer the injection. The nurse quickly grabbed other medicine held by the assistant, thinking it was for her, and rushed towards the Archdeacon's room. As she approached the room, the alarm went off and all nurses and doctors ran in, including the nurse with the injection.

The attending doctor quickly grabbed the injection and inserted it straight into the Archdeacon's heart. All stood back, expecting a spike in the readings of the monitors, but they could see only a straight line showing something had gone wrong, as the Archdeacon was not responding as expected.

The doctor stared at the monitor in disbelief and then looked at the label on the injection and just about collapsed. It read 'Warfarin for blood thinning'. He had given the Archdeacon blood thinner, preventing the heart from working rather than inducing the heart to work. He was speechless, holding his trembling hand out momentarily so all could see what it was.

One by one they all read the label on the needle and realised the error. The matter would have to be investigated, and the doctor stood down until the authorities were notified and could come up with their preliminary investigation as to how this occurred.

Lucifer was standing in the background with a big smile on his face. He had gotten rid of one thorn in his side, another one that cannot oppose his aspirations to dominate the world and control and rule the earth.

He knew that soon, a new archdeacon would be elected, and he was going to make sure it was one of his Antichrists that filled that position, someone whom he could trust to oppose the teachings of Jesus Christ.

CHAPTER 58

PETER WAS ABOUT TWENTY MINUTES from Castle Hill when the hospital called. Vince took the call, as he was in the passenger seat. When told of the passing of the Archdeacon, he froze and turned white; he could not speak or believe what he had heard.

Peter, sensing something was wrong, pulled over and took the phone out of Vince's hand.

Peter said, 'Hello, can I help you? Vince, unfortunately, is not in a condition to take this call. Can you repeat what you have said?'

The doctor said, 'Yes, by all means. We phoned to advise that the Archdeacon has died owing to the coronavirus. His heart unfortunately could not sustain the workload, and, unfortunately, a medical error occurred that caused it to stop functioning. Instead of insulin being administered, warfarin was injected by mistake, causing the heart to stop.' The doctor explained the situation and advised that the attending doctor was not at fault other than, procedurally, he should have checked before administering the drug.'

Peter thanked the doctor for calling and hung up, deeply shocked at the news conveyed to him. He got out of his utility and stood staring out across the vast open spaces that were in front of him, not knowing what to say. He stood momentarily and prayed to ask the Lord to care for His son, the Archdeacon, and as he prayed, Vince got out of the utility and walked across to where Peter was praying and joined in the prayer, bowing his head in sorrow. As they prayed, they noticed a third person with them, the old man. He said to them, 'Do not worry about the soul of your brother, the Archdeacon, for I have brought him home to heaven as I had planned. His body remains on earth, but his soul is with Me. Satan has not won a victory through this accident, but I have taken the opportunity of Satan's criminal act to bring my son home. Do not grieve for him but rejoice, for he is now free and will have eternal life because of his faith in Me.'

Peter was going to ask the Lord about the rest of His plans for them, but as soon as he talked, the image dissipated, and they were staring at each other. Momentarily, they stood there not knowing what to do other than stare in amazement at each other. After a moment, they agreed they should continue their journey, and both men got in the utility, and they recommenced their journey still thinking what had happened.

Not a word was said on the way to Castle Hill until they reached Helen's residence, and both men got out of the utility and walked up to the front door, followed by the escort party that was in the other vehicle.

They walked up to the front door ready to ring the doorbell when, suddenly, it flung open, and Helen was on the other side, quickly embracing Peter and bursting into tears.

Peter hugged her, while she wept continuously for a minute until she regained her composure and started reaching into her pocket for a tissue. She led everyone into the house and took them into the lounge room, where everyone sat down and listened to her conversation as to what had happened to her husband, Paul. She described the agony he went through with the virus and how it affected his breathing, causing him to be put on respirator and finally causing blood clots to form, bringing on the stroke, which eventually killed him.

The funeral was arranged for two days' time, and Peter was asked to administer, as Tim could not bring himself to officiate over his father.

The next day, Tim and Alice arrived with their two children, and all greeted each other warmly, with Helen again bursting into tears, upsetting the children.

Eventually, she quietened down, and everyone made their way to the house and ended up having a family reunion with Vince and the boys joining in.

Paul's funeral was a solemn affair with strict rules applying as to spacing and gatherings.

Peter said, 'Coronavirus is showing us that this is a global and not just regional or country epidemic. It has no borders and is transmitted by our desire for free movement and to deal with life the way we want and not the way God has directed.'

'What happened at Babel was God's way of breaking up the nations, but Satan found a way over the years to overcome this by creating a new Babel by men's desire for currency, power, and personal satisfaction. By mankind believing in himself and not God, mankind and not God has become the centre of the universe. We now have a world that understands one language, English, and one currency, the U.S. dollar.'

'Coronavirus is showing us visually and painfully that nothing in this world gives the security and satisfaction that we find in the true faith in Jesus Christ.'

'This pandemic has taken away our freedom that we have become accustomed to—the freedom of air travel, movement, business activity such as employment, and face-to-face activity and relationships. It has put a stop to enjoyment, pleasures, schooling, theatre, and has made many seek unemployment benefits or loan relief to stay in business and avoid bankruptcy.'

'While coronavirus takes away our freedom, privileges, security, and comfort, it also has revealed that it may also take our lives. You have all heard the statistics of the number of people worldwide being affected and the number of deaths throughout the world.'

'Many fear coronavirus because they believe in the material things that this life can afford and do not base their faith on a rock-solid foundation in Jesus Christ. They look at their houses and cars and wonder how they can ensure these things are not lost through the virus striking them. It is their lifestyle and assets that concern them, not their life after death. It is now and present that counts, not what has been promised by Jesus.'

'Sin came into the world through mankind, Adam and eve, and death came on the earth through their sin, and death has and will spread to all mankind because all have sinned except one, Jesus Christ.'

'We will all die as part of God's judgement.'

'Some, unfortunately, believe they can avoid this or postpone it by their power or wealth.'

'If your faith is strong, it is irrelevant whether you suffer cancer, have a stroke or a heart attack, are assaulted or mugged in the street, or are affected by the coronavirus. It is irrelevant, as you serve the Lord and trust in His discretion, wisdom, and mercy. He promised you eternal life, and that is what your death will bring you irrespective of how you eventually die, as we all shall since Adam and eve's original sin.'

'The world was created perfectly, a paradise. But now, all its beauty is suppressed to a large degree and has been overcome with evil, disasters, diseases, and frustrations. This is seen by mankind as God's fault. Who asks where God is or why has He allowed this to happen?'

'God created the world perfectly for mankind. But mankind was not satisfied with God and, since that time, has struggled with diseases, wars, earthquakes, and depressions, causing many to lose faith and suicide to overcome their loss.'

'The Bible tells us we are all under God's judgement. He has caused the world to be subjected to death, disaster, and misery as part of the sins of Adam and eve. He has not destined us for wrath, but we die of diseases and disasters for our sin. But for those who are in Christ, the "sting" of death has been removed, as He has promised eternal life. Trust in the hands and word of Jesus and not in the foolish words of men.'

'Nothing on this earth is done without God's knowledge and permission, and that includes coronavirus. we are told that it started in Asia and spread throughout the world.

'This has not been the first of such viruses that have killed many millions. The Spanish flu in 1918 was but another one of these viruses that had taken many lives. Yet mankind still believes they will be immune from these viruses and do not need a solid foundation of faith in Jesus. They will be the ones that will eventually find it too late when they die.'

'Those of you who kneel before Satan kneel before a lesser spirit. Satan is on a leash that is held by God. He does not do without God's leave and must seek God's permission to act and is limited as to what he can do even though he is ruler of this world. God decides what Satan can do and what damage he inflicts. He does not act separate from God's judgement—he serves it unwittingly.'

'Most of you do not think twice about defaming or cursing God, but you care about your fortunes and physical assets. God sometimes uses diseases to bring judgement upon those who reject him and follow a path of sin, to get you to see the error of your ways.'

'Coronavirus is but another message saying we are sinners bound for destruction and disasters, and we better get our lives in shape and repent of your sins before it is too late.'

'The message of coronavirus is to stop relying on yourself and turn to God, as you must face death, and it is God who decides the timing of this, not you.'

'Let us pray . . .'

The funeral ended with everyone being invited to join in some finger foods and sandwiches in the hall attached to the church. Some took part, while the majority left, as Covid-19 was still real and distancing and gathering laws applied. Everyone paid their respects to Helen, who was overwhelmed by the occasion and support offered to her. After an hour, the group broke up, and the rest went home. The family left and walked home without a word being spoken.

The question was, what would Helen do now? She was back on her own.

CHAPTER 59

T HE DAY AFTER THE FUNERAL, Peter was contacted by some of his old friends who attended Paul's funeral and thanked him for mentioning Covid-19 and his opinion of where it fitted into the scheme of things. Many were not sure and God's relationship to the virus. Others phoned just to talk to Peter and catch up on what their position was regarding their farms and mounting debt.

Most that he spoke to advised him that things had changed little since he took up their cause and that very little cooperation was coming from the banks and financial institution other than they were waiting for the opportunity to move in and acquire the farms at rock-bottom prices, but haven't done anything yet to ensure there was no adverse publicity. Many farmers were still suiciding, as they could not get support and help from government institutions that were there to give only lip service and tie the farmers up with red tape.

One farmer, Rod Ridgeway, telephoned Peter asking if he still dropped off groceries, as he had no food to feed his family and was getting desperate. Peter said he would contact Vince and arrange for a drop-off the next day.

Peter contacted Vince, and arrangements were made for Peter to drive out to Rod's farm while Vince made the journey from Bungarby with the trailer, and both would meet up at Rod's farm and make the drop-off.

The next morning, Peter prepared himself to drive to Rod's farm. Helen, who did not want to be alone, went along for the drive. Both set off and arrived a few minutes before Vince turned up with the trailer.

Vince drove the trailer to the rear barn, and Peter and Helen walked in to lend a hand to offload. As they congregated around the trailer, Rod turned up with his wife and their two children.

Rod told his wife to stand by the barn roller door at the entrance and entered the barn carrying a rifle, which he pointed at both Vince and Peter.

Peter said, 'Rod, how are you? It has been a while since we spoke.'

Rod said, 'You better stand back against the trailer. I don't want any trouble from either of you.'

Peter asked, 'what do you mean trouble? Rod, we are here to drop off some supplies, and if there is a problem, we will just go. It will take just a few minutes, and we will be on our way.'

Rod said, 'No, you are not going anywhere. There is a contract out on both you and Vince, and I am determined to collect it. The bank has made it clear I either pay up my loan by tomorrow or they will take my farm.'

Mrs Ridgeway, upon hearing her husband, stepped forward in front of Rod and between him and Peter.

Mrs Ridgeway said, 'No, Rod, this is not the way. These men came to help us, and you are talking about killing them.'

Rod said, 'It is the only way we can keep our farm.'

Mrs Ridgeway said, 'Rod, it is murder. Kill both men to collect on that contract, and I won't let you do it.'

Peter said, 'You won't get away with it, Rod. People know we have planned to come out here, so they will know you were the last to see us. Besides, there are too many witnesses. Vince's boys will know what had happened, and so will your wife and Helen.'

Rod replied, 'That is right. I will go down for killing you two, and my wife and the boys will get to keep the farm. The Dominium Group will pay the money out as soon as I telephone them of your death, and they can verify this with the police.'

Peter said, 'Rod, they are playing you for a sucker. They will never pay you the money, saying you were caught red- handed killing us two. They will only pay on a contract if it is a professional hit man, not a farmer from out here. They want your farm, not pay you a couple of million to kill us.'

Rod said, 'I spoke to the principal of Dominium, who assures me the money will be in my bank account as soon as the police confirm your death.'

Peter said, 'Rod, the good Lord will never let you get away with this. Look at your family and your two children. You will never get away with it and will end up never seeing them again. Please put the gun down, allow us to offload the trailer, and we will get out of here.'

Rod said, 'Love, move out of the way, I mean it. Move out of the way.'

Satan had taken control of Rod, and he was cursed to kill both Vince and Peter. His eyes were enormous, like someone on drugs, and he could not be reasoned with.

Mrs Ridgeway moved aside, leaving Rod with aim at Peter and then at Vince.

Helen, who had frozen and could not move, kept saying, 'Rod, don't do it. You will regret it for the rest of your life. Rod, do not do it. Rod.'

Peter was saying, 'Father, into Your hands, I deliver my spirit.'

As Peter was praying, he could see the old man standing near to Rod and believed the end was near for him and Vince. While Helen was talking, you could see Rod squeezing the trigger when, suddenly, a gigantic explosion came from the rifle as Rod pulled the trigger back to its limit.

Smoke came from the firing pin, and Rod dropped the rifle, clutching his face in agony, screaming, 'I can't see!' It was clear the rifle had exploded in his face, burning his eyes.

Peter and Vince rushed up to him and immediately grabbed a bottle of water and doused his face and eyes, but it was clear from looking at his eyes that he had done permanent damage to his sight and would never see again.

Peter and Vince quickly grabbed a towel and wrapped it around Rod's face and put him in Peter's car and drove off to the hospital. Once there, they took him to emergency, who, after examining him, declared he will never see again and had major burns on his face.

Rod stayed in hospital for a week and was then released.

Peter and Vince did not press charges, as they thought he would suffer for the rest of his life in trusting Satan and not God in this situation.

The Ridgeways were forced to hand their farm to the bank, who sold it to the Dominium Group at a discounted price.

Peter went back to Castle Hill with Helen, and Vince and the boys went back to his farm at Bungarby. Everyone was shocked over the incident, particularly the pressure put on Rod to claim the contract on Peter and Vince to maintain his farm for his family.

One thing was apparent: Lucifer was now making his move to capitalise on the misery of people throughout the world and was making sure his Dominium Group benefited from Covid-19 and became enriched in the process.

CHAPTER 60

Peter went back to Bungarby with Helen. She first decided not to go with him, but after thinking about it, she did not want to be alone and decided the company would be helpful after Paul had passed away for her to decide as to what she was going to do with herself. She always got on well with her brother, Peter, and once again, she leaned on him for mental support.

Helen knew that there was always someone she could converse with in Bungarby, as Vince often popped in, and so did some locals.

Peter, Helen, and Vince were on the veranda with three of the boys having coffee and cake for morning tea when a call came through to Peter from one of the senior ministers of the church advising him that his name has been submitted for archdeacon and asking if he conceded to this.

Peter said, 'Archdeacon? You are kidding. I would not stand up to the Lord's standard. Maybe I should not say that, as I have asked forgiveness, and I know Jesus took my sins to the cross and died for me.'

Upon saying that, the old man appeared.

The old man said, 'Yes, Peter, I died for your sins, and your sins are forgiven for what I did on the cross. The only things that remain on this earth are your memories and Satan, who thought he had you from the start, both in body and soul. He has not forgiven you for seeing the light, hearing My word and following Me. You must be careful, for he will use any excuse to discredit you and my church, and he is a murderer and will not hesitate to facilitate your death.

'The Dominium Group is Lucifer's inner circle. James Coelicola, their chairman, is Satan incarnated. He has adopted my brother's Christian name, James, and surname, Coelicola, which means "God, celestial" in Latin. He will soon pay for the misery he has caused this world. But in the meantime, I use him to sift mankind so mankind may know if they have solid, rock-hard faith in me or their faith is on loose sand. The time will come when all must face God and account for their lives on earth.'

'I will send you to the city and make you archdeacon, and you will clean out my church of Satan's Antichrists. Those that do not want to follow My word have no place in My church and should be removed and made out what they really are—disciples of Satan. They are antichrists, sheep in wolfs clothing.'

'Your sister, Helen, will go with you. She has been with you since you started this long journey and has, time after time, shown solid faith in me. She will assist you, but for a short time when she will return to me. Vince will also assist you and ensure the might of Satan does not prevail. You must try to change the attitude of the directors of Dominium Group, or I will eliminate them for what they have done to the farmers and rob them of their land. There is one director amongst them that will hear my word. Seek him out and encourage him to follow Me. Be on your guard, for Satan will not allow this to go unpunished.'

Peter protested, as he did not want to be archdeacon, and as he stepped forward, he realised the Lord had gone and he was talking to those present, who were also confused and worried as to what had just been said to them.

About thirty minutes later, Peter received a phone call from one contender advising him he was prepared to withdraw if Peter was running.

Peter did not know what to say. The Lord told him he would be an archdeacon, and he knew the Lord would not make a statement unless it was going to be true. Peter persuaded the minister to remain on the list as a contender, as he could have his name removed anytime, but nominations must be done within a short period, and once closed, new entries cannot be added.

Three of Satan's Antichrists nominated for the position and the wealthiest man in the world, James Coelicola, made his intentions known that Paul Elliot, senior minister for many years and well-respected, should receive the post. Mr Elliot received the publicity afforded to diplomats and politicians, making him the choice of the average person. Those in the ministry did not agree and knew that Mr Eliot was not a God-fearing man and had no faith in Jesus Christ. He had frequently been quoted saying things contrary to the word of God and went out of his way to diminish the church rather than support it. If he received the appointment, it would be a bad day for Christians and the church.

Eliot was on every talkback radio station and TV program in the country; he debated controversial matters such as abortion and euthanasia, and what he said was not the Bible's view of these matters but the state's view. He was the man out front, and no one was even close to him. If anyone tried to get close in the poles, they found themselves smeared in the press or accused of pornography or such like. Their character would be brought into question by reporters who were paid to discredit the opposition, making it impossible for them to get a fair hearing.

Coelicola was very confident he was going to nominate his man for this position, and this would be the commencement of turning the mass of Christians against God and towards a religion directed by him, one being more in tune with the modern worldview. He knew God would not like it but believed He could do nothing about it, as mankind had the right to free choice. He was going to make God regret giving mankind this privilege.

While Jesus has said Satan can only do what God permits him to do; Lucifer has another adaptation of this, which in his view, he can do anything he can get away with. This attitude has been installed in his followers and is the basis of their relationship with him and why dishonesty prevails.

Lucifer's attitude is he is doomed to hell for a thousand years, so in the realm of things, what has he got to lose? He has got away with his dishonesty for thousands of years and has successfully convinced mankind that his way is the best and only way for them to achieve their desires on this earth. It is this policy that has gained him support. He knows most of the world's population is aligned with him and has nothing to do with God or the Bible. Materiality and wealth are the sign of success on this earth, not promises regards the future.

Coelicola believes that when the time Christ tries to pass sentence on him, Lucifer, he will have such a vast number of followers that God will have no choice but to capitulate to Satan's demands and will not dare carry out His judgement that was handed out to Lucifer and his angels prior to their eviction from heaven. He knows that God so loves mankind, that this will prevent God from sentencing mankind to the same judgement given to Lucifer. Also, Lucifer believes he will have the majority support, forcing God to agree to his demands and not fulfill the sentence handed down to him and his followers and relinquish control to Lucifer.

CHAPTER 61

J AMES COELICOLA WAS IN HIS office going over the opinion polls
commissioned to be done privately to see what the average person
thought of the three candidates he had nominated for the position
of archdeacon. He was also going over the promises he had made to
senior clerics for donations to either renovate their old churches or
make personal payments to them for their support in voting for any
of his three nominees for the position of archdeacon.

He noted that the younger the person, the more likelihood was
they could be persuaded by being offered money, wealth, or material
things; whereas the older persons who followed the teachings of Christ
could be persuaded by offering them a better job, employment, or
opportunity, and they were less inclined to lie or cheat, unless the
benefit was greater than their belief. They would rather adhere to the
word of God than to collect a few trinkets, and this lot always declared
their belief but would move to the opposing force if it benefited them.

Coelicola knew the way to have the older person turn from Jesus
was to cause a death of a close member of the family or an incident
to occur, causing their belief to be tested. This event always had the
person questioning God's love for mankind and His inability or
will to look after them and therefore cause them to abandon their
belief in God. All that was required was a car accident, a rape, or any
misfortune. Coelicola knew mankind would turn from God when
any of these things happened, and he had the power to cause these at
any time to test mankind's faith.

Coelicola noted the contracts were still out against both Peter and Vince. The Archdeacon was dead, and therefore his contract lapsed. He decided the best insurance against Peter ever being nominated or gaining the position was for him to be dead and not active, as he has always been a thorn in his side, preaching the word of God. He tried to buy him out in the past with a lottery win, but this did not work out, and tried to have him killed by a farmer, Rod Ridgeway, but this again never went to plan. He decided to again renew the contract and limit it to two months, forcing both men to stay indoors and have low profiles. If they could not move around freely, they would get limited exposure.

The word went out, and the money on offer was doubled to $20 million, which was enough to attract the best in the business. The lockdown of the world countries would prevent just anyone being able to attend to the contract, as they could not get into the country without buying their way in. They would also have to fly in on a private jet and leave the same way.

CHAPTER 62

Vince telephoned Peter, but Helen answered the phone and said he was free, and Vince could come on over that day.

Vince turned up at about eleven in the morning and was warmly greeted. On this occasion, he had four men with him and not just the usual two, and each had a rifle.

Peter asked, 'Vince, are you planning an ongoing shooting today with the boys? They could have left their rifles in their cars.'

Vince replied, 'Not really. My contacts overseas tell me that the originator of the contract on us is James Coelicola, none other than the chair of the Dominium Group, and that he has upped the payout to twenty million on confirmation of our death. That is twenty million apiece. Not bad for a few minutes' work.'

Peter said, 'Well, that tells me why the rifles. Where are you going to do it, and how soon do you think you will be able to claim the money?'

Helen said, 'Peter, be serious. There are men out there that will jump at this opportunity and will collect on the contract. You will have to stay indoors for a few months to keep yourself safe.'

Peter replied, 'No way. I have been ordered to take up the position of archdeacon, and the vote will take place soon. I will have to be around and about and speak to as many of the voting group as possible, placing my faith in God and not in the intentions of corrupt men. However, I am getting sick and tired of being just on the receiving end of this type of threat. Why cannot we do some pushing ourselves?'

'Coelicola was to get rid of us while positioning his own people in God's church. We cannot take a contract out on Satan even though we would like to, and God would not support us but, currently, there are four names of the Dominium Group that continually crop up as being at the forefront in trying to steal farms from farmers or manipulate world markets for their own benefits. What happens if a contract is taken out on each of these men?'

Vince said, 'We do not have $40 million to pay out on such a contract. Besides, no one will take us for real, as they know we follow the faith and would not issue such a contract.'

Peter replied, 'That's right, but what happens if the contract is in Coelicola's name? Everyone internationally knows of his power and reputation as a ruthless murderer, so they would not question the authenticity of the contract.'

Vince said, 'I guess you are right, and at worst, we can unearth his stronghold, at best, allow him to do what he does best—killing people. But how do we put out the contract?'

Peter replied, 'That's easy with the internet, and it is untraceable. You still have your drug contacts in Canada. Ring them and ask them to confirm that they have listed the contract on behalf of Coelicola, him being one of their largest clients. They would not have listed the contract, but I am sure they would not want to have made such a big mistake on their heads as not listing the contract. If my lead is correct, they are the ones who have listed the contract on us, and therefore they would assume it is part of the original contract and something went wrong in its notation. They won't argue, as they will not have to deal with Coelicola and his temper if found out to be in the wrong.'

Vince said, 'A good plan. I will get onto it straightaway. One of my men is an expert in these things. I will get him on to it straightaway.'

Vince moved out of the room just when Peter's mobile rang, and a senior minister informed Peter that a meeting had been held with several orthodox ministers who agreed that he was their best candidate for the position of archdeacon. They advised they have had enough of the church and the Bible being misrepresented and intent to fight back using the word of God, not the words of men taken from a Bible changed by men. They would have to have Peter's decision to run immediately as they were advising their decision to support him at a midday news conference.

Vince came back into the room and sat down to listen to Peter's conversation. Peter glanced at Vince, and Vince nodded. Peter said, 'John, I appreciate the vote of support from all concerned, but you are rushing me to make a very important decision. I would like to have more time to talk it over with members of my family. No, I am not married, but my sister stays with me now, and she has just lost her husband to Covid-19. If I cannot have more time, advise the audience that I have not decided to throw my hat into the ring, as I understand James Coelicola is supporting three candidates and, to ensure one of them succeeds, has taken a contract out on me for $20 million. Well, John, you know this is true, as some of your parishioners have already mentioned this to you, but I am sure it just slipped your mind. If I hear it on television, I will agree to be nominated as the world will know. If you will not give me that protection, then throw your own name in the ring and let Coelicola come after you and your family. Thanks for ringing.'

The press conference was held midday and was addressed by the senior cleric.

John said, 'Thank you for coming. We wish to announce that there are four nominations for archdeacon, and we have listed their names on the press release issued to each of you. Three are definite and are supported by James Coelicola, while the other will nominate but has been advised that a contract has been taken out on his life by Mr Coelicola, which prevents him from appearing freely in public. We cannot confirm this is the case and have referred the matter to the police for investigation. The vote will be taken in two weeks' time by the relevant bodies, and a new archdeacon will be announced on that day. Are there any questions?'

The room exploded with newspaper reporters wanting to know more about the contract on Peter Marlow's life, as most knew this to be true and knew it was for $20 million.

Shortly after the broadcast, there appeared in the news a statement from Mr Coelicola's office denying his involvement in the contract but declaring them to have been informed of the existence of the contract on Mr Marlow's life from ex-gangland connections.

Peter, hearing that he had been nominated, knew he was a marked man and realised he had to take better precautions than previously and had to restrict his movements.

He moved back to his city office and lived in Vince's unit under protection of some of Vince's men, who were always with him.

Vince decided to also move from Bungarby to the city until the election of the Archdeacon had been concluded and took care to ensure he was not out in the open for a sniper to take a shot at him.

The cleric had arranged for all candidates to make a public presentation on the steps of the church on Sunday week to allow all those involved to hear from each candidate while still maintaining the distancing rules established by the government. Their order of appearance was decided by lot, and Peter was to be the third speaker. Police were to be on hand to ensure their safety and to control the crowd and reporters.

The week was dedicated to advising the public about each candidate and for what they stood for and how they saw the future of the church. The Coelicola connections made sure that their candidates were well publicised and showing their beliefs that religion must keep up with the times and reflect society's standards even if it meant changing a portion of the Bible.

Most of society agreed with their approach, particularly on matters regarding same-sex marriage, euthanasia, abortion, and homosexual matters. However, the orthodox religious persons did not, and they took the view and believed that God's word is what should be followed, not man's intended misinterpretation of the Bible. They did not get an equal representation of their arguments in the press or news, as the Coelicola's camp had most of the publishers bought, and there were no restrictions on the amount of money that could be spent by any of the candidates, so they obliterated the news and were in everyone's faces with their arguments preventing an alternative view being presented.

Peter could be interviewed at his city office but did not venture out to the broadcaster's studios, as this would mean he would expose himself to anyone wishing to claim on the contract.

CHAPTER 63

T HE DAY OF THE PUBLIC debate was organised to give candidates an opportunity to declare their position and present their arguments as to what they stood for and what they would do for the community and church as archdeacon.

John (elder of the church) said, 'The first speaker shall be Marcus Debranin.'

Marcus, who was sitting at the base of the church's steps, stood up as soon as his name was read out and walked up the church steps to the makeshift pulpit on the top level of the steps. He stood there for a few seconds and then made his presentation.

Marcus said, 'Thank you, John, for your introduction. From the outset, I wish to advise that I consider myself a progressive cleric and not one stuck in two thousand years of tradition. I respect my opponent's views and do not condone them but say that I have my view on what is required by an archdeacon in a modern society and have stuck to these consistently.

'I stand for modernising the interpretation of the Bible to incorporate what the majority view, in that we should progress to accept changes that have been legislated by the state in the areas of same-sex marriage, homosexuality, euthanasia, and abortion—four platforms that society has accepted but conflict with the view of the Bible. Society or modernity declares these issues should be in line with society's view and not that the majority must accept the views established some three thousand years ago.

'As Archdeacon, I will commission the alteration of the Bible to reflect a modern view of these aspects of society so we may worship a God that we consider worthy of worshiping and who graces our progressive view.'

Marcus spent a further twenty minutes outlining his progressive view and, no doubt to the delight of James Coelicola, made a good impression with most, considering he held the view of the majority in the community.

John Clements said, 'Thank you, Marcus, for outlining your position and claim to becoming archdeacon. We now have Peter Marlow as our next speaker, and I ask that he step up and present his stand and claim to the position of being archdeacon.'

Helen, who was sitting between Peter and Vince, hurried to the pulpit, as she was going to assist Peter in his presentation by handing him sections of his speech at a time.

Peter followed her up the stairs.

Peter moved to position himself at the pulpit and then realised he did not have his speech, as this was held by Helen. He reached to take it from her, but she moved into the pulpit to place it on the table in the order as he was to make his presentation. As she moved in front of Peter, a shot rang out, and Helen slumped to a kneeling position first, grasping her chest, and then falling face down on the ground.

Vince, quickly realising what had happened, grabbed Peter, but he resisted, kneeling over Alice, staring in disbelief at her, and placing his hand on her chest to stop the bleeding. Vince quickly grabbed Peter and pushed him away from the scene, leaving Helen on the ground. He called for his men to check on her as he grabbed Peter and pulled him into the church, under cover and out of sight.

One of Vince's men checked Helen's pulse, but there was none, and he shook his head, showing she was dead. Police immediately rushed in and evacuated the area, forcing all present to go into the church for cover. Peter tried to go out to check on Helen, but he was held back by Vince and some of his men. Eventually, Peter realised he could do nothing for her, and paramedics who were on the scene showed she was dead, as the shot was straight to the heart. She had no chance of surviving the shot.

The news of the killing was shown on world television, and all that viewed it were shocked that what was clearly predicted as to what was to happen to Peter would have happened except for a split second, when Helen stepped into the line of fire to put out Peter's papers for his presentation.

Alice and Tim were viewing the presentation from their lounge room when they saw Helen fall to the ground and realised that she had been shot by snipper—a shot that was meant for Peter.

Alice quickly telephoned Peter, but he was too distraught to take the call, which was taken by one of Vince's men, who said he would pass the message on to him.

About an hour later, Peter called Alice to give her the bad news that her mother was shot dead, a shot no doubt meant for him.

Nations throughout the world who originally picked up the story a week ago as to why Peter was reluctant to run and James Coelicola's denial that he had a contract out on killing Peter now placed the blame on James Coelicola, who again declared himself innocent of any knowledge of the contract and any association or dealing with the crime bosses, which was an outright lie.

The feeling worldwide was that Coelicola considered himself above the law and could do anything he desired. This had a negative reaction against his first candidate, Marcus, and against the other two candidates that he was supporting. The view was that if Coelicola thought he was beyond religion and the law, then it was considered his nominees would consider themselves likewise, and voters turned from them.

Coelicola had many supporters in a lot of positions of influence, including universities and churches throughout the world. Many were involved in religion and preached Christ, but few believed in Him and, when possible, gave the impression that it was all assumptions and the Bible had very little support or evidence to back up what it was saying.

When a contentious matter rose, none would appear to defend Christ or the church. They all made a good living out of religion, but none would defend it or the church against Coelicola, as they did not believe in Jesus Christ, let alone have faith in Him.

The rest of the debate was called off, and members were asked to vote for whom they considered the best applicant for the job. The first vote was undecided, making it mandatory to meet in two weeks' time to have a further vote. The delegates' decision, unfortunately, was influenced by threats and bribes to have them vote for one of the Coelicola team with preference to Marcus. It was strange when one delegate declared openly that he would vote for Peter Marlow, as he was the only one who could be trusted to follow God's word. That delegate was involved in a tragic car accident on his way home when a truck ploughed into his car on the highway, killing him instantly. The driver of the truck jumped clear just before impact and sustained a minor injury. A replacement delegate was appointed to ensure the numbers were there for the vote.

A second vote took place, and the vote was split evenly between Peter Marlow and Marcus. A further week would have to be put aside before another vote could be taken.

Many delegates were entertained by senior church members of other religions to persuade them to vote for the Coelicola's nominee, Marcus, as he would be the only one that will liberate the Christian religion and give the people what they want. It would also bring religion under the control of the state, making them one rather than having a separation. Many delegates thought this was not a good idea, but said nothing at the time for fear of their lives and the effect it would have on their families.

Many were promised money through personal bribes and benefits for their family, such as guaranteed university places and fees being waived. Others were offered money to refurbish their churches, and these would not have to be paid back. Offers most times seemed outlandish, and one would wonder where the money would come from, yet when pressed, the money would be paid into a personal bank account upon guarantee the delegate would vote Coelicola's way and after the vote was taken.

The week ended with the delegates again meeting in private and taking the final vote, which gave Peter Marlow the majority, as most delegates did not believe the promises made to them would ever eventuate, and most feared the power and influence of James Coelicola.

The question was raised amongst the clerics as to why God did not do something to ensure a fairer vote and why He did not restrain

Coelicola from making his bribes and threats. The conclusion most agreed upon was God viewed this as mankind's problem, and He had given free choice to man and would not influence man's decision as Coelicola was endeavouring to do. They also viewed that once Coelicola was entrenched in the church, then honesty and truth would fall to the person with the most money and not as God had meant it.

Many feared that the world would be punished by God should the majority vote for Coelicola's appointee, as it was doubtful God would allow the alteration of the Bible and His word and the adoption of substitutes.

He threw Lucifer from heaven when he tried to overthrow Him, and there was little doubt he would not tolerate mankind trying to remove the legitimate God and His church from this earth. It was considered that the heatwaves or climate change were God's warning to mankind to be careful what it voted for, as it may come sooner than expected.

God expects mankind to remember that it was He who created the world and not mankind and not the other way around—a point no doubt not considered by Lucifer when he tried to cause the uprising in heaven many centuries ago.

After much debate, Peter was finally appointed archdeacon and immediately took steps to get rid of those ministers that were there to derail the teachings of Christ and the church. Those ministers that felt they had to change the Bible or refused to follow the word of God were dismissed. No doubt they would establish their own churches or be employed where the emphasis was on reform and not the teaching of Christ, or possibly end up as ministers in cults.

CHAPTER 64

Adrian Marsh, who was deputy to James Coelicola and board member of Dominium Group, was sitting at a café with his wife and daughter on a Sunday morning having a quick cup of coffee before proceeding to his office to collect some papers. He sat peacefully in the open under an umbrella with his family enjoying the sunlight when, suddenly, two men ran up to where he was sitting, who immediately produced guns from their belts and unloaded their revolvers straight into his body and ran out to an awaiting car and drove off.

It caught his wife by surprise, who had frozen from fear, while their daughter, seeing her father gunned down, began screaming hysterically. The proprietor of the café stepped forward to see what was happening and immediately phoned for the police and ambulance. Both appeared on the scene soon after, but nothing could be done, as he had been shot too many times and died immediately.

About an hour later, a second shooting was reported where a board member of the Dominium Group was shot while on his way to church with his family. Again, this was at point-blank range and in full sight of parishioners. No one remembered what the gunmen looked like, as it happened all so quickly.

At around twelve midday, the news reported a third member of the Dominium Group board had been gunned down while answering a knock at his front door. Like the others, it was at point-blank range with no chance of surviving the shooting.

That evening, a fourth Dominium Group member was gunned down while exercising with his personal trainer and bodyguard. The bodyguard was injured in that he tried to return fire and was shot at by the men who killed the Dominium Group board member.

News of the shootings were passed on to James Coelicola, who at first thought it was Peter getting back at the attempt on his life or one of Vince's men attending to a revenge job, but as the killings came through, he realised it could not be Peter or his connections but did not know who was attending to these and what was the purpose, as most of the underworld knew of James Coelicola and feared him. So, who would willingly come up against Coelicola with his connections and power?

James Coelicola immediately telephoned his other three directors and ordered them to stay put until he knew who was ordering the killings and why they were being carried out.

Over the next forty-eight hours, Coelicola could not find out who arranged the killings and why. However, he received notice from his office that four lots of $20 million were withdrawn from his account, and in checking, the reason found out it was a claim by the drug ring for attending to the contracts placed by Coelicola on the four board members who had been gunned down.

James Coelicola, who knew nothing about the contracts, went into a rage, denying knowledge of the killings and demanded the return of the money. The drug boss refused, citing the contracts on the men and completion of the contracts as the reason for payment.

Word got around that Coelicola had arranged the killing and paid the money to have his men killed. No matter what Coelicola did, he could not shake the fact that the men were killed under a contract established under his name and paid out of an account that had been used previously for such a purpose. He was recognised by the murderer that he was.

As Coelicola refused to accept responsibility for the contracts and the killings, the drug gang refused to deal with him on any further contracts and ended all existing contracts that were outstanding, including the ones on Peter and Vince.

The news of the clash between Coelicola and the drug bosses were reported throughout the underworld, and the refusal to handle any further contracts was good news to Peter and Vince.

CHAPTER 65

IT WAS A RAINY DAY, and only a few people turned out to pay their respects at Helen's funeral. Peter officiated and found it hard to hold back his tears and was forced to cut the service short to bring things to a conclusion quickly.

It was decided that Helen would be buried alongside Paul Curtis, her husband, who died of Covid-19 in Castle Hill not that long ago.

After the ceremony, they moved off to the cemetery, and prayers were said over Helen's casket before it was lowered into the plot and covered over by dirt.

A small wake was held in a café nearby, but little was said, and all showed signs of still being upset and shocked as to the killing. Many thought the Dominium Group had not paid enough by the four men that were gunned down, while others said payment was made, or was it retribution?

While they were standing around, there was a news flash describing an emergency landing of an airline at the local airport. The airline was not named, nor were the occupants, which Peter thought was strange.

Peter moved closer to the television screen and noticed the markings on the plane were those of the Dominium Group and wondered whether the last three directors of the group were on board.

Vince noticed Peter's interest in the plane and moved closer to the television set to also see what markings were on the plane. He also concluded it was a Dominium Group plane and wondered if the passengers were the three remaining directors of the group. Vince made some telephone calls, and after about a half an hour, it was confirmed that the three were on their way back to New York and had trouble with one of their jet engines.

Peter mentioned several farmers had telephoned him to advise that they were being forced off their land and the Dominium Group was behind it, trying to buy their farms up for a third of the price. Many did not know what to do, as they would have to bankrupt themselves to clear the debt.

Some advised that they understood that the government was going to legislate to prevent farmers declaring themselves bankrupt, forcing them to carry the debt for the rest of their lives, never being able to get back on their feet. Many that found themselves in this predicament were contemplating suicide, as there was no alternative. The whole situation was inequitable, leaving the Dominium Group again in control and reaping extreme profits at the expense of those who could least afford it.

The farmers held meetings and called on the politicians to attend, but at the end, there was a lot of talk but very little action from the politicians to support the farmers. Promises were made, but these were never followed up by action or legislation, and if anyone really tried to rock the boat, they found themselves in trouble or their reputation smeared.

Peter moved over to where Vince was standing and waited for his opportunity.

Peter said, 'You know, Vince, if these are the remaining directors of the board, we may be able to show them what they are doing to the farmers by forcing them off their land. They may see reason if we get them in front of the devastated families or communities. The worst that could happen is they refuse to accept our attempts to reason with them and remain dogmatic in their ways and go about stealing the farms.'

Vince said, 'it would mean we would have to move now before reinforcements got to them.'

Peter said, 'Get your men onto it and let's hit the airport with a military-style operation and take them around for a couple of hours so they can meet as many families affected by their greed.'

Vince immediately phoned his contact in SWAT for help. They would change uniforms and get new magnetic signage on their vehicles, so no one thought it was a government department arresting them.

They would confront them at the regional airport where they were in a secure lounge terminal and, once they were captured and disarmed, take them and their guards around and eventually bring them back to the terminal.

Peter said, 'Vince, you know this will get up James Coelicola's nose, as his directors will get another view of the world and not just the lies Coelicola is preaching.'

Vince said, 'He most probably will kill every one of them himself. He would not allow a contrary view to be expressed or held.'

The time was planned at twelve that day. They could not let the plan to leak out, as Coelicola would have every man there killed if given the opportunity.

They made their raid on the airport terminal. Men created a camouflage from the front, while most went in from the back door. The guards looking after the three directors were taken by surprise, and when ordered to drop their guns, they did so because they were outnumbered. They were immediately taken to an office at the airport and addressed by Peter.

The men were assured they would not be harmed, and that Peter and Vince would accompany them around with their guards. After three hours, they would be brought back to their hangar and allowed to go on their way.

Peter said, 'Most of you do not know me or any of these men. It really is unnecessary, but no doubt you will have to account to your boss, James Coelicola. So, I will give you my name. I am Peter Marlow, the brother of Helen, whom, three weeks ago, you had shot by a sniper who took her to be me and killed her outside the steps of the church where I was to make my presentation as to why I should be elected as Archdeacon. The man next to me is Vince Marconi, whom you also have a contract out on. We understand that four of your directors were gunned down recently under a contract, and you are the only directors left on the board of Dominium Group. You can tell Coelicola that we thought you would like to see first-hand what your grab for wealth is doing to the average family in these regional areas. Regarding Coelicola, some think he is Lucifer under a disguised name, but that is for another occasion.'

'As we have said, we do not intend to harm you and intend to release you back here in about three hours. We understand you are making aggressive demands to acquire farms in this region and really do not care whether your actions are legal or moral. What you men are doing is leaving farmers no hope to reclaim their lives, and therefore they are suiciding because of the pressure. The banks are not caring what happens to these poor souls, only what they can do to ensure your satisfaction.'

'We intend to take you out to speak to some of these farmers and get first-hand knowledge of what they are experiencing and for you to see first-hand what you are doing to the most vulnerable and poorest section of the community.'

One director said, 'if that is all you intend to do, then you can save your time. We are not their keeper and really do not care what happens to the farmers or their families. They should look after themselves, and we will do likewise.'

Peter said, 'So the fact that God gave you the resources to put you in your current position doesn't amount to anything in your book, does it? You think you are a self-made man, don't you?'

The director replied, 'Yes. My parents sent me to university, and I had some lucky breaks and ended up very wealthy.'

Peter said, 'if you are so much a self-made man, why can't you tell me what is going to happen to you tomorrow?'

The director replied, 'No one can predict what happens, but our organisation, with its influence and power, can and makes things happen for their benefit. Since joining Dominium Group, my wealth has doubled, and I intend for it to continue until I retire.'

Peter said, 'You may find God will end your life sooner than you plan, bring all of your conniving and cheating to an end with you taking a holiday with Lucifer in hell.'

'Gentlemen, we would ask you to move to the bus we have borrowed. Your bodyguards can accompany you, but they will not have their guns, which will be returned to them when we return to the terminal. Because we only have three hours, we cannot go out too far from the town. We would like to show you three or four farms and allow you to speak to their owners. Please move into the bus.'

They all got on the bus, and it was driven off to a farm north of the town. After driving through drought-affected land for forty minutes, they arrived at the farmhouse and all alighted from the bus.

The director asked, 'which farm is this one?'

Peter replied, 'This is the Richardson farm. one of you has told the bank to make sure you get it at rock-bottom price knowing that the debt the farmer owes the bank will never be paid off.'

The second director stepped forward. 'I am the one who has told the bank to arrange for a transfer at a fair price and not at a rock-bottom price. I believe the bank is trying to please its masters rather than trying to arrange for a fair outcome.' The first director said, 'what we see here is they are doing him a favour. He will never get off the land and sell his farm under any condition.'

Peter said, 'The banks told them they were going to repossess their land and sell it to the highest bidder. The farm was held in Mr Richardson's name, and it had been in his family for four generations. Three years ago, his farm was listed as the producer of the best merino wool in the Southern Hemisphere. 'Three years ago, the farm was sought after by world investors who were willing to pay over $5 million for the farm and its stock. Now, the bank offered Mr Richardson five hundred thousand dollars.

Mr Richardson owed the bank $2 million, and because of the new legislation introduced by this government, Mr Richardson could not declare himself bankrupt after his farm was sold. The debt stayed with him for all his life, and should he ever get any money, the bank would take it from him so he could never make money to pay off his debt.

Mr Richardson sought help from councillors, but they only say they are there to support him, but no one ever gave him accurate advice or any worthwhile help. As they told Mr Richardson, they must seem to be there to support the farmers to ensure they get their government paid consultancy fee. They really do not have to do anything to earn the money, as they are never judged on the number of people they have helped. Only saying they are there to support the farmers, and if it looks good, the government will give them their fee.

'Two days ago, the bank said it was revising the five-hundred-thousand deal down to three hundred thousand, as all the stock had been sold, including the scouring plant and presses. Upon hearing this from the bank and knowing he could not negotiate with them, Mr Richardson, on his way home, pulled up at one tree on his property and hanged himself. He left a wife and three children. The youngest is three months old.

'Gentlemen, would you come this way? I will introduce you to Mrs Richardson and her three children. Her parents have also come here to see what kind of God-fearing people you are.' Peter moved towards the homestead when the second director stepped forward and said, 'Look, we do not believe it would achieve anything to speak to Mrs Richardson, only cause the family a lot of grief and anxiety. Let us get on with the next farm, as we only have a limited time.'

Peter said, 'The family has asked to at least speak to those people who drove Mr Richardson to suiciding. Surely this is a just and reasonable request.'

The director said, 'Look, they are looking for someone to blame, and there is little doubt that all the fingers are going to be pointed at us. All we did was make a commercial decision to buy their farm. We did not care about their welfare or anything, as we did not know them. All we did was agree to pay them a lump sum, and after that, it was between them and their banks.' With that, they all piled back onto the bus and sat down.

Peter walked into the farmhouse and stayed there for about five minutes. He came out with Mrs Richardson carrying the baby, accompanied by her father and mother. They walked up to the bus and went inside, staring at the people sitting there.

Mr Richardson Senior said, 'None of you had the guts to come inside and face us. You are just a bunch of money-grabbing bastards, and I hope someday God punishes you for what you have done to my son. None of you care what God says in the Bible. I hope you all rot in hell for what you have done to my son. All of you are just a bunch of money-grabbing mongrels.'

Mr Richardson, his wife, and daughter got out of the bus and went back to the homestead.

Peter said, 'We better move on to our next farm, but before we do, can you tell me, did you ever consider what will happen to your soul by acting in this way? You will never have your sins forgiven, and you are going to follow your master, Lucifer, down the path to hell.'

The director replied, 'Look, God gives you none of these treasures. He just gives you trials, which we do not need. We all are wealthy and have political power to make things happen. We do not need God. we have things we would not otherwise have and things that count. With God, you will get none of these things and die as a poor person. We at least have everything we ever wanted and more.'

Peter said, 'I think you have been intoxicated with the theory of what this world can give you if you only deny God.'

'Just remember your four other directors. They also had the philosophy you have. They also went mad and accumulated as much wealth as they could. What happened to them? They were never given the time to enjoy their wealth—shot dead in the open, leaving all their wealth for others. You may be the same. You think you can control all things, but you cannot. Only God knows when your time is up. The wealth you have accumulated may be a very expensive price to pay for a thousand years in hell. 'Wouldn't you be better off making sure you accumulate your wealth is in heaven and live an eternal life rather than the life here on earth for what, five, ten years, and then end up with Lucifer in hell for a thousand years?'

The director replied, 'Possibly. However, James does not believe God will ever bring on the Second Coming. It is spoken about but will never happen. It is a good pitch to keep the average person on the straight and narrow rather than being an actual event that will happen. Three thousand years had passed since it was first mentioned, and still no sign of it ever happening. I believe my family and I would prefer the wealth we have gained over a promise that may eventuate or could eventuate well past our time in the future, considering we first started off with God's curse. We have enough wealth to buffer anything that can be thrown at us and, if left alone, could live a good life with our family.'

Peter said, 'Life is always unpredictable, and if you think God is going to allow you to thumb your noses at him and get away with it, then you should think otherwise.'

The group moved onto the next farm, which was some thirty-five minutes away. They drove up to the homestead, and Peter gave everyone a summary of what has happened. 'The husband died of cancer, and the property was in joint names. The creditors were advised by the bank to file for bankruptcy, as the farmer could not pay his debts. The creditors, who mainly comprised local businesses, rejected the bank's recommendation and gave the widower time to pay her debts off. They refused to file for bankruptcy. The bank who had the deeds to the property went along even though the owner's mortgage repayments were paid in advance.'

'They dishonestly raised an amount that they said were fees and legal expenses incurred in corresponding and communicating with the farmer to resolve property-related issues that were not specified. Since the farmer's wife knew nothing about the claims, she refused to pay for them, and, eventually, the bank took proceedings to bankrupt her to gain control of the property.'

'The wife has no money or an income and can barely feed her family. She cannot get representation in court and therefore not able to plead her case and argue against the fraudulent actions of the bank. The bank is relying on this and has several barristers representing them in this action. All this is happening because you have instructed the banks to secure the farm at the lowest price, and they are following your orders.'

'Will you now follow me to the homestead, and you can speak to the wife?'

Peter moved off the bus, but no one followed him. All sat in their seats and were not prepared to speak to the wife.

The director said, 'We can't see any purpose to speak to the wife. Again, we have instructed the bank to secure the property by legal process, and it is up to them to do this. We do not get involved in the process and do not meddle in their affairs as to how they do it. If the property becomes available, we decide whether we are interested in buying it, and if one of us is, we nominate a price, and if this is acceptable, we then leave it to the lawyers to transact. There is no benefit to us to speak to her.'

Peter said, 'Surely you would want to speak to her to find out whether she is being forced off her farm by illegal means and whether she will sell or is being forced to sell.'

The director replied, 'No, as all we are doing is buying a property that has come on the market. We are not forcing the sale. If that is happening, then you should get the banks to take one of these trips and not us. All we are doing is agreeing to pay the price.'

Peter said, 'No, you have instructed the banks to secure property for you and are not just an at arm's length buyer.'

The director replied, 'That is your argument and not ours. We do not really care about these people or their predicament. All we care about is the result. If the farm becomes available and we are interested, we will buy it. Otherwise, we would wait for the next one to become available and check it out.'

Peter asked, 'Don't you realise that your action or demands on the banks are forcing them to act in the way they are currently doing? They are in fact, just following your orders. They also don't care what happens to these people. All they care about is your business and not what it is doing to these families.'

The director said, 'We don't see it that way. We are merely buyers. Nothing else. Can we now get back to our plan, as the three hours are just about up?'

Peter said, 'I will advise Mrs Bishop that you won't be meeting with her. She thought she could persuade you to give her some more time to get back on her feet and come to some arrangements with you, but I can see that will never happen.'

Peter walked to the homestead and spoke to Mrs. Bishop. After a few minutes, he came out by himself and got on the bus, and they all drove off towards the airport. No one asked what Mrs Bishop had to say or her reaction. They would not care about her or her opinion. All they were worried about was their wealth.

Vince enquired as to what Mrs. Bishop had to say, but Peter indicated he would tell him later, after they had gotten rid of their guests.

The bus was driven back to the airport, and the men were taken back to their plane, which had been checked over and repaired, waiting for them to embark and take off. The guards were given back their guns and their ammunition with instructions not to reload until all personnel had left the area. After about fifteen minutes, the plane took off carrying the Dominium Group directors.

Peter said, 'well, that was a waste of time, wasn't it? They didn't care to do the decent thing and speak to those people whose lives are being ruined by their greed.'

Vince replied, 'I agree. They did not care about anything except their money and their wealth, not God or their fellow men.'

Peter and Vince drove off to Vince's farm at Bungarby knowing they would be safe there.

CHAPTER 66

James Coelicola was eager to hear from his three directors as to what had happened to them during their stay at Castle Hill airport. He called a board meeting at his apartment in new York and had arranged for lunch to be served while they discussed business and their venture.

The apartment was on the thirtieth floor of a multistorey building, which comprised five bedrooms, a boardroom, a study, and a large balcony leading onto an open area, which had barbecue facilities, chairs, and a lounge. The balcony was surrounded by a wall approximately a metre high.

The meeting started with the chairman advising that the death of the four other directors was a mistake, being poor communications given to the drug barons and that he was overseeing the investigations as to what went wrong. He assured the other three members that their lives were not at risk and that there were no contracts out on their lives.

Reports were tabled as to the extent the Covid-19 virus had spread throughout the world and that it had, at the date of the meeting, killed two hundred and twenty thousand people worldwide. It had, as intended, attacked older adults and vulnerable, including the homeless and street dwellers, who were an eyesore on society in most cities. As for older adults, frail, and disabled, they were considered a cost to society, and the virus was a legitimate way of eliminating them. This meant that no further pensions or benefits had to be provided for their existence. It was considered that most would catch the virus and not be able to resist its destructive force as it attacked the lungs, causing inflammation and preventing the person from breathing, as well as causing blood clots, which would kill the person by way of a stroke.

These people generally had compromised immune systems and could not fight off the virus. The results would be that more and more of these vulnerable groups would die off, leaving countries better off in not having to take care of them by way of pensions and special care facilities. The Dominium Group considered this in their favour and acknowledged they would prosper in those countries where the virus was taking hold.

At about one o'clock, the meeting broke up for lunch, and the group went out on the balcony and sat down to a meal, which was prepared and served by waiters. The talk was mainly about what had happened at Castle Hill, with James keen to hear what had happened during their stay at Castle Hill regional airport. He was concerned as they told him of Peter Marlow's coup and his trips to the farms, so they could speak to the farmers that were being forced off their land.

The second director said, 'Marlow tried to get us to see that what we were doing was not as God would want us to act and continually advised us that if we stayed on this path, we would join you in hell for a thousand years. He kept advising us not to trust you, as you would turn on us just as quickly as you would on anyone who did not follow your ways.'

James asked, 'what was your reply to him?'

The second director replied, 'We advised him we were quite content with our current lives and didn't think his God could or would do anything to benefit us.'

James asked, 'What? He didn't offer you anything to persuade you to trust God instead of what I offered?'

The second director replied, 'He said believing in God and having faith in Him will guarantee eternal life as compared to just life on this earth, and our rewards would come in heaven after death and not as we have it currently on this earth.'

James asked, 'And what do you think of his proposal?'

The second director replied, 'It has merits, something to think about.' With that, James Coelicola grabbed the second director by the throat and pushed him to the edge of the balcony, heaving his head and half of his body over the balcony, and then grabbed his leg and heaved him over and off the balcony and let him drop thirteen floors to his death.

All looked on in astonishment and disbelief as to what had happened and the speed at which Coelicola acted without giving the director a chance to explain himself.

James said, 'If there are any of you who want to think you can now become a Christian or join them in their beliefs, then you will get the same treatment as this idiot got. I will tolerate no one speaking of God or Christianity in my presence. As I have told you, the return of God will never happen because we are undermining the Christian faith, and more and more of them are joining our cause and enjoying the wealth that we offer in preference to eternal life, which most cannot envisage. They want the wealth now, not later, and believe they will bargain an entry into heaven later on if it ever came. Most want the wealth now, not later, and do not care about religion or the Bible. It is the good things of life, the material things that they strive to achieve, and we help them get it. If there are any of you that want to accept the Christian faith, then tell me, because I will find out and deal with you later. It is the same for all you out there that want to adopt Christ. You will all get the same treatment from me if you turn from declaring me king.'

No one said a thing, and the meeting broke up, and all went back to their homes, leaving their colleague lying dead on the sidewalk, with police swarming around the body, wondering what had happened.

CHAPTER 67

Peter's inauguration came within weeks of his election as Archdeacon. it was overwhelming for him considering from where he came from to end up in such a position of authority. He made it clear from the start that he would not tolerate ministers preaching what they wanted to, and those who would not adhere to the teachings of the Bible had no place in the church he was overseeing. Many objected to his dogmatic approach to religion, but he stuck to his grounds and made very clear that he would not accept deviation from what the Bible taught.

He was not concerned with the contract that had been placed on him, as he knew that there was a bitter feud still between the drug barons and Coelicola regarding payment for the last four killings. The previous drug baron mysteriously died of a heart attack when he tried to claim payment from Coelicola. The new appointees decided it would be better to be alive and not enforce the payment agreed with their predecessors. They came to terms with the gunmen on a lesser payment but still were weary of Coelicola and therefore did not force the issue and refused to have any future dealings with him.

Coelicola was trying to recruit new directors, but on this occasion, few people came forward after they heard what had happened to the previous directors and how Coelicola was involved in rigging the vote in the Archdeacon's appointment. Most welcomed the power and wealth from their dealings with Coelicola (Lucifer) but thought that it was a high price to pay for the short-term gain they made in giving allegiance to Coelicola, who stood up to his reputation as a liar and a murderer.

The two remaining directors of Dominium Group Pty Ltd and still pursued their endeavours to acquire as much of the farmland, knowing that, at some time, a dam would have to be built and the area would be opened up and not be drought affected. Once that was done, they would make massive profits, and since they controlled the government, they could decide the timing as to when this was to happen.

Peter, once becoming archdeacon, brought the plight of the farmers to the notice of the public and the world as to what was happening. Again, the banks stood together preaching they have done nothing wrong and that they have abided by the Royal Commission's recommendations even though these were lies and all they were doing was exactly what was happening prior to the Royal Commission.

Instances after instances were recorded in the press and on television, causing mounting resentment against the banks in their practices and support of the underworld and little support of the battler.

The tide was turning, and the banks eased off on repossessing farms. Also, some areas had good rainfall and could replant and look forward to harvesting their crops to generate an income, allowing them to meet their repayments and, sometimes, make up arrears as time went by.

Questions were being asked as to how senior employees of banks could earn large sums of money and acquire property in elite areas, and this sometimes showed that some were aligned with the Dominium Group and were being paid off by them.

Peter called these people out whenever he could and made an example of them as to what they were doing to the farmers and all for their own greed. He was having success and wondered whether he would soon confront the forces of the Dominium Group.

On the religious side, he had battles to wager on the attempts to change legislation affecting abortion and euthanasia, which ran contrary to the teachings of the Bible. The vocal majority quickly took centre stage and declared their position, which basically was the position held by the State and not the teachings of the Bible. Again, there became a wider divide between the State and the Bible, but Peter refused to alter his stand on these matters.

Most of the population did not care about religion. All they wanted is a better job and more money. They would freely bow before Lucifer to get these. They did not worry about the teachings of Jesus or his promise of eternal life. However, when things went wrong in their lives, they quickly criticised God and blamed him for whatever had happened. The comments were again repeated: 'Where is God? He should have prevented this. This proves there is no God. He only is an imagination, not a reality. It is a waste of time in believing in God.'

These people truly have not taken the time to understand the purpose for which they were placed on the earth and where religion and God fitted into the realm of things.

Peter was in his office trying to get through work that had piled up because of him attending talkback shows to convey his message to the public as to where God fitted into their lives. He was in his office with his team, which comprised several secretaries and ministry clerks, when James Coelicola appeared amongst them and asked to see him privately. Peter was taken aback by how he got into the office without being observed by one of the security guards or attendants. Peter asked everyone to leave and, once the door was closed, ushered James Coelicola to a chair and stared at him for a moment, wondering, *Is this the end?*

Peter said, 'Mr Coelicola, what brings you to my office? We have not had a good relationship, and I am confused as to why you would present yourself here.'

Coelicola said, 'You know who I am and what I represent. In fact, in your early days, you were one of my most promising members. You followed my way of life, and everything showed you would remain one of my followers and never turn towards religion or Jesus Christ. In fact, you did everything I commanded from you, including killing people, bashing them, stealing, extortion, prostitution, pornography, extortion—you name it, you were in it and made plenty of money out of all these activities, and so did your friend Vince Marconi. Both of you showed promise and could have eventually been considered prospects of joining the Dominium Group as directors if you continued along the path I had set for you. But something went wrong with both of you turning against me and now preaching a contrary message, which does not please me. I have come here to see if we can come to some agreement where you will act in my interest as Archdeacon and not preach the Bible in the strict religious sense, but allow the average parishioner to be misled and, in time, turn away from God and kneel before me as their king. I will in turn provide you with wealth far beyond what you could imagine or get as Archdeacon and give you power and influence that you could not attain on your own or relying on Jesus.'

Peter replied, 'Yes, I was under your influence and thought that there was no other way on this earth but to get as much for myself and that the only person who I should look after was me and my interest only—not my fellow man, just me. There was never enough money or power, and, yes, I killed for it when attacked or sold out as you had taught me to do—your way, or as they say, the way of this world. But through God, I could see another way, a way that could not be bought or earned through favours or wealth. I saw things being done in His name that your power and wealth could not even attempt to do. I saw the disabled being cured, and the crippled made good in His name and could carry on their lives. I saw the blind see again and the deaf hear. All this was done in His name. All I saw through you is greed and killings. Nothing as He had shown me that was possible in His name. No, you are a poor substitute with all that you offer in this world, as all you can offer is materiality and not the true things of life that God offers to those who believe in Him.'

Coelicola said, 'Yes, you have had the privilege of seeing these things, but the second world will never come. It has been preached about, and people have waited for it for over three thousand years. I have been able to forestall it, and as time goes by, more and more take up allegiance to me, never to return to Christianity. Most that attend church are not Christians— they only think they are. They go to church on Sundays and stay one hour and then continue with their sinful ways, not worrying about Jesus until next Sunday. They are followers of mine in that they, too, only care for material things and do not have faith in Jesus. The more people sin, the better are my chances of forestalling the Second Coming, and, eventually, the mass will be with me and not Jesus.'

'He is waiting to get His number of faithful followers, but He will never achieve His quota, as the average person wants nothing to do with God. All they care about is themselves, their jobs, wealth, the material aspects of life, not forgiveness of sins or eternal life. This, to them, is the only life they are going to have, and, therefore, they are going to make the best of it. They turn on God whenever anything happens on this earth, blaming him constantly for these. Everyone knows God created the earth and, therefore, is blamed for everything that goes wrong on this earth or with their lives. I never get blamed, even though most of the time I have caused these things to take place. You should wise up to yourself and join me and enjoy life and accept what I can do for you and the wealth I can provide you with.'

Peter said, 'Yes, I have been told about you and how you tried to gain control of heaven and tried to arrange a mass attack on God's throne and was toppled and thrown out of heaven and took up residence on earth. Yes, you are referred to as the king of the earth and have powers beyond those possessed by mankind. But you are still restricted as to what you can do and need to seek God's permission before acting. You boast a lot, but you are still on a leash and may do the things you do only because you are God's means by which mankind is tested to see who really has faith in Christ or who shares your character and attributes. No, you are wrong about the Second Coming. It will come, and, yes, the world is becoming more like you, as it was predicted, as mankind forgets Christ and seeks only the material things you can offer. No, I will not return to your camp but will still act in His name and allow His mercy and grace to direct and protect me from you.'

Coelicola said, 'I have many followers in the church that will turn against you within a short period. I have ministers of religion in senior positions in different churches throughout the world, not just in yours, and they serve me and not your God. Most of the academics in the universities and colleges are not true Christians but disciples of mine where they are more concerned about their jobs and wealth than the religion that they write about. None stand up and defend Christ or speak to support Him but keep quiet when controversy is raised. These people are followers of mine and will never support you, as you cannot give them what they seek in this world. You should realise that you can never win with God and should make the move to come back to my camp again and live a life that you lived with and prospered with me.'

Peter replied, 'No. I have the opportunity of living a life with you but have found one far better with Jesus Christ. I will continue to have faith in Him and act in the name of the Father.' Peter, upon saying those words, was left alone in the room and for a moment stared at the chair where James Coelicola was sitting, wondering what was going to happen to him. He waited a moment and then realised he still had to get through his archdeacon duties and called his support team back into his office so he could get through the day's work.

The team, who was waiting outside the Archdeacon's office, were bewildered, as they did not see the Archdeacon's guest leave and wondered what had happened to him, but no one asked.

CHAPTER 68

PETER LEANED BACK IN HIS chair and was trying to understand what was being conveyed to him over the telephone. One of Vince's own men gunned Vince down in the barn on his farm and fled from Bungarby and tried to fly out of the country.

Within an hour of being gunned down, the news spread across the underworld that one of Vince's most trusted men had shot him to claim the $20 million contract. He was found lying face down in the barn on his farm by his bodyguards, who went to investigate after hearing some shots being fired.

The man concerned got to the airport but was spotted by some of Vince's friends, who followed him into the bathroom and beat him beyond recognition and then fired ten bullets into him, leaving him dead in a pool of blood.

James Coelicola knew that the man could never claim the contract and knew that Vince was an influential underworld identity respected by all the families and independent state bosses. Everyone knew he had retired some years ago, and no one ever thought of claiming the contract against Vince. Yet Coelicola encouraged one of Vince's most trustworthy men to kill him and claim the reward.

The man concerned was Rolf Vincent, who was a close friend and brother to Vince. He was one of Vince's right-hand men and had worked for him for thirty years. Not that things had changed between Vince and Rolf, but Coelicola got in the mind of Rolf, convincing him he would be a wealthy man if he carried out the killing and could live a carefree life once Vince was dead.

Rolf was told, 'You can do a lot with $20 million, and you would not have to rely on anyone to pay your wages or be around to ensure the money still came in every month.' He played with Rolf's mind, taking away the obstacles and emphasising the potential benefit in carrying out the contract. The risks were not brought to Rolf's attention, only the benefit of having $20 million. He convinced Rolf that he did all the things for Vince and therefore should be wealthy and that Vince has had a good life living without a care while Rolf had to do the hard work. It was now Rolf's time to live in luxury and that Vince had outlived his usefulness, and to end his life would be of little consequence and, to some extent, a relief to Vince, who had nothing more to live for.

Coelicola convinced Rolf that he was getting older and soon would be of no use to Vince. He would end up in a nursing home, and not a good one at that. He should ensure his future or he would find himself penniless. He played on Rolf's mind till he knew only one thing, and that was he had to go through with it. Over time, Rolf believed his thoughts and concluded the only course available to him was to kill Vince and claim the contract.

Coelicola knew Rolf would not live to claim the $20 million bounty or be allowed to kill a respected underworld identity as Vince without immediate retribution. Vince's men and contacts in the underworld would see that Rolf would experience the same fate that Vince had experienced, and this would happen within hours of him carrying out the killing.

Peter wept as he hung up the phone. His one and only friend was brutally gunned down. There was only one of them left, and it would be just a matter of time before an attempt would again be made on his life, as the contract was a large sum of money, and Lucifer would play on the minds of the meek and stupid of this world. Vince looked after Peter and protected him from the underworld and sharpshooters. Peter came from the same background as Vince, and both knew the underworld well and had the same association with the families and held the same respect.

Peter leaned back in his chair, not knowing what to do. He sat there for about twenty minutes and stood up out of his chair to answer a knock outside his door. He cautiously opened it to see a DHL courier on the other side with a large envelope. He signed for the package and went inside and opened the envelope. It was from Vince and had instructions noted on the outside of the envelope that it should be delivered to Peter, should Vince be killed.

Peter opened the envelope with a very shaky hand. Within the envelope was a letter and several documents in plastic folders.

Vince wrote, 'Peter, by now you have heard that I have been shot and betrayed by one of my own men. I was tipped off by friends that Rolf was likely to betray me, but I would not believe it, as he had been with me for thirty years and had been loyal and supportive over the years. We were like brothers. To some extent, I now know how Jesus felt when he was betrayed by one of his own, Judas, and all for thirty pieces of silver.

'In this envelope are deeds to the farm and other properties that I have willed to you. Also, there are deeds to other properties that I have been able to acquire over the years that I have willed to my men. They are each to get a property and a million dollars cash. This will give them the independence and security they deserve and be able to live a life without worry or relying on others for help or handouts. These men have been loyal to me and deserve a portion of my estate. I would ask you to officiate at my funeral and to ensure they get what I have bequeathed to them. Take the documents to my lawyer, whom you know, and he will take care of everything. The major portion of my estate is to go to the poor and needy, including the farmers in and around Bungarby who have been betrayed by the banks, government, and the Dominium Group. The money is to help those with children and families to get back on their feet and push back against the politicians and banks that have sold them down the creek. Keep up the delivery of the food parcels to the farmers, as they rely on the Lord's help in providing these handouts and, where possible, bless those that are disabled and of need of the Lord's help in making them whole and heal them in the name of the Father. I am grateful to witness what money cannot buy and to see the love and compassion of the Lord and to witness His miracles.'

Peter recalled many months ago the Lord said he would recall Vince shortly to heaven, as his purpose on earth was nearing its end. He stared at the documents and first refused to accept the properties, but then thanked Vince for his bequeath and for considering him. He phoned the boys and advised them he would be at Bungarby in two days' time and would officiate at Vince's funeral. They were grateful for his call and were concerned for Peter's safety, as Vince had left specific orders that his boys were to look after Peter.

The boys advised Peter that the local undertaker was handling everything in relation to the body and coffin, and all would be ready in two days' time.

The news covered the story as to how Vince was betrayed by one of his own and that the gunman was found dead in the toilet at the regional airport. Alice and Tim heard the news and quickly called Peter. They knew Vince well, as he was always treated as part of the family, an uncle. Despite Peter advising them not to make the long trip, they decided to attend the funeral and would stay at Bungarby in the church residence.

The next morning, Peter made the long trip to Bungarby and stayed at the homestead on the farm rather than the church. He at first fitted a revolver to the back of his belt for protection but shortly removed it, as he believed he was protected by the Lord and knew there could be none better. He recalled the number of times people had told him that there was no God, because if there was one, He would have prevented whatever happened. They never stopped to think that even the worst events contrived by Satan are used by God for His purpose. They may not have been planned by Him, but He knew of them happening and used them for His good.

Peter drove up to the homestead and was surprised to see all the boys there, as he thought they would stay in town. After the welcome and general conversation, they came down to Vince's will and what was left to the boys. He read out the will, which they were grateful to hear that he thought so much of them. They were very surprised by Vince's generosity, as they did not know he had acquired all the properties mentioned.

The men advised Peter that they considered it their duty to protect him from any assassins, as he was the last one left, even though they had failed dismally in Vince's case. They believed they should have been smarter and read the signs coming from Rolf. No matter what Peter said to them, that he could look after himself, made no difference, as they had promised Vince that if anything happened to him, they would look after Peter. They would do it in rotation, four men at a time and in two cars.

Peter preferred to operate on his own and stated that, but they would not accept no for an answer, and they were determined not to slip up this time.

It was decided that each of the boys would take the next day to go to their farm and establish their control of the property that was bequeathed to each of them. Peter would arrange for transfer of title to them in due course, once probate of Vince's estate was granted.

It was agreed between them that while the boys were off to check out their properties, Peter would go into town and meet up with Alice, Tim, and their two children and would be accompanied by two of the boys, who agreed to check out their properties after the funeral.

Peter drove into town with two of the boys and went into the residence, making sure that everything was clean and tidy. Alice and the family arrived around midday, and after a lot of kisses and tears, they went inside to settle down and discuss tomorrow's ceremony.

News crews assembled in town and took up accommodation in caravans on the outskirts of the town. Peter made sure he was not interviewed for fear that some sniper may take a shot at him, as they knew what he looked like.

Vince was well known in town, and his generosity was appreciated by families on the breadline. It was expected that possibly fifty to a hundred people would come into town for the day to pay their respects to the man who helped them through the drought and their current fight with the banks and the government. Also, his help with the food parcels meant a lot to the farmers, and even though Vince gave the credit to the Lord, most people thought it came from Vince, as they couldn't understand how the Lord could provide the goods other than giving Vince the money in the first place to buy them in bulk. They never thought of recalling the feeding of the five thousand on the Mount with a few fishes and some loaves of bread.

They estimated that the service and formalities would take about two hours and people would then go on their way back home after stopping off at the teahouse and having a sandwich, which Vince liked to do when he came into town. Tim agreed to assist Peter, so the prayers and obituaries were dignified and ideal for the occasion.

The boys went out to their farms and were very pleased with what Vince had left them. They agreed to look after Peter, even though he did not need a babysitter. The boys returned to Vince's farm and stayed there that night. In the morning, they headed back to Bungarby to attend the funeral. The men were to take the coffin out of the hearse and carry it into the church. Most people would stay outside, as there were still distancing laws present that had to be observed.

The news and press were in force in town, and the television reporters were going to broadcast the service not only State wide but also around the world.

Peter expected that there would be approximately one hundred people attending the service. From early morning, it was obvious that this would be exceeded at least twentyfold, as all of Vince's old mates from the underworld turned up to pay their respects, including members of the judiciary and politicians. There were estimated to be two thousand people who came to pay their respects.

A quick thing had to be organised, and it was agreed that the church was not the ideal place to hold the service. It was agreed that the local sport stadium would be the better place, but the mayor refused to allow them to stage the funeral there. Some heated discussions were held between Peter and some of the traditional families that had flown in specially to pay their respects. It was agreed that some families would meet with the mayor to see if they could persuade him to change his mind. At about ten o'clock that day, the mayor abruptly saw the logic of having the service at the stadium. It was a situation where the service would be held at the stadium irrespective of whether the major agreed. However, there was no guarantee that the mayor would witness the service if he went against the family's wishes.

To allow each person to pay their respects, it was agreed that those who wanted could walk past Vince's coffin and place a flower on the ground under the coffin as a show of respect and brotherhood. The crowd proceeded in an orderly manner, with each person stopping, placing their given flower under the coffin, which stood on supports, and some stopping in front of the coffin to say a brief prayer or making a gesture before moving on.

Within the crowd was a sinister character making his way up to the coffin, but with a different purpose. He was going to complete Coelicola's plan and claim the $20 million reward on the contract out on Peter. As he moved up closer to where Peter and Tim stood at Vince's coffin, he knew what he had to do and that it would all be over within seconds. He would shoot Peter right through the head. No one would expect it so close to Vince being shot, as they would be all concentrating on laying Vince to rest. The families will make sure they were protected and not placed at risk and therefore would not be protecting Peter but ensuring their guards were protecting them. The confusion that the shooting would cause will enable the shooter to escape and get free before anyone knew what had happened.

The only one that knew of this plane was Coelicola, and he did not care what happened to the person planning on killing the Archdeacon, so long as Peter was dead, and he could place one of his own disciples in as Archdeacon.

Unbeknown to the crowd, Vince's men had sourced some modern inventions and personnel who knew how to use modern software. With sensors and scanners placed around the grounds, they had detected the family's security guards carrying weapons and knew that this would be the case and they could do little about it. However, they also detected a lone man carrying a high- powered semi-automatic weapon. The man stood out from the crowd and, in doing facial recognition checks on him, could reveal his identity. He was described as small-time gangster from one of the poor states who was not connected to any of the families. He had a long record of petty crimes and, over the last month or so, was seen in the company of James Coelicola and did some killings for him, yet this, of course, could not be proved. He was thought to be the killer who assassinated two of the four directors of the Dominium Group. Image of the crowd showed Coelicola having a heated conversation with the man for about ten minutes, trying to get him to do something. Security realised something was going to happen and kept both men in sight. Coelicola walked behind the stage and onto the other side of Peter as his man moved up in the procession. He was getting close to Peter, which gave him little time to change his mind. As he passed Vince's coffin, he stopped a moment as if he were bowing his head, but he slipped his hand behind his belt and pulled out his weapon. As he did this, a single shot rang out. A sniper on the roof of the stadium shot the man dead. As he fell to the ground, he looked left, and no doubt could see Coelicola intending to move in and take the weapon. As the man fell, he squeezed the trigger of his weapon, which was pointed at Coelicola and not at Peter, and a volley of shots rang out towards Coelicola, which stopped him in his tracks.

Coelicola fell to the ground as if he was avoiding the shots, and as soon as the police and guards ran in, Coelicola got up to the surprise of all that thought he had been shot dead, yet not a scratch was on him; only his clothes were torn where the bullets hit his body. Peter, who was witnessing everything, knew Lucifer could not be killed on this earth and that, in reality, he was spirit taking the form of man.

Vince's men raced up to Peter and quickly escorted him off the stage, leaving Tim to handle the prayers. After a further hour, all had paid their respects to Vince, and the police had taken away the body of the man who was shot. A search was made for James Coelicola, who they believed had been shot by the man who had the semi-automatic weapon, but he could not be found, leaving the police and the crowd bewildered as to where his body was taken, as it was clear he was shot multiple times and at close range.

The final sermon was left to Peter, as he was Vince's closest friend and the Archdeacon.

Peter moved up to the pulpit and looked at those who had gathered, despite the recent attempt on his life. He hesitated for a moment and then spoke. 'Considering what has happened this week regarding the death of Vince, the way the world stands today, and its values and people's pursuit of wealth and material things, you may ask, "What is Christ all about? Where does He fit in within this chaos, and what has He got to do with me?'

'Lucifer was thrown out of heaven because he wanted to establish in heaven what we have here on earth and wanted to replace God as the ruler in heaven. The created wanted to replace the Creator. If he had succeeded, there would be no Bible, no truth, and what we have here today on this earth would have been established in heaven. If this happened, there is little doubt, chaos would have reigned supreme.'

'God said, "No, I will not allow this, as this is not what I stand for. I am the light, the Truth, and this order must be maintained.'

'We are all born into this environment, and we can settle in and accept where we are and live the way of this world or hear His voice, which says there is something far better, something more truthful, something that is right and has been right for centuries in heaven. This truth and righteousness you can claim and accept rather than what is being offered to you in this world. 'You are born into sin to allow you to understand and to witness what sin does to mankind. The killings and maiming are the doings of mankind, and yet some have the audacity to screech out, "Where is God?" When these things happen rather than to say it was man who decided and what has happened results from man's decision.'

'Before you are let into heaven, you will have to prove you want the same things that those who are there want, and that you are not seeking the insecurity, lies, deceit, dishonesty, and drive for material things that is the norm hear on earth.'

'You must show you want a better life, one that gives you truth, honesty, true love, friendship, and security, that what you have is yours for eternity and not just one lifetime.'

'Well, how do you get to heaven from earth? We are all sinners and are doomed to death. Every one of us. This was the curse given to mankind by God.'

'The only one way you can achieve getting to heaven is through Jesus Christ. Believing in Him and having faith in Him is the only way you can enter heaven. Your faith in Him allows you to leave this earth and what it stands for. Your faith in Him is the only way your sins can be forgiven because He paid the price for your sins on the cross.'

'Many have come to me and have asked where they stand with God, as throughout their life, they have ignored Him didn't care about Him or what He stood for. They just went ahead and did the things that benefited them to the detriment of others.'

'Vince was not one of those, as over the last year or so, he saw the Creator's miracles and the light, so he became closer to God and uncoupled his sinful earthly life and took up a life that brought him closer to God. He knew God can forgive sins and asked the Lord to take his sins to the cross. Many of you here have never seen this side of Vince, only the murder and thuggery elements of his younger days. Yes, he killed and controlled an empire and made a lot of money in sinful process, as many of you have done.'

'The problem stems from the attitude the individual has towards God. Is God just a spirit you really do not care about or have much time for, or is He in your heart and mind as the real Creator? You need to answer this in your own way, because each one of us has been given a free will, as had Lucifer. He was trained and gifted. He was given many God-like features and misused them, as many of you have done. God has given you many natural treasures, such as good health, employment, education, and a wonderful family. You are placed on this earth and are trained as he was, and as you grow, you are gifted with virtues such as grace, foresight, intelligence, and skills to achieve what you desire. You are trained over a shorter period than possibly Lucifer was, and no doubt you have not been given the powers he was given, but like him, you gain from God the elements that you now possess. Your ability to think. To evaluate good from evil. To communicate, have sight, smell, touch and ability to reason are just several things God has given to you.'

'Many individuals take these for granted and believe it is their godly right to have these and more, and never thank God for these treasures. They never look at the disabled and deformed and ask, "Why have I received more of the treasures of life, and they less? Why in this world is there the unequal granting of natural resources to the individual? Why are some born with a head start, while others are miles behind?"'

'There will come a time in your life when you confront God, and you will, like Lucifer, challenge God. You must ongoingly decide whether you are to trust in yourself and be your man, or trust in God and have faith in Him and rely on Him.'

'If you trust in self, you are saying, "God cannot do anything for me. It is up to me, and I know better." In circumstances like these,

God lets you go your own way. It does not take much time before you realise your way may not be the best way, and in these times, seek forgiveness and ask God for His grace and directions. When you avoid doing this, you are taking the position of Lucifer in challenging God. You stand before Him and demand the right to sit at the head of God's table and be the leader. You know best, not God. Like Lucifer, you may find yourself thrown out of heaven to earth and come down with a big thud. Reality is painful, and after the fall, you may realise you are not equal to God. You are his creation with set limitations, not the other way around, as some think it.

'In your life, you must decide whether you are going to repent and ask for God's forgiveness or whether you are still going to be your own man and do things your way.'

'If you decide the latter, you have fallen into line with the king of this world, Lucifer. If you do not, then you will have to confront him, as there can be only one King ruling this earth. If you kneel before Lucifer, he will give you all the material benefits you desire to ensure you do not go back to the Lord. If you try to reclaim your relationship with God, you will find things go wrong in your life, and suddenly, the free-flowing wealth or health that you had just dried up or stopped or went in reverse.'

'Either way, you will have to fall behind God or Lucifer or challenge them for their thrones.'

'When you come to Sunday service and say, "Yes, Lord," for an hour and then go home and do your things your way for the rest of the week, you are being your own man and not really caring about what God wants of you. How can you best serve Him during the week? You really do not care about Him until next Sunday when you come again and rethink your position.'

'Just remember, we are assured of death, and this can interrupt your routine, and there will be no more time left for you to decide as to where your allegiance stands, left or right.'

'If at this point in time you cannot realistically say, "I give my faith to the Lord and believe He knows best," and during the week are consistently speaking to God in prayer and seeking his wisdom and consultation, then you, in reality, have little faith in Him but are trusting in your own decisions and, in reality, have very little faith in God. If this is you, then He will do something with your life to make you decide on which side of the fence you think you belong. You cannot sit on the fence in the middle for much longer and will be forced to decide before death overtakes you.'

'If you believe in God and have rock-solid faith in Him, then nothing will uncouple you from God. However, if your faith is based on materialism, wealth, and self, then you will be invited to join Lucifer and his team, and your punishment will be as has been handed down to them—a thousand years in hell.'

'Today, we officiate at Vince's funeral. A man brutally shot dead by his friend. A man he knew for thirty years. This shows that we are all subject to death and that it can come anytime and unexpectedly. Who would have ever thought that Vince's oldest friend would sell him down the creek for money? Vince, who was gunned down by his best friend, served the Lord and found comfort in His spirit in the last year of his life. I can truly say Vince is in heaven and will be with Christ. He sought God, and his sins were forgiven. The man that shot him did it for money but will never get to spend a cent of his reward on this earth and will end up following his master, Lucifer, to hell without an entry fee or commission.'

'We have many families here and many men of importance, with influence and power. Even Lucifer turned up here at Vince's funeral, as he did at the Crucifixion of Christ. A bit concerning, as Vince is now spirit and is with the Lord. Who knows what he can now unleash against Lucifer? We who remain on this earth must, as Vince did— either accept the Lord with all our hearts or find another King to worship that does not care about you.'

'I would urge you to seek the Lord and ask for His mercy and forgiveness of your sins. Be like Vince and from earth look up to heaven and ask for His help to climb out of this mess and enter a better life, one that is eternal and does not rely on your wealth or possessions gained on this earth. Ask for your sins to be forgiven and for the Lord to lead you to a better and more rewarding life. Seek these and ask for His mercy and forgiveness in the name of the Father.'

'Let us pray . . .'

Peter and Tim stayed back as the crowd broke up, and many made their ways to the airport for connecting flights. Some of the older members of the families came to Peter and asked questions about his sermon and their relationship with God. Most considered someone as truthful, pure, and honest,

as God would not want or have anything to do with them, as they have been involved in killings and crime that the average person would not have ever contemplated or got involved in. They mainly wanted to know how God could forgive them of their sins and, like Vince, how they could get to heaven when they die and not end up with Coelicola in his hellhole.

While most of these men were murderers and did bad things in their lifetime, they didn't just go out to kill someone or beat just anyone up as Coelicola has done to gain a person's following or loyalty. They knew who Coelicola was and what he was like. They also knew he had powers that could and would be used to gain a benefit for himself and could be used to their detriment. Peter said, 'We are all born in sin intentionally, and you must seek God if you wish eternal life. God, the Creator, brings you into this world with resources and benefits that only God can give you. Wisdom, intelligence, and health are just a few of these benefits that you cannot buy or win. Satan cannot bring anyone into this world and cannot give anyone any of the natural benefits that God has given to you freely.'

'God, who brought you into this sinful world, asks nothing of you or demand repayment for the benefits he has given you. Yet Satan does. He wants you to remain in the sinful world and follow his ways. If you do this, he will give you material things, employment, wealth, support, to name a few of his promises. He will offer these to you as a bait, but once you accept, there is no promise he will give you what you believe he has committed himself to. Satan will do anything and say anything to keep you in his camp and stop you from believing in Christ.'

'Jesus makes no offer and does not enter negotiations with you. He says, "I am the only way you can get eternal life, and your sins will be forgiven if you believe in Me, as I have already paid the price for your sins.'

'Believe in Him, and you will also receive internal life and have your sins forgiven. What you must do is change your life to follow His teachings. Ask for forgiveness of your sins and have faith in Jesus Christ. It is never too late, but you must change your ways. You cannot live a life with one foot in the old camp and the other in the new.'

'Ask God, and He will help you if you are sincere. If you do not want to give up what you have, then stay as you are, and you will end up in hell.'

All stood there momentarily and then thanked Peter for his words and went off to the airport and their flights home.

CHAPTER 69

SOMETIME HAD PASSED, AND PETER was back in his city office officiating as archdeacon.

He was having a break and sat back in his chair and thought of his life's journey. He started off as a thug, a gangster, and ended up in jail, where he was nearly killed. God took him under His wing and showed him a better life, one that did not require brutality, lies, killing, or the accumulation of wealth. Only faith and honouring the word.

From the start of his life to the finish has been and will be a learning curve to prove faith in Christ. Life's rollercoaster is designed for this purpose, and the many arguments and disbeliefs he had in God were proven wrong over time. Like most, he cursed the Lord when he thought things were going badly but, unlike most, had faith in God and was proven justified by his faith.

He could not have achieved in his life what God has achieved through him, nor would it have been possible for him to have achieved the position of Archdeacon if it weren't for God. if he hadn't listened to God, he would either be a gangster trying to keep his territory and wealth or be dead. There was no way that he could have manipulated or bought his way to becoming an archdeacon. Only God could have achieved this. Peter was glad he listened to God and followed his way.

Who could have thought at the beginning that Peter was being trained by God to handle the obstacles that confronted him? Without that training, he would not have had the skill or courage to do what had been asked of him or confront Lucifer. Along the way, he was forced to see his sister gunned down and his best friend murdered. No doubt these events turned his soul to the degree where he didn't know what to think and couldn't fathom out why this was happening to him. He didn't even recognise they were tests of faith.

Peter thought of the family he had lost in Helen and Vince and felt alone until he realised he was not alone, but God was with him every second of his life, and he could always converse with God and seek His opinion and guidance. All he had to do was to ask.

He sat back and wondered how people who had discontinued their relationship with God felt. They must be lonely and over time, become depressed.

No doubt a degree of separation would be felt when this happens, as Jesus felt when God turned His face from Him when He was nailed to the cross. But He knew Jesus would leave none of His people and would always be there by their side. All that was required was for them to ask God to come back into their lives. But most would never bring themselves to do this. Pride, wealth, and materialism have, most times, taken over from God. The material items are now worshipped in place of God and stand as an indicator of the worthiness of the person. But the car in the garage never talks to you or comes close to you. It doesn't touch your soul or ease the pain felt from the loss of a loved one. It is there to give you a false opinion of yourself, as does Lucifer, but people with the best cars are still lonely and depressed.

Peter wondered where to go from here. Does he wait for Coelicola's bullet?

No, definitely not. He has God, and if God wants him off this earth, He will arrange for it naturally, and until then, he serves the Lord and does His work 'in the name of the Father'. He realised things will get worse in the future, and more will leave the faith not understanding what is really at stake, and most will not take the time to think about the real purpose why they were born and what God wants to achieve with them, while on this earth.

Peter realised the pandemic will kill many throughout the world, leading to incrimination against God. This, coupled with the economic chaos that will follow and the years of unemployment, will cause families to separate and an increase in the suicide rate. All to the benefit of Coelicola, Lucifer.

God, no doubt, expects this and required an Archdeacon that can relate to the average working class and that has the faith and belief to convince His people to follow the Lord's ways. Lies will be told to the public, and it will take a person of strength and character to stand up to what is happening and to the Truth.

It seems that the Lord has selected Peter for this task, knowing that he will do his best, as he has experienced death, thuggery, and lies in his lifetime. He comes from this background and will use his experience in God's work in the future.

From Peter's perspective, he wondered how he could convince the population that they are on a course of destruction and need to change their ways before it is too late.

As he pondered on this matter, he swivelled his chair around and standing behind him was Coelicola staring directly at Peter with eyes wide open.

Coelicola said, 'You fool. Do you really think the average person will follow God? All the misery in this world is blamed on God, not on me or mankind. The usual question is asked, "Where is God? Why has He allowed this to happen?" I will make sure they ask these questions. They follow me, not God.'

'You are fighting a losing battle, as God cannot get the number, He requires replacing the fallen angels in heaven. You had a better life when I was controlling you, and you did the most to gain wealth and power. Not worrying about sinning or your actions. Look at you now, you do not have any of the material things I gave you. You had power and wealth before and now nothing.'

Peter replied, 'I don't need them. That's why I don't have them, but God does. He controls all these things and you, Lucifer, not the other way around. It is you who seeks my support, not me willingly chasing after you and to get the support you had to pay me off with your trinkets. What you offered me is only available on this earth, and the next day, I will lose all these things when death overtakes me.'

'No, I was under your control once, but now you have sought me out and again are trying to control me with sin, whereas under God, there is no control, as I am my own man. I have faith in Him, and He will look after me. No, I will not join a losing cause like yours, but try to persuade others of your lies and scheming and what they really stand to lose if they decide to follow you.'

'It is not the outer appearance of the person who counts but what is in their heart.'

'You try to convince the person that you will provide them with wealth or material things when, in fact, you cannot do this. You tried to give the world to Jesus when you confronted him in the desert. All he had to do was to bow before you. He refused, as these things were not yours to give and belonged to Him. These days you try the same tricks with mankind, knowing you have nothing of your own which you can give them. Yet mankind falls for your trickery, thinking the best way of gaining or accumulating things is through sin.'

Coelicola said, 'What is in the heart is governed by their wallet. It is rare to find the true Christian willing to give up what they have gained on this earth even if they stopped to think that they came with nothing and will leave the same way, but the majority still think what they accumulate is more important than what God offers.'

'It is by convincing most of this that I have gained control of this world.'

'You will not convince people to change. Those that decide to do so have a hard road ahead of them when they have no wealth, assets, money or employment and I am the only one that can manipulate these.'

Peter said, 'Yes. Therefore, the Lord has said, "He who is bashed, robbed, and criticised in doing My work shall be rewarded in heaven." He is making sure you cannot get your hands on the reward. So whatever you do to the true believer, he will accumulate wealth in heaven.'

Coelicola said, 'Only a few will believe you. The majority will not even try or care to go down that path.'

'You are wasting your time. We will see each other daily, for you will sin as most do on this earth, and it is just a matter of time before you come over to my side.'

Peter said, 'Yes, we will see a lot of each other. You may kneel with me and ask God's forgiveness for your sins. I assume you have already had this discussion with Him. You should come to church to hear what the Lord has to say and to see the number that are converting to Christianity and asking for forgiveness.'

Coelicola replied, 'I do, every Sunday, with all of those who support me throughout the week except for that hour.'